Social Policy & Welfare

Mark Walsh
Paul Stephens
Stephen Moore

STANLEY
THORNES

First published in 2000 by
Stanley Thornes (Publishers) Ltd
Ellenborough House
Wellington Street
Cheltenham
Glos.
GL50 1YW
United Kingdom

00 01 02 03 04 / 10 9 8 7 6 5 4 3 2 1

A catalogue record for this book is available from the British Library

ISBN 0 7487 4591 2

Cover photo: Getty Images
Line illustrations: Steve Ballinger, Clinton Banbury

Typeset by Northern Phototypesetting Co. Ltd, Bolton
Printed in Italy by G. Canale & C.S.p.A., Borgaro T.se, Turin

Contents

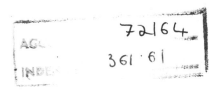

Welcome to *Social Policy and Welfare*. In this first edition our aim was to produce an accessible, clear and interesting text on what are often rapidly developing and very important issues. We sought to strike a balance between, on the one hand, describing and analysing the classic concepts, themes and historical patterns of provision and, on the other, reporting what is happening currently in the area of social policy. As a reader, you will be the best person to judge whether we have achieved a satisfactory balance.

Social Policy and Welfare has been written for readers who are new to social policy. We have produced an introduction to the main issues, concepts and patterns of provision in key areas of social welfare provision in the United Kingdom, such as health, education and housing. An understanding of these matters is of particular value to students studying for GCE A- and AS-level Social Policy and Sociology awards, for GNVQ Advanced Health and Social Care, and for BTEC National Social Care students. However, an understanding of social policy and welfare is also important for students studying on courses such as ACCESS, nurse training and childcare programmes, which contain social care and welfare elements. We hope that the book will be useful to all students who have a need or wish to understand social policy and welfare.

The book makes no assumptions about previous study or knowledge. We have included a significant amount of historical material, to provide background and a context in which readers can locate and understand current debates and issues. We have also tried to remain as current as is possible, with coverage of the New Labour government's 'modernisation' approach to social welfare provision. This is always difficult, given that social policy is a constantly evolving, moving target. As a consequence, the book is supported by a web site (http://www.thorneseducation.com) that aims to remain abreast of new policy issues and developments, and thereby to provide a continuous supply of supplementary material for readers. We hope that you will use and also contribute to the web site, and in doing so shape the next edition of the book.

Because this book is an introductory text on social policy and welfare, we have tried to provide clear and accessible descriptions and explanations of key concepts and issues. We have provided statistical and original source material to illustrate our points wherever we felt that this was appropriate. Should you wish to pursue particular interests further, many books are available on each of the specialist policy-related areas that our chapters cover. These are often referred to in the text, and are detailed in the reference sections at the end of each chapter.

To support learning and understanding of the material, each chapter includes Review Points sections, at the end of each substantive topic area. These act as brief reminders of the essential points that have been covered earlier. There are also Review Activities, to give readers the opportunity to test and assess their own understanding and recall of the material. Try not to skip them – even though you may be tempted to do so! Answering the questions will help you to develop your understanding of the social policy issues that the section covers. We hope that both of these features will be useful in supporting your general learning, and that – if you are using the book as part of an examination course – you will also find them helpful in the revision process.

Social policy can be a very interesting and absorbing subject to study. It is about issues, such as educational opportunity, housing provision and homelessness, and criminal justice policy, that define and influence our lives individually and collectively. As well as being about how British society *actually is*, social policy is very much about how it *ought to be*. As a subject, social policy makes you think and helps you to understand more about the society that you live in now – and about the possibilities for its future. We hope that *Social Policy and Welfare* will be helpful and useful to you in your studies, and that it will encourage you to take further your interest in the issues and debates that it covers.

Mark Walsh, Paul Stephens, Stephen Moore

Acknowledgements

The authors and publishers gratefully acknowledge the help of Patrick McNeill and Graham Ford Williams, who provided useful comments on the manuscript throughout the writing process.

I am indebted to Denis Devine, an inspiring educator and a loyal friend, who taught me that learning should be fun as well as rigorous.

Paul Stephens

The authors and publishers are grateful to the following for permission to reproduce previously published material:

- Blackwell Publishers for the extract from McKeown, T. *The Role of Medicine: Dream, Mirage or Nemesis* (p. 160)
- Butterworth Heinemann Publishers, a division of Reed Educational Professional Publishing Ltd, for the extract from Whitehead, G. *Economics*, 15th edition (p. 96)
- Her Majesty's Stationery Office for extracts from *Social Trends 27* (p. 65); *Social Trends 26* (p. 67); HM Treasury Red Book (p. 82); Department of Health (p. 88); *Social Trends 28* (p. 90), HM Treasury 1990, 1995 (p. 92); *Economic Trends* Dec. 1995 (p. 95); National Income and Expenditure Blue Books (p. 102); *Social Trends 1970, 1976* and *Annual Abstract of Statistics 1984* (p. 103); *Comprehensive Spending Review,* Table 7.1 (p. 105); *Comprehensive Spending Review,* Table 6.1 (p. 106); *Social Trends 1995* (p. 106); Treasury Taskforce Private Finance Projects Team (p. 110); HM Treasury 1998 (p. 121); *Comprehensive Spending Review* (p. 123); Department of Social Security, 1997 (p. 131); *Hansard* (p. 138); *Social Sciences* (p. 149); Acheson, D. *Inequalities in Health: the current position* (pp. 150, 153); Acheson, D. *Independent Inquiry into Inequalities in Health* (p. 151); *Health Survey for England*, Department of Health (p. 152); *General Household Survey,* 1998 (pp. 194, 197); Martin, J. *British Social Attitudes Survey* (p. 213); Martin, J., et al *OPCS Survey of Disability* (p. 225); Department of Health (p. 226); *British Crime Survey,* 1997 (p. 245); *British Crime Survey* 1998 (pp. 244, 246); Hedderman, C., and Hough, M. *Does the Criminal Justice System Treat Men and Women Differently?* (p. 257); White, P. and Woodbridge, J. *The Prison Population in 1997* (pp. 261, 263); HM Treasury 1997 (p. 307); *Tackling Poverty and Extending Opportunity* (p. 318); Department for Education and Employment (p. 276); Department of the Environment, Transport and the Regions, Welsh Office, Scottish Office (pp. 330, 334); *Family Expenditure Survey* (p. 334); Department of the Environment, Transport and the Regions (p. 336). Crown copyright material is reproduced with the permission of the Controller of Her Majesty's Stationery Office.

- Hodder & Stoughton Educational for the extract from Holden, C., Meggitt, C., Collard, D. and Rycroft, C. *Further Studies for Social Care* (p. 44)
- Joseph Rowntree Trust for extracts from Hills, J. *The Future of Welfare: a Guide to the Debate* (p. 105)
- Office for National Statistics for extracts from *Annual Abstract of Statistics 1964, 1969, 1979* (pp. 31, 101) and General Household Survey (pp. 193, 197), © Crown Copyright material
- Open University Press for extracts from Blakemore, K. *Social Policy – An Introduction* (p. 63); and from Hogwood, B. *Trends in British Public Policy: Do Governments Make any Difference?* (p. 98)
- Organisation for Economic Cooperation and Development for extracts from *Health and Health Care in Britain* (pp. 104, 109)
- Oxford University Press for the extract from Hills, Funding the Welfare State. *Oxford Review of Economics,* **11** (3) (p. 106)
- Philip Allan Publishers for the extract from Williams. J. Rethinking Welfare. *Sociology Review* **7** (4) (p. 100)
- Chris Riddell for the cartoon on p. 361
- Routledge for the extract from Brown, R. *Society and Economy in Modern Britain 1700-1850* (p. 32)
- Shelter for extracts from *ROOF*, Jan.-Feb 1999 (pp. 337, 340)
- Times Newspapers Ltd for the extract from the Sunday Times Rich List (p. 67)

Every attempt has been made to contact copyright holders, and we apologise if any have been overlooked. Should copyright have been unwittingly infringed in this book, the owners should contact the publishers, who will make corrections at reprint.

Photo credits

- Chris Schwarz – pp. 115, 140
- Eye Ubiquitous – p. 271 (© Skjold)
- Getty Images – cover photo, p. i
- Help the Aged – p. 136
- Hulton-Deutsch Collection/CORBIS – p. 47
- Hulton Getty – pp. 220, 235, 279
- HWPL – pp. 8 (bottom), 72, 147 (left), 163 (© University of Glasgow), 230 (Tim Woodcock), 270, 320, 354
- London Metropolitan Archives – p. 229
- Mary Evans Picture Library – pp. 31, 33, 36, 39, 40, 350
- North News & Pictures – p. 308
- Popperfoto – pp 45, 75, 147 (right)
- Popperfoto/Reuters – pp. 8 (top), 56, 65, 76, 114, 223, 276, 347, 369
- Thames Valley University (Philip Bigg) – p. 287
- Topham Picturepoint – pp. 24, 125, 219, 299
- UPI/Bettman – p. 368
- UPPA – p. 293

The Nature of Social Policy 1

By the end of this chapter you should be able to:

◎ Explain what social policy as a subject is about, and how it is linked to other social science subjects.

◎ Identify the key characteristics of social policy that make it a distinct area of study.

◎ Describe the political context in which contemporary social policy is developed.

◎ Identify and describe the key factors that influence contemporary social policy development.

◎ Understand the main approaches to and concepts within contemporary social policy.

◎ Understand and describe a number of contrasting conceptions of social policy.

Social policy will be a new subject to most readers of this book. The overall aim of the book is to provide an introduction to key topics, principles and issues in British social policy. The specific aim of this first chapter is to introduce you to the subject, by outlining a number of key topics and concepts associated with social policy.

The chapter begins with a discussion about the range of different reasons for studying social policy. You are encouraged to reflect on your own interests in the subject, and to think about how it may benefit you in your future career and personal life. The chapter moves on to identify the traditional focus of social policy in the United Kingdom, and the relationship between social policy and other social science subjects. While social policy does have close links with other social science subjects, such as sociology and politics, it is also a distinct discipline in itself. In particular, we will look at the nature and significance of political ideologies, the role of the state and the economy, and the focus on real social problems – all of which are important and distinguishing features of social policy.

In order to understand how and why social policy is developed in the UK, you will need to have an understanding of the political and administrative context of policy-making. The nature of 'the state', and the various elements of the state that are related to social policy, are outlined to enable you to understand how social policies are developed. The sections on key social policy principles and contrasting conceptions of social policy address the differing, and competing, reasons for developing social policy initiatives.

Within each chapter, there are periodic Review Points and Review Activities. You are encouraged to use the Review Points sections as revision aids, and to tackle the Review Activities as you come across them. Both of these features are designed to play an important part in helping you to learn about social policy in an effective way.

What is social policy about?

As you begin to read through this first chapter, it may be that the question 'What is social policy about?' is what first prompted you to open this book. Indeed, many of you will probably be asked this same question when you tell your friends, relatives or colleagues that you are thinking about studying, or have begun to study, social policy for the first time. We will explore some of the different features and themes of 'social policy' – both as a subject to study and as an area of practice in this first chapter. This should help you to answer the question.

Government set to tackle homeless problem – target to reduce rough sleeping by two-thirds by 2002

CALLS FOR GOVERNMENT TO TACKLE RISING RATES OF TEENAGE PREGNANCY

Prime Minister identifies eradication of child poverty as key welfare target

TORY ANGER AT POLICY THREAT TO GRANT MAINTAINED SCHOOLS

Crime rate falls – rising optimism as Home Office reports sixth successive reduction

POLITICAL BATTLE ERUPTS OVER PUBLIC SERVICE FUNDING PRIORITIES

The focus of social policy

The key focus of social policy in the United Kingdom is on **social welfare provision**. Social policy is essentially concerned with the practice and study of state, or governmental, social welfare provision, and the healthcare and welfare systems. People who study British social policy focus on why, what and how social welfare is provided by British governments.

Social policy as a subject has its roots in the social sciences, and is relevant to students who have an interest in the provision of 'social welfare' and the operation of health and welfare services. It is now widely studied as a subject in itself, and is also increasingly likely to be a part of social science and health and social care courses. These kinds of courses cover key 'social welfare' issues such as health, poverty and education.

Thinking about 'welfare'

Because social policy investigates social welfare provision, it is important to explore and understand what we mean by 'welfare'. A dictionary definition of 'welfare' says that it means 'well-being; help given to people in need' (*Collins English Dictionary*, 1995). This definition expresses two important, and slightly different, ways of understanding 'welfare' that are also reflected in how people approach social policy.

The first part of the definition says that 'welfare' means 'well-being'. In turn 'well-being' might be seen to mean things such as the sense of security, happiness and comfort that people seek or want and perhaps even have a 'right' to in their daily lives. A desire to improve the well-being of individuals who belong to certain social groups is often given as a reason for the development of social policies.

The second part of the dictionary definition of 'welfare' suggests that it has something to do with the 'help given to people in need'. Social policy as a subject does focus on 'welfare *services*' (help) and on particular groups of people (those 'in need'). The welfare services typically studied in social policy are the state-funded health and social services. Social policy tends to focus on the ways in which state services are provided to protect and support particular social groups whose members *lack* well-being. These include, for example, people who are experiencing poverty and people who have health problems.

The *social* aspect of welfare

Social policy is concerned with *social* welfare provision. It is important to understand that social policies address welfare needs and service provision in a *social* context. While social welfare is fundamentally about the needs of people, the policy level focuses on collective needs and well-being, as well as the collective response to them, rather than on individual cases. For example, in practice, social policies aim to promote and improve collective human well-being by targeting welfare services and interventions on the communities and settings in which people live their lives. The subject of social policy focuses on the different ways in which governments try to change the social circumstances of specific social groups and communities, by distributing and redistributing the resources (such as housing, financial and educational opportunities, for example) that influence health and well-being.

How is social policy related to other subjects?

Social policy is a relatively new academic subject. Until very recently, social policy could only be studied in any depth at degree level. Students who took social policy courses at university were usually following **social science-based** programmes (particularly those with a large sociology component) or were training to be social workers.

Ken Blakemore (1998) describes social policy as a 'magpie' subject. By this, he means that social policy takes – or shares – ideas, concepts and methods with a number of other areas of study, which gives it an **interdisciplinary** character. As a result, it is sometimes hard to define what the focus of social policy is, and what it isn't. For example, social policy focuses on many of the same social phenomena as sociology, but not in the same way. The family, education and health are topics that are of interest to both disciplines. However, whereas sociologists study the nature and social significance of 'the family' as a phenomenon in itself, social policy is more concerned with the welfare services and policies that affect families. Despite drawing on the concepts and approaches of a number of different social science disciplines, social policy makes use of them in particular ways. The disciplines that often feature in the social policy 'jigsaw' are outlined in the accompanying figure.

Subjects that social policy is said to draw from

Despite the difference in focus between social policy and sociology, some people continue to see social policy as an 'applied' branch of sociology. There is still a lot of dispute over this, because both subjects are continually evolving and focusing on similar areas of interest – such as 'the family', as we mentioned earlier. Pete Alcock (1996: 2, 3), a social policy academic, points out that '… the boundaries of our study are never closed' and that the development of social policy as a field of study has led to 'boundary disputes' with a number of other disciplines, such as sociology, economics and politics. In an attempt to distinguish between social policy and other disciplines, Alcock (1996: 4) says that social policy is differentiated from traditional social sciences by *'its specific focus upon the development and implementation of **policy measures** in order to influence the social circumstances of individuals,* rather than the more general study of those social circumstances themselves' (emphasis added).

The key characteristics of social policy as a discipline

If social policy is different from the other social science disciplines that it draws upon, what are its key characteristics? In the previous section, we looked at the links between social policy as an area of study and other social science disciplines. In this section, we will focus in more detail on the features of social policy that distinguish it from other social science disciplines.

Social policy is particularly concerned with:

- ideologies, values and beliefs about individuals, society and 'social welfare'
- real-world, contemporary 'social problems'
- the approaches and actions of governments and the state to 'social welfare' issues
- the political, social and economic context of social policy-making and its implementation
- the nature and effectiveness of health and social welfare provision in the UK

Ideologies, values and beliefs

The study of social policy and the practice of social policy-making are inextricably bound up with the analysis and use of **political ideologies**. In social policy, the term **ideology** is used to refer to a relatively coherent 'package of ideas' and values that affects how people define social welfare issues and formulate social policy responses to them. A number of different ideologies have influenced the nature and development of social policy in British social policy over the past 200 years. As a student of social policy, it is important for you to know about and understand the different features of these ideologies. The concept of ideology and the key ideological approaches to social policy are explained in more detail on pages 12–14.

Values and beliefs – the normative approach

One of the key differences between social policy and other social science disciplines is that social policy academics often admit to having a preference for a particular ideological approach, and let this guide aspects of their work.

> '... the identity of social policy is ... bound up with values: that is, expressing what you believe in, and what you think social policies *should be* trying to achieve to make society better for everyone'
>
> (Blakemore, 1998: 5)

This doesn't mean that social policy researchers collect or analyse their data in a way that is deliberately 'biased'. When collecting and analysing data on social problems and policy issues, social policy researchers – like other academic researchers – are expected to adopt a rigorous approach and should maintain high professional standards. However, they do tend to make clear their values and preferred ideological positions when selecting topics to study and when making recommendations. Put another way, they are likely to comment on how society *ought* to be and what social policies *ought* to be trying to achieve. This is sometimes referred to as

a 'normative approach', and it makes social policy a *prescriptive* rather than just a *descriptive* discipline. Paul Spicker (1995: 10) captures this difference succinctly when he says that 'many people in social policy have no interest at all in being dispassionate about the subject; they are in it for a reason, and that reason is to bring about change'. This leads us on to the real-world focus of social policy.

A concern with practical problems

The study and academic treatment of social policy has traditionally been focused on real-world, practical social welfare problems and how they can be tackled. For example, social policy academics and policy-makers have long been concerned to establish the 'facts' about poverty as a real social problem in the United Kingdom (for a discussion, see p. 119). Social policy is also concerned with different ways of addressing the needs of those affected by poverty. The areas of welfare need and service provision on which British social policy has tended to focus are outlined in Table 1.1.

Social policy also focuses on the social welfare needs of particular groups in society. These 'need groups' are 'people in similar circumstances which require some kind of collective response' (Spicker, 1995: 41). They tend to include:

- people who are vulnerable to – or who are experiencing – poverty, homelessness, sickness or unemployment, or other difficulties that reduce their well-being
- older people, children and marginalised groups, such as people with physical and learning disabilities, long-term health problems or who are socially isolated in some way, who require support and protection to maintain their well-being

Table 1.1 Social problems and social policy issues

Welfare need / problem area	Welfare provision / social policy area
Poverty/income maintenance	Social security
Issues concerning education	Provision of education and training
Housing standards/homelessness	Housing
Issues concerning disease and illness	Health and community care services
Unemployment	Work and training services
Issues concerning crime	Criminal justice services and policy
Issues concerning families and children	Personal social services

Table 1.2 The interacting parts of the 'whole system' of social policy in the UK

Social structure	Political system	Economic system
Social problems 'Need groups'	Government Ideologies The state The European Union Health and social welfare issues	The economy

A focus on the role of the state

Various parties are involved in the development and implementation of social policies (for a discussion, see p. 10). It is important to know about and understand the different roles that these parties play in the social policy field. However, in the UK it is the state that has been the key player in the development and funding of social policy and welfare provision since the late 19th century. Since this time statutory organisations, under the direction and control of government, including the National Health Service, local authorities and the various police forces, have had the job of implementing social policies that have been developed at government level.

Together, the government and government-controlled health and welfare institutions represent the interests of the **state**. An understanding of the evolution, structure and role of the state in Britain is a necessary prerequisite to a better understanding of social policy. You will need to understand how the state has come to play such an important social welfare role, what this role involves, and how the system is structured and operates to provide social welfare services.

The role of the economy in social policy-making

Management of the economy is a key task for all governments. Social policy-making and social welfare provision are very much influenced by the strategies that a government uses to manage the economy, and by the extent to which this is successful. As a student of social policy, you will need to know about the different approaches to managing the economy. The two approaches that have been most important over the past 50 years, and which you should be aware of, are known as **Keynesian economics** and **monetarist economics**. These are discussed in more detail in Chapter 4, on pages 87–89.

The issue that links the economy and social welfare provision is 'public spending', which means government spending. Since 1948, the bulk of government spending has been on social welfare provision. Since this time, there has been a continuing debate about how much the government should spend on providing social welfare services, how this money should be raised, and on what kind of social welfare it should be spent. Some social policy-makers and commentators have also asked more fundamental questions about whether the government should manipulate and use the economy to fund social welfare at all. The state of the economy, and arguments over how governments should manage it, are central to understanding how and why governments develop and implement particular social policy measures.

Interactions between different parts of a 'whole system'

Earlier (see p. 3), we said that social policy was a 'magpie subject', that it took concepts and ideas from a number of different subject areas and applied them in particular ways. We also made the point that there is a lot of overlap and interaction between social policy and other social science disciplines. This is very much a reflection of the fact that, in the UK, social policy as a practice (social policy-making) results from, and needs to be understood in the context of, what Jones (1985) refers to as a 'whole system' of influences. That is, there is an overlap and continuing interaction between aspects of the political system, the economic system and the social structure (see Table 1.2). Together, these influences make up the 'whole stystem'. Social policy as a subject focuses on all the component parts of the 'whole system', so that it is partly about politics and it does involve some economics, while at the same time it is very much about social problems. In essence, social policy is characterised by the particular way in which it brings these subjects and concerns together. In doing so, social policy focuses on how, why and what policy measures and approaches are used to address social welfare issues.

Social policy and you

So, why do *you* want to study social policy? This is a question that you might already have been asked, perhaps by a teacher or lecturer, or by your friends or relatives. It's always useful to reflect on what attracts you to study a subject, because wrapped up in your answer are your own insights and your expectations about what you hope to get out of it.

Activity

Take a few minutes to think about and jot down some of your thoughts about social policy. You could try answering either or both of the questions we've asked so far.

- What is social policy about?
- Why do *you* want to study social policy?

If possible, share the thoughts and ideas in your answers with a fellow student. This may help you to expand your current understanding of, and motivations for studying, social policy.

You may have thought about some of the following when reflecting on your interest in social policy:

'I have an interest in society and social issues.'

'I'm interested in social problems and how they might be solved.'

'I've got some views and ideas about how society should be.'

'I want to know how health and social welfare services work.'

'I would like to work with people in need, and I want to understand the circumstances they face.'

'I like social science subjects.'

People choose to study social policy because:

- the subject helps them to prepare for professional roles as social, housing and education workers in 'welfare' organisations
- they're able to use the knowledge and understanding that studying social policy provides to participate in and make a difference to the policy-making process, and to the lives of people who require 'welfare services'
- studying social policy helps them to think differently, and with 'insight', about the social and political aspects of the welfare issues on which their studies focus

REVIEW POINTS

The nature of social policy

- Social policy is a relatively new area of academic study. It is an interdisciplinary social science subject that draws on ideas and concepts from sociology, politics and economics in particular.
- In the UK, social policy has traditionally been concerned with social welfare provision by the state.
- Social policy is distinct from other social science subjects in the way that it focuses on real-world social problems (such as unemployment, poverty, crime and education) in a *prescriptive* rather than a *descriptive* way.
- In practice, social policies usually try to address the circumstances of social groups who lack health and well-being in some way. These policies focus on collective human needs, and on the ways in which these are identified and can be met.
- Social policies deal with issues, such as poverty, poor housing and disability, that threaten or prevent 'well-being' in families, communities and other social contexts.
- Social policies are the result of interactions within a 'whole system' of social, political and economic factors.

REVIEW ACTIVITIES

1 What has been the traditional focus of social policy in Britain?
2 What does the term **welfare** mean?
3 In your own words, briefly explain how a knowledge and understanding of social policy might be helpful to a care worker.
4 'Social policy is a "magpie subject".' What does this mean?
5 Identify, and briefly explain, two characteristics of social policy that make it distinct from other social science disciplines.

The practice of social policy-making

In this section, we will look in more detail at the political context in which contemporary social policy is made.

As well as being a subject that people study in an academic way, social policy is a practice that many people are involved in and which affects us all. Some people directly 'make' and develop social policies, while others implement them in their work. The key social policy-makers in the United Kingdom are elected politicians, who are also members of the government. When politicians are in government, they are able to translate their ideas about how the country ought to be run into practical social (and, indeed, other types of) policy measures. Social workers, civil servants, teachers, healthcare workers and police officers are all directly involved – whether or not they are aware of it – in putting social policies into practice. To understand how these social policies are developed, you need to have an awareness of the political and administrative context of social policy-making.

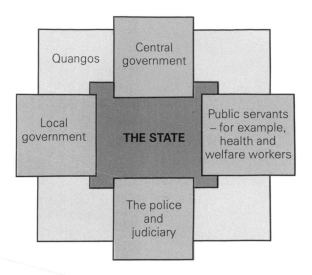

The structure of the state. The state is a set of interrelated institutions or structures that have the legal and political authority to develop, adminster and express health, welfare and justice policies in the public domain

The political context of social policy-making

The government is elected to 'run the country'. As a result, it must make all sorts of policy decisions. It must decide, amongst other things, on how to approach management of the economy (economic policies), what to do about defence (defence policies) and what to do about crime (criminal justice policies). Policies are the plans of action, or approaches, that governments adopt. **Social policies** are the plans, strategies and approaches that governments adopt when deciding what to do about issues and problems that affect social welfare. Members of the government, together with the people who are employed in government-controlled health, social welfare and criminal justice institutions, are said to develop and implement social policies on behalf of 'the state'.

'The state'

The term **the state** refers to the formal political institutions of a society, through which government power is exercised (Spicker, 1995). Using this definition, the state is made up of a number of distinct but interrelated parts. These include central government, public servants, local government and a variety of quangos (see p. 8).

Central government

Central government is nationally elected and is the main source of political power in the United Kingdom. In the UK's electoral system, the government is formed out of the political party that wins the most seats in a general election. The leader of the winning party becomes Prime Minister. It is the **Prime Minister** and his or her **Cabinet ministers** who develop a social policy strategy and produce various social policy initiatives. **Senior civil servants** and other **government ministers** work out the details of important social policies.

Public servants

These include teachers, social workers and junior civil servants who, through their work, administer and put into practice key social policies.

Local government

Locally elected councillors and employees in local authorities, as well as people who participate in locally elected bodies, such as school governers and members of local community health councils, administer and implement key social policies at a local level.

The Prime Minister and his or her Cabinet ministers develop a social policy strategy and produce social policy initiatives

Teachers form one large group of public servants. Through their work, public servants administer and put into practice key social policies

Quangos

Quangos (Quasi-Autonomous Non-Governmental Organisations) are bodies set up by central government to supervise or implement particular aspects of social policy. For example, the Child Support Agency is a quango set up in 1993 to assess, review, collect and enforce child-maintenance payments.

The government generally makes the key decisions about the areas or issues for which they wish to develop social policies, and about the aims and objectives of those policies. For example, the government may decide that they want to reduce the amount that they spend on providing social security benefits for unemployed teenagers, that they want to reduce class sizes in primary schools or that they will increase the amount of the state retirement pension. All of these ideas need to be put into practice. This is where public servants, local government and quangos play their part in finding practical ways of implementing and administering the social policies.

The structure of central government

The social policy work of central government is divided up and carried out in a number of central government departments.

Each of the departments is led by a **secretary of state**, who is a politician elected to Parliament and then appointed by the Prime Minister to run a particular department. The secretary of state will also be a member of the Cabinet, and will take the lead in developing social policy ideas for his or her departmental area.

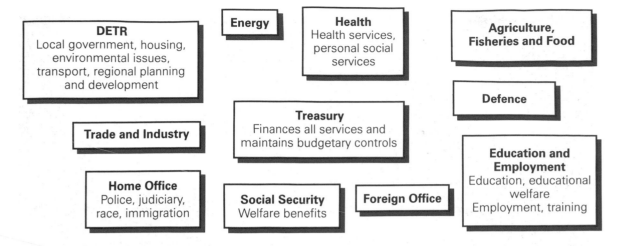

Central government departments

There are a number of central government departments that have a direct impact on social policies relating to health and welfare, while others have a more indirect influence on social policy (see diagram).

The Department of Health is responsible for all matters relating to health and social care. Health and social care policy is formulated by the department, and the various statutory (or state-provided) health and social care services are administered through the department. The department has to make a case to the Treasury for funding to provide these services.

The Department of Social Security is responsible for the welfare benefits system. Social security policy is developed by the department, and members of the Cabinet, in London. The administration and implementation of the benefits system is now carried out by 'agencies', such as the Benefits Agency and the Child Support Agency, which are quangos.

The Department for Education and Employment is responsible for policies relating to these two areas. The current department is an amalgamation of the previously separate departments of education and employment. This

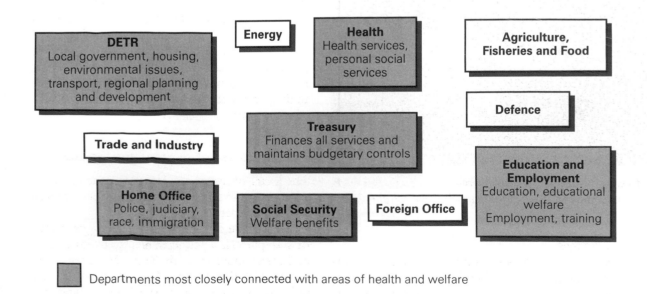

Departments most closely connected with areas of health and welfare

The central government departments most closely connected with health and welfare policy

expresses a deliberate policy objective on the part of the New Labour government, to link education and employment more closely.

The **Department of the Environment, Transport and the Regions** has a very wide range of functions relating to policy concerning the physical environment. This includes housing and inner-city policy, as well as public transport.

The **Home Office** is the key department responsible for law and order policies, including areas such as the police, prisons, immigration, the Probation Service and the courts.

The **Treasury** looks after the finances of the state, and has considerable control over public spending on health, welfare, education and employment services. Each year, the health, education, employment and welfare-related departments have to bid for the money that they wish to spend on their social policy programmes. After discussion of all of the departmental bids, a budget allocation for each department is announced. The departments then have to carry out their policy programmes within the constraints of these budgets. The funding of social policy is discussed in more detail in Chapter 4, on page 86.

The **Cabinet** is made up of the secretaries of state for each major central government department, as well as a number of other senior political figures. All of the Cabinet members will discuss the social policy proposals of the secretary of state for each health- and welfare-related department.

The European Union

The European Union (EU) now plays an important political role in shaping social policy in the United Kingdom. Through the European Parliament, the European Union has powers to develop social policies that relate to a wide range of welfare issues. It is able to influence social policy throughout the member states. These issues, and the impact that the development of the EU has had on British social policy are covered in more detail in Chapter 2, on pages 56–59.

Influences on social policy development

As we indicated earlier, social policy priorities are fundamentally determined by central government. But how do members of the government decide what these priorities should be? What factors influence a government to adopt one particular approach policy rather than another? In this section, we will look at a number of key influences on social policy-making (see diagram).

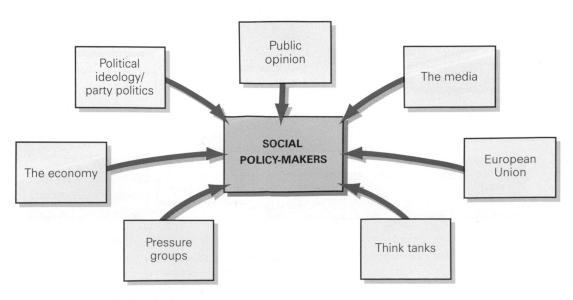

Influences on social policy development

Pressure groups and social policy

Pressure groups play a very important role in influencing governments to develop social policies. Two main types of pressure group can be identified:

- ◎ **Protective** pressure groups work to defend their own members' interests. The British Medical Association is an example of this type of pressure group. It works to represent and protect the interests of doctors.
- ◎ **Promotional** pressure groups **put forward new ideas** aimed at reforming and improving society for particular, usually vulnerable, people. One example of this type of pressure group is the Child Poverty Action Group, which works to represent and raise awareness of the experience and effects of poverty on children.

Pressure groups are usually 'single-issue' groups, or represent the interests of people with a specific set of needs. For example, ASH (Anti-Smoking for Health) is a single-issue group concerned with tobacco smoking, while MENCAP seeks to represent the interests of people with learning disabilities.

Pressure groups use a number of different strategies to try to influence social policy-makers in central government. **Lobbying of Parliament** is a strategy that involves representatives of the pressure group meeting or making contact in other ways with key government ministers and MPs to try to raise awareness of particular issues, and to get them to support the pressure group's proposals for change. **Publicity and use of the media** is another commonly used and powerful way of raising awareness of issues that pressure groups regard as important. Pressure groups try to get their issues covered through stories and interviews in newspapers and on television and radio. By bringing issues to the attention of both the general public and key social policy-makers, awareness and pressure for change can be built up. **Protest** is a dramatic, but often a last resort, measure that can be used to raise awareness of issues and put pressure on the government to develop new social policies. Pressure groups that resort to protest usually do so because they have relatively little power and influence to raise awareness and influence change in other ways. Marches and demonstrations can help a group to get their cause better known through the media when their protest is reported on by journalists.

Think tanks and social policy

The 'think tank' is another source of external influence on government policy-making. It is an organisation set up to carry out research and develop policy ideas, independently of government, which can then be communicated to, and perhaps developed by, those in power. Many 'think tanks' have close connections with politicians and political parties. In this respect, 'think tanks' are different from pressure groups, which try to remain independent, and seek to influence all political parties and governments. In contrast, 'think tanks' tend to try to influence the social policy decisions of specific parties. Pressure groups tend to have a fairly narrow social policy focus. They try to influence government social policy-making on 'single issues' or in relation to the specific client groups whom they represent. On the other hand, 'think tanks' have a broader social policy focus, and have explicit political and ideological goals, although they do not seek to get their employees/members elected to Parliament.

Think tanks in the UK
The Adam Smith Institute
The Institute for Public Policy Research (IPPR)
The Institute of Economic Affairs
The Social Market Foundation
The European Policy Forum
The Fabian Society
Demos

'Think tanks' work to come up with new ideas that can form the basis of social policy recommendations. They carry out research, and present their findings and supporting data as policy proposals to the political party whom they aim to influence. The earliest influential 'think tank' of relevance to social policy was the Fabian Society. The number, and influence, of 'think tanks' grew significantly during the 1980s.

REVIEW POINTS

The context of social policy

◎ Social policy is essentially a political activity. Elected politicians who are members of the government are the key social policy-makers in the UK.

◎ The state is the key provider of social welfare provision in the UK. The state consists of the formal political institutions, such as government departments, and public servants including teachers, social workers and NHS staff who deliver health, education and welfare services.

◎ The European Union now plays an important role in determining social policy priorities in the UK. Other key influences include pressure groups and 'think tanks', who operate outside of government with the specific aim of influencing and changing aspects of social policy.

REVIEW ACTIVITIES

1 Explain what the term **the state** means and identify its different elements.
2 Name, and briefly explain the responsibility of, four government departments that play a role in social policy development.
3 'The making of social policy is essentially a political activity.' What does this mean?
4 What is a 'pressure group'? Describe what pressure groups do to try to influence social policy-makers.
5 What role do 'think tanks' play in the social policy-making process?

Ideologies and social policy

Social policies are plans of action, or approaches, for dealing with 'social problems'. There are usually many different ways of dealing with a problem. In the health and social welfare area, different political parties are likely to take different approaches, and suggest different plans

of action, for dealing with what is essentially the same situation. Why is this? Why do New Labour, the Conservative Party and the Liberal Democrats, and the smaller nationalist parties such as Plaid Cymru and the Scottish Nationalist Party, all have different approaches to, for example, the provision of health services?

The answer is that each party bases its approach on a different 'package of ideas', or ideology, that guides its way of viewing, and method of dealing with, social welfare issues. There are now a number of ideological approaches to social policy. Before we look at these different approaches to social policy, we need to explore, and understand, the concept of 'ideology' a little more.

What is an ideology?

The term **ideology** is difficult to define in a precise way. It was first used by the French writer Antoine Destutt de Tracy, in his book *Elements d'Idéologie* (1805), to refer to the need to develop a 'science of ideas' in politics. At the time, it was believed that 'ideologies' could provide objective, truthful and scientific approaches to politics. While there are various uses of the term, we shall refer to the work of Roy Bentley, and take it to mean:

> 'a reasonably coherent structure of thought shared by a group of people. It is a means of explaining how society works and of explaining how it ought to work.'
>
> (Bentley *et al.*, 1995)

This use of the term 'ideology' is derived from political science. In sociology, the term is sometimes used differently, and is usually associated with Karl Marx's suggestion that an ideology is a set of false and misleading beliefs, propagated by a ruling elite to oppress and exploit the masses. An 'ideology', in the way in which we are using the term, has four main features or components:

◎ a theory about human nature
◎ an explanation of history
◎ an analysis of the role of the state
◎ implications for social policy proposals

A theory about human nature

Ideologies contain a view of what, in essence, people are really like. For example, it is possible to take a very optimistic view of human nature, and believe that most people can be trusted and are able to make important decisions about their lifestyle and behaviour. Alternatively, it is possible to take a more pessimistic view of the qualities of people, and view them as essentially selfish, untrustworthy and in need of monitoring and control. Your view on human nature is likely to influence your preferred ideological approach to social welfare issues.

As well as views about the essence of human nature, ideologies incorporate views on what it is that influences the development of human nature. For example, do you believe that people are born with the characteristics and personalities that they express throughout their lives – or do continuing social experiences influence and shape their behaviour? Your response to this question will again say something about your beliefs regarding human nature and will affect your preferred ideological position. Some ideological approaches see these aspects of human nature as fixed and unchanging from birth, while others incorporate the belief that people can change. When it comes to criminal justice policies, for example, policy-makers' beliefs about human nature can have a significant influence on how they respond to people who commit crime.

An explanation of history

Social policy-makers are usually involved in trying to make society better, as they see it, in the future. Whichever 'ideology' social policy-makers draw on to develop their policies, they need to interpret the past before being able to suggest a better future. In effect, social policy-makers develop a particular version, or understanding, of history to justify their actions. History isn't just about dates, events and 'facts'. It is also about what these things mean – what their significance is. For example, a National Health Service that offered comprehensive healthcare services – free to all at the point of delivery, and based on 'real need' – came into being as a result of the Labour government passing the National Health Service Act in 1948. This event and the dates involved are not in dispute. Some social policy-makers and analysts believe that this was a massively positive historical moment for social welfare. Others, particularly New Right thinkers, would say that it was at this point in our history that the state went too far, and set up a system that has encouraged and supported 'welfare dependency'. Neither view of history is more factually correct

than the other. Each simply interprets the evidence differently, because they view it through different ideological 'spectacles'. As 'packages of ideas', ideologies always include, and involve, a way of interpreting and explaining history.

An analysis of the role of the state

We said earlier that, amongst others, the state consists of central government, civil servants, social welfare and criminal justice staff. Ideas about the role that the state should play in people's lives are central to all social welfare ideologies. Should the state play a major, important role in people's lives or should the state avoid 'interfering'? What should the state aim to achieve through social policies? There are a number of possible goals – such as social control, order, equality and freedom. What, ultimately, are the effects of state intervention in social welfare? Some ideological approaches see positive benefits in terms of the improvements that the state can make in people's lives through social policies that re-engineer society. Others see state intervention as a dangerous development – as encouraging and trapping people in 'welfare dependency', or reliance on the state. From this kind of perspective, state intervention is seen to discourage self-help.

Social policy, as a subject, focuses on the approaches and responses (and the ideas behind them) of governments to major social problems and welfare issues. One of the key issues – and the focus of continuing debates – in social policy has always been the extent to which the government (or state) should intervene in people's lives, to provide them with welfare services and to regulate their behaviour. Throughout this book, the issue of 'state intervention' is a recurrent theme.

Implications for social policy proposals

Ideologies always include a position on each of the features outlined above. Each of the parts of an ideology is linked, and supports the others. For example, where human nature is viewed in an optimistic, positive way (people are capable of making their own decisions), it follows that the state should have a limited role in people's everyday lives, and should not dictate how people ought to behave. If, on the other hand, human nature is seen in a more negative, pessimistic way (people are untrustworthy, selfish and reckless), then it follows that the state should play a greater role to control and guide people's behaviour.

Ideologies offer different 'packages of ideas' to social policy-makers. They influence and guide their decision-making in different ways. This is why three social policy-makers can come up with three different solutions to what appears to be the same 'social problem'! We will look at this in more detail as we work through the main ideological approaches that have been evident in social policy over the past 200 years.

On paper, ideologies tend to look like relatively coherent, consistent 'packages of ideas'. It is usually possible to identify the principal ideological approach that a particular government adopts in its social policy-making. However, it is not necessarily the case that a political party or government always, or inevitably, bases its social policy programmes on a specific ideological position. In the real world, social policy-makers tend not to use ideologies in a direct way, as though they are following a 'recipe'.

Ideological approaches to social policy

Given the central role of governments in social policy-making, ideological approaches to welfare provision, and academic analysis of it, have tended to be linked to the left–right spectrum of political viewpoints that has existed over the past 100 years or so.

It is possible to locate some of the key ideological approaches to social policy within this spectrum, but others don't fit quite so easily. The New Right approach to social policy is a politically right-wing approach. Radical socialism is a politically left-wing approach. The New Labour government elected in 1997 seeks a 'middle way' between right-wing and left-wing political viewpoints. The extent to which this is a significant ideological development in itself is discussed later (see p. 55). The social democratic ideology is the nearest ideological position to New Labour's policy-making approach, but doesn't completely or adequately match it.

A number of ideological approaches to social policy fall outside of the party political spectrum. Feminism, anti-racism and environmentalism are ideological approaches that challenge the left–right model as providing an incomplete and inadequate representation of the interests of marginalised

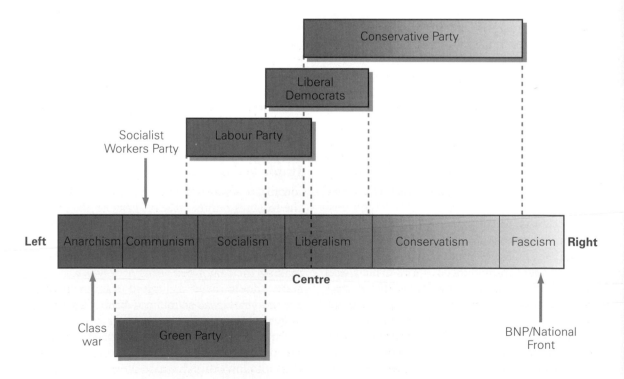

A linear model of the left–right political spectrum

groups such as women and minority ethnic groups, and of broader environmental concerns. These approaches are sometimes referred to as new social movements: they have gradually been developed and become more significant from the 1960s onwards.

Each of the main ideological approaches to social policy-making is outlined briefly below. They are all discussed in further detail in Chapter 13, on pages 356–365.

New Right approaches

This approach to social policy is also sometimes referred to as **market** or **economic liberalism**, a **neo-conservative** or **anti-collective** approach. Variations of New Right thinking have been around since the 17th and 18th centuries. The term **New Right** came about in America in the 1970s and, as an influence on social policy-making, was most powerful in the 1980s during the years of the Thatcher government.

People who adopt a New Right approach to social policy-making believe that the government should avoid becoming involved in regulating individuals' lives. New Right approaches put a lot of stress on **individual freedom** and **liberty** (for further discussion, see p. 20). New Right policy-makers believe that government intervention in social problems is a form of 'interference' in people's freedom, and that it makes social problems worse rather than better. These policy-makers usually prefer 'market' solutions to social problems.

New Right thinkers and policy-makers tend to make a distinction between, on the one hand, individuals who 'deserve' welfare services and help and, on the other, 'undeserving' individuals who should not receive government welfare and support (this is a theme that is discussed in more detail in Chapters 2 and 5). For example, those who are poor through no fault of their own are 'deserving' of help and welfare services, whereas those who are poor because they deliberately remain jobless, or who 'waste' their money or abilities through laziness, are 'undeserving'.

The New Right approach puts a lot of emphasis on **individual responsibility** and **choice**, and the motivating effect of a '**free market**' on both the purchasers and providers of health and social welfare services. New Right thinkers tend to believe that free, state-funded welfare services result in inefficient and expensive state organisations and '**welfare dependency**' on the part of their users. A better approach,

according to New Right thinkers, is to ensure that health and welfare organisations have to compete against each other for 'purchasers'. Competition will make the business of providing welfare services more efficient and cost-effective, and will drive up standards of service. New Right policy-makers see low taxation as a way of giving people who need health and welfare services the 'purchasing power' needed to exercise their right to choose which welfare services they will use.

The New Right approach opposes the idea of a state-provided health and welfare system, and argues that the current public system should be drastically reduced. Social policy-makers who were adopting a New Right approach in the 1980s developed policies that encouraged individuals to buy services from private providers or use voluntarily funded charitable services.

Social democratic approaches

The social democratic approach to social policy is also sometimes referred to as '**social liberalism**' and a '**collective**' approach. This type of approach to social policy-making results in the state providing far greater levels of social welfare services, and in regulating people's lives to an extent that is unacceptable to New Right thinkers. Social policy-makers influenced by social democratic approaches see central government – and, indeed, the state in general – as having an important role to play in 'managing society'. They believe that the state should protect its citizens from the extremes of poverty, and should act to prevent the development, in society, of major social and economic inequalities. The key principle that guides many social democratic social polices is **equality**. This is explained in more detail on page 19–21. New Right thinkers believe that financially 'successful' individuals should be free to choose what to do with their wealth. One choice that these people have is to contribute some money to charities that help the 'deserving' poor. In contrast, social democratic thinkers believe that it is the duty of the better-off to support people who are 'in need'. When this is translated into social policy-making, it means that social democratic policy-makers are more likely to impose taxes on high-earning individuals and use this money to fund health and social welfare services.

Social democratic thinkers often judge people's 'need' for welfare in terms of their 'objective' social, medical or psychological situation, rather than in 'moral' terms of whether they are 'deserving' or 'undeserving'. In addition, social democratic thinkers adopt the view that people's behaviour should, to some extent, be regulated and controlled by the state through the law. This use of state, or **collective, responsibility** is rejected by New Right thinkers on the grounds that it limits individual **freedom** and liberties. Freedom and liberty are important social policy principles, and collective responsibility is a key issue in social policy-making. All of this is discussed in more detail on pages 20–23.

The radical socialist approach

This is also sometimes referred to as the **Marxist**, **neo-Marxist** or **conflict** approach. People who hold radical socialist views oppose the capitalist economic system and blame it – and the small minority of very wealthy people who benefit from it – for inequality and social problems. Norman Ginsburg (1998) says that people who adopt a socialist approach to social policy-making make two assumptions about capitalism. First, they propose that capitalist societies can't meet the social welfare needs of all their members. This is because capitalism is founded on, and sustained by, 'competitive individualism'. Second, capitalism sustains fundamental social inequalities and divisions that are 'morally unacceptable and socially debilitating'.

Socialist approaches tend to see people as co-operative and, in essence, compassionate with regard to each other. Socialists also see behaviour as being shaped by social influences. As a consequence, it is important, in the socialist scheme, to create the kinds of environment in which all people can develop and thrive. Poor standards of housing, high levels of unemployment and the experience of poverty are seen as consequences of the capitalist system – and also as factors that create certain types of social problem (crime and ill-health, for example). This contrasts with the New Right, and, to some extent, social democratic approaches, which locate the causes of many social problems within individuals themselves, seeing them as bad, weak or less able people.

It follows from socialist analyses of human behaviour, and their blaming of capitalism for many social problems, that the state should play a major role in tackling social problems and creating appropriate social conditions and opportunities. The goal of radical socialism is the transformation of capitalism. Radical socialist social policy would use extensive state intervention to challenge the capitalist system and 'capitalist class', in its mission to create a new, more co-operative, supportive and egalitarian society.

One key goal of social policy would be to redistribute wealth and resources in society in order to achieve **equality** (for more discussion of this principle, see p. 17) and the **universal provision** of welfare. The socialist approach is based on the idea that there are universal human needs, and that there is also a **universal (collective) responsibility** for ensuring that those basic needs are met. This leads to the idea that people have **'social rights'** (that is, to have their needs met) and to the requirement that welfare services should be publicly funded (collective responsibility) in order to achieve social equality of outcome. It is for these reasons that socialist approaches to social policy-making and welfare provision are associated with higher taxation.

The United Kingdom has never been a socialist state. It has always been, and remains, a capitalist state. Radical socialism and Marxism are ideologies that have always been on the far left of the British political spectrum. The ideology adopted by the old Labour Party (pre-Blair) was a milder form of gradualist reformism rather than revolutionary socialism.

The feminist approach

Feminism offers a relatively new approach to social policy analysis. It does not fit within the party political spectrum, as do the New Right, socialist and social democratic approaches. In fact, Jane Lewis (1998: 86) argues that it is 'a mistake to think that it is possible to identify a single feminist approach to social policy'. There are various ways in which the perspectives of women can be used to challenge the assumptions and practices of social policy-makers and welfare providers.

Feminist approaches share the characteristic of viewing social issues from the perspective of women. Lewis (1998) indicates that feminist analyses of social policies began to appear in the 1970s. Feminists are often very critical of the welfare state, and the way in which 'traditional' (male) social policy works against women or fails to support them. A theme of many feminist analyses is that social policies have articulated in-built male assumptions about gender roles, and have implemented a 'patriarchal welfare state'. For example, in the not too distant past it was assumed by the benefits system that if a woman was cohabiting with a man he would take responsibility for supporting her, and so women in this

Table 1.3 Approaches to social policy

Issues	New Right	Social Democratic	Radical Socialist	Feminist	Anti-racist
		Perspectives			
ECONOMICS	A free market unfettered by government interference. People should have very low taxes, and decide what to do with their money.	A free market, but with government control to even out the extremes of wealth and poverty. Relatively high levels of taxation.	State to own all businesses and commerce. Salaries and conditions related to government decisions.	A radical approach to what is considered work, therefore housework is of equal status to employment. Work should be made more flexible to respond to more demands on women (such as family).	Employment practice should be radically examined. Positive action programme should be introduced to give blacks and Asians preference in employment to compensate for past discrimination.
INEQUALITY between people	Good, necessary and a spur to make people work harder. People should be rewarded for their hard work and should not pay high rates of tax.	Acceptable and inevitable, but *extremes* cannot be allowed. So a welfare state would provide for the less well-off and this will be paid for by heavy taxes on the rich.	Inequality is wrong, and needs to be eliminated by state action. There should be, as far as possible, a classless society. No wealth and no poverty.	Inequality is wrong, women have always been discriminated against, and economic/social policies need to be introduced specifically to benefit women.	Inequality is wrong, blacks and Asians have always been discriminated against, and economic/social policies need to be introduced specifically to benefit ethnic groups.
WELFARE STATE	Bad, creates a **dependency culture**, where people rely on the government for help, instead of self-help or family. Welfare is enormously expensive, wasteful bureaucracy.	Good. Welfare state helps pull people together by providing sense of shared citizenship. Compensates those who 'lose out' in a market economy.	Majority and minority views which differ. *Majority* – welfare state is good and should be improved. The result of working-class pressure. *Minority* – bad, introduced to stop the people demanding a radical overhaul of the capitalist system.	Concept is good, but is based on the exploitation of women, both as low-paid carers/professionals and as unpaid carers in the home. Needs to be restructured, taking into account the specific needs of women.	Concept good, but institutional racism exists. Needs to be more aware of, and responsive to, needs of blacks and Asians.
HEALTH CARE	Should be private, insurance-based for the majority of people, for those with limited incomes, there would be assistance with fees or a residual state healthcare sector.	National Health Service, free and fully funded by the government.	National Health Service, but also a belief that much illness is a result of capitalism and therefore eliminating capitalism would reduce ill health.	Provided cheaply by women, both formally and informally. Women suffer worse health than men but some areas of women's lives have been 'medicalised'; for example, drugs for depression, childbirth.	Greater awareness of ethnic groups' needs by the NHS. Large numbers of poor paid black workers in the NHS labour force.

SOCIAL POLICY AND WELFARE

situation had their social security benefits withdrawn. There are many examples of social policies and welfare services that are based on 'traditional' or as feminists would say, 'patriarchal' ideas about male and female roles and family life.

Feminists are in favour of a woman-centred approach to social policy-making, one which deals with the inequality that women experience as a social group, and which addresses some of the specific issues that are important to women.

Anti-racist approaches

The particular focus of anti-racist social policy-makers is the situation of black and other minority ethnic groups. People who seek anti-racist social policy want government to recognise racism as a major social problem, and anti-racism as a central social policy goal. It is argued that effective social policy measures can be used in positive ways to counter individual, organisational and societal racism.

The anti-racist approach to social policy – when applied to past and existing social policy measures, and to the social welfare system as a whole – tends to identify racism as an existing, endemic feature of 'welfare' provision and the ideologies that underpin it. Ahmad and Craig (1998: 91), for example, state that 'racism in state welfare has a long history.' As a subject, social policy has tended to ignore the issues of 'race' and racism, and the social divisions and inequalities between different ethnic groups.

Anti-racism is an approach to combating inequalities. It is built on the notion that racism is institutionalised and is an everyday part of life for many people in British society, rather than just being the 'unacceptable behaviour' of a small, 'bad' racist minority. This approach emphasises the need for broad social policies that challenge and change the ways in which racism is institutionalised, as well as measures to deal with overtly racist behaviour.

Environmentalism

Environmental, or Green, approaches to social policy emerged and have grown in influence from the 1970s onwards. **Environmental ideologies** claim to be outside of the left–right party political spectrum, and centre on a concern for the maintenance of an appropriate, **sustainable** balance between people and the natural environment.

Environmentalism can be thought of in two forms – **light Green** and **dark Green** (Ferris, 1991).

The 'light Green' approach has now become a part of the policy approach of successive Conservative and Labour governments, both of which have claimed that they take the public's environmental concerns seriously. Dark Greens are much more critical of governments and of the welfare state itself. There tends to be little explicit debate about social policies, and rather more of a critique of government policies and actions as being the result of over-industrialisation and over-population.

Environmentalism has an indirect impact on social policy and welfare debates, through the growing significance of, and concern for, the creation of a sustainable environment. Welfare issues are addressed in the very broad sense of the relationship between people and the natural world. Environmentalism offers a critique of the large-scale, bureaucratic state health and welfare systems that have developed in Western societies to cope with the effects of industrialisation. Environmental ideologies do not suggest specific social policy responses or principles, but they are now influencing social policy-makers to take environmental impact and sustainable development into account when addressing both long-standing and new social problems and policy issues.

REVIEW POINTS

Ideological approaches to social policy

- Ideologies are 'packages of ideas' that guide and influence social policy-makers in identifying and responding to social welfare issues.
- The key ideologies that have traditionally been associated with British social policy are known as the New Right approach and the social democratic approach.
- In the UK, the New Right and social democratic ideologies have strongly influenced the social policy approaches of the Conservative Party and the Labour Party, respectively, during the latter part of the 20th century.
- Radical socialist, feminist and anti-racist ideologies offer non-party alternatives to social welfare issues, and are critical of the assumptions and principles on which the New Right

18

and social democratic approaches are based.

- ◎ Environmentalism offers a radically different ideological approach to social policy issues that challenges, in certain respects, the party political and 'marginalised group' approach of other ideologies.

- ◎ Social policy-making does not follow a 'pure' ideological approach. Ideologies offer general sources of guidance to social policy-makers. Social policies can often include a mix of differing and competing ideologies.

> ### REVIEW ACTIVITIES
>
> 1 In your own words, explain what the term **ideology** means in social policy.
> 2 With which British political party is the New Right ideology associated?
> 3 Identify two of the key principles that characterise the New Right approach to social policy-making.
> 4 What are the key principles of the social democratic approach to social policy? Explain within your answer how these principles contrast with the New Right approach.
> 5 What is the key goal of the radical socialist approach to social policy-making? How do radical socialists suggest that this could be achieved?
> 6 Why are feminists critical of 'traditional' social policies and the welfare state? What are the main goals of feminist social policy?
> 7 What key social problem can be tackled by anti-racist social policy? Why, according to the anti-racist approach, has this proved to be so difficult to deal with?

Key principles in social policy

Social policies are guided by a number of key principles. These principles are what drives, or gives direction to, and are also sometimes the goals of, social policy. Social policy principles partly express moral beliefs and 'a vision of how things ought or ought not to be' in society (Blakemore, 1998: 17). As we saw in the previous section on ideology, there are a number of different possible 'visions' of how the world 'ought' to be. Each ideological approach makes use of the key social policy principles in a particular way.

Equality

'Equality' has been a key principle, and goal, for left-wing social policy-makers since the beginning of the 20th century. Politicians and policy-makers

from the social democratic, socialist and anti-racist traditions, for example, note that there are unacceptable social inequalities in British society. For these people, social policy should be used to create a fairer, more equal, society.

In contrast, right-wing thinkers, and New Right social policy-makers, tend to believe that it is wrong to attempt to *make* society more equal through the use of social policies. One classic way in which governments have tried to 'engineer' greater equality is through imposing high taxes on people who have high incomes, and then redistributing this money – through health, education and welfare services – to people on lower incomes (for a longer discussion of 'social engineering', see p. 23). Social policy during the postwar consensus period was based on such a 'tax-and-spend' approach.

The redistribution of wealth

Right-wing social policy-makers contend that the goal of 'equalising' society in this way can only be achieved at the 'cost' of those people who have got themselves into the best positions in society. They also argue that society in general suffers, because attempts to impose 'equality' require a very active, interventionist state bureaucracy that 'interferes' in people's lives and reduces their **freedom** and **liberty**. This doesn't mean that the New Right, or right-wing social policy-makers, ignore all forms of 'equality'. They believe, for example, in social policies that promote 'equality of opportunity' but not equality of outcome. The accompanying cartoon illustrates the different ways in which social policy-makers interpret the principle of 'equality'.

Egalitarianism is based on the idea that people have *equal rights* and that there should be *equal outcomes* for all. In practice, egalitarians tend to tolerate some degree of inequality because of individual differences. Whereas some people are motivated, capable and work hard, others are lazy, incompetent and dishonest. What if the cake in our cartoon was a *reward* for clearing snow? Should everybody get the same amount of cake simply because they took part in the work? Is this not unfair and unjust to the people who worked hardest and achieved the most? There are various points of view on this. The cake doesn't have to be a *reward* for work. It could be seen simply as nutritious food, offered to meet people's physical needs. In order to achieve 'equality' in nutritional status/energy levels, it might be

The equality dilemma

necessary to treat the 'snow clearers' differently rather than equally. This sounds strange at first, but treating people differently can result in a kind of equality. We might say that the people who have greater nutritional needs should get more cake! In social policy terms, this is known as 'equity'.

Equity means that people with greater needs are treated more favourably than people with fewer unmet needs, to equalise 'outcomes'. The problem with the 'equity' approach to equality is that it does not *look fair*. Equity approaches also require social policy-makers to come up with acceptable and accurate definitions and ways of measuring 'need'.

Both **egalitarianism** and **equity** involve attempts to ensure equality of outcome. There is another approach that does not do this. A third way is to use social policy to ensure that people have '**equality of opportunity**'. This usually means giving people an equal chance in, or equal access to, competitive situations. Equality of opportunity policies work a little like a competitive athletics race.

Social policies that aim to promote equality of opportunity are criticised on the grounds that they fail to take into account existing social

inequalities, and the relative advantages and disadvantages that people have when they enter 'the race'. Some of the athletes in our example may be better prepared because better pre-race training opportunities were available to them, or they may know other runners who will work to help them during the race.

Needs

'Need' is an important concept in social policy. It is usually used to refer to the requirements of different groups in society, such as 'the needs of people in poverty' or 'children's needs'. The rationale for much social policy is that it targets the social welfare needs, or more usually the *unmet* social welfare needs, of particular social groups. So, what are 'needs'? Len Doyal and Ian Gough (1991) have identified **physical health** and **autonomy** as universal basic human needs. They list a number of factors that they say contribute to the attainment of physical health and autonomy (see box).

Everybody starts from the same point and races under the same conditions. All runners enter on the same terms (equal access) and, theoretically, any one of them could win (equality of opportunity). In reality, it is highly likely that some will do better than others. Individual differences in potential and ability will result in a range of different outcomes. Is this fair and just?

Universal basic human needs
Nutritional food and clean water
Protective housing
A non-hazardous work environment
A non-hazardous physical environment
Appropriate health care
Security in childhood
Significant primary relationships
Physical security
Economic security
Appropriate education
Safe birth control and child-bearing

You will probably be able to suggest other items that you think should be in the list (see box), and you might dispute some of the items that are already included! It is very difficult to identify 'needs' objectively. One reason for this is that there are a number of ways of thinking about 'need'. Jonathon Bradshaw (1972) has identified four different ways of defining 'need' (see Table 1.4).

Table 1.4

Ways of defining 'need'

Felt need occurs when individuals are aware of their own needs. Not all 'felt need' is expressed, as inequalities in power and status can prevent less powerful groups from voicing their needs. Should social policy seek out and try to meet unexpressed 'felt need'?

Normative needs are those that are defined according to the norms, or standards, of health and social welfare professionals. Should social policy be based on the 'professional', normative judgements about 'need'?

Expressed needs are those that are known about, publicised and which become demands. Should social policy always respond to 'expressed need'?

Comparative needs result from making relative judgements between different social groups; that is, the 'needs' of one group are defined in relation to what others have or don't have.

'Need' is a concept that keeps appearing in social policy debates. There is a continuing debate, for example, over the extent to which the state should be responsible for meeting human needs. Should the state assume responsibility for providing social welfare services to all people in all need areas? Left-wing policy-makers are likely to be more comfortable with this position than right-wing policy-makers. What is the role of the individual in meeting his or her own needs? How much 'self-help' responsibility should be placed on people? Right-wing policy-makers are more likely to support a greater degree of self-help as being the means for meeting 'need'.

Freedom and rights

Individual **freedom** and **rights** are also concepts that have occupied the minds of social policy-makers and thinkers for a long time. These social policy principles are most often associated with right-wing social policy ideologies. Right-wing advocates of freedom and rights suggest that human beings should be free from control and coercion in their lives, and that all people should

have an inalienable right to freedom. Infringement of personal freedom therefore involves a denial of individual rights, as it restricts an individual's opportunity to realise his or her potential. The key issue for social policy-makers is to decide what freedom and rights mean in practical terms.

Right-wing thinkers believe that freedom springs from the way in which the economy is managed. For them, 'free markets' promote freedom for everyone. However, social democrats (and others) maintain that the state should step in to control the market and mitigate the inequalities that it causes (see Chapter 2). The issues of 'freedom and rights' and the role of the state are central debates in discussions about social policy. To what extent should the state act to ensure the 'freedom' and 'rights' of every citizen to enjoy a certain standard of living and welfare?

The use of key principles in social policy-making

There is rarely a clear, unambiguous set of principles underlying specific social policies. In practice, social policies are often based on conflicting principles, and apparently different ideological approaches can make use of 'equality', 'needs' or 'freedom' in their social policy measures. Nevertheless, debates over how governments should act in dealing with important social welfare issues often include, at one level or another, some thinking about and application of ideas about 'need', 'equality' and 'freedom'.

REVIEW POINTS

Principles in social policy

- Social policies are often driven by ideological goals such as equality and freedom.

- 'Equality' is an ideal that is most often associated with left-wing policy approaches, while 'freedom' is a principle that is most often associated with right-wing approaches.

- There are at least three ways of interpreting the principle of equality.

These are known as 'egalitarianism', 'equity' and 'equality of opportunity'.

◎ The concept of 'need' is central to social policy-making, but is difficult to define. The various definitions of need centre around ways of identifying the 'basic requirements' of human beings.

REVIEW ACTIVITIES

1 Why is 'equality' such an important principle for left-wing social policy-makers?
2 On what grounds do right-wing social policy-makers object to 'equality' as a policy goal?
3 What are the three main types of 'equality'? In your own words, briefly explain what each involves.
4 'Need' is a key social policy concept that can be defined in different ways. Identify and explain two ways in which this concept can be defined.
5 Which ideological approach to social policy is most likely to promote 'freedom' and 'individual rights' as key principles?
6 Why do New Right notions of 'freedom' promote minimal state intervention in welfare provision?

An overall view – contrasting conceptions of social policy

In this section, we will look at some of the contrasting ways of understanding the nature of, and reason for, social policy. The short discussions that follow are cross-referenced to other sections of the book. This will enable you to check your understanding of related social policy ideas and concepts – and it will also enable you to follow up debates, themes and issues that interest you. The areas covered touch on central debates about, and conceptions of, the rationale for social policy, such as 'Why does social policy exist?' and 'What should social policy be used for?'

Social policy and social engineering

As we have seen earlier, in the sections on the political context of social policy and on ideology, social policy-making is a very political and 'contested' practice. A simple answer to the question 'What should social policy be used for?' would be to say that social policies should be used to produce a better society. But what is better? What is a good society? These are questions that provoke a large amount of political debate and

conflict. Nevertheless, governments do develop and implement social policies in order to 'engineer' – that is, design and construct – a better society. This is sometimes referred to as the **social engineering** approach to social policy.

Blakemore (1998: 211) defines social engineering as 'a philosophy or approach to government which suggests that it is possible to plan solutions to social problems and to create a new social order'. A government committed to using social policy for 'social engineering' purposes would, in the extreme, plan and deliver welfare services to achieve deliberate political goals. Blakemore (1998) argues that the 'social engineering' motive was a significant element of the public housing and urban planning initiatives from 1918 to the end of the 1920s. During this period, social policy-makers believed that social divisions could be reduced and a better quality of life achieved through the adoption, by the state, of a policy of funding and providing social housing and new urban landscapes in the form of 'garden cities'.

Cumbernauld was one of several new towns built or designated under the New Towns Act of 1946, an example of social engineering in housing policy

The postwar consensus on social policy (see p. 10) has also been described as being based on an acceptance of the social engineering approach to social policy. During this period, there was an assumption, by all governments, that the gradual development and extension of the 'welfare state' would improve society. The assumption was that, through social policy, governments could reduce inequality and create a better, fairer society. But 'better' in what way? 'Fairer' for whom? In the 1980s the Thatcher governments challenged the whole idea of the 'welfare state' (see pp. 50–53), in order to bring about what was then felt, by the Conservative Party, to be a 'better society'. For example, the Thatcher governments used a number of deregulation and privatisation policies to bring about, or 'engineer', a reversal of the state's role in building and providing mass 'public housing'. The sale of council houses was a deliberate attempt to create a 'property-owning democracy' as well as to reduce the state's house-building bill.

Social policy-making does implicitly involve an attempt to change society, but there are always political and ideological battles over what is good, right and ought to happen. In reality, the social engineering approach to social policy involves a paternalistic use of state intervention to bring about changes that are seen as 'desirable' and beneficial for people (Blakemore, 1998). For some people, social policy should be used to 'engineer' a more equal society. For others, it should be used to promote individual freedom and rights. There are yet others who believe that it should be used primarily to promote a society that treats women and people of all ethnic groups fairly and justly.

Social policy as a statement of collective conscience

The idea of social conscience

'The history of social policy is portrayed as a process of progressive social betterment. This is often linked to the idea of a gradually developing *social conscience*.'

(Burden, 1998: 69)

Why does social policy exist? That is, why is it necessary? What are the reasons for the development, and continued existence, of the government's social policy role? One way of answering these questions, and of explaining the rationale for social policy, is to say that an objective need and *public pressure* for social policies developed in the 19th century (see pp. 33–34), and still remains.

The suggestion is that the world faced, and continues to face, a number of significant social problems that required 'solutions' – or, at the very least, government responses. In the increasingly complex society that emerged in 19th-century industrialised Britain, there was, and has continued to be, a need to support people who were unable to cope without state social welfare provision, and to bring order to social life. During the late 19th century, the increasing social policy intervention of governments into areas of British social life was, according to this argument, stimulated by the growth and expression of a 'collective conscience' in British society that demanded social policy intervention. So, what does the 'collective conscience' involve?

A person who has a 'strong conscience' has clear moral values. He or she has reasonably clear beliefs about what is right and wrong, acceptable and unacceptable. Sociologists, particularly those who use a 'functionalist' perspective, suggest that 'society', as an interdependent collection of people(s), exists because people share and accept common values. They contend that there is consensus, or agreement, on what is acceptable and unacceptable in relation to important issues, such as how people ought to behave towards each other, and about the social and physical conditions in which people live.

The 'collective conscience' approach is based on the idea that social policy is an expression, or statement, of shared values and beliefs about social welfare, and the behaviour and social conditions that can and can't be tolerated in society. Many social policy developments have been explained as being reactions against unacceptable social conditions in society. The discovery, and periodic rediscovery, of 'poverty' in Britain is one such example. In the late 19th century, a number of major studies of living standards, particularly those by Charles Booth (1840–1916) and Joseph Rowntree (1836–1925) exposed the existence of widespread poverty in Britain (see p. 119). This stimulated public opinion and was a spur to the development of the benevolent, paternalistic interventions that have become known as the 'social conscience approach'.

The implication of the 'social conscience' explanation is that governments develop social policy as a reaction to collective beliefs and values about basic social welfare standards and values, and do so out of benevolent motives, to do with social betterment. It is the case that policymakers sometimes try to correct 'social wrongs', such as poverty or homelessness, when they become aware of their existence – and also of strong public opinion on the matter. However, governments, especially those that have a strong ideological viewpoint and a commitment to reform, also aim deliberately to influence the 'social conscience' and set the social policy agenda themselves.

The 'social betterment' explanation of the purpose of social policy can be criticised for failing to acknowledge that social policy has also been used for **social control** purposes. Social policy measures can be analysed and interpreted as a catalogue of ways of monitoring and regulating people's behaviour, and as a way of imposing social controls – and the dominant ideas of powerful groups – on less powerful groups in society.

The balancing of public support and self-help within social policy initiatives

There has been a long-standing historical debate about *the extent to which* the state should intervene in social welfare issues, and what the individual's own responsibilities should be. There are two obvious extremes in this debate: that the state should provide for all the welfare needs of its citizens; and that the state should not intervene in the area of social welfare, because these issues are essentially 'private responsibilities'. Neither of these positions reflect what actually happens in terms of social welfare provision in the UK, which is that social policies tend to produce a compromise position, so that they involve elements of both public support and self-help.

'Public support' refers to state intervention in social welfare issues. State support for individuals who were unable to meet their own welfare needs began at the end of the 19th century (see p. 42). This began a gradual process of moving away from a 'self-help' system in which welfare needs were seen as personal responsibilities, and social problems as 'personal misfortune'. The 'self-help' ideal was a very strong value in the 19th-century Victorian era. The belief that the government should intervene to support those who were actually unable to help themselves gradually evolved and became accepted during the 20th century. Despite this, and for various reasons, the 'self-help' principle never disappeared, and remains an important feature of social policy.

From both moral and political perspectives, 'self-help' has been seen as a good thing and a goal that people should seek to achieve. 'Self-help' is considered to be important in promoting personal responsibility and avoiding 'welfare dependency'. A continuing theme of the Thatcher governments' social policy initiatives in the 1980s – and something that was taken up by the Blair government in the 1990s – is the idea that the state should provide 'selective' welfare (public support) to people most in need. This should be combined with a requirement that individuals in receipt of welfare should take as much responsibility as possible for meeting their own needs. For example, the early attempts to introduce 'unemployment benefit' following the National Insurance Act 1911 were based on the important principle that workers should pay contributions that would be supplemented by the government.

The balance of public support and self-help within social policy initiatives tends to shift depending on the political ideology of the government in power and the state of the economy. Public support for welfare initiatives has tended to be greater under Labour governments, particularly during the prosperous postwar period when the 'welfare state' developed and expanded. The years of economic recession and the emergence of New Right influenced policy in the 1980s under the Thatcher governments saw a shift back to 'self-help'. Despite a reduction in public support for welfare initiatives in the 1980s, it was never withdrawn.

The debates about how much welfare should be provided – that is, what the balance of public support and self-help should be within social policy initiatives – is closely linked to the issue of individual rights and responsibilities in relation to welfare.

REVIEW POINTS

Contrasting conceptions of social policy

- The purpose and use of social policy is a contested issue. Governments tend to develop and implement social policies that express their own political/ideological beliefs about how society 'ought' to be.
- The use of social policy deliberately to change and develop society in particular ways is referred to as a 'social engineering' approach.
- From a 'functionalist' perspective, social policy emerged and continues to

exist because it is a means through which the 'collective social conscience' is expressed.

- The 'social conscience' explanation for social policy can be criticised on the grounds that it fails to take due account of the social control function of much social policy and the power of elite social policy-makers.
- There has been a continuing debate within social policy about how much public support should be provided relative to the amount of self-help. The balance shifts according to the ideological position of the government in power.

REVIEW ACTIVITIES

1 Why is it inadequate simply to say that the purpose of social policy is 'to produce a better society'? Explain what this statement *doesn't* say!
2 In your own words, explain the term **social engineering** as it is applied to social policy.
3 'Social policy expresses the "collective social conscience".' How can this claim be explained in functionalist terms?
4 What are some of the problems associated with the idea of a 'collective social conscience'?
5 Why might a government place a high value on 'self-help' in its social policy initiatives?

References

Ahmad, W. and Craig, G. (1998) 'Race' and social welfare. In: *The Student's Companion to Social Policy* (ed. Alcock, P., Erskine, A. and May, M.). Blackwell, Oxford.

Alcock, P. (1996) *Social Policy in Britain*. Macmillan Press, Basingstoke.

Bentley, R., Dobson, A., Grant, M. and Roberts, D. (1995) *British Politics in Focus* (ed. Roberts, D.). Causeway Press, Ormskirk.

Blakemore, K. (1998) *Social Policy – an Introduction*. Open University Press, Buckingham.

Bradshaw, J. (1972) A taxonomy of social need. In: *Problems and Progress in Medical Care: Essays on Current Research, 7th Series* (ed. McLachlan, G.). Oxford University Press, London, for the Nuffield Provincial Hospitals Trust.

Burden, T. (1998) *Social Policy and Welfare – a Clear Guide*. Pluto Press, London.

Doyal, L. and Gough, I. (1991) *A Theory of Human Need*. Macmillan, London.

Ferris, J. (1991) Green politics and the future of welfare. In: *Social Policy Review 1990–91* (ed. Manning, N.). Longman, Harlow.

Ginsburg, N. (1998) The socialist perspective. In: *The Student's Companion to Social Policy* (ed. Alcock, P., Erskine, A. and May, M.). Blackwell, Oxford.

Jones, C. (1985) *Patterns of Social Policy: an Introduction to Comparative Analysis*. Tavistock, London.

Lewis, J. (1998) Feminist perspectives. In: *The Student's Companion to Social Policy* (ed. Alcock, P., Erskine, A. and May, M.). Blackwell, Oxford.

Spicker, P. (1995) *Social Policy: Themes and Approaches*. Harvester Wheatsheaf, Hemel Hempstead.

2 The Development of Social Policy in the 20th Century

By the end of this chapter you should be able to:

- ◎ Understand the historical origins of social policy in the United Kingdom.
- ◎ Outline the role of the Liberals and the birth of welfarism.
- ◎ Describe the contribution of Beveridge to the development of the modern welfare state.
- ◎ Understand the significance of Thatcherism and Blairism in the reconstitution of social policy in late modernity.
- ◎ Describe the emergence of the European influence and the role of the European Union in the evolution of social policy in the United Kingdom.

Modern social policy-making and welfare provision in Britain has its roots in the 18th and 19th centuries. This chapter describes and explores the development of social policy in Britain from that period until the present day.

The chapter begins by considering the reasons why an historical perspective is important in understanding British social policy development. We then explore the influence of 19th-century social, economic and political change, particularly the processes of industrialisation, urbanisation and the development of capitalism, and the significance of these in stimulating social policy initiatives. While these major social changes are important, there are a number of ways of understanding the link between social change and social policy development. We look at the 'functionalist' explanation, which explains social welfare provision as being a response to newly emerging 'needs' in the 19th century; and the 'conflict' approach, which relates social policy development to the emergence of the labour movement and concerns about 'class conflict'.

Nineteenth-century approaches to the problem of poverty, and to the significant public health problems that existed at this time, are outlined to provide an illustration of early welfare provision, and also of the

emergence of some of the key themes that have run through social policy ever since. The late 19th and early 20th centuries saw a significant increase in state intervention in welfare provision. The role that the Liberal Party, and the philosophy of 'social liberalism', played in extending welfare provision through policy development is described, and the range of welfare provision that existed in the era before the welfare state is illustrated.

The development of a national, government-funded system of health and welfare after the Second World War was a watershed in British social policy development and welfare provision. The political commitment to this new 'welfare state' is discussed and illustrated in the section on the postwar 'welfare' consensus. The next watershed in social policy-making and welfare provision occurred in the 1980s, when the 'postwar consensus' was challenged by the New Right approach of the Thatcher-led Conservative governments. We will look at the consequences of this and the extent to which it has been continued or changed since the emergence of the New Labour government in 1997. The chapter ends by outlining the role that the European Union now plays in influencing the direction and development of social policy and welfare provision in the UK.

The historical origins of social policy-making in the United Kingdom

Introduction

You may already be wondering why a history of social policy is necessary. Isn't social policy about the future, about making society a better place? Why do we need to look at the past? These are questions that students sometimes ask, and probably more often think to themselves, as their teacher begins a lesson by saying 'In the 18th century ...'. Nevertheless an understanding of the historical background to present-day, or contemporary, social policy is important, and ultimately helpful to all people interested in social welfare issues.

Richard Brown (1991) identifies a number of ways in which 'history' can help students to understand the general social and economic development of British society. We can usefully adapt and apply these to our more specific need of understanding social policy and welfare development in British society:

- ◎ History tells us about the variety of ways in which people have already thought about social policy and provided social welfare. It tells us that social policy thinking and welfare provision have gradually *evolved* over time. To understand what people think and do (in relation to social policy) today, we need to understand the thinking and practices of the past.

- ◎ History allows us to draw on, and hopefully benefit from, people's experience of policy-making and welfare provision in the past. If social policy-makers know about the principles and patterns of welfare provision and experience that have already occurred, they can avoid 'reinventing the

wheel'. Knowledge of the past also gives some insight into the possibilities of what might happen in the future.

Many of the ideas and debates that feature in contemporary social policy do have a long history and repeat earlier themes. Modern social policy in the UK has evolved over the past two centuries, and continues to do so, with new social policies building on, responding to and sometimes extending pre-existing ideas and approaches. Ken Blakemore (1998: 40) identifies a number of key social policy themes that link current and historical social policy issues. These are outlined in Table 2.1.

What does an historical account of social policy development involve?

As we explore the historical background to the development of UK social policy, we will be looking at the actions, beliefs and experiences of people in a changing society. We are trying to identify and understand what people – as individuals, in communities, groups, institutions and, on a very general level, as a society – believed and did about what we now call 'social issues' and 'problems'. We will need to identify and refer to specific social policy events and achievements in the past, and also to the general themes and patterns of social policy thinking and welfare provision.

An historical analysis looks at social policy development in the UK in relation to both change and continuity. However, we are not suggesting that we are presenting the 'True Facts'. Neither will we be saying that the events and factors that

Table 2.1 Repeating themes in social policy over time

Present-day social policy issue	Historical example of the theme
Welfare dependency; 'workfare'; dealing with 'social exclusion' and the possible formation of an underclass	The reform of the Poor Law; the 'workhouse test'; distinctions between 'deserving' and 'undeserving' poor
Renewed interest in public health and preventive policies; health promotion	Public health reforms; government regulation of sanitation, housing and working conditions

we refer to are connected in precise, specific ways – such as 'A happened, which led to B and then C'. There are many possible 'histories' of social policy development, because history always involves interpretation of the past. It is impossible to say precisely which of many coexisting influences in the past *caused* social policy to develop in the way that we describe it.

Nevertheless, it is possible to use historical evidence to try to understand the origins and evolution of social policy-making, by identifying and describing a number of social, political and economic influences that seem to have stimulated social change and subsequent social policy development over time. We will focus on trying to describe these influences, and we will explore the ways in which these factors may have influenced governments to become involved in 'forms of state intervention which affect the social opportunities and conditions under which people live[d]' (Burden, 1998: xi).

Key influences on social policy development in the 18th and 19th centuries

Think about the following two questions for a moment:

- ◎ At what point did social policy-making first become a feature of government activity in Britain?

- ◎ Why did social policy develop in the way that it has?

If you understood the points being made about history in the previous section, you will know that there is no way of providing a *'correct'* answer to these two questions. The historical development of social policy is not an unproblematic, linear chain of events. There is no definitive beginning point, no moment or event that we can point to and say 'this is when social policy making first began'. This would seem to pose something of a problem for you in understanding the origins of social policy development in the UK!

Many social historians and social policy writers link the origins of social policy development to major changes that occurred in British society between the beginning of the 18th and the end of the 19th centuries. These social changes resulted in the evolution of new, problematic social conditions, new forms of economic relations and new political institutions, which made government-led social policy-making

possible and necessary. We will begin trying to 'locate' social policy development historically, by looking at how society changed from the beginning of the 18th century onwards, and then we will consider how different types of explanation link these changes to the emergence of welfare provision.

Social change during the 18th and 19th centuries

The **Industrial Revolution** is often referred to as a key period in the economic and social history of Britain. **Industrialisation** refers to the gradual change from traditional, agricultural methods to those involving some form of mechanised, factory-based production. Britain was the first nation in the world to go through the process of becoming industrialised. The Industrial Revolution is thought to have begun at some time in the 18th century, and it continued into the 20th century. Historical evidence shows that, during this period, industrialisation transformed British society and the lives of British people. Social transformation did not happen suddenly, as though one year Britain was a pre-industrial, agricultural society and the next it was 'industrialised'. There was a gradual change in methods of production and the location of people's work that – combined with other important social, political and economic developments – are linked to the development of major health and social welfare problems.

In the following sections, the general process of social change during industrialisation, and the problematic social conditions to which these changes led, are described. These social conditions were important in stimulating thinking about, and early interventions in, the provision of social welfare.

The growth of the industrial society

At the beginning of the 18th century, Britain was primarily an agricultural country with most people living in rural areas. The population of Britain was only 9 million (Jones, 1994: 5), but was about to expand rapidly (see the graph).

The majority of workers and industries operated within a **domestic system**. This involved people working in their own homes to produce goods, or components of goods, and also to cultivate food on their own farm or piece of land. The advantages of this system were that workers and their families were free to work for themselves at their own pace, work and family

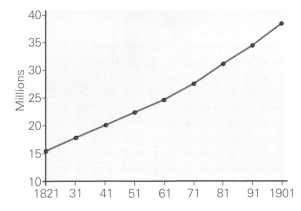

The population of Britain, 1821–1901

In a pre-industrial domestic system, people worked in their own homes to produce goods

life was relatively integrated, and working conditions could be controlled by workers.

During the 18th century there was a gradual move away from this way of working. The invention of machines led to a revolution in the ways in which goods could be produced and the speed and scale of the process. Work was gradually relocated into factories that housed the machines. This gradual move from domestic to factory-based systems of production did not occur at the same pace in all areas of industry, and varied across the regions of Britain. There is extensive historical evidence, however, that the general process of industrialisation was well under way by 1800 (Brown, 1991).

The growth of urban society

The 18th and 19th centuries saw significant changes in the size, location and lifestyle of the British population. Industrialisation was a very important influence in stimulating this movement. The growth of factories and the availability of work in them attracted people from rural areas and sustained higher densities of people in particular areas. This gradual but major shift in the location of the population, and the growth of towns and cities around them, is known as **urbanisation**. The accompanying maps provide some historical evidence of this process occurring during the 18th and 19th centuries.

The social consequences of urbanisation and industrialisation

The huge social upheaval of the 18th and 19th centuries had a major effect on the physical and social conditions in which people had to live. The consequences of a large mass of people moving to live around new factories in a relatively short space of time included:

- housing shortages and squalor
- sanitation problems
- public health problems and regular outbreaks of disease
- exploitation of workers and widespread poverty

The accompanying illustrations and extracts from 18th- and 19th-century documents provide some historical evidence of social conditions, and public concern about them, during this period.

Changes in the political order

In addition to the social changes that occurred in British society during the Industrial Revolution, important changes also took place in the political order. At the start of the 21st century, the United Kingdom has a system of **parliamentary democracy** in which people are elected to Parliament, in freely held general elections, by citizens over the age of 18 who have the right to vote. This system has evolved over the past 200 years, and contrasts with the previous system.

In the previous system, access to Parliament, and government, was based on privilege, tradition and royal appointment. The right to vote did not become universal for men and women over the age of 21 until 1928. The qualifying age was reduced to 18 for both men and women in 1969. The lack of democracy in the period leading up to

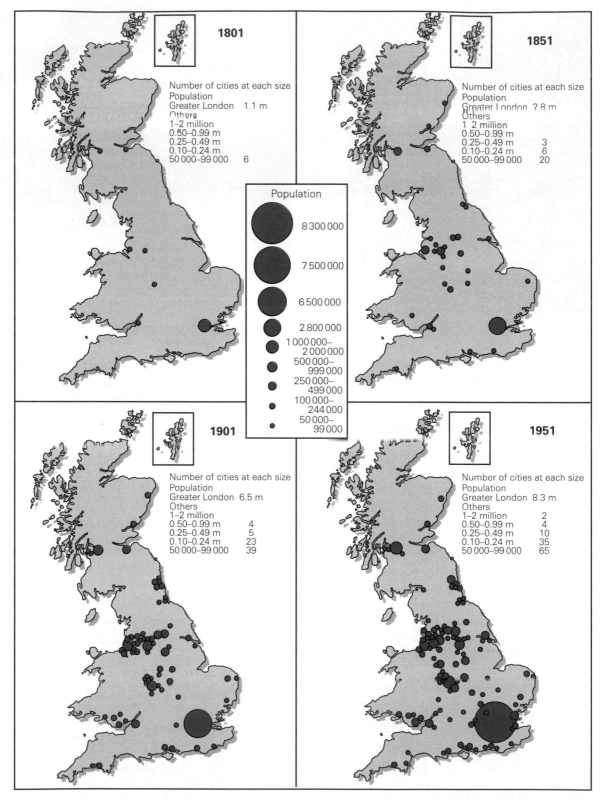

(Brown, 1991)

The process of growing urbanisation can be seen in the population maps above

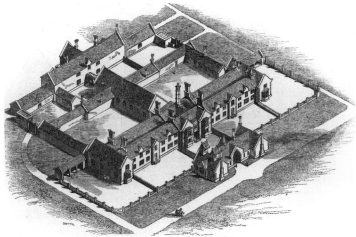

Concern about housing shortages and squalor (left) led to the creation of workhouses, like the one shown above

industrialisation meant that the small section of society that held political power tended to use it to protect its own interests, rather than dealing with social problems or issues that affected the general population. Brown (1991: 25) states that governments were 'concerned with the external security of the country, promoting and protecting commercial interests, and maintaining law and order at home'.

The **Parliamentary Reform Act 1832** began a slow process of 'democratising' Parliament, when it extended voting rights to small property owners. This gradually led to a change in approach to government. The growth of a new class of industrialists and entrepreneurs in the 19th century also stimulated a further challenge to the 'traditional' authority and position of the aristocracy and the landed gentry. Gradually, political power was being extended to different sections of the population.

The changing role of government

Political change occurred slowly and gradually through the 18th and 19th centuries. The general approach to government remained a conservative, non-interventionist one, and tended to be limited to issues relating to law and order and the economy. Governments were not particularly active in reforming society or providing social welfare, and were not generally expected to do so. As political power gradually spread through society, expectations changed and governments tended to become a little more involved in social welfare issues. Nevertheless, in the 19th century

the role of the state, and government, only extended to regulating and controlling 'social problem' areas, rather than promoting positive social change. This role has been described as that of a 'nightwatchman' (Driver and Martell, 1998).

Explanations of the emergence of state welfare

The emergence of state welfare provision, as set out above, is presented as being the result of the major social, economic and political changes that took place in the 18th and 19th centuries. There are a number of ways of explaining *why* state welfare developed in the context of these changes, at this particular time.

Welfare as a needs-led response

One explanation, sometimes called the 'functionalist' approach (for more on functionalism, see p. 350), is that the processes of industrialisation and urbanisation led to major social problems and, consequently, to unmet 'needs' in the population. The 'functionalist' explanation is that governments became involved in welfare provision in order to meet the new 'needs' that emerged at this time. But what was their motivation to do so? The main problem, and key criticism, of the functionalist explanation is that it pays insufficient attention to another significant development during the 18th and 19th centuries. Specifically, it underestimates the impact of new social class relationships – and of class conflict – in Britain. As a result of the Industrial Revolution, a capitalist, 'market' economy emerged. This profoundly affected the social structure of Britain and the nature of social relations between people.

The role of 'conflict' and commodification

Capitalism is an economic system in which the majority of the population work for a smaller number of employers who own the 'means of production' (factories and other productive capital). The workers produce goods, or commodities, that are sold for profit rather than being used to meet the workers' own needs. While the workers/employees are paid a wage for their work, it is the capitalist employer who benefits most, through keeping the profits that result. In this alternative 'conflict' explanation, state welfare provision is seen to have emerged out of the ways in which both the capitalist class (employers/owners) and working classes (employees/workers) dealt with the 'conflict' that resulted from this new form of socio-economic relationship.

The new capitalist economic relationship between employers and employed workers led to the development of two main groups in society with significantly opposing interests. The workers were relatively powerless until they organised themselves and engaged in political action through trades unions and socialist political parties, collectively known as the 'labour movement'. The capitalist class, the employers and owners of the means of production, held the powerful positions in society and formed a ruling elite.

The role of the labour movement and the significance of class conflict in the development of welfare provision form the basis of Esping-Anderson's (1990) approach to explaining welfare provision as a 'de-commodified' aspect of life in a capitalist state. Esping-Anderson (1990) uses the term commodification to describe the way in which capitalism turns all aspects of life into 'commodities' that can be packaged, bought and sold. As matters such as health, education and leisure become 'commodified', people's access to these 'goods' depends on their ability to pay for, or buy, them. Esping-Anderson (1990) argues that the existence and activities of strong labour movements have led to many aspects of welfare being 'de-commodified'. That is, they become freely available to people when the state, under pressure from the labour movement, intervenes to provide them as a 'right' for all citizens.

The 'conflict approach' suggests that state intervention provides 'de-commodified' welfare in order to avoid greater class conflict, and to placate the labour movement. The labour movement is placated because it gains welfare that is funded out of higher taxes on the wealthy effectively redistributing resources to the less wealthy, who receive welfare. The history of welfare provision in Britain indicates that when state welfare began to emerge at the end of the 19th century, there was indeed an emerging and growing 'socialist' movement that sought to represent the interests of the working class. Nevertheless, it is also the case that many of the early examples of state welfare provision resulted from Liberal and Conservative Party government action (see p. 42). Despite this, it is probably true to say that the growing power and influence of the labour movement was significant in stimulating social policy debates and welfare provision.

⊚⊚⊚⊚⊚ REVIEW POINTS ⊚⊚⊚⊚⊚

⊚ An understanding of the historical background of social policy development and welfare provision in the UK enables current policy and practice to be understood in an appropriate context. It also gives insights into the repeating themes and patterns that have occurred over time.

⊚ The origins of modern social policy in the UK can be traced back to early government intervention in the areas of poverty and public health in the 18th and 19th centuries.

⊚ Social changes – particularly industrialisation, urbanisation and the growth of the labour movement – and the emergence of parliamentary democracy and a capitalist economy, played a central role in creating the social conditions and possibilities for the emergence of social welfare provision.

⊚ The 'functionalist' approach to explaining the emergence of state social welfare provision is based on the idea that new health and welfare 'needs' developed as a consequence of social change, and that governments responded to public demand to improve poor social conditions.

◎ The 'conflict' approach explains the emergence of state welfare as being a consequence of a strong labour movement, that pressurised governments into 'de-commodifying' health and welfare provision.

Nineteenth-century social welfare issues

At the start of the 21st century, two areas of social policy intervention that we take for granted as being the responsibility of government social policy-makers and service providers are ensuring adequate public health provision and tackling poverty. This was not the case a few hundred years ago. The way in which 19th-century governments thought about and approached these issues provides a good illustration of ideas about 'social welfare' during this period, and introduces some of the classic themes and debates that have been a part of social policy-making over the past 200 years.

Dealing with poverty 1700–1900

Poverty is a social problem that has faced the people and governments of Britain for centuries. It is the issue that has prompted a huge range of social policy developments and welfare services, in efforts to counter the destructive effects that it has on the health and well-being of the individuals, families and social groups who experience it.

Poverty was a serious, and worsening, problem in 18th- and 19th-century Britain. The combination of a growing population and a change from agricultural to factory work meant that there were too many people looking for work.

This meant that employers could keep wages low. Many jobs that had been performed by hand (such as weaving), and had provided employment for a large number of people, could now be performed far more cheaply and efficiently by machines in factories. When trade slumped, factory owners could lay off workers at short notice just as they could take them on again rapidly when conditions improved. There was no redundancy pay, social security or other support available at the time.

Coping with the poor – the Poor Law system

The early system for dealing with the poor was based on the Poor Laws of 1598 and 1601. These required each parish to look after its own poor. The local **justices of the peace** appointed **parish officers** to levy a 'poor rate', which was a form of local tax, on every householder in the parish. The needy people who could work were classified as 'able-bodied poor' and were set to work in the local **workhouse**. People who were poor because of their old age, or because they were sick, were given money called '**outdoor relief**', or were put into almshouses (early hospitals). Children were often put out as apprentices, in order to learn a trade and become self-sufficient as they grew up.

This system of parish workhouses and poor

relief continued until the end of the 18th century. It eventually failed because of the changing nature of work – from agriculture to factory production – and because of population growth and movement. There were too many poor people for parishes to cope with. The costs of supporting the poor rose rapidly during the 18th and early 19th centuries.

Views about poverty

The ways in which individuals and governments respond to poverty depend on the views that they hold about its causes. Are people poor through no fault of their own, or is poverty their own fault? Is poverty an inevitable feature of society, or can it be eradicated?

In the 19th century, some people, such as the Reverend Thomas Malthus, believed that poverty was an inevitable feature of society and that it was a mistake to help the poor. Malthus believed that intervention in 'natural processes' caused overpopulation and subsequent social problems. In his view, paying 'poor relief' created the poor and made the problem worse. Criticisms such as those made by Malthus, and claims that the costs of poor relief were too high resulted, in 1832, in the government setting up a Royal Commission.

The Royal Commission on the Poor Laws involved an investigation of the workings and effects of the Poor Laws in a sample of 3000 parishes throughout Britain. Three commissioners and 26 assistant commissioners were appointed. Their report was published in 1834 and was very critical of the Poor Laws, recommending drastic changes. The aim of the commissioners who wrote the report was to change attitudes to work, as well as the system of supporting the poor. The commissioners' main recommendations are set out in the accompanying box.

Recommendations of the Royal Commission on the Poor Laws, 1834

1 To restore the self-respect of working people, it was necessary to treat the poor more harshly than the worst-paid labourer. People would then choose to work rather than receive poor relief. This is now known as the principle of 'less eligibility'.

2 To test whether people really needed poor relief, it would only be offered in the workhouse – and it would be so unattractive that people would only accept it as an alternative to starvation. Men and women would be separated, food would be adequate but uninteresting, and there would be strict discipline. This was called the 'workhouse test'.

3 All 'outdoor relief' payments (to the poor in their own homes) would be stopped.

4 People who simply could not work (the elderly, children and the sick) would be looked after in separate institutions.

5 Parishes should join together to form unions. Each union would have a workhouse, run by a Board of Guardians elected by those who paid the poor rate. A central Poor Law Commission would be set up in London to inspect the work of the local guardians.

With the exception of number 4, the commissioners' recommendations became part of the **Poor Law Amendment Act 1834**. This Act saw the introduction of a much harsher, more punitive approach to people in poverty. It was hated by the majority of poor people for the next 100 years, because of the separations that it caused, the requirement to wear a workhouse uniform and the harshness of the workhouse regime.

In the five years following the Poor Law Amendment Act 1834, 350 workhouses were

The Poor Law Amendment Act 1834 saw the introduction of a more punitive approach to people in poverty. Workhouse conditions became much harsher

built. In the North of England, attempts to introduce the system were met by opposition and riots. However, the new Poor Law did succeed in reducing the costs of supporting the poor. 'Outdoor relief' was never abolished and was, in fact, found to be less expensive than keeping people in workhouses. Increasingly, workhouses came to contain only orphans, the old, the sick and people who were mentally ill.

Alternatives to the Poor Law system

From the mid-19th century onwards, in order to avoid the Poor Law system, working people turned increasingly to self-help schemes, such as those provided by friendly societies, trades unions and co-operatives.

Philanthropic voluntary action was also a significant source of social welfare during the late 19th century. The Victorians were keen philanthropists, with many people – particularly the rich, but also less wealthy middle-class individuals – developing and running 'charity' schemes for the poor. Kathleen Jones (1994) describes various forms of philanthropy, and makes the point that many of the more active philanthropists were women, or people with strong religious convictions. Quaker families such as the Frys, Tukes, Cadburys and Rowntrees were prominent in providing social welfare through voluntary, philanthropic means. Help, support and services from philanthropists provided an alternative to the harsh and minimal provision of the Poor Laws. Philanthropy was increasingly organised in the late 19th century, and many contemporary voluntary groups can trace their roots back to this period. While philanthropists were altruistic and wished to help people in poverty, they often required that the people who they helped should also conform to their own religious beliefs and moral standards.

Mutual aid was another source of social welfare provision in the late 19th century. Trades unions and friendly societies have their roots in the mutual aid arrangements in which workers engaged. This involved groups of workers voluntarily pooling resources to support each other in times of hardship. Mutual aid societies operated locally, and on a small scale, although there were many such unions and societies throughout Britain in the 19th century. As they grew in size, a number of them moved into areas such as housing and worker co-operatives. The mutual aid movement provided buffers between the workers and the workhouse in times of hardship.

Self-help also played a significant role in 19th-century social welfare thinking. Samuel Smiles (his real name!) wrote a famous book called *Self-help* (1859). In it, he states that 'heaven helps those who help themselves'. Personal effort and hard work were seen as an important solution to the social problems that people faced. Self-help was an important Victorian value. Self-improvement could be achieved through a combination of self-denial, sobriety and thrift. People could improve their social and financial situation through their own behaviour, by taking personal responsibility for their lives. It was argued that they should not rely on state welfare to get themselves out of difficult situations. Smiles, and many other Victorians, saw undesirable consequences in philanthropy.

By the end of the 19th century, the belief that poverty could be avoided by care and hard work was widely held to be false. There was less of a tendency to blame the poor for their situation, and attempts were being made to provide different forms of support to the people in the workhouses – largely children, older people, the sick and the mentally ill, for whom the workhouse test was never intended. Schools were set up, hospitals built and foster homes provided for orphaned children.

Key features in the approach to poverty in the 19th century

The 19th century saw the development of a number of key features of social policy in relation to poverty:

- A moral distinction was made between people, in terms of whether they were 'deserving' or 'undeserving' of social welfare.

- The concept of 'less eligibility' was explicitly developed, and the principle was established that welfare support should not place people in a better position than if they worked.

- Access to welfare was gained by passing certain 'tests' for example, of willingness to work, willingness to give up certain liberties, and of existing financial means. The tests were used to assess whether or not a person was 'deserving' of welfare, and also to deter people from taking up welfare support.

- Concern about the costs of providing welfare led to a continuing debate about who should pay and how much welfare should be provided.

During the 19th century, governments used social policy to contain and deter the growing demand for social welfare. The *laissez-faire* ('let well alone') approach that dominated economic and political thinking suggested that it would be wrong to assist the poor, because 'income security' benefits would interfere with the natural processes of the labour market. The state's regulatory role gradually expanded, but did not form the basis of a statutory social welfare service. Charity, mutual aid and self-help were all seen as methods through which people could look after themselves and their families in times of hardship.

Public health problems in the 19th century

The poor physical conditions in urban areas in the mid-19th century led to major public health problems. Rapidly growing cities experienced major outbreaks of disease, epidemics and other problems, because of:

◎ overcrowded, damp and poorly ventilated housing

◎ the lack of an effective sewerage system

◎ industrial pollution

◎ the lack of a clean water supply

◎ a lack of understanding about how infectious diseases were spread

Most people living during the 19th century died at a relatively young age of infectious diseases that were contracted because of the public health conditions, or lack of services, at that time (see Table 2.2).

Throughout the 18th and 19th centuries, there were regular disease epidemics.

The reform of public health in the 19th century

The present decline, and continued low incidence, of infectious disease as a cause of death, and the general improvement in public health in the United Kingdom, is largely due to social policy that reformed public health provision in the 19th century. The main reforms occurred between 1840 and 1900.

Initially, widespread opposition and a lack of medical knowledge were major obstacles to reform of the public health situation. The efforts of reformers such as **Edwin Chadwick** had a major impact on the eventual development of public health policy in the UK. Chadwick set up an investigation into public health that resulted in the 1842 *Report on the Sanitary Condition of the Labouring Population of Great Britain*.

Chadwick's investigation concentrated on three aspects of public health – drainage, refuse and the water supply. In 1840, drains were only designed to take away rainwater. They often consisted of ditches or brick tunnels that would be cleaned every few years by teams of men known as 'scavengers'. Householders were expected to make their own arrangements for getting rid of their sewerage and other refuse. Some houses had cesspits; others had open privies, shared with several other houses, as described in the Babbage Report (see box). The cesspits would be cleared out

Table 2.2 The average age at death in 1842

	Rural (Wiltshire)	Urban (Liverpool)
Professional person/gentry and family	50	55
Farmers/tradesmen and family	48	22
Mechanics and labourers	33	15

(Culpin and Turner, 1987)

The Reverend Patrick Brontë

A summary of the conclusions of the Babbage Report

1 That the annual mortality of the hamlet of Haworth is 25.4 in the thousand, whilst the mortality of the neighbouring hamlet is only 17.6 in the thousand.

2 That a large pecuniary loss, equivalent to at least 6s. in the pound, falls upon the inhabitants of Haworth in consequence of this excessive mortality.

3 That 41.6 per cent of the people born die before attaining the age of six years.

4 That the average age at death is 25.8 years, which corresponds with that of some of the most unhealthy of the London districts.

5 That 21.7% of the population die without receiving any medical assistance, and that this fact offers great facilities for the commission of crime.

6 That the number of privies [lavatories with no drainage] is unusually small, averaging only one to every four-and-a-half-houses.

7 That no sewerage exists to carry off the refuse and decomposing matter, and that the exposed cesspools are very offensive and injurious to health.

8 That the present water supply is extremely limited in quantity, and that in the summer, much of it is deleterious in quality.

9 That the parish churchyard is so full of graves that no more interments be allowed.

10 That an efficient system of sewerage may be laid down at the weekly charge of ¾d. per house, that an ample supply of water would cost 1¼d. per house weekly upon average, and that such houses as may require it may have water laid on, be properly drained and have the present offensive privies converted into water closets at a weekly charge of 1d.

occasionally by scavengers, who would pile the excrement in the street before taking it away to sell to farmers. By the middle of the 19th century, public health problems were well documented and, given their scale, were leading to calls from the public for government intervention.

In 1850, the Reverend Patrick Brontë (the father of Charlotte and Emily Brontë), helped to initiate an enquiry into 'the sewerage, drainage, and supply of water, and the sanitary condition of the inhabitants of the hamlet of Haworth'. The Babbage Report (1850) presented a detailed account of social conditions in Haworth.

The main recommendations of the Haworth inquiry were that a sewerage system should be installed and cesspools abolished, that burials be stopped in the churchyard, and that a clean water supply should be 'distributed through branch mains and service pipes'. It should be noted that the assumption was that the people of Haworth, rather than the government, would pay for changes to be made.

Public health reform was an important focus of social policy development in the 19th century. Edwin Chadwick was very critical in his 1842 report of the state of public health, and of the vested interests that prevented improvement from being made. The report recommended to Parliament (see box) that urban sanitation should be forcibly improved through the building of drainage and sewerage systems and a clean water supply.

An extract from Chadwick's Report

'After an examination of the evidence I conclude

First: That the various forms of epidemic disease amongst the labouring classes are caused by atmospheric impurities produced by decaying animal and vegetable substances, by damp and filth, and close and overcrowded dwellings.

The annual loss of life from filth and bad ventilation is greater than the loss from death or wounds in any war in which the country has been engaged in modern times.

Second: The most important measures and the most practical are drainage, the removal of all refuse from the streets and roads and the improvement of supplies of water.

The expense of public drainage and supplies of water would save money by cutting the existing charge resulting from sickness and mortality.

For the prevention of disease it would be a good economy to appoint a district medical officer with special qualifications.

(Edwin Chadwick, *Report on the Sanitary Conditions of the Labouring Population of Great Britain*, 1842)

The Public Health Act 1875 gave local authorities responsibility for laying drains and sewers

The controversial aspect of Chadwick's report was his suggestion that the public health reforms he proposed should be paid for by individual citizens, out of the rates. There was considerable opposition to this, and a lot of criticism of Chadwick, because it was seen as an **infringement of liberties** and **choice**. The **Public Health Act 1848** was the eventual result of Chadwick's 1842 report. This provided for the setting up of a Local Board of Health to control sewerage, drainage and water supply, as well as parks, roads and slaughterhouses. Because the Act was 'permissive', and could not force people to set up or comply with the Board, it was largely ineffective. A contemporary letter to *The Times* newspaper (see box) clearly expresses the opposition that existed to Chadwick's ideas, and the view that individual liberties and 'rights' are more important than collective health.

'There is nothing a man so much hates as being cleaned against his will'

'The Board of Health has fallen. We prefer to take our chance of cholera than be bullied into health. Everywhere the Board's Inspectors were bullying, insulting and expensive. They entered houses and factories insisting on changes revolting to the habits or pride of the masters and occupants. There is nothing so much a man hates as being cleaned against his will, or having his floors swept, his walls whitewashed, his pet dung heaps cleared away, all at the command of a sort of sanitary bumbailiff. Mr Chadwick set to work everywhere, washing and splashing, and Master John Bull was scrubbed and rubbed till the tears came to his eyes and fists clenched themselves with worry and pain.'

(*The Times*, 1 August 1853)

A series of cholera epidemics, the extension of the vote to men in towns and cities, and the discovery of a link between germs and disease were all factors that influenced the development of the **Public Health Act 1875**. This finally made it compulsory to appoint sanitary inspectors and a Medical Officer of Public Health. Local authorities were given powers to lay drains and sewers, and to build reservoirs, parks, swimming baths and public conveniences.

Themes in the approach to public health during the 19th century

Concern about poverty, squalid living conditions, the widespread use of child labour in industrial production, and the lack of literacy in an uneducated and potentially threatening general population were important triggers for the development of social policy in the 19th century.

The most important development in state intervention in social welfare in the pre-1948 welfare state era was the enactment of public health legislation at the end of the 19th century. The development of public and environmental health services occurred before the development of large-scale personal medical and social services.

Nineteenth-century public health reforms

1831	A Central Board of Health was set up by government to deal with a major outbreak of cholera.
1842	The *Report on the Sanitary Conditions of the Labouring Population of Great Britain* was published. This was a pioneering and critical report on the environmental causes of disease, led by Edwin Chadwick.
1846	The Liverpool Sanitary Act. This was an example of how all the major cities required specific legislation to permit them to bring about public health improvements.
1848	The Public Health Act set up a national General Health Board. Local authorities were permitted, but not obliged, to set up local boards to improve sanitation and other amenities.
1865	The Sewage Utilisation Act laid down national standards for safe sewage disposal.
1866	The Sanitary Act required local authorities, for the first time, to comply with previous legislation.
1872 and 1875	The two Public Health Acts were pieces of legislation that consolidated and clarified all earlier regulations. They laid down the duties of local authorities with regard to environmental health up to 1936.

REVIEW POINTS

- Two of the earliest welfare issues in which government became involved were the relief of poverty and public health problems.
- The Poor Law system was an early attempt to limit the damaging effects of poverty. It gradually failed to achieve this aim, as the numbers in poverty rose during the 18th and 19th centuries.
- People who saw poverty as 'natural' or a 'personal misfortune' criticised government intervention, and believed that access to help should be limited to the 'deserving poor' only.
- A review of the Poor Law system led to a harsher, more limited system that sought to deter reliance on state help wherever possible.
- Alternative methods of meeting welfare needs, such as voluntary organisations, mutual aid and self-help, developed in the 19th century to enable people to avoid the harsh, stigmatised Poor Law provision.
- The process of urbanisation led to rapidly growing cities, in which there were major public health problems due to the lack of basic environmental health services.
- Support for the work of reformers such as Edwin Chadwick wasn't universal. Public health reforms were resisted by those who considered that they were economically and politically threatened by the potential changes.
- The public health reforms that emerged in the late 19th century illustrate how the government gradually became involved in ensuring minimum standards of public health.

1   Explain what each of the following terms mean in relation to 19th-century Poor Law provision:
    ◎ outdoor relief
    ◎ the workhouse
    ◎ less eligibility
    ◎ deserving and undeserving poor

2   Why was the Poor Law Amendment Act 1834 so unpopular with people in need of welfare?

3   What is 'philanthropy'? In your answer, explain what philanthropists did in their attempts to relieve poverty and other social problems.

4   Why were 19th-century governments reluctant to provide social welfare services that would relieve poverty?

5   From what type of illness did most people die in the 19th century?

6   How did urbanisation contribute to this cause of death?

7   What, according to the Reverend Patrick Brontë, were health conditions like in rural Yorkshire in the mid-19th century? Give a brief description in your own words.

8   Why did some people oppose public health reform in the mid-19th century?

The Liberals and the birth of welfarism

During the 18th and 19th centuries, the most powerful and influential political ideology was economic liberalism. This encouraged individualism and free trade. It discouraged governments from spending public money on welfare services. However, in the decades leading up to the beginning of the 20th century, attitudes to social welfare gradually changed. Economic liberalism was challenged by the development of new forms of *social liberalism*, and by the emergence of the new ideology of socialism. During the first half of the 20th century, this change in approach led to a gradual move away from individualist to collec-tivist ideas about the provision of welfare. It was increasingly felt that the state ought to create adequate conditions and opportunities for *all* people to live healthy and fulfilling lives.

The Liberal governments and welfare reform

The reforming Liberal governments of the early part of the 20th century extended the role of the state in the provision of social welfare. From the late 19th century, it had been clear to a growing number of reformers and politicians that the state would have to play a greater role in dealing with the mounting social problems and inadequacies of the Poor Law system. Gradually, the 19th-century system was overhauled and redeveloped. Reforms were built on an existing growth in interest in social welfare issues.

The late 19th century had seen an increasing involvement by various members of society in the provision of social welfare. Workhouse visiting, mainly by middle-class women, improved work-house conditions and made life in them more humane. The public health movement gained influence and made progress as a local government system began to develop. Various areas of social welfare provision, from public health to housing and education, were also gradually addressed by the state at central and local government level. Health and social services were still haphazardly divided between the public, voluntary and private sectors. The rich paid for medical care from GPs in private practice while, at the other end of the social scale, the Poor Law Amendment Act 1834 provided for the treatment of the poor.

Reforming welfare

The **Poor Law Amendment Act 1834** embodied the new 'economic liberal' principles of the 19th century. It rested on the assumption that public expenditure for the sick poor should be severely restricted, and where possible reduced, and that 'undeserving' able-bodied paupers were the authors of their own misfortune and should not be helped by the state. At the beginning of the 20th century, a **Royal Commission on the Poor Laws** was established to review the operation of the Poor Law system and make recommendations about its future.

A battle was fought out within the Commission, between conservative members keen to preserve the status quo and a smaller number of **Fabian socialists**. For the Fabians, the best way to reform society was through the extension of state activity and a gradual transformation to a socialist society. The Fabian group set out their ideas for reform in the **Minority Report** of the Commission. The **Majority Report**, representing the conservative views, recommended a continuation of the Poor Law system. The Fabian proposal was that the state should accept responsibility for preventing poverty, and should establish minimum welfare standards that should be available to all through universal services.

Despite the two sets of recommendations from the Commission, the Liberal government pursued a different strategy: it found a 'third way' of introducing welfare reform based on 'social insurance'. The **National Insurance Act 1911** was the watershed in this respect.

The National Insurance Act 1911 offered unemployment and health insurance to workers, 90% of whom were male. It involved the individual worker making a 'National Insurance' contribution from their wages, which was supplemented with further contributions from their employer and the state. The aim was to build up an insurance fund, out of which contributors could be paid when they became unemployed or suffered ill-health that prevented them from working. The scheme worked well at first and built up large surpluses. It failed as a result of the economic depression of the 1920s and 1930s. Unemployment rose dramatically during this time (see figure) and, without continuing contributions, could not support all who needed it. In addition, many groups, particularly women and children, were not covered in the first place. The ability of 'social insurance' schemes to fund adequate social welfare provision was soon to be questioned.

The 1920s and 1930s saw the introduction of a broad range of new, landmark social welfare legislation (see p. 44), and there were improvements in health, education and housing that 'were contributing to a better society' (Jones, 1994). The Poor Law was dying out and the non-interventionist role of the state with its minimal levels of provision had clearly been challenged.

From the turn of the century, but particularly during the inter-war period, governments demon-

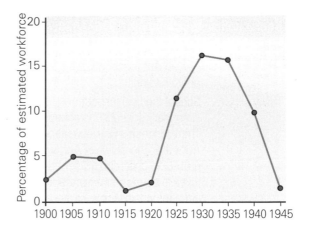

Unemployment in Britain, 1900–1945

strated that they were prepared to intervene far more than their 19th-century predecessors and provide social welfare services. While there was a movement during this period towards a welfare state, the Liberal government still believed that **individual responsibility** and **self-help** were important components of welfare provision. New socialist ideas, which proposed that social policy should be used to promote **equality**, were becoming more influential, but were not part of the Liberal government's approach.

During the inter-war period, it was realised that there were severe limitations to the insurance principle as a way of providing security of income and health to everyone. Government schemes for pensions, health and unemployment insurance were all extended and improved, but mass unemployment and persistent poverty in the 1930s meant that large sections of the population were not covered by insurance. This undermined the initial success of the scheme.

The Liberal governments of the early 20th century played a very important role in expanding the scope of state provision of social welfare. The box on page 44 gives some indication of the range of areas in which they developed state provision of health and social welfare services.

SOCIAL POLICY AND WELFARE

Social policy development, 1906–1939	
1906	The Education (Provisions of Meals) Act – school meals for poor children
1907	School medical inspections; secondary school scholarships The Workmen's Compensation Act 1908 The Children Act, which protected children and set up juvenile courts; non-contributory old-age pensions established The Education (Administrative Provisions) Act The Incest Act The Probation of Offenders Act The Labour Exchanges Act The Old Age Pensions Act
1909	The People's Budget – graduated taxation; trade boards established; labour exchanges set up
1911	The National Insurance Act
1918	The Representation of the People Act; the Education Act raised the school-leaving age to 14
1010, 1023 and 1924	Subsidised Housing Acts provided for local authority council housing
1920	The Unemployment Insurance Act extended insurance to most workers and their dependants
1925	Contributory old-age, widows and orphans' pensions
1926	The Hadow Report – recommended state secondary education for all
1928	Women over 21 allowed to vote
1929	The Local Government Act abolished the Poor Law Unions
1931	The 'Means Test' brought in
1934	The Milk Act; the Unemployment Assistance Board for the long-term unemployed

(Holden *et al.*, 1996)

REVIEW POINTS

- The Liberal governments of the early 20th century used social policies to extend the role of the state in providing social welfare services.
- There was a gradual shift away from the economic liberal *laissez-faire* approach of the late 19th century, towards a more supportive form of social liberalism.
- In the 1920s and 1930s, 'social insurance' failed to provide adequate welfare for large sections of the population of the UK.
- Emerging socialist ideas gradually challenged Liberal welfarism and led to a demand for greater state intervention in welfare provision.

REVIEW ACTIVITIES

1 Explain how 'social liberalism' is different to 'economic liberalism'.
2 Why was the National Insurance Act 1911 a watershed in social policy?
3 Give two reasons why the 'social insurance' principle ultimately failed to provide adequate welfare for the population of the UK in the 1930s.
4 What happened to unemployment levels during the Depression of the 1920s and 1930s?
5 The Liberal governments of the early 20th century are associated with the growth of 'welfarism'. Using the box on the left to illustrate your points, briefly explain what this means.

Beveridge and the modern welfare state

Sir William Beveridge (1879–1963) is often referred to as the architect of the 'welfare state' in Britain. In 1941 he was commissioned by the wartime Prime Minister, Winston Churchill, to investigate the welfare schemes of the time and suggest ways of improving them. He developed a set of ideas and principles that effectively led to the development of the National Health Service, and to a national system of social security benefits, the so-called 'welfare state'. As a consequence, the state's role in social policy-making and welfare provision expanded significantly.

Developments in social welfare that can be traced back to Beveridge	
1942	Beveridge Report on social insurance
1944	Butler Education Act provided secondary education for all
1945	Family Allowance Act
1946	National Health Service Act; New Towns Act; National Insurance Act; National Assistance Board; Children Act; Industrial Injuries Insurance Act
1947	The Town and Country Planning Act; The Housing Act
1948	5 July was 'The Appointed Day' when the 'welfare state' began
1948	National Assistance Act

Sir William Beveridge (1879–1963)

Beveridge's investigation and recommendations

Sir William Beveridge was the Master of University College, Oxford when he was appointed to lead an interdepartmental committee of civil servants in an investigation and review of policies for National Insurance. The results and recommendations of the investigation went much further than the original terms of reference given to the committee. In the final report, *Social Insurance and Allied Services* (1942) (also known as 'the Beveridge Report'), the committee set out a plan for social security reform and a framework for a 'welfare state' that would tackle Britain's major social problems. The Beveridge Plan for developing welfare provision

was based on tackling five 'giant evils' that were identified as existing in British society, and as forming barriers to postwar reconstruction:

- want (poverty)
- disease (ill-health)
- ignorance (lack of education)
- squalor (poor housing)
- idleness (unemployment)

Beveridge's plan was primarily designed to attack want (poverty) through the development of a national social security system that would, for the first time, give British people real income security. The plan for income security would establish a new degree of co-operation between the state and the individual. It was proposed that the state would provide a national minimum level of income for all, in the form of social security benefits. This would not be means-tested and would be available to everyone as a right. Jones (1994) provides a detailed explanation of how this scheme to abolish 'want' was targeted to 'provide for all the basic and predictable needs of the population'. Compared to previous levels of state intervention, the scheme involved a considerable extension of social welfare provision by the state.

As well as developing a scheme to attack 'want', the Beveridge Plan proposed that the state should work to develop a comprehensive health service and full employment. The Beveridge committee saw connections between the five 'giant evils', and argued that they needed to be tackled through the development of a number of welfare services and government-led strategies.

Beveridge's 1942 report was initially recognised by the media, the public and politicians as 'a blueprint for a new and more egalitarian Britain, which could heal the scars of war and the older but enduring scars of the thirties' (Jones, 1994: 130). While all political parties recognised the importance of the report and its proposals, Winston Churchill, the Conservative Prime Minister at the time, did not initially debate or act on the proposals. In his autobiography, Beveridge stated that 'while the British people and the free world outside Britain were applauding the Beveridge Report, the Government of Britain ... showed to the report an attitude of marked reserve, and to its author an attitude which developed from ignoring him to boycott' (Beveridge, 1953: 323). Despite the initial official reservations about the proposals, Jones (1994) describes how, in the closing years of the Second World War, they were widely debated by members of the public, as the 'reconstruction' of Britain became the main topic of public discussion. Jones (1994: 132) states that 'never before or since has there been so much committed public debate in Britain about the shape of social policy'.

The Conservative-led coalition government of the war years was replaced in the 1945 general election by a Labour government. This government took on the task of setting up a 'welfare state' that would systematically tackle Beveridge's 'five giants'. The creation of a new, more equal society was the key task of government. Social policy was at the top of the public and political agenda. The development of welfare services extended the role and intervention of the state further than ever before.

The founding of a 'welfare state'

The 1940s saw the development of social legislation aimed at setting up the 'welfare state'. The term **welfare state** refers to both the idea of state responsibility for welfare provision and to the institutions and services through which this is delivered. Each of Beveridge's five 'giant evils' was targeted through new legislation, and through the development of state-funded and -run services.

Want

The existence of 'want', or poverty, was the main reason for Beveridge's initial investigation. Following his report and recommendations, a series of legislative measures were introduced to tackle this problem (see box).

Policy initiatives related to 'want'

◎ **The Family Allowances Act 1945** introduced an allowance for all children under 16, except for the first-born child.

◎ **The National Insurance Act 1946** introduced a new insurance scheme that would provide those who contributed to it with a range of benefits, including – amongst others – unemployment benefit, sickness benefit, maternity benefit, retirement benefit and widow's benefit.

◎ **The National Assistance Act 1948** introduced provisions for people who were not covered (because they couldn't or didn't contribute) by the benefits related to National Insurance. The Act provided grants of money and/or accommodation for people who were unable to meet their own needs. Part 3 of the Act related to accommodation for people 'in urgent need' or 'in need of care and attention'. Aneurin Bevan, the Minister of Health, introduced this clause to the House of Commons by saying 'The workhouse is to go.'

The details of these Acts of Parliament have been updated many times since they were first enacted. They established a range of state-provided benefits and social welfare services that lasted for many years and, in some cases, are still available today.

Disease

The National Health Service Act 1946 was the key piece of legislation that set out the principles on which a national, comprehensive and free health service would be established. The **National Health Service (NHS)** came into being on 5 July 1948.

Before the arrival of the NHS, healthcare services were provided through uncoordinated and fragmented private, voluntary and local authority (municipal) organisations and individual practitioners. The outbreak of the Second World War was seen as a key factor in forcing the government to intervene for the first time, and exercise some control over Britain's healthcare providers. The Emergency Medical Service was organised, to provide a coordinated and state-controlled hospital bed service, a national blood transfusion service and an ambulance service for the country. Blakemore (1998) argues that the idea of a nationalised, comprehensive system of health care was the subject of much earlier discussion, as it was clear from the turn of the century onwards that health service provision in Britain was inadequate to meet the needs of the population.

After the end of the Second World War, all types of hospital were 'nationalised' and brought under the control of the Ministry of Health. The Beveridge Report placed tackling the 'giant evil' of disease in Britain high on the political agenda. It can also be argued that the promise, and later introduction, of a national health service was calculated to 'maintain the morale of the population during the war, and to provide them with a vision of a bright future, including free health care for all, if Britain won the war'.

The NHS was founded on three key principles:

- that services would be free at the point of delivery
- that it would be comprehensive in terms of covering all people in all areas of the country
- that access to services would be on the basis of 'real' – that is, clinical – need, rather than ability to pay, chance or other social criteria

This approach to providing healthcare services put into practice the ideological principles of a Labour government that believed in 'democratic socialism', and which also felt that there was a strong moral case for providing free, universal health care.

Idleness

One of the recommendations of the Beveridge Report was that the government should act to ensure 'full employment'. This was later changed to 'high and stable employment'. Following the end of the Second World War, the high unemployment that people feared would happen as soldiers returned to Britain did not materialise. In the immediate postwar years, the Labour government nationalised many of the so-called 'public utilities', such as the gas, electricity and

Aneurin Bevan (1897–1960)

Aneurin Bevan, the Labour Minister for Health, is quoted by Jones (1994: 143) as commenting on the National Health Service Act 1946 in the following terms:

'The field in which the claims of individual commercialism come into most immediate conflict with reputable notions of social values is that of health … preventable pain is a blot on any society. Much sickness, and often permanent disability, arise from failure to take early action, and this is due to the high costs and the fear of the effects of heavy bills on the family … You can always "pass by on the other side". This may be sound economics. It could not be worse morals.'

water industries, as well as coal, steel and the railways. This enabled politicians to plan and, to some degree, to manage important parts of the economy and to have an influence on employment levels. Relatively high employment levels lasted up until the early 1970s. During this period there was a lot of optimism that government planning and regulation of the economy could create and sustain stability in this area.

Ignorance

Before the Second World War, the education system in Britain was, like the healthcare system, patchy and fragmented in terms of what it offered and to whom. **The Education Act 1944** was a key piece of legislation that brought coherence to this system by 'nationalising' much of the provision before the end of the war. Free, compulsory education for all children from the age of five years was established as both an entitlement and a requirement. The school-leaving age was 14 in 1945, and was later raised to 15, and then to 16 years of age in the 1960s. Equality of opportunity was a key goal of the legislation, because education was seen as an important means by which all sections of society could progress and benefit.

Squalor

Poor housing and living conditions, and the recon-struction of many areas destroyed by wartime bombing, were tackled through legislation such as **The Town and Country Planning Act 1947**. This ultimately required all local authorities to plan the built environments of their local areas in coherent ways that benefited the local population.

The social legislation that resulted from the Beveridge Report is described by Jones (1994) as 'evolutionary rather than revolutionary'. It tended to build on earlier legislation, and extended the already growing role and influence of the state in providing health and social welfare services in a more comprehensive and rational way.

The postwar political and social policy consensus

The period between the end of the Second World War and the late 1970s is notable for the 'consensus', or general agreement, that existed between political parties in their approach to social policy-making. This is often referred to as the **postwar consensus**. The Labour government that was elected after the end of the war in 1945 held power until 1951. When the Conservative Party was subsequently elected to government in 1951, they continued to support the work done on establishing a 'welfare state'. This acceptance of the key principles of the welfare state, and of government support and funding for the provision of a wide range of social welfare services, was a feature of all government approaches to social welfare until 1979.

The expansion and later contraction of the 'welfare state'

The initial years of the welfare state saw expansion in terms of the proliferation of new state-run and funded welfare services, and an increasing amount of intervention in people's lives. After the end of the Second World War, 'social reconstruction' was urgently required. Social policy seemed to offer a way of rebuilding society in a different, more equal way.

The social ideals of the new Labour government ran into difficulties because of postwar economic problems. Postwar Britain was short of money and faced financial difficulties. The population, while in favour of many of the social reforms, lost faith in the Labour government when prices and taxes increased and basic commodities continued to be rationed because they were in short supply. By 1951 Winston Churchill was back in power, as the Conservative Party won the general election in that year. Nevertheless, the fight against the five 'giant evils' continued, as the new Conservative government accepted the need for, and basic approach to, social reform through welfare policy.

Idleness and **want** were not major problems in the postwar years due to the relatively high levels of employment.

Postwar housing

There was a considerable need for housing after the end of the Second World War. Many houses had been destroyed during the wartime 'blitz', slums still existed from the pre-war days and there had been no house-building during the war. Under the first postwar Labour government, local authorities were given powers (see box) and funding to embark on a house-building programme. Between 1950 and 1955, over 1 million new council houses were built.

Legislation aimed at dealing with 'squalor'

- ◎ The New Towns Act 1946
- ◎ The Town and Country Planning Act 1947
- ◎ The Housing Act 1947
- ◎ The Housing Rents and Repairs Act 1954

Most of the housing redevelopment that occurred in the first decade after the Second World War was funded and directed by the government, through local authorities.

Healthcare services

Health and social care services evolved and developed a great deal between 1948 and 1970. Myfanfwy Morgan (1985) identifies various factors as being significant features of the changing face of health provision during this period (see box).

The postwar development of the National Health Service

- ◎ There was an initial decade of reconstruction, re-equipment and consolidation.

- ◎ From 1960 until 1974, there was a period of innovation, expansion and strategic planning.

- ◎ An attempt was made to address the uneven distribution of GPs and services.

- ◎ Some services that had been provided outside the hospital (for example, midwifery) now moved in, and community services took on a preventive role.

- ◎ The seeds of the community movement were sown, particularly in respect of mental health care.

- ◎ Resources and services were centralised, usually around a district general hospital.

The development of education services

The intended aim of the new postwar education system was to provide equality of educational opportunity for all children and young people. The existing system of education was developed into three types of secondary school: grammar schools for the academically minded, technical schools for the practically orientated and secondary modern schools for the rest. The original idea was that the three types of school should have 'parity of esteem', and that the 11-plus exam would be used to guide students into the most appropriate type of school. This 'tripartite' system had political and policy support from both Labour and Conservative governments until the mid-1950s. Although the 11-plus exam was originally intended to be a means of distinguishing between types of ability, it was gradually subverted into being a means of selecting students on social rather than educational criteria. The policy of the Labour Party changed in the 1960s to one of supporting comprehensive schools. Their argument was that grammar schools were educationally and socially divisive. The state education system slowly changed as the 11-plus examination was gradually abandoned, though it never quite went away. As comprehensive schools developed in the 1960s, the policy focus shifted to educational opportunities for children of average and less than average ability, and also to further education and training opportunities for school-leavers.

The 1960s also saw growth in higher education provision, with the development of several new universities – including Aston, Warwick and Sussex – and the emergence of polytechnics and colleges of higher education. From a policy perspective, education was seen as an important means of healing social divisions in UK society, as well as having a critical role in preparing the labour force to meet the UK's future economic needs.

During this period, both the Labour and Conservative parties agreed on the fundamental issues in relation to social policy. That is, there was a need for state support and funding of health and social welfare provision. However, they differed on the way in which they felt this ought to be delivered. T. H. Marshall, a professor at the London School of Economics and a major academic figure in social administration at the time, commented on the consensus approach to social policy and the provision of social welfare services by suggesting that Britain might be approaching 'the end of ideology'. Public provision of welfare seemed to be the accepted approach.

The postwar consensus

'There had been "a convergence of principles and an integration of practices" to which all political parties had made some contribution: "there is a growing measure of agreement on many of the fundamentals. It is realised that many of the old antitheses are largely imaginary ... there is little difference of opinion as to the services that must be provided, and it is generally agreed that, whoever provides them, the overall responsibility for the welfare of the citizen must remain with the state".'

(Jones, 1994: 164; quoting from T. H. Marshall, 1965: 97)

The breakdown of the postwar consensus on social welfare provision

All British governments in the postwar period accepted that they had a responsibility to maintain the 'welfare state'. Arguments against the public funding of universal welfare provision held little sway, but gradually increased in influence as the 'welfare state' ran into practical and funding problems. In the late 1960s, adverse economic conditions led to questions first being asked about the assumptions on which the 'welfare state' was based. Collective and universal state provision of social welfare services were based on the belief that full employment could sustain the public funding of services, because enough money could be collected through income taxation to pay for services. Both Conservative and Labour governments had operated 'tax-and-spend' policies to fund welfare during the postwar years.

Low growth in the economy in the 1970s meant that high public spending on welfare could not be sustained. Gradually the consensus broke down, and new ideas – particularly from the developing New Right movement – began to emerge to challenge long-held beliefs about how and why social welfare services ought to be provided. As these problems came to a head, James Callaghan, then the Labour Prime Minister, told his party conference in 1976:

'We used to think that you could just spend your way out of a recession and increase employment by cutting taxes and boosting government spending. I tell you in all candour, that option no longer exists, and that in so far as it ever did exist, it worked by injecting inflation into the economy. And each time that happened the average level of unemployment has risen. Higher inflation was followed by higher unemployment. That is the history of the last twenty years.'

Social policy commentators on the Left also questioned whether social welfare provision had made society any more equal. It had not led to a socialist state. By the mid-1970s, the Conservative Party had abandoned its commitment to the consensus 'middle way' on social welfare that had begun in 1951. In the face of a national economic recession and increasing unemployment, in 1977/8 the Labour government cut welfare spending and ended their commitment to full employment: 'It was the moment which marked the first great fissure in Britain's welfare state ... the magic prescription of growth, public expenditure and full employment paid for by higher taxation and perhaps slightly higher inflation, had ceased to work' (Timmins, 1995). In 1979, the Labour Party lost the next general election and a new era of welfare reform began.

The New Right had gained influence in the Conservative Party when, in 1975, Margaret Thatcher had replaced Edward Heath as leader of the Conservative Party in opposition. Mrs Thatcher led the party to victory in the 1979 general election. The Thatcher governments of the 1980s introduced a significant shift in approach to thinking about, and to the actual provision of, social welfare – a shift that challenged decades of social democratic thinking.

REVIEW POINTS

Beveridge and the modern welfare state

- The National Health Service and a national system of social security provision were developed by a Labour government following the recommendations of William Beveridge.
- The system of state-funded and -provided health and welfare is often referred to as the 'welfare state'.
- The aim of the 'welfare state' was to tackle the five 'giant evils' of poverty, ill-health, lack of education, poor housing and unemployment that affected the 'welfare' of British citizens in the 1930s and 1940s.
- The 'welfare state' system involved a massive increase in the amount and scope of state intervention in the provision and funding of welfare.
- Between the end of the Second World War and the late 1970s, there was a general political consensus that state intervention and funding of welfare was a good thing.
- During the 1970s, an economic crisis and the emergence of New Right ideas challenged, and ultimately led to the breakdown of, the postwar consensus.

REVIEW ACTIVITIES

1 Who was William Beveridge and why is he associated with the 'welfare state'?

2 Name the five 'giant evils' that Beveridge identified and sought to tackle through state welfare provision.

3 What did the postwar Labour government do to tackle 'want', or poverty, in Britain?

4 Identify the three principles on which the National Health Service was founded. Explain, in your own words, what each means.

5 Which piece of legislation introduced the current system of free, compulsory education for all children between the ages of 5 and 14 years old?

6 What did the 'postwar consensus' on welfare involve?

7 Explain why the postwar consensus started to collapse in the 1970s.

Thatcherism, Blairism and the reconstitution of social policy in late modernity

In 1975, Margaret Thatcher became the first woman to lead the Conservative Party. She was also the first woman to become Prime Minister, when the Conservatives won the general election in 1979. She resigned as leader of the Conservative Party and Prime Minister in November 1990, after almost 12 years in office. During this period, the governments that she led implemented a wide range of often radical social policies that expressed a distinctive set of ideas and beliefs about 'welfare'. These became part of what was known as Thatcherism.

What is Thatcherism?

The term **Thatcherism** is used to describe the political and ideological framework of the Conservative Party, and the corresponding governments, led by Margaret Thatcher in the 1980s. It refers to a mixture of ideas that are basically drawn from, and reflect, New Right thinking on welfare, the role of government and the state, and the economy. **Milton Friedman** and **Friedrich von Hayek** were the two recent key academic thinkers from whom Thatcherite social policy-

Margaret Thatcher

makers drew inspiration. They both envisaged the 'free market' as being fundamentally important, and believed that governments should 'interfere' in the market as little as possible. New Right thinkers, such as Friedman and von Hayek, contend that the real focus of government should be economic problems, such as tackling inflation, and goals such as 'wealth creation', rather than social welfare issues and the pursuit of equality.

A number of 'think tanks', including the Institute for Economic Affairs, the Centre for Policy Studies and the Adam Smith Institute, set out to promote the ideas of von Hayek and Friedman in the 1970s and 1980s. They succeeded in doing so, and became influential in shaping the ideas of Thatcherite Conservative Party politicians and social policy-makers during this period. Thatcherism has a number of key features that have important consequences for social policy:

- *A monetarist approach to the economy*. The main aim of a monetarist economic policy is to keep inflation under control. A government that adopts a monetarist economic policy limits its economic interventions to controlling the money supply. Thatcherism is strongly associated with this approach. Previous Labour and Conservative governments had adopted a Keynesian economic policy (see p. 87), in which the main economic aim was to maintain high levels of employment. Governments that adopt a Keynesian approach intervene much more and 'manage' the economy in a more active way. For example, they borrow money to provide welfare services, 'nationalise' (take into state control) some industries and subsidise them using government money.

- *Privatisation of nationalised industries and services*. One consequence of adopting a monetarist approach to the economy was that the Thatcher governments sought to reduce government borrowing and the subsidisation of various industries. They did this through privatising them. Privatisation involves selling nationalised and government-funded services to private investors – ordinary individuals and companies with money to invest. The aim of privatisation was to raise money that could be used to pay off government borrowing, improve the efficiency of the nationalised industries, and encourage

'popular capitalism' and a 'share-owning democracy'.

- *Centralisation of political power*. While the New Right and Thatcherist approach emphasises the importance of individual freedom and a limited amount of government intervention in the economy, the centralisation of power is also a key feature. During the 1980s, much of the power of the trades unions and of local government bodies was removed and redistributed to central government. In effect, it was the power of organisations that might have opposed Thatcherism that was removed.

- *Authoritarianism*. Thatcherism is strongly associated with the adoption of authoritarianism. It was thought that the credibility and authority of the state had been damaged in the years of postwar consensus, because of inappropriate over-involvement in social welfare and nationalisation of key industries. Thatcherism saw a need for the state to be strong, and to have authority in the areas of law and order and defence. Authoritarian social policies were considered justifiable and desirable in areas relating to social control and public order.

Thatcherism and social policy

The Conservative governments of the 1980s began a process of 'rolling back' the welfare state. The general strategy was to limit a 'welfare state' that had seemed ever-expanding, and to shift responsibility for welfare from the state to personal, private and voluntary providers. In many ways, the social policy approaches of the Thatcher governments were based on what the state wouldn't and shouldn't do. It was felt that the state had gone too far in providing welfare and was, in fact, creating 'welfare dependency'. The approach of the Thatcher governments was to focus less on making social policy on welfare issues and more on the economy.

The Thatcher governments' reversal of 'welfare state' expansion was finance-led. They didn't initially pass legislation to nullify, overturn or stop previous developments. Instead, they attempted to use financial controls to limit expansion and change the focus of welfare provision in many areas in which the state had, during the consensus period, funded and provided universal services.

The **social security system** continued to pay out large amounts of welfare benefits during the 1980s. Repeated attempts were made to tighten up eligibility criteria, the real monetary value of many benefits fell as the link between benefit levels and wages was broken, and some people were taken off benefits and moved into training and work schemes. Despite ideological opposition to increased welfare spending, the amount of public spending on social security benefits actually rose during the 1980s (see Chapter 4, p. 90) as a result of an increase in the number of people becoming unemployed during this period.

The **National Health Service (NHS)** was not privatised by the Thatcher governments, although many of the support and ancillary services, such as catering and cleaning, were. The overall structure of the NHS was streamlined through a number of reorganisations. Charges for prescriptions and other services were also extended and increased. The National Health Services and Community Care Act 1990 intro-duced the most radical changes seen in the NHS.

NHS Trusts, which were to operate within an 'internal market' in health care, took over the provision of secondary-level health care from district health authorities. They were given limited budgets and were required to work within them and balance the books at the end of the current financial year. The funding controls that were introduced into health care were also expressed through the development of GP fundholding, in which GPs were given a limited budget and were also required to work within it.

One of the key social policies goals of the Thatcher governments was the creation of a 'property-owning democracy'. This meant that a concerted effort was made to sell council housing to tenants, and to encourage people to buy their own homes rather than rely on public housing. Local authorities had restrictions placed on them to prevent them from continuing to build and provide new council homes. The number of new houses built by councils fell from 107 000 in 1979

to 30 000 in 1987. During the same period, home ownership increased from 55% to 64% of all types of tenancy. Local authorities were required to make business partnership arrangements with the private and voluntary sectors to fulfil any residual housing need.

Education was also 'reformed' by the Thatcher governments, to reduce the amount of state control and increase 'freedom of choice'. The Education Reform Act 1988 gave schools the right to 'opt out' of local authority control, and take on a more independent 'grant-maintained' status. Further and higher education had major budget restrictions imposed on them. People who opposed these measures often referred to them as 'financial cutbacks'. The Education (Student Loans) Act 1990 also saw the welfare state principle of 'free education' come to an end, when it introduced a requirement that higher education students should take out loans in order to pay for part of their maintenance fees. As a result, the previously mandatory state 'grants' were gradually reduced.

Jones (1994: 204) argues that legislation such as the Education Reform Act 1988, the Children Act 1989 and the National Health Services and Community Care Act 1990 expressed a Thatcherite approach in relation to social welfare. This amounted to:

- limiting financial expenditure on state health, welfare and education provision
- breaking up large public welfare agencies
- increasing the scope of the private sector
- bringing in business management and ideas, to influence the running of health and welfare services
- reducing the power of health and welfare professionals over how services were run and budgets spent

Thatcherism effectively ended the postwar consensus approach to the public funding and provision of health and welfare services. The purpose, goals and approach to social policy-making were redefined by the introduction of New Right ideas and policy strategies. While Thatcherism under Margaret Thatcher ended when she was replaced as leader of the Conserv-ative Party by John Major in 1990, the profound effects that it had on social policy remain.

Blairism and New Labour's approach to social policy

In May 1997, the Labour Party won the general election and ended 18 years of Conservative rule. New Labour, as the government refers to itself, can be viewed in ideological and social policy terms as 'post-Thatcherite' (Driver and Martell, 1998). Nevertheless, the experience, approach and achievements of Thatcherism are important to the 'New Labour project' and its approach to social policy.

The experience of Thatcherism has ensured that the approach of New Labour is significantly different from that of the 'Old' Labour postwar governments. State ownership of major industries, economic planning and full employment, and 'tax-and-spend' welfarism are not a part of the New Labour approach to social policy-making. New Labour's approach to social policy has had to accommodate the effects of Thatcherism – an approach that rejected and/or overturned the social democratic welfare consensus.

In a speech to the Fabian Society in 1995, Prime Minister Tony Blair argued that the party's new social policies 'should and will cross old boundaries between left and right, progressive and conservative' (see Blair, 1998). Driver and Martell (1998) suggest that New Labour's approach to social policy can now be understood in terms of how they address three questions:

- ◎ Who pays, and who benefits?
- ◎ How should welfare be delivered?
- ◎ What should welfare do?

Who pays, and who benefits?

New Labour has questioned whether social welfare should be provided on a universal basis. It is evident that social welfare provision does not redistribute resources in society. Le Grand (1982), for example, has shown that the middle classes benefited most from health and education provision during the welfare state era of universal provision. New Labour now departs from this 'Old Labour' approach by targeting welfare at particular groups.

The purpose of state 'welfare' has been refocused under New Labour. While the state is still seen as having a responsibility to support vulnerable individuals in need, the New Labour approach also requires welfare recipients to accept that they too have an obligation to help themselves out of 'welfare dependency'. Welfare reform now aims to provide opportunities for **'social inclusion'**, rather than attempting to redistribute wealth to equalise society. The New Labour governments will structure welfare services and support to provide social opportunity for people who are experiencing 'social exclusion', but – if they are to continue receiving support – the 'socially excluded' must also fulfil their responsibilities, and their obligation, to help themselves.

How should welfare be delivered?

Under the Thatcher governments there was a move away from centralised, bureaucratic provision of social welfare. New Labour is continuing this, and sees the private, voluntary and state sectors as part of a complex, 'pluralist' welfare system, one that can meet needs but can also promote freedom, choice and value for money. New Labour's approach to social policy aims to provide for a diverse society, in which there are many needs and interests. It does not accept that the state should be the key provider of uniform, comprehensive services, in the 'Old Labour' welfare consensus manner.

In many ways, New Labour is developing and revising ideas about how welfare should be delivered that originated in the Thatcher era. For example, it is seeking to offer a new model in which 'welfare providers' must be responsive to the needs of the 'consumers' of their services. Driver and Martell (1998) argue that the New Labour approach is a reform of a conservative reform not the abolition of conservative policy and a return to postwar social democracy. New Labour also accepts that there are limits to the governments role in welfare. The state will no longer be the main provider of welfare services. It will act as purchaser and regulator of services, making partnerships with the voluntary and private-sector providers.

New Labour's approach to how welfare is delivered marks a significant shift from the individual versus collective, state versus market, public versus private debates of the past. The 'Third Way' that New Labour claims to have developed recognises the interdependence of many of these 'opposites', and crosses what were once seen as boundaries in an either/or approach to the different ways of delivering health and social welfare services. Individual choice, personal independence and responsibility are New Labour principles at the same time as equality of opportunity and social justice.

What should welfare services do?

Postwar social welfare provision was based on the idea that social policy could and should be a counterweight to the effects of 'free market' capitalism, and that it should be used to make society better for those disadvantaged by its operation. It was maintained that social policy ought to be about promoting social justice, which was often seen as requiring a redistribution of income and wealth.

New Labour now accepts, and is committed to, the existence and operation of a market economy. Social policy, for New Labour, should aim to enable people to work in and benefit from the economy, rather than ameliorate the market's worst effects on 'disadvantaged' social groups. The aim of New Labour social policy now is to 'promote personal autonomy and choice', giving individuals the 'confidence and capability' to manage their own lives (Commission on Social Justice, 1994: 113). New Labour is seeking to develop social policies that conceptualise social welfare as a 'trampoline' rather than as a 'safety net'.

Is the 'Third Way' a new social policy ideology?

There has been much discussion about the approach to social welfare issues adopted by the government since New Labour came to power in 1997. Many people with 'Old Labour' sympathies were hopeful of a return to the 'welfarist' approach of the postwar years, and have professed their disappointment about the fact that this has not happened. In answer to critics from both 'Old Labour' and the Conservative Party backgrounds, New Labour claims that they are pursuing a new, radical approach. They call this the 'Third Way'. It is neither a socialist or a New Right approach to social welfare provision. There remains a lot of debate over whether the 'Third Way' is a new approach that charts a course between these ideologies, or whether it is a clever, careful compromise between the two. Driver and Martell (1998) argue for the latter.

They suggest that 'rather than a synthesis or transcendence of opposites into something new, this is the balancing of opposites, an attempt to combine them into interdependence with one another ... the new politics is a management of old opposites: both are still in tension with one another'.

It will take some time before New Labour's approach to social policy at the end of the 20th century can be analysed and evaluated in terms of whether it brought about a significant shift in approach to social welfare. At the beginning of the 21st century, with New Labour in power and adopting a 'Third Way' strategy, it is possible to say that there is now a centre-right consensus whereas, for much of the 20th century, there was a centre-left consensus. Social policy has been 'reconstituted' as a result of the experience of Thatcherism and, under New Labour, this would seem to result in welfare policies that are both an accommodation of and a reaction against significant features of Thatcherism.

REVIEW POINTS

- The conservative governments led by Margaret Thatcher in the 1980s ended the postwar consensus on welfare. They rejected the 'tax-and-spend' approach of postwar governments in favour of New Right ideas, and reduced the role of the state in welfare provision.

- Thatcherism was based on a monetarist approach to the economy, a reduction in the public spending on welfare and an increase in the role of non-statutory provider organisations.

- The Thatcher governments did not privatise the NHS, and they failed to reduce overall levels of spending on welfare benefits. They did *restructure* the NHS, and they introduced more means-testing and 'selective' welfare provision.

- Thatcherism led to decisive changes in the structure and funding of health and social welfare provision, which have been accommodated by the New Labour government.

◉ New Labour claims to have found a 'Third Way' between New Right ideas and the 'tax-and-spend' postwar consensus.

◉ There is continuing debate about whether or not New Labour's attempts at balancing public support and private funding constitute a new approach to welfare.

> ### REVIEW ACTIVITIES
>
> 1 What were the four key features of Thatcherism?
> 2 Identify three ways in which the Conservative governments of the 1980s reversed, or 'rolled back', the welfare state.
> 3 One of the policy goals of the Thatcher years was the creation of a 'property-owning democracy'. What did this involve?
> 4 What, according to the New Labour government, should be the purpose of state welfare?
> 5 What is meant by the 'Third Way' in social policy?

The influence and role of the European Union in the evolution of UK social policy

The European Parliament building in Strasbourg, France

If you were to ask a friend, relative or colleague 'Who makes the social policy that applies to the United Kingdom?', most relatively well informed people would identify the central government of the UK as the key source. For most of the past 200 years this has been true. Social policy-making in Britain has been the role of central and, to a lesser extent, local government. The social policies made have been specifically designed for and implemented in Britain. However, as you are probably now aware, Europe – in the form of European Union (EU) bodies – is beginning to influence the UK's social policy-making agenda. The UK joined the European Economic Community (EEC) in 1973 and became a member state of the European Union following the **Single European Act 1986**.

Before we look at the impact of the European Union on social policy in the UK, it is necessary to understand the structure and function of the various parts of the EU.

What is the European Union?

The **European Union (EU)** is made up of a group of countries in Western Europe and Scandinavia. The member states belonging to the EU have signed a treaty (the main form of legislation) that allows them to join and sets the ground rules for their membership. The EU is the latest stage in a process of integration and co-operation between European countries.

The European Union is organised around a number of political, administrative and judicial institutions. These are the bodies that develop European policy and legislation. They include the following.

The Council of Ministers

The Council of Ministers is based in Brussels, Belgium and consists of one government minister from each of the member states. The main purpose of the Council is to set the social (and other forms of) policy agenda for the EU and to make policy decisions. The Council of Ministers is really several councils. Where the matter under discussion is a health issue, the relevant health minister from each member state will attend, to represent the views and interests of his or her country. Where the matter is related to, say, crime or to education, a different minister from each country would attend.

The Council of Ministers takes all of the important EU policy decisions. It has the power to issue regulations, directives, decisions, recommendations and resolutions (see box). The member countries take it in turns to hold the Presidency for periods of six months. The Council of Ministers is the most powerful body in the European Union.

The four main types of European law

◎ *Regulations*. These must be enforced by all of the member states and have immediate effect once passed. They take precedence over national laws on the same subject-matter. They are made by the Council of Ministers. Examples include the Unfair Terms in Consumer Contracts Regulations 1995 (no unfair small print in consumer contracts) and the Food Labelling Regulations (which set out a uniform system).

◎ *Directives*. These apply to some or all of the member states of the EU. National governments can decide how to put them into effect, thereby retaining a degree of national autonomy.

◎ *Decisions*. These apply to individual persons, corporations or member states, and are legally binding on them. They must be carried out as directed. The decisions are the result of the deliberations of the Council of Ministers.

◎ *Recommendations and options*. These have no binding force, but represent the view of the European Commission or the European Parliament.

The European Commission

The European Commission is based in Brussels, Belgium. It is one of the four governing institutions of the European Union. Its main function is to initiate and develop proposals for European legislation. The Commission is made up of 20 commissioners nominated by member state governments. It is required to act independently of the member state governments in ways that are in the interests of the EU as a whole. The Commission administers EU funds and subsidies, manages and implements policies, and makes sure that policies are put into effect.

The European Court of Justice

The Court is based in Luxembourg. It consists of one judge from each member state plus one more, who are assisted by six advocates general. The judges are appointed for six years. The Court hears

SOCIAL POLICY AND WELFARE

cases that involve any infringement of community law. Its rulings on European law are final and take precedence over the decisions of courts in the member states. The Court can quash (overrule) any Commission measure. The European Court of Justice is separate from the European Court of Human Rights, which is not a part of the European Union body of organisations.

The European Parliament

The Parliament is based in Strasbourg, France and is an elected, political body. It is composed of 626 European Members of Parliament (MEPs) from the member states, who are elected in 'European elections' every five years. The number of MEPs per country is determined by the size of the population of that country. The outcome of the last election, in June 1999, was as follows:

Austria	21	Netherlands	31
Belgium	25	Portugal	25
Denmark	16	Republic of Ireland	15
Finland	16	Spain	64
France	87	Sweden	22
Germany	99	UK	87
Greece	25		
Italy	87		
Luxembourg	6		

In June 1999, the UK Conservative Party won 36 seats, Labour won 29 seats, the Liberal Democrats ten seats, the Scottish National Party two seats, Plaid Cymru two seats, the UK Green Party two seats and UK Independents three seats; while in Northern Ireland, the Social Democratic and Labour Party, the Ulster Unionist Party and the Democratic Unionist Party took one seat each. All citizens of EU member states who are over the age of 18 have a right to vote for, or stand as, an MEP representing their own member state. The European Parliament debates the proposals put forward by the **European Commission**. It has the right to put forward amendments to these proposals, and the power to approve or reject the yearly budget to pay for the work of the EU. The European Parliament is the world's first and only existing democratically elected body that crosses national boundaries. To date, European MEPs have been reluctant to disrupt the proposals and policies of national governments in cases in which they have conflicted with the intentions of the European Parliament.

The European influence on British social policy

When the **Treaty of Rome (1957)** originally established the **European Economic Community (EEC)** six countries – Belgium, France, Italy, Luxembourg, West Germany and the Netherlands – joined. The United Kingdom didn't join until 1973, when the EEC was expanded to nine member states. The original aims of the EEC were as follows:

- to strengthen peace in Europe
- to achieve economic integration and harmonise economic development
- to achieve the closer union of people in Europe

The original Treaty of Rome proposed close co-operation between member states on welfare issues such as education and training, social security and employment, but left decisions about fundamental social policy issues to the governments of the separate member states. During the postwar consensus period, the objective of European social policy was to promote co-operation between member states, so that the free movement of labour could occur. It was felt that this would lead naturally to harmonisation in social welfare provision.

By the 1970s, the European Economic Community was proposing a more active approach to social policy. There was a gradual move towards trying to get member states to agree that social welfare objectives and the social rights of workers should be standardised throughout Europe. Through initiatives such as the European Social Fund, the European Regional Development Fund and the European Programme to combat poverty, the European Union has engaged in attempts to forge greater social links between EU member states. Funding has been directed at priority issues in particularly 'needy' regions of the EU.

European welfare 'harmonisation' has proved very controversial, particularly within the Conservative Party, who fear a loss of sovereignty and an erosion of the UK's right to 'self-determination' if Europe gains greater political influence and power in the area of social policy. The proposals of the Single European Act 1986 were particularly problematic for the Conservative Party.

The **Single European Act 1986** amended the Treaty of Rome. The main purpose of this legislation was to create a Europe-wide free trade area by 1993. The Act also gave the **European**

Commission authority to act in new areas, such as the environment and social policy. The UK still had a Conservative government at this time, and remained opposed to these new powers.

In 1992, the Conservative government of the UK signed the **Maastricht Treaty**, along with the 11 other member states. The Treaty had five main objectives:

1 A closer European Union, with more co-operation between governments.

2 A common foreign and security policy.

3 All EU states to have the same home affairs and justice policies (the same laws in Britain, France, and so on).

4 A single currency, controlled by a European Central Bank, by 1999.

5 European citizenship for all EU nationals.

Opposition to the developing social policy role of the European Union led to the British government refusing to sign the **Community Charter of the Fundamental Rights of Workers**, also known as the 'Social Chapter', of the Treaty. The aim of the Social Chapter was to ensure that all EU citizens had access to common social rights and employment laws. These cover health and safety regulations, a minimum wage and an agreed maximum number of hours in a working week. Following the election of the New Labour government in 1997, the UK signed up to the Social Chapter and has implemented a number of its provisions.

The current New Labour government is more positive towards the European Union than its Conservative predecessor. Despite the various social welfare initiatives that have been developed within the context of the EU, the social policy-making role of central government in the UK remains largely unaltered by its contact with, and commitment to, the EU. At present, the EU does not appear to have an agenda that will involve attempts to harmonise the differing health, education or welfare systems of the various member states. Most new European legislation and policy-making that touches the social welfare area is on 'employment' issues. The UK has implemented European policy directives on equal treatment of workers since the 1970s, and looks set to continue to do so. The European Union's influence on social policy-making in the UK is worthy of note, but is perhaps not such a significant factor as many anti-European commentators and politicians claim at the present time.

REVIEW POINTS

◎ The British government has engaged in formal political, economic and social co-operation with other European countries since joining the European Economic Community (EEC) in 1973.

◎ The UK became a member of the European Union following the Single European Act 1986.

◎ The key institutions in the EU are the Council of Ministers, the European Commission, the European Court of Justice and the European Parliament.

◎ The EU has influenced social policy in the UK since the 1970s. The key areas of influence have been workers' rights and health and safety.

◎ The expansion of the EU's social policy role is politically controversial, but has been relatively limited in its impact on major areas of social welfare provision.

REVIEW ACTIVITIES

1 Name the piece of legislation that established the European Union in 1986.

2 Which EU institution is the most active and influential in setting the European policy agenda?

3 Why did the Conservative government have reservations about the Single European Act 1986?

4 To what extent has the EU taken over the social policy-making role of the British government?

References

Beveridge, W. (1953) *Power and Influence*. Hodder and Stoughton, London.

Blair, T. (1998) *The Third Way: New Politics for the New Century*. Fabian pamphlet 588. The Fabian Society, London.

Blakemore, K. (1998) *Social Policy – an Introduction*. Open University Press, Buckingham.

Brown, R. (1991) *Society and Economy in Modern Britain 1700–1850*. Routledge, London.

Burden, T. (1998) *Social Policy and Welfare – a Clear Guide*. Pluto Press, London.

Commission on Social Justice (1994) *Social Justice: Strategies for National Renewal*. Vintage, London.

Culpin, C. and Turner, B. (1987) *Making Modern Britain*. Collins Educational, London.

Driver, S. and Martell, L. (1998) *New Labour – Politics after Thatcher*. Polity Press, Cambridge.

Esping-Anderson, G. (1990) *The Three Worlds of Welfare Capitalism*. Polity Press, Cambridge.

Holden, C., Meggitt, C., Collard, D. and Rycroft, C. (1996) *Further Studies for Social Care*. Hodder and Stoughton, London.

Jones, K. (1994) *The Making of Social Policy in Britain 1830–1990*. The Athlone Press, London.

Le Grand, J. (1982) *The Strategy of Equality*. George Allen and Unwin, London.

Marshall, T. H. (1965) *Social Policy*. Hutchinson, London.

Morgan, M. (1985) *Sociological Approaches to Health and Health Care*. Croom Helm, London.

Timmins, N. (1995) *The Five Giants: a Biography of the Welfare State*. HarperCollins, London.

Inequality and Social Policy 3

By the end of this chapter you should be able to:

◎ Describe and evaluate different ways of defining equality and inequality.

◎ Map the extent of inequalities of income and wealth in the United Kingdom.

◎ Identify the defining characteristics of inequality in relation to life chances based on social class, gender, ethnicity, age and disability.

◎ Identify and evaluate debates surrounding social policy measures to tackle inequality.

On 12 May 1999, the *Daily Telegraph* reported that an upper-middle-class London family with an income of £100 000 was at great risk of discomfort, a 'hundred grand' being the 'poverty line' of the capital's upper-middle class. You can imagine the absurdity of trying to 'explain' this kind of discomfort to someone living on the streets. London shares the dubious status of being one of the richest cities in Europe, while also having some of the poorest communities in the United Kingdom. Over the course of a year, at least 2400 people spend some time sleeping rough in the capital (Social Exclusion Unit, 1998).

The income gap between the upper-middle class (city traders, lawyers and other professional elites) and the rough sleepers is vast. This is economic inequality, clear and simple. Once differences in income and wealth become solidified into rankings that are perpetuated over time, as they are in the UK, we speak of a class society.

However, inequality isn't just about the unequal distribution of income and wealth. Older and disabled people are more likely to experience lack of access to transport; women and black people are more likely to encounter harassment at work; and working-class pupils are more likely to be excluded from school. These are only a few examples of how the status attached to gender, ethnicity, age and disability can affect life chances.

Although social policy in the UK seeks to influence a wide variety of outcomes, one of its main objectives is to tackle inequality. In large part, this means introducing policy measures that will (at the very least) narrow the growing gap between the poor and the rich by redistributing resources.

This gap is starkly portrayed in the *Britain Towards 2000* report (cited by Julia Hartley-Brewer, 1999). Using fictitious characters, the report presents a very unequal society. At one end is Rachel, single, in her 30s and with her own advertising company, and at the other end, Craig, who left school without qualifications and who lives off welfare and drug dealing.

Because of medical advances, Rachel is able to delay having a child until she is 45 or older. She lives alone in an inner London neighbourhood with a low crime rate. Craig lives with Maria who, in addition to working in a supermarket, cares for her elderly parents and her two children from previous relationships. The children are logged as 'at risk' by their school and are being monitored for emotional and psychological difficulties.

Britain Towards 2000 paints a picture of life that the government wants to avoid through social policy – a nation in which some people will have lots of freedoms and choice, whereas others will lack the knowledge and resources to fit in. As a result, predicts the report, by 2010 the UK will be plagued by enduring divisions between a prosperous majority and a poor minority – not, we might (hopefully) add, if anti-equality policies kick in and free the poor from poverty.

This chapter documents the extent of inequality in the UK and examines how social policy tries to tackle it.

Definitions of inequality

For the social scientist, inequality describes socially produced differences in well-being between different groups in society. Some policy-makers applaud this. Others loathe it. There is, in short, a politics of inequality.

If, for example, a policy-maker thinks that inequality is acceptable, he or she might invoke terms such as 'competitive spirit' and 'survival of the fittest'. On the other hand, policy-makers who consider inequality to be a bad thing tend to claim that it is the result of 'exploitation' and 'social injustice'. If it's actually possible to be neutral about inequality, one could simply document its different forms without further comment.

In British government circles, the term 'inequality' is negatively charged. It's seen as a problem, and as something to be tackled. This wasn't the case, however, in early 19th-century England, when aristocratic politicians regarded inequality as a necessary condition for the existence of a stable society, in which each person knew – and accepted – his or her place in the 'natural' scheme of things. Our main focus in this book is, of course, on 21st-century issues, which largely means looking at how policy makers tackle inequality, rather than wanting or accepting it. There is a fairly broad consensus in British politics that some types of inequality (with the emphasis on *some* types) are unfair and problematic, and should be rooted out.

Types of inequality

In a broad sense, **inequality** refers to the unequal distribution of valued resources and opportunities in society. It's a multidimensional concept that includes, for example, disparities of income, wealth, prestige, power and access. The opposite of inequality – equality – also logically contains a number of dimensions. One might, for example, live in a society in which there's some equality of opportunity (say, the same chances for girls and boys to enter medical school) but a great deal of income inequality (for instance, higher male earnings).

It's helpful to distinguish between equality and inequality of *opportunity* and equality and inequality of **condition**:

- *equality of opportunity* refers to equal access to the chance of obtaining society's prizes (a good education, a decent income, a healthy life and so on) on the basis of merit rather than social background

- *inequality of opportunity* refers to unequal access to the chance of obtaining society's prizes owing to social background

- *equality of condition* refers to equal access to society's prizes for everyone, irrespective of social background or merit

- *inequality of condition* refers to unequal access to society's prizes owing to social background or merit

Definitions and policies

The extent to which social policy in the United Kingdom can be seen as an attempt to make society more equal can only be fully understood if we're clear about the kind of equality that we're talking about. The way in which a problem is defined affects how we seek to solve it.

Social policies whose aims are to ensure that people enjoy the same (or nearly the same) life outcomes are rare. They exist more in the minds of socialists than in the policy instruments of government. Even in the 'egalitarian' Nordic countries, which use redistributive taxation to reduce the extremes of economic inequality, the goal hasn't been so all-encompassing as to embrace equality of outcome.

Social policy-makers in the UK have never sought to create an equal society. Rather, the aim has been to remove barriers to equality of opportunity. In that context, it comes as no surprise to learn that the body whose brief it is to tackle gendered inequalities is called the Equal *Opportunities* Commission.

What's actually meant be equal opportunities isn't always clear-cut. For, as Ken Blakemore (1998: 26) points out, 'equal opportunity means different things to different people'. Thus, for example, says Blakemore, the political Right stresses equality of *opportunity*, whereas the political Left emphasises *equality* of opportunity. Such differences of emphasis have important consequences for social policy. Blakemore illustrates this point in his typology of 'minimalist' (right-wing) and 'maximalist' (left-wing) equal opportunity strategies (see Table 3.1).

As you can see, the left-wing version – maximalist equality of opportunity – is, at times, hardly different from the principle of equality of outcome. In practical policy terms, however, UK social policy has stopped short of introducing positive discrimination (or 'affirmative action', as

Table 3.1 Equal opportunity strategies

'Minimalist' principles	'Maximalist' principles
Equality policies aim to ensure that people are treated fairly or on an equal basis. Discrimination on grounds of gender, 'race', disability or other irrelevant criteria is unjust and illegal in most cases.	Equality policies aim to create equal outcomes. Policies and the law must go further than banning unfair or negative discrimination; they must also positively encourage or discriminate so that minorities and other disadvantaged groups benefit equally from employment opportunities or the welfare system.
'Fair competition' on a 'level playing field' is the hallmark of this approach. The end-result or outcome (for example, being employed or receiving a benefit) must be decided on merit or according to need.	There is no 'level playing field'. Historic advantages enjoyed by those in control mean that they decide how 'merit' and 'need' are defined. Although merit is important, it may have to be redefined to avoid in-built bias against women, the disabled and so on.
Individuals must be treated 'in like fashion'. The end-result is unequal, but fair. Any discrimination, positive or negative, is wrong.	Individuals may be treated differently according to the social group or category they belong to. 'Positive action' or 'positive discrimination' may be necessary to make sure that under-represented groups obtain benefits or employment they have previously been excluded from.
Quotas, or reserving a certain number of jobs, educational places or services for members of minority and disadvantaged groups, are unjust.	Quotas, or at least targets, to bring the *proportions* of people in various groups (women, disabled people and so on) in line with the proportions receiving employment, education and welfare are necessary, because without them little will change.
'Minimalist' principles fit best with liberal or conservative principles and values.	'Maximalist' principles fit best with social democratic or egalitarian principles, though 'tough' equal opportunities policies are found in the right-of-centre dominated USA.

(Blakemore, 1998: 27)

it's also called), instead using what Blakemore terms 'measures of positive action'. Such measures include steps to encourage more disabled people to apply for jobs by improving mobility access in the workplace.

Whether they support 'maximalist' or 'minimalist' ideas of equality of opportunity, most UK social policy-makers agree that there must be **equity of access** to the public services that the welfare state provides. Equity of access to public services is based on fairness, not equality. If, for example, your medical need is greater than mine, you get more treatment. It would be absurd to suggest that I should get an equal share (half) of the treatment if you needed all of a particular medication and I needed none of it.

Equity adjusts the impact of inequality in a way that is designed to be pro-poor. It makes us care about inequalities in the sense that we recognise some needs as more pressing, and therefore more deserving of priority. But as a policy tool, equity isn't radical. It reduces the worst effects of inequality without tackling root causes.

When the Labour Prime Minister Tony Blair calls for a more equal society, we can be fairly certain that his idea of equality is based on 'equity' (benefits for those who need them, treatment according to clinical need, and so on) and 'equality of opportunity' (equal right of access to education, absence of discrimination on grounds of disability, and so on), rather than on equal outcomes. In his annual Labour Party Conference speech in 1999, the Prime Minister put his case for 'a society that treats us all equally', but not for a society of 'equal incomes', or of 'uniform lifestyles or taste or culture'. His notion of 'true equality' is a society with 'equal worth, an equal chance of fulfilment, equal access to knowledge and opportunity'. What we have here is an outlook that generally (but not exclusively) errs towards Blakemore's 'minimalist' model of equality policies.

Most forms of inequality in society spring from economic disparities. A rich family can buy their child a good education. A poor family might have to settle for less. Top earners can afford to buy healthier food than the low paid and unemployed. One can add to the list of advantages that are, by and large, the result of economic inequality. Even the inequalities linked to gender, ethnicity, age and disability are, to a large extent, based on relative economic advantage. Men earn more than women, white people more than black people, working age people more than pensioners and non-disabled people more than disabled people.

Of course, it often happens that certain vulnerable groups in society suffer the disadvantage of low income and more. Thus, for example, sociologists Stephen Castles and Godula Kosack (1973) found that immigrant workers in Europe who belong to the working class not only form a bottom stratum within this class, but also encountered racial discrimination.

Before looking at the various ways in which inequality (in its various forms) affects different groups in society, we'll first map the bold outlines of economic inequality in the UK. We'll then move on to consider inequality in relation to the relative life chances of specific social groups.

The extent of inequality

President John F. Kennedy once remarked that 'A rising tide lifts all the boats.' That note of optimism might be applied to the United Kingdom in the period after the Second World War up to the late 1970s, when economic growth benefited all income groups. However, during the period from 1979 to 1994/5, the general trend was towards increased inequality, as real net incomes at the bottom of the social scale rose very slowly, or not at all, and those at the top soared. This, according to John Hills, was despite an average income growth of 40% (Hills, 1998).

Not only has the gap between the richest and poorest increased over the past couple of decades, but the amount of movement between income groups has been limited, and damaged life chances have been transferred across generations (HM Treasury, 1999). Children who grow up in poor families do less well at school and are more at risk of social disadvantages in adult life. Moreover, their own children's life chances are often adversely affected.

Income and wealth distribution

Income and wealth are very unevenly distributed in the United Kingdom, which is another way of

Material advantages are very unequally shared in the UK

saying that the UK is a massively unequal society. While both terms denote access to resources, **income** is a money flow, with wages and salaries being by far the largest source of income for most people, and **wealth** is a (relatively) fixed asset, with homes being the most common example.

Income

People receive income from a variety of sources but, as already indicated, the lion's share derives from wages and salaries. Table 3.2 summarises the main sources of household income in the UK from 1971 to 1995.

Table 3.2 Household income in the UK

Source of income	Percentages					
	1971	1976	1981	1986	1991	1995
Wages and salaries[1]	68	67	63	58	58	56
Self-employment income[2]	9	9	8	10	10	10
Rent, dividends, interest	6	6	7	8	9	7
Private pensions, annuities and so on	5	5	6	8	10	11
Social security benefits	10	11	13	13	11	13
Other current transfers[3]	2	2	2	3	2	3
Total household income (= 100%) (£ billion at 1995 prices[4])	314	365	398	472	573	599

[1] Includes forces' pay and income in kind.
[2] After deducting interest payments, depreciation and stock appreciation.
[3] Mostly other government grants, but including transfers from abroad and non-profit-making bodies.
[4] Adjusted to 1995 prices using the consumers' expenditure deflator.

(adapted from *Social Trends 27* (1997: 90), using figures from the Office for National Statistics)

Earnings between occupations differ markedly, with professionals and managers receiving much higher pay than unskilled workers. Moreover, the proportion of people with incomes below half of the average income rose from 8% in 1982 to 19% in 1993. Since the late 1970s, the living standards of people in the bottom 20% or 30% of the income league table haven't increased significantly. However, top income earners, says John Hills, have gained much more rapidly than the average (Hills, 1996). With reference to income distribution in 1996/7, the Department of Social Security reported that:

- In the bottom fifth of the income distribution, about 20% of people were in families with an unemployed head or spouse, and around 30% were non-pensioners in families that were otherwise economically inactive.

- People in unemployed families were particularly likely to have low incomes. About two-thirds of individuals in families where the head or spouse was jobless, and about one half of persons living in other non-working families (mainly, lone parents, the sick and the disabled) had incomes in the bottom fifth of the income distribution.

- Over 75% of people in lone-parent families were in the bottom two-fifths of the income distribution, with more than 40% falling in the bottom fifth. Pensioners were over-represented in the bottom half of the income distribution, but not markedly in the bottom fifth.

- Almost three out of ten children were in the bottom fifth of the income distribution. About four out of ten children were in the top half of the income distribution.

- Women accounted for 55% of adults in the bottom fifth of the income distribution and 47% of adults in the top fifth. Men were under-represented in the lower part of the distribution, and over-represented at the top, with women being more evenly spread.

- Single women with children were over-represented in the bottom fifth of the income distribution. Among pensioners, single women were more likely than single men to have a low income. This wasn't the case, however, for non-pensioners without dependent children.

- The income distributions of families headed by a member of an ethnic minority were skewed towards the bottom. This pattern was especially marked for Bangladeshis and Pakistanis, of whom about seven out of ten were in the bottom fifth of the income distribution.

Wealth

Inequality of wealth is also massive, even more so than income, with the top 10% of the UK population owning half of all the wealth (Joseph Rowntree Foundation, 1999c). There are two main kinds of wealth:

1 *marketable wealth* – assets that can be sold or cashed in (for example, homes, shares, racehorses and paintings)

2 *non-marketable wealth* – assets that can't be sold or cashed in, or are hard to do so (for example, occupational and state pension rights)

The value of personal wealth (mainly owned by individuals, but including unincorporated private businesses, life assurance and pension funds) in the UK in 1994 exceeded £2500 billion. Most people hold the largest part of their wealth (between 40% and 60%) in the form of their homes. Only individuals whose wealth is above £500 000 (about 1% of the population) hold more of their wealth in shares than in other assets. Big shareholders constitute an upper (or ruling) class in the UK.

Table 3.3 shows the distribution of wealth in the UK from 1976 to 1993.

The exceedingly wealthy people in the UK can be narrowed down to about 1000 individuals who, between them, are worth almost £115 billion (*Sunday Times Rich List 1999*, April 1999). At the top of the list – in April 1999 – was Hans Rausing, a British-based Swedish industrialist who made his fortune in the food packaging industry. Rausing was then worth £3.4 billion. Lord Sainsbury and family (of the supermarket chain) were ranked second, with a wealth rating of £3.1 billion. The *Sunday Times Rich List 1999* is made up of 1022 men and 71 women – 709 of the richest 1000 are self-made millionaires, while 291 inherited their wealth and 137 are aristocrats.

Table 3.3 The distribution of wealth[1] in the UK

	Percentages				
	1976	1981	1986	1991	1993
Marketable wealth					
Percentage of wealth owned by:					
Most wealthy 1%	21	18	18	17	17
Most wealthy 5%	38	36	36	35	36
Most wealthy 10%	50	50	50	47	48
Most wealthy 25%	71	73	73	71	72
Most wealthy 50%	92	92	90	92	92
Total marketable wealth (£ billion)	280	565	955	1711	1809
Marketable wealth plus occupational and state pension rights					
Percentage of wealth owned by:					
Most wealthy 1%	13	11	10	10	10
Most wealthy 5%	26	24	24	23	23
Most wealthy 10%	36	34	35	33	33
Most wealthy 25%	57	56	58	57	56
Most wealthy 50%	80	79	82	83	82
Total marketable wealth (£ billion)	472	1036	1784	3014	3383

[1] This applies to the adult population aged 18 and over. The estimates for 1976, 1981, 1986 and 1991 are based on the estates of persons dying in those years. The estimates for 1993 are based on estates notified for probate in 1993–1994. The estimates are not strictly comparable between 1993 and earlier years.

(adapted from *Social Trends 26* (1996: 111), using figures from the Inland Revenue)

There are:

155	in land and property
142	in industry
86	in food production and retailing
82	in finance, banking and insurance
74	in computers, technology and software
70	in media and publishing
61	in construction
60	in non-food retailing
52	in music and entertainment
51	in leisure
38	in distribution and car sales
37	in transport
26	in pharmaceuticals and health care
24	in textiles and fashion
19	in business services and recruitment
12	in mobile phones
11	in the Internet

In today's UK, more than 70% of the super-wealthy have made their fortunes themselves, with inherited wealth slipping below 30%. This is in stark contrast to 1989, when 57% of the then wealthiest people had inherited their wealth.

Inequality and poverty

According to the Institute for Fiscal Studies (see Gregg *et al.*, 1999), inequality and poverty have risen very sharply in the UK since the late 1970s. Children have been particularly badly hit, with many more of them now growing up in disadvantaged circumstances. Among some of the findings reported by the Institute (Institute for Fiscal Studies, 1997; Gregg *et al.*, 1999) are the following:

- the richest 10% of the population now have as much income as the whole of the poorer half of households

◎ since the late 1970s, income inequality has risen faster for families with children than for those without

◎ families with children have come to comprise a much greater proportion of the poorest group

◎ over 4 million children were in poverty in 1995/6, three times the number 20 years earlier

◎ on virtually any measure, poverty has increased very significantly

Taking stock of the unequal social landscape that it says it has inherited from the previous Conservative government, the Labour government released the findings of a major Treasury study on the causes and scale of inequality (HM Treasury, 1999). Among the main findings, based on 1997 figures, were these:

◎ 12 million people in the UK, almost a quarter of the population, live in relative poverty – nearly three times the number in 1979

◎ inequality increased by a third between 1977 and 1996 – this is virtually unique among developed nations

◎ inequality is passed across generations – the children of the low paid are much more likely to be low paid

◎ two out of every five children are born poor, many to families who weren't poor before the birth of a child – as many as one in six families are pushed into poverty after the birth of a child

◎ poverty damages a child's life chances: by the time children are 22 months old, clear social class differences in their rate of educational development are evident – these differences widen even more when children start school

◎ in the mid-1990s, half of those leaving unemployment were jobless again within the year

◎ people get stuck in a 'low-pay, no-pay' cycle – the number of men caught in this cycle, or in a long-term but low-paid job, has doubled since the early 1980s

REVIEW POINTS

◎ The UK is a massively unequal society, in which income and wealth are very unevenly distributed.

◎ Income inequality and poverty have risen very sharply in the UK since the late 1970s. The richest 10% of the population now have as much income as the whole of the poorer half of households.

◎ Children have been particularly badly hit. Over 4 million children were in poverty in 1995/6, three times the number 20 years earlier.

REVIEW ACTIVITIES

1 What's the difference between **income** and **wealth**?

2 What evidence is there to support the claim that, in economic terms, the UK is a massively unequal society?

3 Describe the main changes that have occurred in sources of household income between 1971 and 1995 (see Table 3.2).

4 What is the key source of wealth of the wealthiest 1% of the UK population?

5 According to HM Treasury, how many people were living in poverty in the UK in 1997?

Inequality in relation to life chances

The most important life chance in any society is the opportunity to live a long, healthy life. In the United Kingdom, as in many other countries, this opportunity is unevenly shared. The roots of good health and ill-health are notably traceable to social class, gender, ethnicity, age and disability.

For example, people in the unskilled working class are more likely to have a serious long-term illness than professional people; women usually live longer than men; Scottish-born people are more likely to die from lung cancer than people born in England; the highest suicide rates are found among men aged 25–44 and those over 75 years; and some disabled people aren't eligible for heart transplants.

Often, the single most important predictor of health and other life chances is **social class**, a social scientific category that defines a person's economic ranking in society. In the UK, sociologists conventionally identify three main classes **upper**, **middle** and **lower** (also commonly called **working**). Each class is further differentiated in relation to 'in-class' economic gradations and other aspects of social stratification, notably gender, ethnicity, age and disability. For example, skilled workers earn more than unskilled workers, a higher proportion of middle-class men enter politics than middle-class women, and so on.

Many social scientists believe that class is the bedrock of stratification, arguing that economic security (the basis of class) tends to eclipse the independent effects of gender, ethnicity, age and disability. This doesn't mean that non-class dimensions are unimportant, but that they should, whenever possible, be considered together with class position.

The following sections examine health, employment and educational inequalities in relation to social class, gender, ethnicity, age and disability, indicating – as appropriate – linkages between these groups. These three dimensions aren't exclusive, nor do they cover all possibilities, but they are centrally important in so far as key life chances are concerned. Because the same (and other) dimensions are examined more fully in other chapters (see Chapters 6, 11 and 12), what follows is a broad overview.

Social class

Before plotting life chances against social classes, it's helpful to outline the form that class stratification takes in the UK. A 'three-class pyramid', with an upper class at the top, a middle class midway, and a lower (or working) class at the bottom, works well here.

The upper class

Comprising only about 1% of the UK population, the upper class mainly consists of big property owners, with massive capital asset and share incomes. The richest 1000 of these people have been referred to earlier, in the *Sunday Times Rich List 1999*.

The lifestyles and life chances of the upper class are well-documented: see, for example, the work of Malcolm Hamilton and Maria

Hirszowicz (1993). Upper-class people move and marry within the same (relatively closed) social circles, and display a high degree of social cohesion (that is, people of similar backgrounds tend to stick together), marked by lavish entertainment and travel, membership of prestigious London clubs, education at the top public schools and 'Oxbridge', attendance at hunt balls, Ascot, the Henley Regatta and the 'London season', and grandiose residences. They're disproportionately over-represented – often through 'elite self-recruitment' – in the top positions of business, the military and the judiciary and – directly or indirectly – they hold considerable sway in politics.

The middle class

Sociologists often identify two groupings within the middle class. These are the **'old' middle class** of relatively prosperous proprietors – either self-employed (for example, a barrister) or employers of only a small number of employees (for example, a country practice vet) and the **'new' middle class** of non-manual employees. There's wide diversity within the 'new' middle class: the university professor, the school teacher and the school secretary. The best-paid rub shoulders with peak privilege and power, having reached the foothills of the upper class. The worst-paid earn less than skilled manual workers, and are sometimes referred to as the 'non-manual section' of the working class.

The working class

Sociologists often identify two main groupings within the working class:

- *skilled and semi-skilled employees* (for example, plumbers and telephone operators), who earn about the same as lower-middle-class employees (for example, nurses and social workers)

- *unskilled employees* (for example, cleaners and dishwashers) and non-working people on low fixed incomes (for example, long-term unemployed, pensioners and 'rough sleepers'), some of whom encounter varying degrees of social exclusion from mainstream society

Although economic position is the defining feature of class, distinct social lifestyles (themselves linked to income and wealth) set different classes apart. Dress codes, holiday destinations, newspaper readership and restaurant preferences are among the tell-tale signs.

Back in the 1970s, tailored suits and bowler hats were obligatory office wear for 'old-middle-class' city gents

Class and health

In the first chapter of his book *Durable Inequality* (1998), Charles Tilley introduces the reader to Britain's first professional cartoonist, the 18th/19th-century caricaturist, James Gillray. In Gillray's witty portrayals of the then British class system, beefy, red-faced aristocrats towered over small, gaunt paupers. The pictures, though savage, reflected real events. At the start of the 19th century, poor 14-year-old boys averaged 4 feet 3 inches tall, whereas aristocrats and gentry of the same age averaged around 5 feet 1 inch (Tilley, 1998).

Why was this so? It was because the children of the poor suffered malnutrition, while the children of the landed class ate well. In the 1840s, it was found that London 'gentlemen' lived, on average, twice as long as 'labourers'. From 1911, British death certificates have been coded for social class based on occupation, which has enabled researchers to study the links between class and mortality rates.

UK research has consistently shown that an individual's class position in society strongly affects his or her health and life expectancy. Moreover, people most at risk of ill-health tend to have the least satisfactory access to the full range of preventive health services – this is the so-called **Inverse Prevention Law**.

One of the more important studies in health inequalities was prompted by Richard Wilkinson who, in 1976, wrote an open letter in *New Society* magazine urging the then Labour government to set up an urgent inquiry into the causes of different mortality rates between the classes. What subsequently became known as the Black Report appeared in 1980, when Sir Douglas Black, then President of the Royal College of Surgeons, produced evidence of marked class-related inequalities in health chances. People in unskilled jobs had a two and a half times greater chance of dying before retirement than professional people.

The Black Report disclosed that the gap in mortality rates between rich and poor had widened between 1930 and 1970. In 1930, unskilled workers were 23% more likely to die prematurely than professional workers. By 1970, the likelihood was 61%. The Black Report was branded by right-wing politicians as being part of a left-wing cause. As a result, it wasn't seriously acted upon by the Conservative government in office at the time of its publication. However, evidence from later research has shown that the health divide increased during the 1980s.

The Black Report was re-published in unabridged form in the 1990s, which indicates, perhaps, a renewed interest in the links between health and inequality. This seems appropriate, given that, as we enter the 21st century, people at the bottom of the social ladder are still in much worse health than those at the top, a point forcibly made by Sir Donald Acheson in his 1998 Report, *Independent Inquiry into Inequalities in Health*.

Sir Donald found that although inequalities in health occur throughout all classes, the weight of scientific evidence points to strong class-linked health chances. By the early 1990s, the mortality rate among men of working age was nearly three times as high for those in class V (unskilled) as for those in class I (professional). Moreover, improvements in life expectancy were greater from the late 1970s to the late 1980s for women in higher classes. There are also clear differences in infant mortality rates, with babies in lower classes being more at risk.

Morbidity rates often show a marked class gradient. For example, in 1996, 25% of women in class V were classified as obese, compared to 14% of class I women. Men in class I also had lower rates of obesity. Another indicator of poor health, raised blood pressure, is more likely to affect women in manual classes than those higher up the social scale (Acheson, 1998). Major accidents are more common among men in the manual

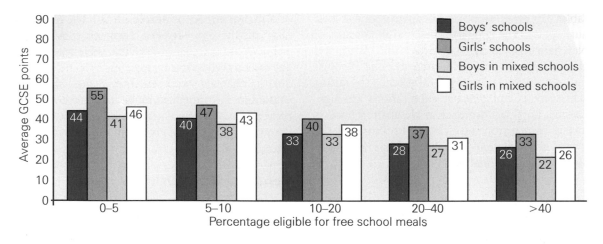

(Ofsted)

Achievement of boys and girls in single-sex and mixed schools: average GCSE points scores (grade A = 5 points, grade E = 1 point) banded by eligibility for free school meals

classes for those aged under 55. But, between 55 and 74, the non-manual classes have higher major accident rates (Acheson, 1998). As far as psychological health is concerned, all neurotic disorders were more common among women in lower than in higher social classes. However, such differences weren't found among men. On the other hand, more men in lower classes were dependent on alcohol than those in higher classes (Acheson, 1998).

Class and employment

This issue has already been addressed in the section on social class. The important thing to remember is that occupation is one of the most accurate predictors of all other life chances. Put simply, people in top jobs are more likely to have healthier longer lives, to remain in and obtain more from full-time education, and to pass these and other benefits to their children. The opposite applies to people in low-paid work and to the long-term unemployed.

Class and education

A massive volume of research points to marked and enduring inequalities in educational outcomes that are linked to class. Children from higher social classes not only perform better than those from lower social classes; they also attend the most successful schools. For some, this means elite private schools, and for others, 'middle-class' state schools in middle-class areas.

Class-based markers are apparent early on, with poorer reception-aged children obtaining lower baseline scores in reading, writing, speaking and maths. By the time they take GCSEs, children

from poor neighbourhoods are a long way behind their middle-class peers. The proportion of pupils living in these areas who leave school with no graded GCSEs is well above the national average. The accompanying figure shows how average GCSE point scores are related to numbers of pupils eligible for free school dinners (a good proxy measure of low-income households):

As can be seen, even after allowing for gender, and for single-sex or mixed establishments, pupils in schools where a higher proportion is eligible for free school meals are more likely to underachieve relative to pupils in schools where this proportion is lower. For example, in mixed schools where more than 40% of pupils are eligible for free meals, the average GCSE points score for girls is 26, whereas in mixed schools where only 0–5% of girls are eligible, the average score is 46.

With regard to school resource allocation and provision for school-building renewal, evidence suggests that inequalities have widened over the past 20 years or so. Schools in poorer neighbourhoods are more likely to be hard pressed for space, and to have the environment degraded by graffiti and litter. Such conditions contribute to more stressful working and learning conditions (Acheson, 1998).

While it would be wrong for schools in poor neighbourhoods to take refuge in class-based explanations of relative educational failure, it is unwise to ignore the obvious impact of class on educational outcomes. In areas in which low income, poor health and bad housing set up real obstacles to school improvement, good teachers can and do make a difference, but their (and their pupils') achievements often don't show up in raw league es. For example, despite being the poorest local authority in the country, the London Borough of Newham has made concerted and successful efforts to raise pupil achievement. The borough has developed a strategic approach to raising achievement, and teacher expectations are high. Overall, pupil performance in Newham schools is low in comparison with national norms, but the rate of improvement at GCSE level has been at, or ahead of, the national trend in recent years.

Gender

Although social scientists distinguish between **sex** (a biological characteristic woman or man) and **gender** (a cultural attribute – femininity or masculinity), the two terms are often used interchangeably in the literature. In this section, unless otherwise indicated, 'sex' and 'gender' both refer to biological difference.

Even if some 'sex-specific' behaviours are linked to genes, the way in which a person is socialised has a big impact on his or her life chances. Many little boys ask for dolls, but their parents quite often prefer to give them 'boys' toys'. This reinforces gender-stereotyped play, thereby affecting the way in which boys behave. Similar things happen, with worrying consequences, when societies make cultural judgements about 'women's activities' and 'men's activities'. In most cases, women lose out here

and men gain. For example, in the UK there's a clear distinction between domestic/female and public/male spheres of activity, which is one of the reasons why women earn less than men. Even health chances between the sexes, although undoubtedly influenced by biology, have cultural dimensions. Rough-and-tumble play, more common among boys, is also more likely to lead to injury.

Gender and health

Mortality (death) rates are higher at all ages for males than for females. Between the ages of one and 14, more boys are likely to die from poisoning and injury, including motor vehicle accidents, fire and flames, accidental drowning and submersion. The gender gap in mortality widens during the teenage years so that, by age 15, boys have 65% higher mortality than girls (Acheson, 1998). Throughout adult life, mortality rates for men are higher than for women, for all the major causes of death. In youth and early adulthood, this is largely due to motor vehicle accidents, other accidents and suicide. In the 25–40 age group, mortality rates for women have decreased over the past two decades, whereas for men of the same age they've increased. Life expectancy is five years longer for women than for men (Acheson, 1998).

On the other hand, women have significantly higher rates of disability than men, especially at

This picture may be dated, but women are still often associated in the public mind with domestic work

older ages. One probable reason for this is the increased incidence of osteoporosis (a disabling bone disease) among women. Women also suffer more than men from poor mental health, particularly in areas related to anxiety and depression. Men, however, have higher rates of alcohol and drug dependence (Acheson, 1998).

Gender and employment

The number of women who go out to work has steadily increased over the past few decades, yet women still earn less than men in paid employment. More than 20 years after equal pay legislation, women's average pay in 1999 was only 80% of men's. Income inequalities are affected by, among other factors:

- stereotyped educational, training and work 'choices'
- over-representation of women in part-time and low-paid jobs
- sexual harassment and other forms of discrimination
- balancing paid employment and assumed family roles
- limited childcare facilities

Findings from a survey conducted for the Equal Opportunities Commission (EOC) (1999) confirm not only that fundamental barriers to real sex equality remain, but also that there's a worrying degree of complacency among some senior policy-makers. The survey asked MPs, MEPs, life peers and political advisors about their awareness of sex equality issues and their attitudes. Although 88% were aware of the pay gap between women and men, and 76% thought that promotion opportunities for women were much worse than for men, only 43% believed that more needs to be done to tackle sex discrimination.

Gender and education

In 1988, social scientists spotted a 4% achievement gap between girls and boys at school, with the girls ahead. These days, hardly a week goes by without a story about boys' underachievement in schools. According to Ted Wragg, a distinguished professor of education at Exeter University, the underachievement of boys is one of the biggest challenges facing schools and society. A number of factors are said to have led to the phenomenon of girls outperforming boys at school. These include:

- the (virtual) abolition of the 11-plus exam, which was weighted in favour of 'masculine' knowledge and skills
- increased awareness on the part of teachers towards gender issues at school, particularly in relation to improving girls' performance
- the transition to coursework-based GCSEs, which tends to favour 'homework-conscientious' girls
- a rise in 'laddish' culture, with image-conscious (working-class) boys seeing academic achievement as 'naff', or 'uncool'
- a mounting body of evidence that girls learn to speak earlier than boys, and that much of this stems from talk between daughters and mothers
- research showing that fathers rarely help at home with literacy activities, leaving this to mothers

Whatever the causes, the fact remains that girls are outperforming boys in almost every subject in GCSE. Differences between girls' and boys' achievements are especially marked in areas of urban disadvantage. Up to age 16, girls are doing well in countries as far afield as the UK, the USA, Australia and Finland. Unesco reports that the phenomenon of girls outpacing boys has also appeared over the past few years in a number of 'developing' countries.

After age 16, the situation isn't as clear-cut. Girls have closed the gap with boys at A and AS level, but boys are over-represented at the very high and very low scores. Moreover, relatively few girls take A-level courses that are wholly mathematical, scientific or technological, thereby denying themselves certain career opportunities later on. At university, there are slightly more female than male undergraduates in the UK (based on figures for 1998), quite a transformation given that, in 1970–1971, there were twice as many male undergraduates as female.

Ethnicity

An ethnic group is a group whose members identify with a distinct (often national) culture. Many ethnic groups have easily identifiable customs of dress, art, music, language (including accent and dialect) and religion. Skin colour is often a defining feature of ethnicity, but only because cultural significance is usually attached to this (for example, 'Black is beautiful').

Social scientists often distinguish between ethnic majorities and ethnic minorities. In the UK, the ethnic majority are white English Britons. Non-English British-born citizens who strongly identify with their ethnic origins (many of them black and Asian, but also Scottish, Welsh and people of Irish descent) are ethnic minorities, as are non-Britons. Some social scientists reserve the term 'ethnic minority' for oppressed ethnic groups, such as African Caribbeans and Bangladeshis. However, strictly speaking, white non-Britons who rarely encounter ethnic discrimination (for example, Australians and Swedes) are also ethnic minority groups.

In the 1991 Census, just over 3 million people, 5.5% of the population, identified themselves as members of one of the nation's non-white ethnic minorities. Nearly half of these people were UK-born. White minority ethnic minorities weren't counted, but recent estimates show that the Irish are the biggest single ethnic minority, comprising about 4.6% of the population.

Ethnicity and health

It's actually quite difficult to find comprehensive data on the mortality rates of ethnic minorities, because country of birth, rather than ethnic group, is recorded on death certificates. This means that mortality figures are restricted to migrants, including migrants from Scotland, Northern Ireland and the Republic of Ireland. In 1989–1992, deaths from all causes (including perinatal mortality) for nearly all migrant groups were higher than average (Acheson, 1998).

Data is available for most ethnic groups in relation to illness. People from ethnic minorities are more likely than the ethnic majority to describe their health as 'fair' or 'poor'. Available data also suggests that Irish people have higher rates of illness, as well as mortality (Acheson, 1998). However, it's unhelpful to generalise about ethnic minorities as a whole, because health chances vary between different groups. For example, mortality rates for lung cancer are low in migrant groups born in the Caribbean, Africa and Asia, and high for people born in Ireland and Scotland (Acheson, 1998).

Ethnicity and employment

A large body of research (see Joseph Rowntree Foundation, 1999a) shows that, on average, ethnic minorities suffer a substantial amount of economic disadvantage. Indeed, sometimes all that varies is the relative degree of disadvantage

suffered. Thus, for example, rates of male unemployment are somewhat higher for Indians (7.4%), and considerably higher for African Caribbean (20.5%) and Bangladeshi and Pakistani groups (15.9%). Even more striking, though, is the greater proportion of people from all ethnic minorities who are in poverty, as defined by less than half the average income. On that measure, for example, four out of five Bangladeshi and Pakistani households are poor (Acheson, 1998).

Although we must guard against portraying economic life chances as uniform outcomes, the broad patterns of inequality are clear – people from ethnic minorities are more likely to be concentrated in low-paid, low-status manual work, doing shift work, with long hours and with limited access to training and occupational benefits.

Ethnicity and education

According to Sir Herman Ouseley, then chair of the Commission for Racial Equality, 'Education in Britain is institutionally racist and racism is an inherent part of the education system' (see Ghouri and Barnard, 1999).

Why is it, Sir Herman asked, that after nearly 40 years of analysing and campaigning, so many black children are underachieving? Sir Herman's isn't a lone voice. According to government inspectors, many of the UK's schools are institutionally racist. By **institutional racism** is meant internal arrangements in schools and education authorities (not always consciously planned) that work against ethnic minority pupils. For example, black and white pupils often start school with similar levels of attainment but, by secondary school, white pupils are usually markedly ahead in academic terms. Something in the system is creating this gap. It certainly doesn't help that the stereotype of the disaffected, underachieving black pupil is still entrenched in school culture. If we consider exclusion rates, for example, black pupils are more than three times more likely to be permanently excluded than their white peers.

The fact that two-thirds of all excluded pupils never return to mainstream education might explain part of the relative underachievement of the over-represented black boys amongst this group. But what about the majority of black boys who aren't excluded? Why are they underachieving? Perhaps there are too few black teachers to act as positive role models and spur black pupils on. Or perhaps the over-representation of pupils from ethnic minorities in lower-ability groups in itself fosters low achievement. Low expectations beget poor results.

Explanations for relative black under-achievement are many and complex. For one thing, there's a wide discrepancy between black African pupils and black Caribbeans, with pupils of African origin generally doing better. If we look at other ethnic minority groups, the picture gets even more complicated, with some Asian children obtaining significantly better GCSE results than white pupils.

Age

People tend to think of children, young adults, middle-aged adults and older people as distinct homogenous groups. Yet inequalities exist both within as well as between age groups. For example, middle-class children often do better at school than working-class children, and young adults typically earn less than middle-aged adults.

True, ageing involves universal biological processes, but the social categorisation of age is very much a product of culture. For example, in the UK, reaching the chronological age of 18 is socially defined as entering early adulthood. But this transition could just as easily be defined at the age of 16 or 21, in which case adult status would come earlier or later in a socially defined timetable.

Age and health

Allowing for the fact that health chances at different stages of the chronological life course are affected by class, gender and ethnicity, ageing itself eventually leads to a deterioration in health and finally to death. This isn't to say that being old necessarily means ill health and senility. On the contrary, many older people remain fit and active in later life, and rightly contest the notion that old age and feebleness go hand in hand.

When failing health does occur, it hits harder among poorer older people. Lung cancer and respiratory disease, breathing problems, coronary heart disease, high blood pressure and stroke are more frequent among lower-class older people, as are rates of tooth loss. Long-standing illness has a higher incidence among unskilled men over 65 than among men from professional backgrounds, but there's no corresponding difference for women (Acheson, 1998).

Age and employment

People of working age in well paid, full-time employment, especially, those at peak career in

The US senator and astronaut, John Glenn, on board the space shuttle Discovery at the age of 77, hardly fits the stereotype of a senile old man

middle adulthood, are – in almost all cases – financially better off than the unemployed, children and pensioners. Unemployment can occur at any time during working life, but when older people become jobless, it's often harder for them to get back into work. Research by Alan Walker shows that people aged 50–60 face widespread discrimination from employers, with age restrictions in job advertisements being a common barrier (Walker, 1998).

Children's economic life chances are closely tied to the incomes of their parents. Children from prosperous backgrounds are comfortably off, whereas those from poorer households fare much less well. At the dawn of the third millennium, some 40% of children were born poor, as defined by being in families in the bottom one-third of the nation's income distribution. There are also clear links between child poverty and future earnings, so that today's poor children are more likely than other groups to become tomorrow's poor adults.

Older people are particularly vulnerable to poverty, whether this is defined as below half the average income or on means-tested benefits (Acheson, 1998). Beveridge had intended that the National Insurance (NI) pension would rid the giant 'want' of poverty in old age. However, when it came to calculating the NI pension level, this was set below that of 'national assistance' (now called income support). This meant that a pension in itself wasn't enough to lift an old person out of poverty.

Although occupational pensions have since helped to improve the living standards of many pensioners, older people are still one of the largest groups living in poverty in the UK. In 1992/3, households in which the head or spouse were aged 60 or over represented nearly one-quarter of the poor, defined as those living on below 50% of average income, after deduction of housing costs. (Walker, 1998). Old age is 'gendered', with men generally better off (though not well off) than women.

Age and education

In the (not so distant) past, formal education stopped for most people at the end of compulsory schooling. A minority stayed on for a couple more years to take A-levels, and a smaller 'subsample' went to university. Even undergraduates (unless they did higher degrees or postgraduate training) left 'learning' behind for the world of work. Things are changing. The past ten years have seen an increasing shift from an elite towards a mass system of higher education. In 1979, just over one in ten young people entered higher education. By 1997, the figure had risen to almost one in three.

This physically imparied athlete is much fitter than many able-bodied adults

Some commentators lament this and cry 'More means worse.' But it doesn't.

There's no evidence that the provision of greater educational opportunity (including 'second chance' access for adults who failed at the school hurdle) has compromised quality of provision. The move towards more inclusive higher education has brought new confidence and opportunities to people who might have imagined that college or university wasn't for them. The rallying call isn't 'Dumb down', but 'Wise up'!

Disability

Disabled people are amongst the most widely marginalised groups in the UK. Until relatively recently, many of them were tucked away in 'total institutions' – homes for incurables and so on. 'Mainstreaming' strategies play an important part in the new Labour government's manifesto commitment. But, says Marilyn Howard, if they are to be more than a civil servant's 'tick box exercise', the culture of policy-making on disability issues needs a good shake-up (Howard, 1999).

Although important progress is being made in a number of policy areas (for example, a New Deal), disabled people are still more likely to have low-paid jobs, to live on benefits and to have restricted access to the labour market, transport and the built environment. Moreover, there's still a climate of mistrust over largely unsubstantiated claims of massive fraud in the disability benefits system.

Yet, in the tens of thousands of cases investigated by the Benefit Integrity Project (inherited from the last Conservative government), not one single case of confirmed fraud was found. Notwithstanding these findings, Department for Social Security officials have continued to swoop on the homes of many thousands more disabled people without finding any evidence of fraud. According to Lord Morris of Manchester (Labour's first Minister for Disabled People, from 1974 to 1979), these investigations have brought some disabled people to the brink of suicide.

Impairment and health

It's easy, but often wrong, to equate disability and ill-health with each other. Some disabled people are very ill because of their impairment (for example, people with cystic fibrosis), whereas others lead very healthy lives (for example, deaf athletes). Whether impairment in itself leads to a greater likelihood of illness and premature death is very much linked to the nature of the impairment.

Worryingly, some disabled people are considered by some health professionals as less deserving. The Downs Syndrome Association is particularly concerned that people with Downs Syndrome are unlikely to be put on heart transplant waiting lists. According to a spokeswoman from the Association, a number of health professionals don't think that people with Downs Syndrome are worth making an effort for – and this doesn't just apply to heart patients. A report from the Association, published in 1999, found that 28% of parents of Downs Syndrome children who were questioned believed that they had suffered ill treatment from medical staff.

The unequal treatment and social inequalities experienced by disabled people in education and employment are discussed in some detail in Chapter 8 (see pp. 217–241).

REVIEW POINTS

⊚ The most important life chance is the chance to live a long, healthy life. In the UK, these and other life chances (notably, educational and occupational prospects) are clearly linked to social class, gender, ethnicity, age and disability.

⊚ Many social scientists believe that class lies at the heart of stratification, tending to eclipse, in life chance terms, the independent effects of gender, ethnicity, age and disability.

⊚ This doesn't mean that non-class dimensions are unimportant, but that they should, whenever possible, be considered in conjunction with class position.

⊚ In general, the health, educational and occupational life chances are better the higher one's class – and also for men, white people and non-disabled people. There are, of course, exceptions to this pattern. For example, girls outperform boys at GCSE.

REVIEW ACTIVITIES

1 Describe the 'three-class pyramid'.
2 What effect does an individual's social class appear to have on his or her health, employment and educational opportunities?
3 Describe the apparent links between gender and an individual's health, employment and educational 'life chances'.
4 Briefly outline the apparent links between ethnicity and life chances with reference to health, employment and education.
5 How does impairment affect a person's access to health, employment and educational opportunities?

Tackling inequality through social policy

United Kingdom social policy set limits on the range of inequalities to be tackled by government. Few, if any, policy-makers have seriously sought to put Britons on an equal footing (*equality of outcome*). Rather, the objective has been to put them on an equal starting line (*equality of opportunity*) in an unequal society. Note, for example, how the word 'opportunity' is inserted in an article that outlines a Labour politician's view on the best way to reduce poverty:

'By running the economy well you can do more for those most in need ... We all want to be part of a successful economy. We all want to do the best we can for ourselves and our families. But we want everyone to have that *opportunity*.'

(Alistair Darling, Social Secretary, *The Observer*, 22 August 1999)

(in other words, the more you earn, the more you pay) – would boost the incomes of the low paid. It would also give the government more revenue for social security spending. Higher taxes for those who can afford to pay them would mean a better, more socially inclusive life for the poor. This arrangement operates in the Nordic countries, where it helps to keep poverty at bay. If the UK were also to return to this system, which linked benefits to earnings rather than prices (it was abandoned in the early 1980s), at-risk groups would fare better.

A minimum wage

Crucially linked to welfare-to-work New Deals is the argument that work must pay. There's ample evidence to show that low pay causes poverty, and so a national minimum wage is intended to tackle low-waged poverty. The Low Pay Commission, whose brief was to recommend a national minimum wage level, proposed £3.60 per hour from April 1999 for workers aged 22 or over, and this was approved by the government.

Many thousands of workers will gain from the **national minimum wage (NMW)**. However, because the level is very modest ('Could those who legislate the wage of others live on it themselves?' seems a relevant question), many workers will have to be paid top-ups in the form of benefit credits. The fact that the government didn't even endorse the Low Pay Commission's far from generous recommendation of an increase of 10p from June 2000 doesn't bode well for the use of minimum wage legislation as an anti-poverty measure.

Under existing legislation, workers who are below the minimum school-leaving age are excluded from the NMW, and workers aged 18–21 are on the reduced rate of £3.00 per hour. What we have here is a system of unequal rates of pay for the same work, a clear case of ageist (in this case, 'anti'-young worker) legislation. A minimum wage is, in principle, an effective instrument in any war on poverty. The important thing to remember, though, is that it mustn't be too minimum!

Peter Townsend, a British sociologist and one of the world's leading experts on poverty, would like the government not only to provide a generous minimum wage but also to set limits on high earnings and levels of personal wealth. This makes good social scientific sense, but it isn't what social policy-makers have in mind. British governments consistently reject even the policy, much favoured in Nordic countries, of taxing top earners heavily to help fund welfare programmes.

Eliminating child poverty

Prime Minister Tony Blair has called for the elimination of child poverty within a generation – a 20-year mission. Between 1968 and 1995/96, the proportion of children with no working parent rose from 2% to 10% of those in two-parent families, and from 30% to 58% of those in lone-parent families (Joseph Rowntree Foundation, 1999b). This growth in the number of children living in families without work is closely linked to a rise in child poverty, with workless families accounting for 54% of all poor children in the mid-1990s, compared with 31% in the late 1960s. Over the same period, the proportion of poor children living in lone-parent families has risen from 19% to 43% (Joseph Rowntree Foundation, 1999b).

While the increase in lone-parent families in itself accounts for part of the overall increase in child poverty, the rising risk of unemployment for lone- and two-parent families has been a bigger cause for concern (Joseph Rowntree Foundation, 1999b). Given that poor families have poor children, it makes good policy sense to improve family incomes. Welfare to work deals will help here, but the measures on offer – such as improved education, more child-care and Sure Start for children at particular risk – although helpful, won't, by themselves, guarantee more income for poor families.

Innovative and radical measures, such as Education Action Zones, will undoubtedly help to improve vulnerable children's early potential. But it takes time for some advantages to kick in. Being poor until one goes to university or starts work is tough going. That's why it's important to introduce poverty-reducing measures (benefits, grants, and so on) into life trajectories that are on course for a better future but haven't got there yet. This principle also applies, for example, to unemployed adults on training courses.

If an end to child poverty is to be more than a tabloid headline, increased benefits must play a role in meeting this pledge. Research evidence shows that payment to the first-line (or only) caring parent (usually the mother) raises the prospect of the benefit being spent on children. Giving women more child benefit is crucial, but it doesn't tackle one of the main causes of 'feminised poverty' – unequal pay. Better childcare facilities and higher in-work credits might persuade more mothers to raise children and earn a living simultaneously, but if New Deals don't lead to equal pay, there seems little prospect that poor children will escape poverty.

Another thing that the government might want to do is to look and learn from France, where child poverty is less widespread than in the UK (around 24–25%, compared to 40%). *All* children in France have access (at no cost to parents) to high-quality pre-school education at Ecoles Maternelles from the time they're potty trained. Attendance is almost universal from ages 3 to 6, which means that most poor children go to, and gain from, these nursery schools – not just those in action zones or pilot schemes, or those whose parents can afford to pay fees.

Given that the UK Treasury is on record as saying that 'The seed of inequality in adulthood is denial of opportunity in childhood', were it to provide non-fee paying, pre-school education to *all* British children, poor children might grow up with much better prospects, both in terms of jobs and higher education.

Raising benefits

The present and last governments have both played down the importance of raising benefits (and not just child benefits) in tackling poverty. The non-working poor have been told to get a job. Some have even been threatened with benefit withdrawal or suspension if they don't find work, or if they refuse to enter a government-approved training programme.

The present government is prepared to go along with raising (but not by much) some benefits, notably, the kind that alleviate life-cycle poverty, such as child benefits and retirement pensions. Within such provision, all recipients are potential contributors. Most people who receive child benefit and pensions have and/or continue to pay National Insurance and taxes. They don't, so to speak, receive 'money for nothing'. Yet, even in this area of social security, the government has decided not to uprate pensions in line with average earnings, instead keeping them in line with inflation. Because of this decision, more older people will become and remain poor.

In the case of unemployment benefits and income support, the government is taking a tougher line. Not all who receive these benefits are, or have been, in a position to make significant contributions. Moreover, people in work pay, through their taxes, for people who aren't in work. This means that people on income support

who haven't previously made contributions are, say some commentators, receiving 'money for nothing'. There's little public sympathy for this group, a fact that the government knows and uses to its advantage.

Unemployment and income support benefits aren't the solution to inequality, argue policy-makers. Ministers note that today's offerings were designed 50 years ago as a stop-gap for men during infrequent and short spells out of work. The government's prescription is that it's better to get a job.

But what happens if the job offers poverty wages? At best, the low paid might obtain tax credits. Clearly, the threat of benefit withdrawal can force people into exploitative jobs. Political rhetoric about the minimum wage being the nail in the coffin of dead-end employment is, of course, just that – rhetoric. Who wants to work as a security guard for 60 hours a week, on a minimum wage that still makes it hard to eke out a living?

Combating social exclusion

In the 1960s, the Swedish social scientist, Gunnar Myrdal (1969: 138), coined the term **underclass** to describe 'unemployed and, gradually, unemployable and underemployed persons and families at the bottom of a society ...'. Innocently and unwittingly, Myrdal had opened a sociological Pandora's Box. The term became expropriated by New Right commentators in the UK and the USA to denote 'undesirables' at the bottom of the social pile, who both excluded themselves from and threatened mainstream values.

According to some New Right commentators, all of the following groups are said to belong to the underclass: black youth, the unemployed, lone parents, teenage mothers, football hooligans, people on benefits, benefit fraudsters and hunt saboteurs. Quite a collection! But they hardly constitute an under*class* because the term 'class' denotes sameness, not difference. What do a teenage mother and a hunt saboteur have in common? – very little, in terms of objective characteristics. But they have quite a lot in common if you want to stop being a social scientist, and attack them using terms such as 'underclass', because their lifestyles don't fit into the mainstream!

More recently, but not without some debate, the term 'socially excluded' has become the political euphemism for 'underclass'. 'Socially excluded' avoids the notion of class and thus common social identity, but still manages to suggest that certain members of society are 'beyond the pale'. Would you like to be described as 'socially excluded'? It doesn't flatter, does it? Nevertheless, 'socially excluded' looks set to stay, with both politicians and academics using the term. The government has set up a Social Exclusion Unit, and the London School of Economics has created a Centre for Social Exclusion (CASE).

So who are the socially excluded in today's UK? A concise and an accurate reply – but not an all-encompassing one – would be 'the poor'. For, as CASE point out (in their 1997–1998 Annual Report), while income poverty crucially affects the extent to which people can take part in society, social exclusion isn't just about low income. For example, the income poor find it difficult to take part in social and political activities, and have relatively little access to the legal system.

While lots of factors (including, for example, disability, ethnicity and gender) can and do lead to social exclusion, poverty remains the central problem, and economic inequality is still the major factor that keeps the social layers apart in British society.

Redistributive economic policies

Policy-makers are using the tax system to help the poor back into work. This includes, for example, Working Families and Childcare Tax Credits to provide a guaranteed minimum income, lower tax for low-paid workers, and a tax credit scheme for disabled people who move from benefits into full-time work.

Commenting on the 1999 Labour budget, Julian Le Grand (*Financial Times*, 10 March 1999) wrote:

> 'The government has put in place a strategy for improving the lot of the poor without punishing the rich.'

This budget, says Le Grand, clearly benefited families and children through child tax credit (see the accompanying figure). In terms of redistribution, the low paid also gained, with the introduction of a 10p basic income tax rate. Money was redistributed towards older men in the years prior to retirement through the New Deal (a welfare-to-work measure) for the over-50s. Pensioners received extra benefits, such as increased winter payments for heating, and their minimum income guarantee was increased.

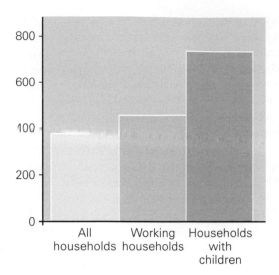

The annual change in disposable income (£ per household), from the 1998 and 1999 budgets

On the other hand, the 1999 budget left the wealthy relatively untouched, with thresholds for capital gains tax and inheritance tax raised and tax rates unchanged. Middle-class families gained from the children's allowances, and because middle-class people tend to outlive working-class people, more middle-class pensioners will be around to receive benefits in later life. However, as homeowners, the middle class lost most from the abolition of mortgage interest tax relief, and through an increased emphasis on means-testing.

Social policy outcomes

Social security, whether through Elizabethan Poor Laws or Beveridge's National Insurance, has long been the major instrument of tackling inequality in Britain. In the mid-1990s, social security expenditure was running at over £80 billion a year, by far the biggest item of public expenditure (Alcock, 1999).

However, the present government, with statistics as hard evidence, argues that social security hasn't and isn't succeeding in the war on poverty and inequality. The politicians seem reluctant to believe that this might be because benefits have been too low, instead focusing on the alleged dependency that state support has encouraged.

The government's promise is to help the poor to help themselves. At the heart of current social policy initiatives is a swathe of welfare-to-work programmes. The debate on the problems of poverty and inequality has become one on how best to put the poor into a position to determine their own future. There's little or no attempt here radically to redistribute economic resources, but there is a shift towards more equality of opportunity, of helping the poor to gain access, through education and training, to (allegedly) well-paid jobs.

It's difficult to gauge the extent to which government initiatives are reducing the gap between the rich and poor. Recent (1999) figures show that the gap is still very wide. That said, Labour government policy-makers are determined to make it smaller, and have set a series of year-on-year targets for tackling inequality by which the public will be able to judge actual progress.

In late 1999, *The Independent on Sunday* commissioned David Piachaud, a professor of social policy at the London School of Economics, to assess inequality trends over the previous two years. His verdict was encouraging. The number of people in poverty, said Piachaud (1999), has been reduced by nearly 2 million since New Labour took office in May 1997. Furthermore, the number of children being brought up in poverty has gone down by about 800 000.

These figures don't give grounds for complacency in the war on poverty and inequality. There's much to be done, and 20 years (the Prime Minister's deadline to end child poverty – itself an unspoken target for the eradication of poverty as a whole) is a long time for anyone to remain poor. As we enter the third millennium, the UK remains a stubbornly unequal society in economic and social terms. The government recognises this and is judging its own performance in tackling the problem against annual poverty audits.

REVIEW POINTS

◎ Few, if any, policy-makers have sought to put Britons on an equal footing (*equality of outcome*). The goal has been to put them on an equal starting line (*equality of opportunity*) in an unequal society. That said, differences of emphasis across the political spectrum are discernible, with Labour ideologically more committed to reducing inequality than the Conservatives.

◎ The Old Left support **egalitarian redistribution**; namely, shifting more of the good life from the top to the bottom of the social hierarchy by taxing the rich until their buttons pip. This position represents a move towards greater, but not full, equality of outcome.

◎ The New Right endorse social policies that promote the pursuit of self-interest. The goal is **trickle-down redistribution**; letting the advantages of one group's good fortune trickle down upon other groups.

◎ In between these two positions, New Labour's Third Way seeks to redistribute opportunities rather than income and wealth. 'Equality' is about opportunities to get on and to have a voice, and also to make this advantage available to others (by working, paying taxes, and so on) in a 'stakeholder society'.

◎ New Labour policy-makers see equity of access to job opportunities and to public services as having equalising effects, by raising the living standards of the relatively disadvantaged. Inequalities aren't removed, but just ironed out to some extent.

◎ 'Welfare to work' is the linking theme across the current government's welfare policies. This is supported by measures such as a minimum wage, tax breaks for the poor, tackling social exclusion, and setting a formal target for the elimination of child poverty.

◎ Unemployment benefits and income support don't figure prominently in the government's war on poverty, with ministers arguing that today's offerings were designed 50 years ago, as a stopgap for men during infrequent and short spells out of work. The government's message is that it's better to get a job.

◎ Preliminary assessment of current government policies on tackling inequality offer some encouragement.

Between 1997 and 1999, the number of people in poverty has been reduced by nearly 2 million, and the number of children being brought in poverty has gone down by about 800 000.

1 Explain what the terms 'egalitarian redistribution' and 'trickle-down redistribution' mean.

2 How does the New Labour government's welfare-to-work policy aim to tackle inequality?

3 Describe two policy measures that might help to tackle chilld poverty.

4 Explain why the policy of providing social security benefits seems to have failed as an anti-poverty strategy.

References

Alcock, P. (1999) *Understanding Poverty*, 2nd edn. Macmillan Press, Basingstoke.

Blakemore, K. (1998) *Social Policy – an Introduction*. Open University Press, Buckingham.

Castles, S. and Kosack, G. (1973) *Immigrant Workers and Class Structure in Western Europe*. Oxford University Press for the Institute of Race Relations, London.

Ghouri, N. and Barnard, N. (1999) Racism 'inherent in school system'. *Times Educational Supplement*, 19 February.

Giddens, A. (1998) *The Third Way*. Polity Press, Cambridge.

Gregg, P., Harkness, S. and Machin, S. (1999) *Poor Kids: Trends in Child Poverty in Britain 1968–96*. Joseph Rowntree Foundation, York.

Hamilton, M. and Hirszowicz, M. (1993) *Class and Inequality*. Harvester Wheatsheaf, Hemel Hempstead.

Hartley-Brewer, J. (1999) New millennium likely to create a tale of two Britains. *The Guardian*, 18 October.

Hills, J. (ed) (1996) *The Changing Distribution of Income and Wealth in the UK*. Cambridge University Press, Cambridge.

Hills, J. (1998) *Thatcherism, New Labour and the Welfare State*. Centre for Analysis of Social Exclusion (CASE), London School of Economics, August.

Howard, M. (1999) Social exclusion zone. *The Guardian*, 28 July.

Institute for Fiscal Studies (1997) *Inequality in the UK*. Oxford University Press, Oxford.

Myrdal, G. (1969) Challenge to affluence the emergence of an 'under-class'. In: *Structured Social Inequality* (ed. Heller, C. S.). Macmillan, New York, pp. 138–143.

Oliver, M. (1998) Disabled people. In: *The Student's Companion to Social Policy* (ed. Alcock, P., Erskine, A. and May, M.). Blackwell, Oxford, pp. 257–262.

Piachaud, D. (1999) Leader column. *The Independent on Sunday*, 19 September.

Social Exclusion Unit (1998) *Rough Sleeping*. July.

Social Trends 26 (1996). HMSO, London.

Social Trends 27 (1997). The Stationery Office, London.

Tilley, C. (1998) *Durable Inequality*. University of California Press, Berkeley.

Walker, A. (1998) Older people. In: *The Student's Companion to Social Policy* (ed. Alcock, P., Erskine, A. and May, M.). Blackwell, Oxford, pp. 249–256.

Internet sources

Acheson, Sir Donald (1998) *Independent Inquiry into Inequalities in Health*:
http://www.official-documents.co.uk/document/doh/ih/ih.htm

Equal Opportunities Commission (1999):
http://www.eoc.org.uk/html/body_press_releases_1999_7.html

HM Treasury (1999) *The Modernisation of Britain's Tax and Benefit System. No. 4. Tackling Poverty and Extending Opportunity*. 29 March: http://www.hm-treasury.gov.uk/pub/html/docs/tackpov.html

Institute for Employment Studies (1999) *The New Deal for Young Unemployed People: a Summary of Progress*: http://www.employment-studies.co.uk/index.html

Joseph Rowntree Foundation (1999a) *Ethnic Groups and*

Low Income Distribution. Ref. 249, February:
http://www.jrf.org.uk/jrf.html

Joseph Rowntree Foundation (1999b) *Child Poverty and its Consequences*. Ref. 389, March:
http://www.jrf.org.uk/jrf.html

Joseph Rowntree Foundation (July 1999c) *Income,*

Wealth and the Lifecycle. Ref. 759, July:
http://www.jrf.org.uk/jrf.html

Scottish Poverty Information Unit (1998) *Disability and Poverty*. Briefing 7, December:
http://spiu.gcal.ac.uk/B7DisPty.html

4 The Funding of Social Policy

By the end of this chapter you should be able to:

- ◎ Describe the links between social policy and welfare provision and the management and performance of the economy.
- ◎ Explain the basic features of Keynesian and monetarist approaches to managing the economy.
- ◎ Describe the emergence of publicly funded social policy through taxation, public borrowing, fees and charges, and a system of National Insurance.
- ◎ Describe the patterns of funding in key areas of social welfare.
- ◎ Understand reasons for the increasing role of the private and voluntary sectors in social policy delivery.
- ◎ Discuss the nature and effects of the public–private finance initiative.
- ◎ Describe the increasing focus on client funded provision and selective delivery.

Social policy initiatives cost a lot of money. Regardless of how good or worthy a government's social policy proposals are, the implementation of any welfare initiative depends on whether it can be funded.

Social welfare provision in the United Kingdom is traditionally thought of as being funded by central government. While the state is now the most significant source of funding for health and social welfare provision, this has not always been the case. It is important to note that social policy is also partly funded through, and delivered by, private- and voluntary-sector resources. In this chapter we will examine the general issue of funding health and welfare services and address a number of key topics within this. We will begin the chapter by considering the role that the economy – and the approach that a government takes to managing the economy – plays in the funding of social policy. We will look in particular at the Keynesian and monetarist approaches.

Following this, we will look at the main sources of state funding for social policy. The key source is **taxation**.

Social policy and the economy

One of the key tasks facing any government is management of the economy. Public expenditure, and how it is funded, is central to this 'macro-economic' policy. The performance of the economy is at the foundation of what the government does, and largely determines what it can do in any area of policy-making. Economic trends and changes, such as trade recessions, have social consequences, such as higher levels of unemployment, which affect the level of spending on social policy. When the economy is functioning well there is more money, but perhaps less demand, for social policy spending – and vice versa when it is functioning poorly.

Nevertheless, each year the government must find ways of funding, or paying for, it's health and social welfare commitments. As an important area of government action, social policy-making and welfare provision is therefore very much influenced by the way in which the economy is managed.

Ways of managing the economy

Different governments manage the economy in different ways, depending on their **economic** and **political ideologies**. Since the end of the Second World War, governments have tended to adopt either a 'Keynesian' or a 'monetarist' type of approach to economic management. While individual governments have tended to develop their own particular variations of either Keynesian or monetarist economic management, these two approaches have very different implications for the public funding of social policy. In the next section, we will briefly explore three key approaches to economic management that have been used during and since the emergence of social policy and welfare activity in the United Kingdom.

Classical economics

During the 18th and 19th centuries, 'market forces' were left to decide on the level of **national income** and the rate of growth (or decline) of the economy. Governments adopted *laissez-faire* ('let well alone') economic policies, and saw cycles of growth and recession occur regularly in the 'free market'. For a while the British economy would grow, or 'boom', and then it would progress much more slowly, or 'slump'. During 'slump' periods social problems – such as increases in levels of poverty, ill-health and unemployment – tended to occur, or were exacerbated, and more vulnerable groups in society suffered the consequences.

Whitehead (1996) identifies 15 cycles of economic 'boom' and 'slump' between 1792 and 1913. Each 'boom' period of economic growth lasted for about three and a half years, and the 'slump' for about four and a half years. At the end of a strong trade cycle during the First World War (1914–1918), a 20-year 'slump' (the Depression) began. This ended the belief that the economy could recover automatically after a slump, without major government intervention, and led to a new 'Keynesian' approach to the management of the economy.

Keynesian economics

In *The General Theory of Employment, Interest and Money* (1936) John Maynard Keynes (1883–1946) outlined ideas that were subsequently developed during the period after the Second World War into the accepted approach to managing the economy. **Keynesian economics**, as it became known, was very important in stimulating and providing an economic context for, and a way of funding, the development of social policy during this period.

Keynes came up with a new 'interventionist' approach to economic management that attempted to control and direct the economy rather than 'letting well alone' through cycles of 'boom' and 'slump'.

Keynes ideas were radical when compared to previous non-interventionist approaches to the economy. Classical liberal economists had believed that the government should leave the economy alone, and allow market forces to decide prices and levels of employment. In contrast, Keynes argued that the government could and should directly intervene to influence the level of demand for goods and services, by promoting and supporting full employment, and by increasing or decreasing taxes.

Keynes believed that if demand for goods and services could be kept high, then the 'boom' and 'slump' economic cycle – and many of the social problems that went with it – could be avoided. He felt that the government held the key to ensuring that there was 'effective demand' for goods and services. He believed that the government should develop economic and social policies that promoted full employment. They could do this through nationalising industries, and by developing social welfare and other public services that would provide employment opportunities. The logic was that if more people were employed and earning an income, demand for goods and consumer spending would be stimulated. High demand for goods and services would itself help to support high levels of employment. Keynes' system involved the government injecting 'purchasing power' into the economy. Expenditure on socially valuable projects could provide employment and restore 'life' and growth into the economy.

The inflationary spiral (see page 88)

One consequence of the Keynesian approach to economic management was high wage and inflation rates. Near-full employment levels led to a shortage of labour. This led to increased wage claims and inevitably to increased prices in the shops. This led to a further demand for higher wages, and hence an **inflationary spiral**.

Keynesianism was unable to resolve the problem of high inflation at times when there was full employment. Nevertheless, forms of Keynesianism were used by governments to manage the economy and develop health and welfare services until the mid-1970s. The approach had the effect of supporting relatively high levels of public expenditure during this period. When economic crisis occurred in the mid-1970s, unemployment rose and the government was forced to increase taxes and cut public expenditure. In the 1970s, the Keynesian approach to economic management was questioned and criticised because of it's ineffectiveness in dealing with the crisis that struck. The alternative way of managing the economy that gained popularity was called 'monetarism'.

Monetarist economics

Monetarist management of the economy involves a rejection of many of the aims and methods of Keynesianism. The main economic priority for monetarists is to keep inflation low. Monetarists do not believe in making policies to support full employment, and are even prepared to use unemployment as a way of keeping inflation down.

Monetarists believe that the government should avoid 'interfering' in the workings of the economy too much. They reject the Keynesian approach of manipulating demand for goods and services, but do see the government as having a key role in controlling the money supply. Monetarists feel that the amount of money circulating in the economy affects the price of goods and services. When there is an increase in the money supply, prices rise and inflation occurs.

The Conservative governments of the 1980s adopted a monetarist approach to managing the economy. In order to control the amount of money circulating in the economy, they tried to reduce public spending and public borrowing. The logic was that if public spending was greater than the government's income, then the money supply increased through borrowing. The solution was to reduce public spending and put a limit on government borrowing.

In the early years of the Thatcher administrations, income tax rates were lowered, some

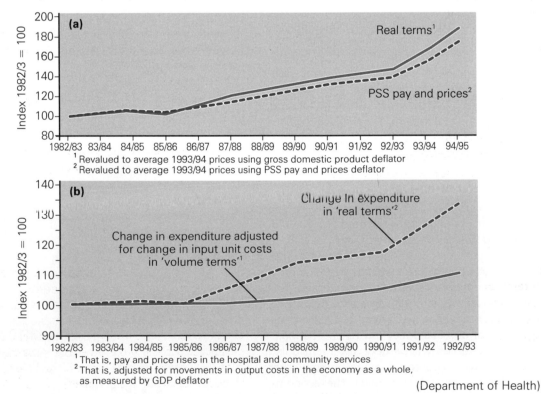

(Department of Health)

(a) Real and volume terms spending on local authority social services, 1982/3 to 1994/5. (b) NHS spending in real and volume terms, 1982/3 to 1992/3

national assets were 'privatised' and indirect taxes on spending (VAT, tax on petrol, alcohol, and so on) were increased. A lot of the money raised was used to reduce public-sector borrowing (the PSBR; see p. 96). Despite their success in reducing public-sector borrowing, the Thatcher governments were unable to reduce overall public spending, which actually increased throughout the 1980s (see the accompanying figure).

The growth in unemployment during the 1980s led to greater demand for social security benefits, and at the same time less revenue was being received from indirect taxes on spending and from income tax on earnings.

In many ways, social and economic policy need to be understood together. As we saw in Chapter 2, when looking at the emergence of social policy following industrialisation, economic developments have significant social consequences. Alcock (1998: 247) makes this point clearly when he says that 'social and economic policy interact; therefore they need to be planned and developed together – and in practice in Britain, and elsewhere, this is just what happens'. Some understanding of the way in which governments try to manage the economy is helpful in gaining an appreciation of these social and economic policy links. In the next section, we will look at the consequences of economic activity – income and expenditure – and try to identify where social policy funding fits in.

REVIEW POINTS

- ◎ Social policy initiatives and welfare provision are closely tied to the performance of the economy.

- ◎ The implementation of policy initiatives largely depends on public funds being available to pay for services.

- ◎ In the second half of the 20th century, governments tended to manage the economy through either a Keynesian or monetarist approach.

- ◎ Keynesian economics is concerned with active management of the 'level of demand' in the economy through full employment. It is associated with the approach adopted by governments from 1948 to the mid-1970s.

- ◎ Monetarist economics is concerned with management of the money supply, and is associated with welfare funding and provision in the 1980s.

REVIEW ACTIVITIES

1 Name three different sources of social policy funding.

2 Explain why the performance of the economy is closely tied to the funding of social welfare in the UK.

3 What were the key points made by John Maynard Keynes that distinguished his 'Keynesian economics' from the ideas of 'classical economics'?

4 What are the key ideas on which 'monetarism', as a system of economic management, is based?

5 What effect did the emergence of monetarism in the 1980s have on government welfare spending?

Government income and expenditure

In order to understand how the government obtains income – or **revenue** – and to understand some of the terms used later in the chapter, a brief explanation is necessary of how the national economy works.

Government income

As an economic entity, the United Kingdom is sometimes likened to a large firm or a company –

'UK Plc'. The monetary value of all goods and services produced domestically, or within the UK ('UK Plc'), is known as the **gross domestic product (GDP)**. Some of this income is sent out of the country to foreign shareholders of UK businesses. At the same time, UK businesses and citizens receive income from being shareholders in businesses that trade outside of the UK. The 'net flow' resulting from taking this foreign 'out flow' from the foreign 'in flow' of income is

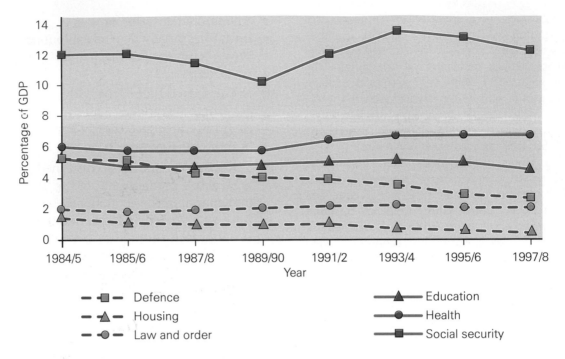

(HM Treasury, 1998)

Public spending on selected functions as a percentage of GDP, 1984–1998

Table 4.1 General government expenditure, by function, £ billion at 1995 prices[1]

	1981	1986	1991	1994	1995
Social security	61	76	83	100	102
Health	26	29	35	40	41
Education	28	29	33	37	38
Defence	25	29	26	25	23
Public order and safety	9	10	15	15	15
General public services	0	10	13	13	14
Housing and community amenities	14	12	10	11	10
Transport and communication	8	6	8	7	9
Recreational and cultural affairs	3	4	4	4	4
Agriculture, forestry and fishing	3	3	3	3	3
Other expenditure	44	39	27	37	43
All general government expenditure	230	247	257	292	302

[1] Adjusted to 1995 prices using the implied GDP market prices deflator

(*Social Trends* 27; source for figures, Office for National Statistics)

added to the GDP to give a figure called the **gross national product (GNP)**. These two measures of **national income** are often referred to in statistics that aim to show how much the government spends on social policy.

The government obtains a large part of its income, or revenue, by taking a slice of the national income by imposing 'levies' – or **taxes** – on the earnings of workers and on the profits of the companies for whom they work. The government then spends part of this money on it's various health and welfare commitments.

Government spending

As well as having social policy commitments, the government must find funds for a wide range of other areas of activity, including defence, industry and foreign policy. Historically, governments in the UK have found that they need to spend more than they are able to receive. The result has been that a **national debt** has developed, and the government has needed to finance the difference between income and expenditure through **public borrowing**. The amount that the government needs to borrow each year, combined with the existing amount of national debt, is known as the public-sector borrowing requirement (PSBR). This is discussed in more detail later in the chapter (see pp. 96–97).

Many of the government's public spending commitments are of a continuing nature, in the sense that a government cannot just stop paying for them overnight, to save money or reduce the national debt. In the area of social policy, all newly elected governments inherit a costly health and social security system, on which many sections of the UK population depend. The government cannot abandon paying for, or radically alter the levels of spending on, these

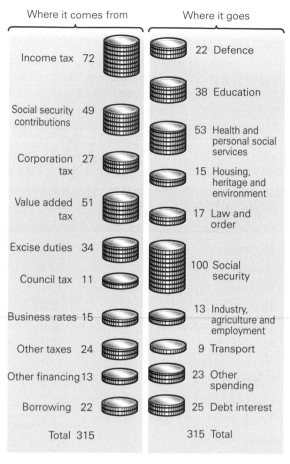

Where it comes from		Where it goes	
Income tax	72	22	Defence
		38	Education
Social security contributions	49	53	Health and personal social services
Corporation tax	27	15	Housing, heritage and environment
Value added tax	51	17	Law and order
Excise duties	34	100	Social security
Council tax	11		
Business rates	15	13	Industry, agriculture and employment
Other taxes	24	9	Transport
Other financing	13	23	Other spending
Borrowing	22	25	Debt interest
Total	315	315	Total

(HM Treasury)

The planned receipts and expenditure (in £ billion) of the British government, 1997/8

services over a short period of time. Therefore, new priorities and approaches to funding social policy tend to be introduced, and to show themselves, over relatively long time scales.

In the next section, we will look at the key sources of government revenue, and social policy funding, in more detail.

Sources of social policy funding

Central government is always faced with the difficult task of finding and collecting enough money to fund health and social welfare services. How do they do this? What are the different options available to them? In the United Kingdom there are four main sources of

government funding for social welfare provision: taxation, National Insurance, public borrowing, and fees and charges. Taxation provides the main source of funding. The different forms of taxation are discussed in more detail below.

Taxation

The Liberal government elected in 1905 was the first to utilise public taxation as a means of supporting social welfare provision. Prior to this, taxation had been seen primarily as a means of paying for wars. Glennerster (1997: 113) defines taxes as 'a compulsory levy on individuals and firms made by law and levied by government'. **Direct taxes**, such as those levied on the earnings of individuals (income tax) and companies (business, or corporation, tax), and **indirect taxes**, such as those on consumer goods (VAT, for example), provide the bulk of the money that government uses to fund social welfare services.

Table 4.2 Sources of tax revenue in the UK, 1948–1994/5

Tax	Percentage of total taxes				
	1948	1964	1982	1990/1	1994/5
Income tax	31.8	32.1	26.5	27.4	25.2
Tobacco	14.3	9.7	3.3	2.8	3.0
Beer, wine, spirits	10.2	5.7	3.1	2.4	2.2
National Insurance	8.0	14.8	20.2	17.2	16.8
Local rates/council tax	7.6	9.3	11.2	5.1	3.6
Purchase tax	7.2	6.5			
Value added tax			12.8	15.2	16.7
Profits tax	6.8	4.2			
Corporation tax			5.0	10.6	7.8
Death duties and inheritance taxes	4.4	3.2	0.5	0.6	0.6
Customs duties	2.7	2.0	1.8	0.8	0.8
Stamp duty	1.4	0.8	0.8	0.8	0.7
Petrol and diesel	1.3	6.6	4.7	4.7	3.0
Vehicle licences	1.2	2.0	1.7	1.7	1.5
Entertainment tax	1.2				
Capital gains			0.6	0.9	0.4
North Sea oil			4.7	0.4	0.2
National business rate					5.1
Other	1.7	0.9	1.9	9.6	8.5

(*The Economist*, 17 December 1983; HM Treasury, 1990, 1995))

Direct taxation

A direct tax is one that is levied on the income that an individual, household or company receives. The most well known direct tax is called **income tax** and is levied on people's earnings above certain 'tax-allowance' limits. There are various income tax rates in the UK, so that people who are wealthier pay more tax as their earnings get larger. Those who are on lower incomes pay a smaller amount of their income in tax. This makes income tax a 'progressive tax', as the amount of income paid in tax grows progressively larger as the level of earnings rises (see box).

> ### Income tax as a 'progressive' form of taxation
>
> John James earns £8000 per year before tax as a waiter. He pays £1600 in income tax in a year. This amounts to 20% of his earnings.
>
> Gemma Johnson earns £80 000 per year as a hotel manager. She pays £16 000 in income tax in a year. This also amounts to 20% of her earnings.
>
> The figures show that the more a person earns, the more money he or she pays in income tax.

For most people, income tax is collected through the Pay-As-You-Earn (PAYE) system. Under this system, employers calculate and deduct tax payments and hand them over to the Inland Revenue, the taxation department of the government (see Table 4.3).

The historical background to income tax

Income tax was first imposed on the people of Britain in 1799. William Pitt the Younger was the Prime Minister and Chancellor of the Exchequer, and he imposed the tax at a rate of 10% in order to fund a war against Napoleon. The cost of the war had already drained Britain's resources and the government had run up a considerable national debt to finance it. Following the defeat of Napoleon at the Battle of Waterloo in 1815, income tax was repealed. It was originally intended to be temporary, but it never quite went away. It was reintroduced and repealed on several occasions during the 18th and 19th centuries.

By the middle of the 19th century, with industrialisation stimulating major social changes (see pp. 30–32), income tax was seen in a more positive light by government. In 1842 the Prime Minister, Sir Robert Peel, was faced with an empty Exchequer and a growing national debt. He imposed a tax on incomes above £150 per year. Again, the tax was supposed to be temporary, but increasing national expenditure ensured that income tax was continually imposed. Income tax is now an accepted, familiar part of life in the UK. It is still a 'temporary' tax, as it expires on 5 April each year and is re-levied through the annual Finance Act.

Other direct taxes levied and collected by central government include corporation tax, capital gains tax, property taxes, National Insurance contributions and taxes on the inheritance of wealth. These are described briefly in Table 4.4.

Indirect taxation

Indirect taxes are also known as expenditure, or spending, taxes. They are taxes levied on the goods and services that people buy and sell. There is an increasingly wide range of indirect taxes in Britain, the most significant of which are as follows:

- *Customs and Excise duties.* These taxes are levied on imported goods, such as tobacco, wine, beer and spirits, and oil (including petrol).
- *Value Added Tax (VAT).* This is the main source of indirect taxation, and is a significant source of government income. It is a sales tax levied on products or goods that are sold by one person to another. Some goods, such as children's clothes, food and books, are exempt from this tax, and some small businesses and all charities do not have to pay it.
- *Vehicle licensing taxes.* All cars and lorries, as well as motorcycles and scooters, must display a current tax disc before they can be driven on a public road. Drivers pay a flat yearly rate regardless of how often they use their vehicle or how much they make use of public roads.

Indirect taxes tend to affect people in low-income groups to a greater extent than those who earn higher salaries. Many of the indirect taxes imposed by governments in the United Kingdom fall on goods that are more heavily purchased by

Table 4.3 The approximate proportion of tax revenue from direct and indirect taxation sources in the UK, 1948–1994/5 (figures rounded in this simplified presentation)

Tax	Proportion of total taxes collected (%)				
	1948	1964	1982	1990/1	1994/5
Direct taxes	60	66	71	69	68
Indirect taxes	40	34	29	31	32

(adapted from Glennerster, 1997:119)

Table 4.4

Other direct taxes levied by central government

Corporation tax
This is a tax on the earnings/income of companies. It has tended to provide a relatively small proportion of government income (see Table 4.2).

Property taxes
With the permission of Parliament, local authorities levy taxes on the value of property in their area. Most individuals over the age of 18 currently have to pay 'council tax' unless, like full-time students, they are exempt. The amount that an individual has to pay will depend on the value of the property in which he or she lives. Businesses also have to pay a property tax, the national business rate, which is linked to the value of their business premises.

Capital gains tax
This tax is imposed on the 'gain', or profit, that people make when they sell an asset that has increased in value between the time at which they bought it and when they sold it. Assets such as owner-occupied houses are exempt. Capital gains tax has not been a major source of income for governments (for figures, see Table 4.2).

Taxes on inherited wealth
Inheritance tax is levied on the capital and wealth that people inherit, usually from family members or close friends. Inheritance tax is a form of 'death duty', although it doesn't yield much income for government in comparison to other sources of taxation (see Table 4.2). One reason for this is that it is possible to 'avoid' (not evade!) the tax by passing wealth on to the next generation a few years before death.

people in lower-income groups. For example, taxes on alcohol and tobacco are especially high, and VAT is imposed on a wide range of everyday goods and services. While people with higher earnings do potentially have more money to spend, those with lower incomes 'spend', or lose, a larger proportion of their available income in

tax. Table 4.5 outlines the impact of indirect taxes on people in different income groups.

National Insurance

National Insurance is oddly named, since it is, in fact, a tax that pays for social security benefits. The National Insurance scheme has its origins in the early years of the 20th century, when the Liberal government of David Lloyd George developed a limited scheme of weekly contributions to a sickness and unemployment benefit scheme. Following the **National Insurance Act 1911** only men earning less than £160 per year could make contributions and receive benefits. The National Insurance scheme was extended by the proposals of the Beveridge Report and by the National Insurance Acts of 1946 and 1948 that followed it. Under the Beveridge proposals, National Insurance was to be:

- **comprehensive**, in that it was applicable to the whole of the working population
- based on **flat-rate contributions**, which meant that all employees, and employers, would pay in the same amount, and that employees would be able to claim a flat-rate benefit payment when they needed it
- a means of ensuring an adequate, **minimum level of income**, the idea being that benefit payments would ensure that people avoided falling into poverty

The initial idea was that the money from contributions would be kept in separate National Insurance Funds.

The nature of National Insurance has gradually changed. Initially, people made flat-rate contributions and received flat-rate benefits. This meant that the level of contribution had to be set low so that the poorest workers could afford to participate. As a consequence, benefit levels were also low, as they were made from these contributions. Gradually, the level of contribution was raised and was linked to earnings. People who earned more had to pay more in National Insurance contributions.

Under the present compulsory National Insurance scheme, workers, their employers and the government all pay into a National Insurance Fund. This money is used to pay welfare benefits to those who experience unemployment or sickness, or who are eligible for a state pension following their retirement. National Insurance is less

Table 4.5 Taxes as a percentage of gross income, by income group in the UK, 1994/5, by decile

Taxes	Percentage of total income				
	Bottom	3rd	5th	8th	Top
Direct					
Income tax	2	4	8	13	19
National Insurance	1	2	3	5	3
Council tax	—[1]	6	4	3	2
Total direct taxes	3	12	15	21	24
Indirect					
VAT	12	8	8	7	5
Tobacco and alcohol	7	4	4	2	1
Car tax, TV, betting	6	4	4	3	2
Intermediate[2]	7	5	4	4	3
Total indirect taxes	32	21	20	16	11
Total taxes	35[3]	33	35	37	35
Average gross equivalised household income, including cash benefits (£ per annum)[1]	5 757	8 296	14 366	24 525	49 391

[1] Housing benefit meets council tax for poor familes
[2] Taxes on employers deemed to be passed on in prices
[3] Excluding council tax from taxes and housing benefit from income
[4] Household income is adjusted to take account of the number of people in the family, counting children as less than one

(Central Statistical Office)

progressive than 'direct' income tax, as higher earners benefit from an upper limit on the amount of their earnings on which National Insurance is payable. National Insurance contributions are not payable on earnings above a certain limit. National Insurance has gradually become relatively more important as a source of government revenue. Nevertheless, it still provides only a small proportion of the overall revenue that the government requires.

REVIEW POINTS

- Public funding of social policy emerged at the beginning of the 20th century and has gradually increased in importance as a source of welfare funding.
- Governments obtain their revenue through a number of different sources. These include taxation, National Insurance, public borrowing, and fees and charges.

- ⊚ Taxation is the key source of government revenue and welfare funding. It is obtained by means of the government taxing a proportion of 'national income'.

- ⊚ There are a number of forms of taxation. These can be classified as being either 'direct' or 'indirect' taxes.

- ⊚ Income tax is the most well known and significant direct tax. It is a 'progressive' tax, in that people pay more as their income grows.

- ⊚ Indirect taxes are also known as 'spending taxes'. They are taxes on the goods and services that people buy and sell.

REVIEW ACTIVITIES

1 In your own words, explain how the government obtains revenue through taxation.

2 To what does the term **gross domestic product** refer?

3 With reference to Tables 4.2 and 4.5, explain the significance of the different forms of taxation as sources of government revenue.

4 Why are indirect taxes also known as 'spending taxes'?

5 Outline the arguments for and against the strategy of increasing 'indirect taxes' as a way of raising more government revenue.

Public borrowing

When the government requires more money than it can collect through taxation it has to borrow funds, usually from members of the public. It does this by issuing, amongst other things, Treasury bills, bonds, National Savings certificates and Premium Bonds. The amount of borrowing required to fund government activity is known as the **public-sector borrowing** requirement (PSBR). The total amount of borrowing that remains unpaid at any one time is known as the **national debt**.

The national debt first developed in 1694, when the Bank of England was established. It made its first loan, of £1.2 million, to the government. The amount of national debt has grown larger ever since (see Table 4.6).

Table 4.6 The national debt

Year	Amount of national debt (£ million)	Increase/decrease in year (£ million)
1984	172 209	15 712
1985	189 712	17 503
1986	197 589	7 877
1987	205 342	7 753
1988	213 527	8 185
1989	200 080	−13 447
1990	189 730	−10 350
1991	193 415	3 685
1992	205 528	12 113
1993	231 435	25 907

(from HMSO *Financial Statistics*, quoted in Whitehead, 1996)

The national debt increases each time the government finds that it cannot raise enough money from taxation to pay for its planned expenditure. There have always been big increases in the national debt when Britain has been at war. However, the growth of social welfare provision by governments during the period since the end of the Second World War has been a major factor in the significant increases that have occurred over the past 30 years. A commitment to the funding of extensive social welfare programmes since 1945 has required governments regularly to spend more than they have received in revenue.

Postwar politicians who based their management of the economy on 'Keynesian' economic ideas tended to assume that governments had to borrow money to cover welfare commitments, and that public spending could actually stimulate the economy in times of recession or economic 'slowdown'. The logic was that, as the economy improved, national income would increase, and therefore tax revenues would grow. These tax revenues could then be used to pay off the additional public borrowing. The average level of borrowing has been higher when Labour governments have been in power. At its peak level in 1975, the PSBR formed 19.7% of public expenditure (see Table 4.7). By the mid-1970s, both public borrowing and public spending were increasing, but the economy wasn't growing.

The subsequent criticism of monetarist-minded politicians was that this borrowing was part of the economic problems that beset the United Kingdom in the mid-1970s. They argued that public-sector borrowing introduced too much money into the economy and caused price and wage inflation. The control of inflation became the goal of the monetarist New Right, who saw a reduction in the PSBR – and in public spending in particular – as a key part of their strategy.

The ratio of PSBR to public expenditure gradually fell from the late 1970s onwards, until a repayment was made in 1987 (see Table 4.7). Despite some optimism that the national debt could be paid off, subsequent governments have had to resort to borrowing to finance public-sector spending. Public-sector borrowing remains an important source of government revenue, and plays a part in funding social policy initiatives. Of the various options available to them, it is the source of finance that policy-makers and politicians currently favour least. The key reason for this is that public-sector borrowing always involves a repayment burden and can distort other aspects of the economy.

Fees and charges

Social welfare services that are provided by statutory (government) organisations are typically thought of as being free to service users. However, there are many examples of service users having to pay for some or all of the cost of the health or social welfare service that they receive. This money provides a relatively small source of income for central government. For example, charges levied for NHS services provide only 3% of its income and 9% of the funding of personal social services (Glennerster, 1997: 135).

Glennerster (1997) says that a **fee** typically comprises the full financial cost of providing a service, plus an element of profit. In contrast, a **charge** can be a nominal contribution to the cost of providing a service (for example, everyone must pay £1) or, in some circumstances, it can involve payment of the full financial cost. The system of fees or charges is not based on any particular principle or set of rules. The result of this is that within the health and welfare system as a whole there is a huge range of fees and charges.

The history of charges

The 'welfare state' was founded in 1948 on the principle that it would be 'free at the point of delivery'. This was a move away from an earlier system of mixed welfare funding, in which there was only limited government funding and rather more private payment. Before the 'welfare state' era began in 1948, the bulk of the (relatively limited) services were funded through charitable contributions to voluntary hospitals, or by individuals personally paying the cost of private fees.

The 'welfare state' ideal of free services did not last very long. Jones (1994: 151) describes how Aneurin Bevan, the first Minister for Health, had to resist pressure from his colleagues to charge for medical prescriptions as early as 1949 – and eventually resigned over the issue. Charges for dentures and spectacles were introduced in 1952, as the cost of providing health care through the NHS grew rapidly. Charges for a variety of health services have been a source of government income ever since.

Table 4.9 gives some indication of the relatively minor significance of charges in funding public health services when compared to other sources of government income.

Table 4.7 Trends in the public-sector borrowing requirement (PSBR) in £ billion (at 1989 prices)

Year	PSBR	PSBR as percentage of public spending	PSBR as percentage of GDP	Party in government
1963	7.2	7.6	3.1	Conservative
1964	8.1	8.2	3.4	
1965	9.3	8.8	3.8	Labour
1966	7.3	6.6	2.8	
1967	13.8	11.1	5.2	
1968	9.1	6.8	3.3	
1969	−3.7	−2.8	−1.3	
1970	−0.3	−0.2	−0.1	Conservative
1971	7.7	5.6	2.6	
1972	10.4	7.4	3.5	
1973	20.1	13.4	6.2	
1974	27.2	16.5	8.4	Labour
1975	33.5	19.7	10.5	
1976	25.9	15.4	7.8	
1977	14.0	8.8	4.2	
1978	18.8	11.3	5.4	
1979	25.5	14.6	7.2	Conservative
1980	20.2	11.3	5.8	
1981	16.3	9.0	4.8	
1982	7.1	3.8	2.0	
1983	16.0	8.4	4.4	
1984	13.4	7.0	3.7	
1985	9.3	4.7	2.4	
1986	2.9	1.5	0.7	
1987	−1.7	−0.9	−0.4	
1988	−12.5	−6.5	−2.9	
1989	−9.2	−4.7	−2.1	
1990	−2.0	−1.0	−0.5	

(Hogwood, 1992)

The number, and the financial costs, of charges for health and social welfare services expanded quite significantly in the 1980s under the Thatcher Conservative governments. During this period there was a concerted effort to reduce public spending on social welfare (for a discussion, see p. 120). Charges for health services, such as for prescriptions, increased and charges were introduced across a range of new areas, such as dentistry, optical services, further and adult education, and leisure provision.

The increasing use of charges during the 1980s and 1990s is part of the continuing process of mixing public and private funding in the provision of health and social welfare services. The postwar consensus era of state-funded universal welfare provision ended with the election of the Conservative Party to government in 1979 (for details, see p. 51). The role of the state as a funding source and provider of welfare services has been gradually changing ever since.

Table 4.8 Social problems and social policy issues

Why impose charges for health and welfare services?

Cost reduction

Charges do reduce the amount of public spending on health and welfare services, even if only by a small amount. By imposing charges, public spending limits can be relaxed.

Psychology

The imposition of nominal charges for services can be a way of reducing the 'stigma' that is sometimes associated with 'state' welfare. By paying even some of the cost, people are more likely to feel that they 'deserve' the service.

To prevent abuse and reduce demand

One argument for imposing charges for welfare services is that they have the effect of discouraging people who don't really need them from using up valuable services. Means Tests are sometimes used to decide how much of a charge a particular person has to pay. Poorer people pay less, while wealthier people pay more.

Avoiding cuts and defending services

Where health and welfare service providers face cuts in their budgets, or other financial problems, they sometimes argue that it is best to charge service users some of the cost in order to keep their services going. In this way, they can 'defend' threatened services.

Alternatives to taxation and public borrowing as the key sources of funding, and to statutory organisations as the main providers of welfare services, have been sought by all major political parties over the past 15 years. Over this period, a new consensus seems to have developed. There is now a broad agreement between political parties that services should be funded through joint public and private initiatives, and that the private and voluntary sectors should play a greater role in delivering health and social welfare services. We will look at each of these developments later in this chapter.

REVIEW POINTS

- Public-sector borrowing and revenue from fees and charges supplement the income that governments receive through tax and National Insurance.
- Public-sector borrowing has grown progressively larger since the 'national debt' first developed in 1694.
- Borrowing is a key source of making up the shortfall in revenue from direct and indirect taxation that is needed to finance social welfare commitments.
- Since the mid-1970s, governments have made concerted efforts to reduce the PSBR and public expenditure generally.

Table 4.9 NHS sources of finance from 1950/1 to 1974/5 (%)

Fiscal year	Taxation	Insurance	Charges
1950/1	87.6	9.4	0.7
1952/3	87.6	8.0	4.0
1954/5	86.9	7.9	5.0
1956/7	88.7	6.4	4.7
1958/9	80.3	14.4	5.0
1960/1	81.9	13.3	4.4
1962/3	77.1	17.2	5.5
1964/5	79.6	15.0	5.1
1966/7	84.8	12.4	2.4
1968/9	84.8	11.8	3.1
1970/1	85.8	10.8	3.2
1972/3	87.0	9.0	3.6
1974/5	91.3	5.7	2.6

(Lowe, 1999: 187)

⦿ Fees and charges provide only a small proportion of government revenue.

⦿ The increased use of charges in the 1980s was part of an attempt to reduce public welfare expenditure, but also signalled the end of universal 'free' welfare provision.

Patterns of social policy funding

So far, we have considered how the government obtains the money (revenue) that it needs to fund its key social policy commitments. In this section, we will look at the areas in which this money has been spent, and at the patterns of spending over the past century.

In Chapter 2, we looked at how state social policy and welfare gradually evolved over the 19th and 20th centuries. The trend in total public expenditure between the 19th century and the present day is an upward one, of gradually rising levels of expenditure. Brian Hogwood (1992: 39) shows that there were points at which overall public expenditure rose and fell throughout the 19th and 20th centuries, that it has tended to increase as a result of war, but that spending levels have been maintained through increases in social expenditure.

The emergence of publicly funded social policy

In effect, the state only began to require large amount of revenue for social policy funding in the 20th century. In 1914, at the start of the First World War, the standard rate of income tax was 6%. This produced £44 million in income, with a further £3 million produced by a 'super tax' on the rich. By the end of the war in 1918, the standard rate of income tax had increased to 30%, thus raising £257 million, with £36 million more in 'super tax'. In addition to income tax and 'super tax', an 'Excess Profits Duty' was levied on firms that had made money from the war effort. The tax collected rose to over £580 million.

The Liberal government used much of their taxation revenue to fund growing state welfare provision, aimed at building a 'land fit for heroes'. They extended health and education provision, introduced pensions and began a major council house-building programme. Despite the increasing taxation revenues, government spending on welfare led to an increase in the national debt which, by 1920, had grown to £7875 million.

Public expenditure on social welfare increased significantly after the Second World War as state welfare services expanded. Since 1945, the bulk of public spending has been on social welfare provision, because the government has largely financed the 'welfare state'. The collective provision and public funding of health and social welfare services became established, and was accepted as the best method, during the postwar consensus era from 1945 to 1979. During this period, voluntary and private-sector funding and provision of welfare services played only a minor role compared to that of government.

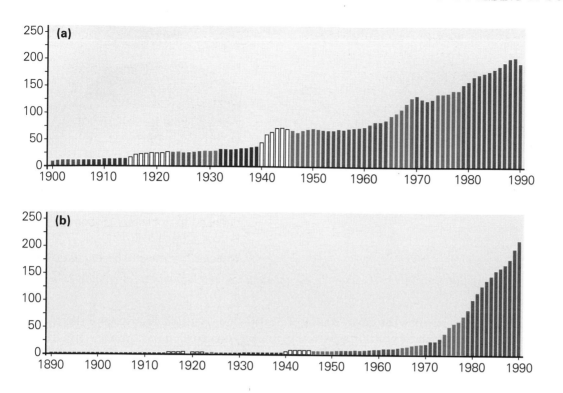

(Hogwood, 1992)

(a) Total taxes, 1900–1990 (£ billion at 1990 prices).(b) Total public expenditure, 1890–1990 (£ billion in cash terms)

Table 4.10 Social expenditure, 1951–1977

	1951/2 £m	1951/2 %	1956/7 £m	1956/7 %	1961/2 £m	1961/2 %	1966/7 £m	1966/7 %	1971/2 £m	1971/2 %	1976/7 £m	1976/7 %
Total public expenditure on social services	2 135	100.0	3 011	100.0	4 396	100.0	7 198	100.0	11 790	100.0	32 145	100.0
Individual service												
Social security	702	32.8	1 068	35.5	1 674	38.1	2 642	36.7	4 578	38.8	11 575	36.0
Personal social services	33	1.5	44	1.5	67	1.5	123	1.7	324	2.7	1 243	3.9
School meals, milk and welfare food	73	3.4	99	3.3	102	2.3	148	2.1	149	1.3	470	1.5
NHS	494	23.1	639	21.2	928	21.1	1 446	20.1	2 362	20.0	6 249	19.4
Education	416	19.5	671	22.3	1 057	24.0	1 827	25.4	3 023	25.6	7 438	23.1
Housing	417	19.5	490	16.3	567	12.9	1 012	14.1	1 354	11.5	5 170	16.1
Current expenditure	1 694	79.3	2 478	82.3	3 714	84.5	5 938	82.5	10 058	85.3	27 652	86.0
Capital expenditure	441	21.7	533	17.7	682	15.5	1 260	17.5	1 732	14.7	4 493	14.0

(Annual Abstract of Statistics)

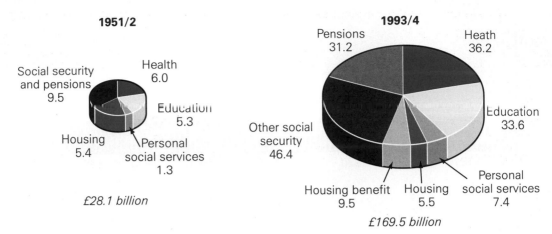

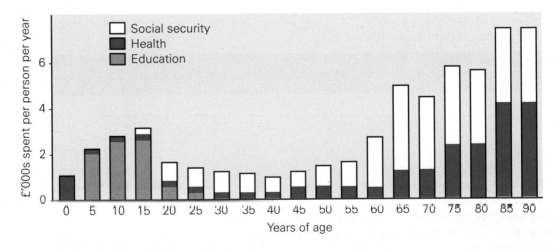

The size of the welfare state in 1951/2 and 1993/4: the sums are in £ billion, expressed in 1993/4 prices on a UK basis

The government remains the main source of social welfare funding, but its position as virtually the sole source of funding has changed. The increasing significance of private- and voluntary-sector funding is discussed later, on pages 107–108. Nevertheless, despite the changes that have occurred, public money still funds most social welfare provision. So, where does the money for 'public spending' on health and welfare go to? We will consider this in the next section.

Patterns of funding

Expenditure (£000s) per person per year on selected welfare services

In the previous section we considered how health and social welfare services have, in their various forms, been provided through a number of different sources of funding. In this section, we will look in a little more detail at some of the historical patterns of funding health, social security and education services.

Paying for health care

In Chapter 2 we saw that, in the late 19th and early 20th centuries, hospital-based health services were provided through a variety of funding methods. Private payments and voluntary donations were important sources of

Table 4.11 The National Health Service: selected current and capital expenditure, 1951–1976

	1951/2 £m	%	1956/7 £m	%	1961/2 £m	%	1966/7 £m	%	1971/2 £m	%	1975/6 £m	%
Current expenditure												
Hospital services	268 }		377 }		538 }		797 }		1462 }		3943 }	
less receipts from patients[1]	−4 }	52.7	−5 }	57.0	−6 }	57.4	−9 }	54.5	−13 }	59.1	−23 }	70.0
General services	165 }		202 }		274 }		387 }		609 }		1134 }	
less receipts from patients	−5 }	31.9	−24 }	27.3	−41 }	25.1	−22 }	25.3	−65 }	22.2	−85 }	18.8
of which (net cost)												
Pharmaceutical	53	10.6	–	–	78	8.4	163	11.3	224	9.1	456	8.1
Dental	36	7.2	–	–	52	5.6	67	4.6	96	3.9	200	3.6
Ophthalmic	10	2.0	–	–	10	1.1	14	1.0	14	0.6	55	1.0
General services	48	9.6	–	–	88	9.5	112	7.8	196	8.0	338	6.0
Local authority health service[1]	39	7.8	55	8.4	81	8.7	132	9.1	151	6.1	–	–
Departmental administration and so on	13	2.6	23	3.5	31	3.3	47	3.3	59	2.4	169	3.0
Total current expenditure	477	95.2	628	96.1	875	94.4	1332	92.2	2203	89.8	5138	91.8
Capital expenditure												
Hospitals	15	3.0	20	3.1	42	4.5	98	6.7	191	7.8	355	6.4
Local authority[1]	3	0.6	2	0.3	8	0.9	14	1.0	54	2.2	91	1.6
Other	6	1.2	3	0.5	2	0.2	2	0.1	5	0.2	12	0.2
Total capital expenditure	24	4.8	25	3.9	52	5.6	113	7.8	250	11.2	458	8.2
Total NHS expenditure	501	100.0	653	100.0	927	100.0	1445	100.0	2453	100.0	5596	100.00

[1] The statistics in these lines were assimilated in a slightly different fashion after 1971/2, and are therefore not strictly comparable

(*Social Trends* and *Annual Abstract of Statistics*)

health service funding in this period. As the demand for services grew, payments were gradually introduced by voluntary hospitals. After the First World War, the government intervened to help the voluntary hospitals out of a severe financial crisis. During the 1920s and 1930s, voluntary hospitals benefited from a new source of income as people began to pay into contributory insurance schemes, such as the Hospital Savings Association.

Running in parallel with the voluntary hospitals was a state-provided hospital sector. Funding for these municipal hospitals was complex and chaotic. This system was rationalised when, in 1945, the Labour government effectively nationalised local authority and voluntary hospitals. The birth of the National Health Service led to the vast majority of hospital care being wholly funded from taxation.

Primary care is that provided by GPs and community-based healthcare staff. This type of care has grown from being privately provided and funded to today's situation, in which the majority of primary care is provided 'free at the point of delivery' and is funded out of general taxation.

Patterns of healthcare funding

One of the founding principles of the NHS was that it should be funded entirely out of taxation. However, successive governments – frightened, perhaps, by the unpopularity of high taxes – have tried to find other ways of getting more service for less money. From the beginning of the NHS in 1948 up to the present time, the amount of money spent on health services has increased dramatically (see Table 4.11). From 1948 until the late 1970s, there was a pattern of continuous

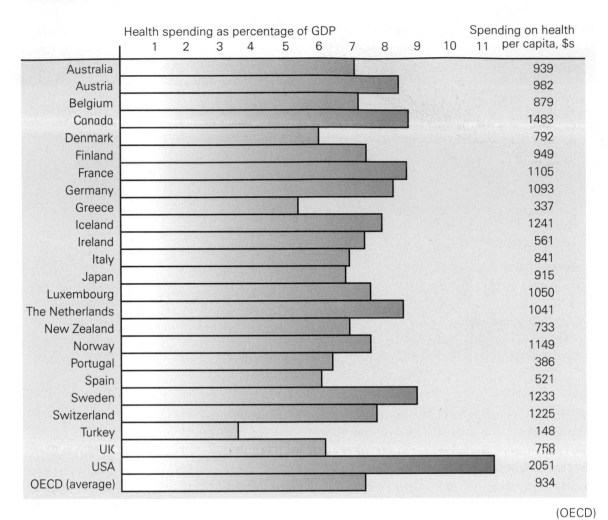

	Health spending as percentage of GDP	Spending on health per capita, $s
Australia		939
Austria		982
Belgium		879
Canada		1483
Denmark		792
Finland		949
France		1105
Germany		1093
Greece		337
Iceland		1241
Ireland		561
Italy		841
Japan		915
Luxembourg		1050
The Netherlands		1041
New Zealand		733
Norway		1149
Portugal		386
Spain		521
Sweden		1233
Switzerland		1225
Turkey		148
UK		758
USA		2051
OECD (average)		934

(OECD)

Cross-national comparisons of health expenditure (OECD countries), 1987

growth in public spending on healthcare services. Whereas in 1948 the total expenditure on the NHS was 4% of GDP, in 1995 it was 6.5% (Glennerster, 1997: 172).

Nevertheless, in comparison with other countries, the UK spends comparatively little on health care (see figure).

Glennerster (1997: 174) argues that the UK's relatively low spending level can be seen, in part, as a tribute to the way in which NHS staff have kept costs down. However, as the population ages, as medical treatments become more expensive, and as people become more aware of the different treatment options available to them, the costs are rising. Since the 1970s, health costs have been a major concern for health policy-makers.

NHS reform is now underpinned by a commitment to increased government spending on healthcare services. The spending plans for

England provide for average increases of 4.7%, in real terms, over the period 1998–2001. Table 4.12 provides an overview of projected health spending up to 2002.

Paying for social security

Social security is the largest single item of government social expenditure. It has grown under all governments in the postwar period (see figure). Rises in levels of unemployment are obviously followed by growth in social security spending. Hogwood (1992: 46) has identified a number of factors that stimulate this pattern of growth:

- an increase in the non-employed numbers of older people

- an increase in non-employed groups, such as single families

Table 4.12 Key figures[1] (£ million)

	1998/9	1999/00	2000/1	2001/2
Total health[2]	37 169	40 228	43 129	45 985
NHS	36 507	39 581	42 415	45 179
of which:				
Current budget	36 279	39 301	42 062	44 768
Capital budget	228	280	352	411
Personal social services	8 477	8 915	9 408	9 906
of which:				
Standard spending assessments	7 815	8 268	8 693	9 100
Funded by department	662	6475	714	806

[1] Figures may not sum due to rounding

[2] This line includes all NHS Spending, plus Department of Health funded spending on PSS

[3] This shows Department of Health funded spending on personal social services, which comprises mainly special, specific and capital grants to local authorities, credit approvals and a grant to the Central Council for Education and Training in Social Work

(Comprehensive Spending Review)

- ◎ decisions by pre-1979 governments to enhance the real value of welfare benefits by linking them to average earnings levels
- ◎ the introduction of a number of new benefits
- ◎ high levels of unemployment

Paying for education

State education has gradually evolved since the Education Act 1870. From this point until the Education Act 1944, public education was provided and funded through a diverse range of state, church, private and voluntary organisations.

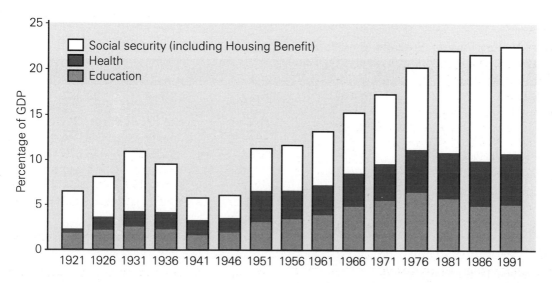

Welfare spending, 1921–1991

(Hills, 1993)

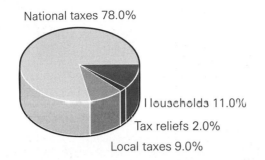

National taxes 78.0%

Households 11.0%

Tax reliefs 2.0%

Local taxes 9.0%

(Hills, 1995)

Sources of funds for education in the UK, 1993/4

Glennerster (1997) provides an interesting and thorough history of education finance. Public expenditure on state education has grown from 3.3% of GDP in 1950 to 6.2% in 1994. Central government currently pays for about 78% of all education in the UK (see figure). This spending is supplemented by a significant private education sector.

Nevertheless, the level of education expenditure in the UK is lower than that of many other countries (see Table 4.13).

Patterns of education spending

State schools are funded through local and central government, and manage about 85% of their budgets. In the main, colleges of further education and universities are generally funded by central government, through so-called Funding Councils. They're also free to raise money from other sources. University students receive grants and subsidised loans to cover their living expenses.

Public spending plans provide for an average increase in expenditure on education in England of at least 5.1% in real terms each year between 1998/9 and 2001/2. Table 4.14 summarises these plans.

The government sees spending on education, training and pre-school provision as cost-effective, because such expenditure is likely to improve productivity. An educated, well trained workforce is a more efficient one.

Table 4.13 Public expenditure on education as a percentage of GDP (at factor cost) in the UK, 1950–1994

Year	% GDP
1950	3.3
1955	3.3
1960	4.1
1965	5.1
1970	5.8
1975	6.7
1980	6.3
1985	5.6
1990	5.5
1994	6.2

(Central Statistical Office)

Table 4.14 Key figures, England (£ million)

	1998/9	1999/00	2000/1	2001/2
Education	10 819	12 142	13 717	14 907
Sure Start	–	84	184	184
Total DfEE and OFSTED[1]	14 166	15 473	17 295	18 612
Current budget	13 424	14 352	15 702	16 670
Capital budget	742	1 121	1 594	1 942
Local authorities (ESSAs)[2]	19 384	20 484	21 737	23 066
Total	33 550	35 957	39 032	41 678

[1] Departmental expenditure limit

[2] Education standard spending assessment

(HM Treasury)

In a society in which it's no longer the norm to leave school at 16 and find a job, the government's investment in education – which could reach £19 billion over the next 3 years – makes the options presented to today's young people very different from those faced by their grandparents.

⊚ Public expenditure on health, education and social welfare services followed a pattern of generally increasing growth during the 20th century, regardless of the political party in government.

REVIEW POINTS

⊚ Public funding of social policy began in the 19th century, but became an increasingly significant part of the government's role during the 20th century.

⊚ The birth of the welfare state after the Second World War was the point at which public spending on education, health and welfare became established as the main way of funding these types of services.

⊚ In the last few decades of the 20th century, private- and voluntary-sector sources of finance grew in importance. However, despite this, public expenditure remains the key source of welfare funding.

REVIEW ACTIVITIES

1 What did the Liberal government do to raise money for public expenditure following the First World War?

2 Explain why public expenditure on health and social welfare increased so significantly following the Second World War.

3 Describe how the UK's spending on health care compares with that of two other countries.

4 Using Table 4.12, explain what the government intends to do in terms of funding healthcare services up to 2002.

5 Describe the sources of finance for education and their relative contribution to overall funding of education in the UK.

The increasing role of the private and voluntary sectors

Health and social welfare services are provided in what has been referred to as a 'mixed economy' of welfare (Wolfenden Committee, 1978). This means that services are funded and provided from government, private- and voluntary-sector sources. In the history of social policy provision, the significance of each of these sectors has, at different times, grown and declined. Chapter 2 described the way in which 19th-century social welfare was mainly delivered through the private and voluntary sectors, with the state providing only minimal, 'last resort' provision (see pp. 35–38). From the start of the 20th century onwards, the role of the state increased, and the voluntary and private sectors became less significant in social policy delivery.

From the beginning of the 'welfare state' era until the mid-1970s, governments provided the vast majority of funding for, and were the key provider of, health and social welfare services. As we have seen (see p. 50), the late 1970s saw a change in both economic conditions and the ideological approach to social welfare. One of the main effects of the end of the postwar consensus has been an attempt to shift responsibility for funding and providing social welfare services away from the state to the voluntary and private sectors.

New sources of funding

During the 1980s, successive Conservative governments looked to the private sector for new sources of social policy funding. Attempts were also made to channel public expenditure through voluntary and private-sector service providers. Private spending on health and social welfare increased significantly during the 1980s. According to Brunsdon (1998), the Conservative governments of the 1980s increased the role of the private sector by:

The public–private finance initiative

'Our aim is to make sure that wherever possible, an injection of private finance improves the quality and value of public services. The PFI is the natural, logical procurement route of choice. As the benefits of the pioneering projects become clear to consumers and contractors, people will wonder how it could ever have been otherwise.'

(Michael Jack, [Conservative] Financial Secretary to the Treasury, 29 November 1995)

The Private Finance Initiative (PFI) was first announced in 1992. The aim of the initiative was to bring public-sector money and management expertise into the provision of public-sector services. The PFI developed out of several earlier projects, in which private capital was used to finance 'infrastructure' projects that would otherwise have required major public-sector capital expenditure (and borrowing) to finance them. Nevertheless, PFI is a significant departure from previous practice of funding social welfare development and services out of public finances.

The concept underlying the PFI, and public–private partnerships generally, is that the government's prime interest in public projects is seen as being in ensuring the provision of a service to users, rather than in developing and building up the capital assets needed to deliver those services. This contrasts with the traditional postwar approach to public projects, in which there was a focus on public ownership of the capital assets and, some would argue, less concern about the quality of the services being provided through them.

The PFI offers the prospect that public projects will provide the services required of them more efficiently and economically. The Conservative government introduced the PFI but, since their defeat in the 1997 general election, the PFI has continued to play an important role in New Labour's approach to social welfare provision.

By 30 April 1998, PFI contracts with a capital value of nearly £9 billion pounds had been signed (see Table 4.17). These had funded a wide range of services, including the new National Insurance Recording System, two new privately operated prisons at Bridgend in Wales and Fazakerley in Liverpool, various hospital and community health service developments, and a number of schools and colleges.

Table 4.17 The value of PFI deals signed by social policy-related central government departments at end of April 1998

Department	£ million
Department of the Environment, Transport and the Regions	5673
Department of Social Security	740
The Home Office	300
Department of Health	629
Department for Education and Employment	253
All central government departments	8990

(Treasury Taskforce Private Finance Projects Team)

REVIEW POINTS

◎ Changes in economic conditions, and the ideological approach of the Conservative government at the beginning of the 1980s, led to attempts to shift responsibility for the funding of health and social welfare services from the state to the voluntary and private sectors.

◎ Private spending on health and social welfare increased during the 1980s as a result of privatisation initiatives, the introduction of prescription charges and fees, and the growth of private pensions and medical insurance.

◎ In the 1990s the Conservative government introduced private funding of health and welfare provision through the Private Finance Initiative (PFI).

◎ The new Labour government elected in 1997 has continued to develop public–private funding partnerships, and also seeks to develop the voluntary sector as a source of welfare funding.

Hills, J. (1993) *The Future of Welfare: a Guide to the Debate*. Joseph Rowntree Foundation, York.

Hills, J. (1995) Funding the welfare state. *Oxford Review of Economics*, **11**(3), 27–43.

HM Treasury (1998) *Public Expenditure Statistical Analyses* [the 'Grey Book']. Cm. 3901. The Stationery Office, London.

Hogwood, B. (1992) *Trends in British Public Policy: Do Governments Make any Difference?* Open University Press, Buckingham.

Jones, K. (1994) *The Making of Social Policy in Britain 1830–1990*, 2nd edn. Athlone Press, London.

Keynes, J. M. (1936) *The General Theory of Employment, Interest and Money*. Macmillan, London.

Laing, W. (1990) *Laing's Review of Private Health Care 1990/1*. Laing and Buisson, London.

Leathard, A. (1990) *Health Care Provision: Past, Present and Future*. Chapman and Hall, London.

Lowe, R. (1999) *The Welfare State in Britain since 1945*, 2nd edn. Macmillan, Basingstoke.

Whitehead, G. (1996) *Economics*, 15th edn. Butterworth–Heinemann, Oxford.

Wolfenden Committee (1978) *The Future of Voluntary Organisations*. Croom Helm, London.

REVIEW ACTIVITIES

1 What is a 'mixed economy of welfare'?
2 Explain the aim of the PFI.
3 Using the figures in Table 4.15, identify the most significant changes that have occurred in welfare funding between 1978/9 and 1993/4.
4 Identify two types of welfare provision that can now be purchased in the private sector.

References

Alcock, P. (1998) *Social Policy in Britain – Themes and Issues*. Macmillan, London.

Brunsdon, E. (1998) Private welfare. In: *The Student's Companion to Social Policy* (ed. Alcock, P., Erskine, A. and May, M.). Blackwell, Oxford, pp. 154–160.

Glennerster, H. (1997) *Paying for Welfare: Towards 2000*, 3rd edn. Harvester Wheatsheaf, Hemel Hempstead.

designed to be accessible to everyone who worked. This meant that the level of contributions had to be set low, so that people on lower incomes could afford to take part. As a result, benefit payment rates were also set at a relatively low level. Beveridge's model was based on universal access and provision, which meant that all people who were eligible, regardless of their level of wealth or income, could claim benefits.

The postwar welfare state

After the end of the war in Europe, the Labour Party was elected in a landslide victory at the polls. The 1945 Labour Manifesto, *Let us Face the Future: a Declaration of Labour Policy for the Consideration of the Nation*, argued that victory in war must be followed by a prosperous peace. Labour's plan for a prosperity and peace were enacted in a series of social reforms from 1945 to 1951 which, taken together, laid the foundation of the postwar welfare state.

Among these key legislative measures designed to tackle poverty and income maintenance issues were the following:

- The National Insurance Act 1946, mainly based on Beveridge's 1942 *Report on Social Insurance and Allied Services*, which created an integrated, universal system of social insurance, whose aim was to cover all major personal risks (for example, sickness) from cradle to grave.

- The National Assistance Act 1948, which established a single, national means-tested allowance for unemployed people whose income fell below a standard set by Parliament, and was intended as a safety net for those not adequately covered by National Insurance.

While it's customary to look at the postwar trail of social reform as the one that *led to* a welfare state, it's important not to forget the one that *led up* to these measures. The UK welfare state didn't just spring out of postwar Labour politics. It had a history – a road to, as well as from, 1945 (see 'Funding issues – past and present' below).

The main structures of the UK welfare system were in place by 1951, and a series of Conservative governments kept the momentum going from 1951 to 1964. In the 1960s and early 1970s, despite differences of emphasis between the two main political parties (Conservative and Labour), both accepted that the state should be the main provider of social welfare, including a growing amount of welfare in the form of social security and other cash benefits. Referring to the period up to 1979 (when Margaret Thatcher became Conservative Prime Minister) as one of cross party consensus on welfare, Ken Blakemore (1998. 55) says that 'as Conservative and Labour governments succeeded one another, they were unlikely to rip up the social policies of the previous government and were predisposed to expand the role of the state as a provider of welfare'.

Signs of change, however, had been apparent even before the Thatcher era. Cutbacks in public spending began in 1976 under a Labour government. Hills (1998: 3) is very clear about this when he says that 'as far as welfare spending is concerned, 1976–77 marked the end of the postwar *growth* in its share of national income. The lid went down on spending when the IMF came to visit, not when Mrs Thatcher was elected.'

But once the lid was shut, the first Conservative government lead by Margaret Thatcher was quick to signal its unease with postwar policies on public expenditure, and the social security bill in particular. The new government's first White Paper on its own public spending plans began with the statement that 'public expenditure is at the heart of Britain's present economic difficulties' (cited by Hills 1998: 1).

Rolling back the state – rhetoric or reality?

The rhetoric of welfare politics in the 1980s revolved around the need to 'roll back the state' (that is, to reduce its impact on public affairs) and cut public spending. However, history tells a somewhat different story. Although, from 1979 to 1997, the Conservatives changed the balance of welfare spending (towards health and social security, at the expense of education and housing), they devoted almost the same share of national income to the main welfare services as previous Labour governments – at or around a quarter of national income. The accompanying figure illustrates this point.

At the same time, notes Hills (1998), there were some ways in which welfare was cut back during the Conservative years (1979–1997). These can be summarised as follows:

- *Breaking the index link*. In the early 1980s, the link was broken between the value of social security benefits, such as the flat-rate basic state pension, and measures of other

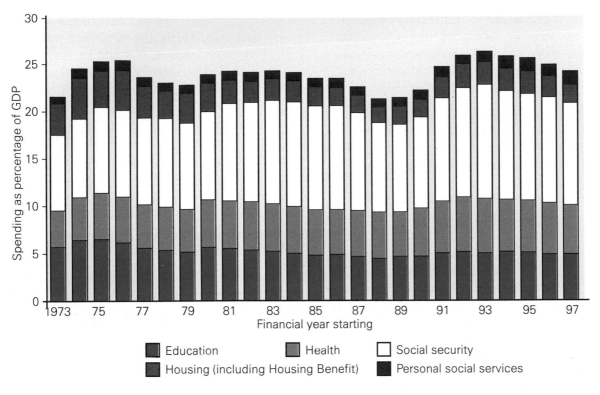

(HM Treasury, 1998)

UK government welfare spending, 1973/4 to 1997/8

incomes or earnings. Cash benefits no longer increased in line with national prosperity and higher wages; instead, they were generally set to increase in line with price inflation. The relative value of these benefits has therefore steadily fallen in relation to the incomes of people at work.

◎ *A series of privatisation measures*. The most notable of these was the 'Right to Buy' scheme, under which, between 1981 and 1995, 1.7 million council homes were sold to their tenants at discounted prices. Private-sector provision was also encouraged and increased in pensions and in residential care for the elderly. Importantly, private provision rose only slightly in health care under the Conservatives. Similarly, the role of private-sector education didn't expand much.

◎ *Increased use of means-testing*. To give one example, the number of families who relied on means-tested benefits for their basic income through Income Support (social assistance) or Family Credit (wage supplements) rose from 8.5% in 1979 to 21% in 1994.

◎ *The development of 'legal welfare'*. As an illustration of this, a Child Support scheme required absent parents (usually fathers) to contribute towards the costs of maintaining their children, thereby offsetting some of the welfare costs that would otherwise have fallen on the state.

Despite these and other attempts to reign back public spending, it might come as a surprise to learn that, in its final year of office, 1996/7, the Conservative government spent almost the same share of national income on the main welfare services as its Labour predecessor had done 20 years before.

REVIEW POINTS

◎ The first significant steps in providing the English poor with access to 'social welfare' were taken with the introduction of the Elizabethan Poor Laws in 1598 and 1601. These statutes envisaged that the 'deserving poor' would be cared for in almshouses. People who could work were expected to find a job. The Royal Commission on the Poor Laws in 1834 recommended that unemployment benefits should only be provided as a last resort, and that all able-bodied individuals would have to work, even if this meant entering a workhouse.

⊚ Many Victorian Britons experienced severe poverty, and pioneering research by Charles Booth, and later by Seebohm Rowntree, at the start of the 20th century identified causes of poverty beyond individual control. It was time for a new approach. In the 1940s, Sir William Beveridge brought together an uncoordinated range of welfare benefits into a single, coherent **welfare state** (although he didn't like this particular term!). Beveridge recommended a National Insurance contribution plan to establish a benefits 'safety net'. A Labour government implemented the plan after the Second World War.

⊚ The main structures of the UK welfare system were in place by 1951, and a raft of successive Conservative governments kept the momentum going from 1951 to 1964. In the 1960s and early 1970s, the two main political parties (Conservative and Labour) both accepted that the state could, and should, be the main provider of social welfare. Cutbacks in public spending began in 1976 under a Labour government. From 1979 to 1997, the Conservatives changed the balance of welfare spending towards health and social security, at the expense of education and housing.

REVIEW ACTIVITIES

1 Explain the term 'deserving poor'.
2 How did Sir William Beveridge try to tackle the 'giant evil' of 'want'?
3 Using the chart on page 121, describe the pattern and trends in spending on social security payments between 1973 and 1997.
4 How did the Conservative governments try to reduce state spending on social security between 1979 and 1997?
5 To what extent did the Conservative governments succeed in 'rolling back the state' between 1979 and 1997?

Paying for welfare

A central consideration in social policy is how to allocate a limited amount of funding and services in order to promote welfare and reduce or eliminate poverty. Tackling poverty through social security is expensive and, say some politicians, sometimes counterproductive. Social security accounts for a third of all government expenditure and, at any given time, about one-third of the population will be receiving one social security benefit or another.

Projected spending on social security during the period 1998–2002 is given in Table 5.1.

Funding issues – past and present

The difficult issue of who should pay for social welfare has attracted considerable debate for a very long period of time. If we go back to the early 19th century, the landed MP, Samuel Whitbread, complained about the mounting burden of the Poor Law rate which, he said, weighed heavily on the shoulders of the landed class. Whitbread proposed to reduce Poor Law expenditure through rate-funded popular education. He didn't seek to abolish the Poor Law but to make it, in his own words, 'almost obsolete' (Poor Laws Bill, 19 February 1807), by teaching the working class to become 'too proud to beg'. Educated workers would, he thought, aspire to improve their economic position through hard work and thrift rather than relying on Poor Law benefits.

Whether or not popular education produced the kind of worker Whitbread envisaged, members of the landed class were no longer prepared to bear the costs of a system that, in their view, encouraged dependency on the state. If education turned lazy workers into industrious employees, all well and good. But if this didn't

Table 5.1 Proposed spending (in £ million) from the *Comprehensive Spending Review*

	1998/9	1999/0	2000/1	2001/2
Benefit expenditure[1]	92 267	97 119	99 529	105 274
DSS administration[2,3]	2 880[4]	3 330	3 410	3 490
Total	95 147	100 449	102 939	108 764

[1] Annually managed expenditure.
[2] Departmental expenditure limit.
[3] Includes £160 million of non-DSS administration grants.
[4] Net of £350 million receipts.

happen, the harsh measures introduced in 1834 by the Royal Commission on the Poor Laws would root out dependent poverty.

The philosophy of the 1834 Poor Law was in step with the capitalist doctrine of *laissez-faire* which, in this case, meant letting the poor fend for themselves in a free labour market. Partly in response to the distress caused by the reformed Poor Law, working people developed their own self-help movement. Trades unions, co-operative savings 'banks' and friendly societies were to play a prominent role here. Alongside working-class self-improvement societies, the Victorian age also witnessed an expansion of charitable and voluntary activities. Indeed, in the second half of the 19th century, the funds available in London charities alone were more than the amount spent on official poor relief.

In 1909, the first brick of the British welfare state was laid when a Liberal government introduced a **non-contributory pension scheme** (one in which you don't have to contribute payments to receive benefit). A five shilling 'Lloyd George Pension' (named after the then Prime Minister) became payable to men and women from age 70. The government estimated that the pension would cost about £6–7 million annually. By 1914, however, the actual costs had almost doubled, to £12.5 million. As an indication of the inadequacy of the old system, the Poor Law had earmarked only £2.5 million for the relief of the elderly poor. Next, Liberal politicians focused on sickness and unemployment, introducing a National Insurance Act in 1911 that produced compulsory health insurance, employees and employers each paying flat-rate contributions.

Approved friendly societies provided minimum cash benefits that could be topped up by extra contributions to the societies themselves. A state contribution also provided entitlements for workers who weren't previously insured through a friendly society. This flexible partnership between state and non-state welfare providers lasted for 37 years, until it was finally replaced in 1948 by the social security system and other strictly state-funded arrangements.

By the 1940s, most of the basic elements of a welfare state were in place. There were contributory benefits for old age, sickness, unemployment and widowhood, as well as a special safety net for the elderly and the jobless. But provision was patchy and poorly coordinated, a state of affairs that Beveridge sought to put right.

A key argument of the Beveridge Report (and here we have a clue as to why Beveridge didn't like the term 'welfare state') was that the British people wanted benefits in return for contributions, rather than free allowances from the state. This contributory principle was enshrined in Attlee's 1946 National Insurance Act when, in conjunction with the National Assistance Act of 1948, Attlee's Act introduced:

- sickness and unemployment benefits
- retirement pensions for women at 60 and for men at 65
- maternity benefits, widows' benefits and a death grant
- a National Assistance Board that replaced the Poor Law

The contributory principle

The **contributory principle** – that the people should pay for welfare – still holds sway. The government relies almost overwhelmingly on national taxes to pay for public services, and it's the people, of course, who are the first-line providers of the money. Households and firms are taxed either directly on income or indirectly through spending taxes (for further explanation, see Chapter 4, pp. 92–93).

Part of what social policy does when it provides public services from public funds, says Howard Glennerster (1998: 208), is 'to shift the time at

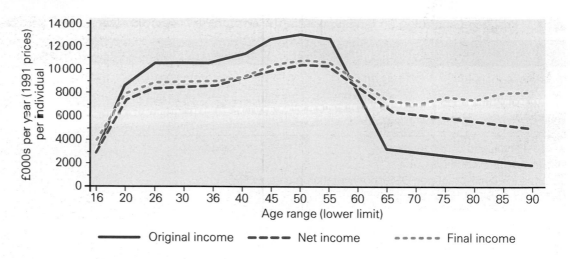

(Hills, 1993)

Incomes by age as affected by 1991 tax and social security systems in the UK

which people pay for the services they need from periods when they cannot pay to times when they can. Social policy is acting like a lifetime savings bank.' Glennerster's point is illustrated in the accompanying figure.

The unbroken line indicates the average incomes that individuals would earn at different ages if the world were 'frozen' in 1991 economic terms. **Net income** is the income that remains after tax is deducted. **Final income** includes income after tax plus the value of state benefits – not just in cash, but also the value in kind of benefits such as health and personal social services.

Earnings during working life not only provide taxes to help pay for the heavy costs of old age, but they also provide a wage or salary rather than benefit income. This is why the Labour government elected in 1997 has set out to invest so heavily in employment, with a 'Welfare to Work New Deal' to help the young unemployed move from benefits into work.

The New Deal

The New Deal is a policy developed by the new Labour government, and is based on a 'contract' between the government and the welfare recipient. It gives the individual rights and responsibilities, as well as removing the option of 'doing nothing' while on full benefit. Young people in receipt of benefits will now have to accept respon-

sibility for improving their own suitability for employment, by taking educational or training courses, or by working on job training schemes in order to continue receiving benefit. There are also New Deals for the long term unemployed, lone parents and disabled people.

New Deals might reduce social security spending, but they are unlikely to replace it. There's still a need for the provision of benefits to certain groups who are unable to meet their own financial demands at particular moments in their lives, or because they have no other ways of obtaining income. For example, there are lone parents who believe that looking after their children is best done by staying at home, severely disabled people who can't function in work environments designed for the able-bodied, and mentally ill people who are unable to hold down a job. For these and a number of other groups in society, social security is seen by welfare rights activists as an indispensable safety net that the government has a public and a moral obligation to provide.

Social security spending is an important part of a poverty reduction policy. Some politicians believe that, on its own, social security isn't enough. The Old Left continue to believe much more could and should be achieved through a 'fairer' tax system – one that shifts the tax burden from regressive to more progressive forms of tax (for an explanation of these terms, see Chapter 4,

Old Labour, seen here at conference in Blackpool in 1968 but a dwindling force in today's government, argue that higher taxes on big earners would provide more money for social security spending

pp. 92–93), thereby boosting the incomes of the low paid. Old Left critics of New Labour policy contend that this would also give the government more revenue for social security spending. And if the United Kingdom were also to return to the system (abandoned in the early 1980s) in which benefits were linked to earnings rather than to prices, vulnerable groups would fare even better.

However, the government – which is keen to shed Old Labour's 'tax and spend' image – is placing more reliance on welfare to work than on social security benefits and redistributive taxation. As we enter the third millennium, the major goal of the late-modern welfare state is to rebuild the system around work and security: work for those who can work, and security for those who can't.

- ◎ The issue of who should pay for social welfare has attracted debate for a long time. In the early 19th century, the landed MP, Samuel Whitbread, proposed to reduce Poor Law expenditure, which weighed on the shoulders of the landed class, through rate-funded popular education. Educated workers would, he thought, aspire to improve their economic position through hard work and thrift rather than relying on Poor Law benefits.

- ◎ In 1909, the first brick of the UK welfare state was laid when a Liberal government introduced a **non-contributory pension scheme**. In the 1940s, Beveridge argued that the British people wanted benefits in return for contributions, rather than free allowances from the state. The **contributory principle** – that the people should pay for welfare – was enshrined in Attlee's 1946 National Insurance Act.

@ The contributory principle still holds sway. The government relies almost overwhelmingly on national taxes to pay for public services, and it's the people who are the first-line providers of the money. Today, the government – which is keen to shed Old Labour's 'tax and spend' image – is placing more reliance on 'welfare to work' New Deals than on social security benefits.

REVIEW ACTIVITIES

1 How did Samuel Whitbread seek to reduce Poor Law expenditure?
2 What's a **non-contributory pension scheme**?
3 What's the **contributory principle**?
4 What advantages arise from using public funds (notably, tax revenue) to provide public welfare?
5 What's meant by a 'welfare to work' policy?

The late-modern welfare state

When New Labour entered government in 1997, it inherited a welfare state not unlike – in terms of the share of public spending on welfare – that inherited by New Right (and Old Labour) governments in the past. Moreover, it fought the 1997 election on a pledge to hold public expenditure levels for its first two years in office to those planned by its Conservative predecessor.

You might therefore ask 'What's so new about New Labour?' To answer this question, and thus to gain a better understanding of the late-modern welfare state, we need to look at the defining characteristics of New Labour social policy. It's helpful, in that context, to examine the government's position (and, as appropriate, that of its critics) on a number of key welfare-related issues:

@ public and private spending
@ universal and targeted welfare
@ work and the work ethic
@ benefit levels
@ social exclusion
@ inequality
@ demographic factors

Public and private spending

In the UK, welfare is based on a complex mix of public and private activities. Thus, for example, a public institution such as a school might buy a contracted-out private service (catering, for example) or an individual might privately pay for a publicly run facility, such as an NHS 'pay-bed'. Tania Burchardt (1997) has identified a number of

different mixtures, including:

@ public provision/private finance/public decision (for example, council home rents)
@ private provision/public finance/public decision (for example, hospital catering)
@ public provision/private finance/private decision (for example, NHS pay-beds)

She has also highlighted two 'pure' models:

@ 'pure public' – public provision, finance and decision (for example, child benefit)
@ 'pure private' – private provision, finance and decision (for example, private-sector education)

The above examples suggest that the boundaries between public and private welfare are sometimes quite fluid, so we must guard against using oversimplified 'public' or 'private' labels. Nevertheless, it's both possible and helpful to distinguish (at least, in broad terms) between **publicly funded** and **privately funded** welfare.

One-quarter of UK national income is spent on welfare. The government relies almost overwhelmingly on national taxes to pay for public services. The role of private-sector welfare did increase under the Conservatives, but more in relation to service provision than in terms of finance.

Public welfare

In the UK, the Treasury is the central government department that is responsible for advising the Cabinet as to how much society can afford to spend on public services. It also plays a significant role in negotiations between government departments about how much money goes to health, education, child benefits and so on. While central (and also local) government are the bankers of public funds, the people, through taxation, are the investors.

In his analysis of public spending from 1973 to 1997, Hills (1998) draws out three key points:

- ◎ overall public spending went gone down in relation to national income, from a high point of almost 50% in 1975/6, but welfare spending remained a steadily rising share of all public spending

- ◎ public spending restrictions didn't begin in 1979, when the Conservatives took office, but in 1976 under a Labour government

- ◎ the overall tax burden wasn't cut under the Conservatives – income taxes were reduced (especially for the highest-income groups), but taxes were increased in other ways (notably, through higher VAT and increased National Insurance Contributions)

As the time of writing, the New Labour government has produced three budgets, whose overall effect has been to redistribute money towards children and the working poor. Public spending has involved 'redistribution by stealth'. The Chancellor of the Exchequer has redistributed incomes and resources to poorer people by means of 'backdoor' tax rises that are not particularly noticeable.

In his first budget (1997), the Chancellor left income tax rates alone, just as promised. However, by levying big tax rises on corporations, he was able to promise a series of welfare policies specifically directed at poorer households. The Chancellor also used most of the cash from a £5 billion reserve fund (money held for crises, and for distribution in later years of the public spending round), thereby releasing early and substantial funds for education and the NHS.

In the second budget (1998) – after allowing a little extra for education and health, as well as for public transport – the *Financial Times* (Editorial comment, 17 March 1998) reported that, after allowing for inflation, the full effect of the Chancellor's measures 'will be broadly neutral this year'.

According to Julian Le Grand (*Financial Times*, 10 March 1999), the Chancellor's third budget (1999) was redistributive in a number of ways, directing more money towards children and families (for example, through Working Families Tax Credit), towards older men in the period prior to retirement (for example, through the New Deal for the over-50s), and towards older women and men during retirement (for example, through increased payments for winter heating). Despite these measures, adds Le Grand, the tax burden of the rich was left relatively unchanged.

New Labour has coined a new principle for funding public services – 'money for modernisation'. This implies a contract. The government says that more money will be provided, but with strings attached. In return for investment, there must be reform. Investment and reform are the twin pillars of the New Labour social policy agenda led by Prime Minister Tony Blair.

The government is therefore creating a number of cross-departmental budgets to fund particular initiatives. For example, the 'Sure Start' programme aims to provide targeted support for young children and their families across a range of services. Local agencies are also encouraged to pool resources. Thus the Probation Service, local councils, the police and health authorities are working together to set up Youth Offending Teams.

Private welfare

A few economists on the Right argue that government should ensure that we all have money and then step aside, allowing us to buy whatever private educational, health and other service providers sell on the open market. This is a rather radical position: in practice, private services coexist with public ones. The Right wants to see more private provision in areas such as education, health, housing and social security. For example, governments can offer financial inducements to encourage people to go private, as happened with the Conservative government's Right to Buy scheme for council home tenants in the 1980s.

According to Edward Brunsdon (1998), private welfare has grown significantly over the past two decades. Banks and high-street chain stores now compete to provide alternatives and additions to state welfare. In like manner, Conservative and Labour governments have fostered a climate in which people are encouraged to consider self-help and self-provision.

Brunsdon (1998: 155) describes private welfare as 'a range of markets trading in welfare products and services'. These, he says, can be considered under two broad headings:

1   Markets that trade in financial services, such as education plans, health insurance, mortgages, pensions, and social care insurance.

2 Markets that trade in welfare services *per se*, for community health, home care, hospital provision, housing, long-term care, and schooling.

It looks as though private welfare is here to stay, and will indeed expand. In other areas of social policy, (for example, prison reform) the private sector has played, and will continue to play, an important role in a private–public mix. A crucial question to consider is whether private services will lead to the erosion of public provision. The present government is on record as saying that the public and private sectors should work together to ensure that, wherever possible, people are insured against foreseeable risks and can make provision for retirement (Green Paper, 1998). Noting that, for most people of working age, paid work is paramount, government claims that for others (especially pensioners), the rapid growth of private–public partnerships for saving has been the key to rising prosperity. In that context, claims New Labour, occupational pensions are arguably the biggest welfare success story of the 20th century, helping to provide many pensioners with a comfortable retirement.

It seems unlikely that private provision will replace all public provision. There may even be more public regulation of private markets – itself a form of state intervention. Whether private provision will eventually offer an alternative that challenges state provision remains to be seen (see Brunsdon, 1998).

Universal and targeted welfare

The 'consensus welfare state' of the postwar period was based on universal provision. By contrast, Thatcherism saw a more targeted role for welfare, a safety net for the poor rather than a pot for everyone. New Labour's Third Way offers a mixture of the two: a general pot for universal welfare in some areas (for example, health), and a safety net for targeted welfare in others (for example, social security).

Benefits 'in kind' (that is, provision of a service, such as hospital treatment) are often universal, whereas cash benefits (for example, Income Support) are frequently targeted. In both cases, the distribution of these benefits is predominantly pro-poor. Nevertheless, the government is committed to a welfare state that provides public services to the whole community, as well as cash benefits to the needy.

An important area of intense debate in the UK concerns the costs of long-term care arising from frailty or disability among older people. Should these costs be met by the state, on a universal or a means-tested basis? Some commentators think that the costs should be borne by the 'patients' themselves or by private insurance. Others note that Britons get free care in the NHS, and argue that this should also apply to council residential homes. In particular, the prospect of older people having to sell their homes to raise money for long-term care is strongly objected to.

Universal welfare

The principle of universal welfare is based on the notion that certain universal welfare needs exist – for example, free medical care – and that society as a whole must meet these needs. Universality, says Ruth Lister, means that everyone should have the same access to the same rights, instead of sectioning off the poor from the rest of society through means-testing (Lister, 1998).

In some welfare areas, traditional taxing and spending are the government's preferred strategy. The 'general pot principle' prevails, for example, in education and health, and goes hand in hand with free, universal provision. The 1997 and 1998 New Labour budgets increased spending above previous plans in both these areas. This was made possible by raising some taxes (for example, on petrol and tobacco), by squeezing other areas of public spending (for example, social security), and – linked to the last point – making use of the 'peace dividend' (namely, dipping into the pot normally used for defence budgets).

Some benefits are universal, non-contributory and non-means-tested. These include Child Benefit and Disability Living Allowance. Everyone who fits the eligibility criteria is entitled to claim and receive these benefits.

While the Old Left traditionally pushed for universal welfare, New Right policies in the 1980s and 1990s moved public spending in areas such as cash benefits and social housing towards means-testing. The principle is a simple one: test people's economic means and, where there are serious shortfalls, target welfare accordingly. It's a principle that New Labour favour in certain areas, but one which they believe should exist alongside universal provision in others.

Targeted welfare

In contrast to universal welfare, which provides welfare for all, targeted welfare is selective, generally limiting assistance to those whose incomes fall below a defined level, as determined by means-testing. The number of people in families who rely on means-tested welfare for their basic income, either through Income Support (social assistance) or Family Credit (means-tested wage supplements), increased from 8.5% in 1979 to 21% in 1994.

Targeting looks set to remain an important instrument of the late-modern welfare state, with some benefits only available for particular 'need groups'. Such benefits are increasingly offered as part of a 'welfare package' of education, job-training and 'supported work' opportunities, aimed at getting benefit recipients back into self-supporting paid work.

The state will continue to involve itself in targeted welfare for as long as politicians recognise that there are times when, through no fault of their own, people suffer great misfortunes – disability, illness, redundancy and so on. In such circumstances, borne of 'brute bad luck' rather than the result of personal choice, individuals have a legitimate claim to public support. This is where mean-testing plays a crucial role – helping those who need help rather than offering universal cash benefits for all.

'Security for all', the slogan of postwar welfare, didn't fit the Conservative government agendas of the 1980s and early 1990s, and it doesn't chime with New Labour's Third Way. In particular, New Labour policy-makers want to cut back on middle-class welfare spending. Benefits, they argue, must be focused on the very worst off people in society (and preferably those who are 'deserving' poor)

Targeting need rather than distributing welfare indiscriminately appeals on both sides of the political spectrum. For New Labour, it promotes social justice by targeting the most needy. For Conservatives, it represents a more economical use of public resources. It's debatable whether or not more means-testing will appeal to the middle class. A policy of denying higher-income earners entitlement could diminish their willingness to pay, through taxes and national insurance, for a system in which they no longer have a stake.

Work and the work ethic

The Conservative governments of the 1980s nostalgically equated a hard work ethic with 'Victorian values'. New Labour uses more contemporary language but, like its predecessors, believes that work is a potent form of welfare. 'Ethics' aside, being in work makes good economic sense. It increases productivity and

yields a salary or a wage rather than a welfare cheque. Besides, a lot of people on benefit would rather be in a job.

In line with its efforts to move people from social security benefits into work, the current Labour government has introduced a series of welfare-to-work reforms, with a particular focus on the low-wage labour market. Extra resources are provided for training, and subsidies are available for employers who hire young people who have been out of work for six months, and older people who have been jobless for more than two years.

Much of the official discourse around these reforms, says Hills (1998: 26), 'borrows from the US "welfare to work" agenda, in the process beginning to change the way the word "welfare" is used in Britain towards meaning cash benefits for the poorest as in the US, rather than the much wider concept generally used in British debates over the welfare state'. Hills (1998) also notes that the government has started to use language, borrowed from Continental Europe, of 'social inclusion' and 'social exclusion'. It's here that New Labour emphasises the link between paid work and social inclusion. The New Deal, claim Labour politicians, will help those detached from the labour market to find a job and enhance their prospects of long-term employment.

But what if people don't want to work? Education and training to get them into work, and work placements with voluntary organisations or an Environmental Task Force, are other alternatives. However – at least in the case of the young unemployed – continued life on benefits is no longer an option.

Yet, according to the best official estimate (as reported by the Social Exclusion Unit in 1999), in England, one in eleven of young people aged from 16 to 18 aren't in education, training or employment. The Unit is very keen to find out why these young people haven't taken up the government's 'offers' and is investigating the matter. It's particularly interested to discover what factors prior to age 16 might predispose some young people not to continue in education, and not to enter training or employment.

So what will happen to those young people who reject the government's schemes and, as a consequence, don't receive benefits? The short answer is that that no one knows. Some might suffer increased poverty, while others might turn to crime, and – in the extreme – to drug dependency or even suicide. It's one thing to link welfare to work in social policy terms, but there's

THOUSANDS OF ELDERLY PEOPLE WILL STOP FEELING THE COLD THIS WINTER

About 21,000* probably. That's how many died last year. Not because of old age or natural causes. But as a direct result of cold-related illnesses.

The mild winter couldn't save them. Even the new government's one off payments couldn't save them.

And the way things stand, there will be nothing to save elderly people from the cold this year either.

750,000 pensioners are now at risk of hypothermia. One cold night, or even a few frozen hours, could kill them.

And yet the Cold Weather Payment of £8.50 is only available after seven consecutive days of freezing temperatures.

Help the Aged believes this is a national disgrace.

In order to save lives, we are planning to give out thousands of heating grants. But we need the support of people like you.

You can help us with a donation today by phoning **0800 75 00 75** or sending the coupon to the address shown below.   *Source: Office for National Statistics*

Lisa Banton, Help the Aged, FREEPOST LON13041, PO Box 203, London EC1B 1DG.

Please send whatever you can afford, just £14 could heat a room for three weeks. Thank you.

I enclose a cheque for £_____ or debit my credit card

Visa ☐   Mastercard ☐   CAF ☐   Expiry Date ___/___

Card number | | | | | | | | | | | | | | | | |

Mr/Mrs/Ms

Address

Postcode

Telephone No.   9892MCXXX02   **Help the Aged**

The controversial Help the Aged advertisement, designed to raise awareness about deaths caused by cold weather

- ethnic minorities, many of whom are disproportionately represented in low-paid work and among the unemployed
- families with children – children increase the cost of essentials, particularly at a time when one of the parents, usually the mother, stops paid work to care for them
- pensioners who depend on state benefits or small occupational benefits

The last group, older people, constituted the largest category among the poor for most of the postwar period. This dubious status changed in the 1980s, when unemployment soared and the then Conservative government reduced unemployment benefits. By the 1990s, the old and the unemployed were just as likely to be poor. In 1992/3, households in which the head or spouse was 60 or older comprised 23% of the poor (defined by the government as earning below 50% of average income after housing costs), and the unemployed represented 22% (Walker, 1998).

Statistics on poverty are disturbing but, on their own, convey little of the ravages of the problem. To raise public awareness about the effects of poverty on older citizens, Help the Aged released a series of advertisements in 1998, showing old people's bodies in a mortuary (see figure). Posters from the charity displayed pairs of tagged feet on mortuary slabs, with the slogan 'Thousands of elderly people will stop feeling the cold this winter'. *The Times* and *The Daily Telegraph* refused to carry the advertisements, but Help the Aged defended the shocking images because, as the charity put it, the facts are shocking. More than 20 000 older people were expected to die from the cold that winter, said Help the Aged. It believes that the government's fuel payments to pensioners are not enough to reduce the number of cold-related illnesses, such as pneumonia, heart failure and hypothermia.

Whatever your views on the Help the Aged campaign, the facts about cold-weather deaths are stark. There were 21 462 deaths among older people between December 1997 and March 1998, and that winter was a mild one. Why did these older people die? In most cases, it was because they were poor, and couldn't afford to pay heating bills. Put simply, pensions for the elderly in the UK don't provide enough for many of them to keep warm.

REVIEW POINTS

- Among the main *proposed* causes (which often allegedly work in tandem) of poverty in the UK today are: individual weakness; a cycle of deprivation; the formation of an underclass; a dependency culture; government policies; low pay; the decline of heavy industries; changing employment patterns; the declining importance of trades unions and of minimum wage protection; the price-linking of benefits; and having a child.

- The casualties of poverty include: pensioners who depend on state benefits or small occupational benefits; lone parents and their children; certain ethnic minority groups (notably the Bangladeshi and Pakistani populations); unemployed and low-paid people; 16- and 17-year-olds who have no job, no youth training place and no benefits; and disabled people, and families with a disabled child.

REVIEW ACTIVITIES

1 What arguments and evidence suggest that individual weakness isn't the main cause of poverty?
2 Identify six groups who are at risk of being poor in the UK
3 How have changes in the nature of employment contributed to levels of poverty in the UK over the past 20 years?
4 Explain why the failure to link welfare benefit levels and average income levels may 'trap' some people in poverty.
5 How can visual images bring home the lived experience of poverty in a way that statistics can't?.

...s of health and illness

...social distribution of health and ...ess

...esearch data suggests that there are significant and enduring social inequalities in health and illness experience in the United Kingdom. Far from being an individual matter, the statistics show quite definitively that health and illness are linked to a range of social factors, including social class, ethnicity, region and gender. In this section, we will describe and explore the data on the unequal social distribution of health and illness in the UK.

Inequalities in health

People generally assume that health is a product of a combination of a person's genes and of their lifestyles, and to some extent this is true. Usually, they then assume that, having taken this into account, standards of health and expectation of life are randomly distributed across the population. That is, if genes and lifestyle are taken out of the equation, everyone in society has the same chance to experience 'good health'. However, this is not true – length of life and standards of health are closely linked to social characteristics, such as social class, ethnic origin, gender and geographical location. When we look at inequalities of health, in the next section of this chapter, we will see clearly that patterns emerge to support the claim that health is 'socially determined'.

Mortality

Mortality refers to death. Mortality statistics are compiled from information provided by doctors, who complete a 'death certificate' when a person dies. Taken together, all of this information describes the social distribution of death in society. The statistics that are developed from analysing death certificates are sometimes referred to as 'death rates'. They indicate that there are social patterns to mortality.

Over the past 20 years, death rates have fallen across all social groups and for both sexes. However, although all death rates have fallen, the chances of people from the higher social classes (see the accompanying figure) dying early are falling faster than those of people from lower social classes. In other words, the difference in the expectation of life is widening between the more affluent and the poorer groups in society.

Typical occupations of each social class – the Registrar General's scale	
Occupations are listed in alphabetical order, and are mainly basic titles: foremen and managers in the occupations listed are allotted to different classes.	
I Professional and so on	Accountant, architect, chemist, company secretary, doctor, engineer, judge, lawyer, optician, scientist, solicitor, surveyor, university teacher, veterinarian
II Intermediate	Aircraft pilot or engineer, chiropodist, farmer, laboratory assistant/technician, manager, proprietor, publican, member of parliament, nurse, police or fire brigade officer, schoolteacher
IIIn Skilled non-manual	Auctioneer, cashier, clerical worker, commercial traveller, draughtsman, estate agent, sales representative, secretary, shop assistant, typist, telephone supervisor
IIIm Skilled manual	Baker, bus drive, butcher, bricklayer, carpenter, cook, electrician, hairdresser, miner (underground), policeman or fireman, railway engine driver/guard, upholsterer
IV Partly skilled/semi-skilled	Agricultural worker, barman, bus conductor, fisherman, hospital orderly, machine sewer, packer, postman, roundsman, street vendor, telephone operator
V Unskilled	Chimney/road sweeper, kitchen hand, labourer, lift/car park attendant, driver's mate, messenger, railway stationman, refuse collector, window/office cleaner

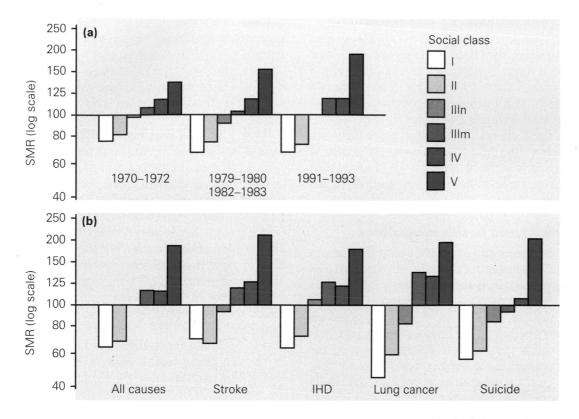

(*Social Sciences*, June 1997)

Standardised mortality rates (a) by social class (based on occupation), males, England and Wales, 1970–1993; and (b) from selected causes (based on occupation), mean aged 20–64, England and Wales, 1991–1993

In the early 1970s, the mortality rate among males of working age was twice as high for those in the lowest social class as for those in the highest. By the late 1990s, the figure was *three* times higher! As we said before, this is caused by a faster decrease in mortality rates for more affluent groups in the population. Mortality rates fell by 40% between 1970 and the late 1990s for social classes I and II, by 30% for classes III and IV, but by only 10% for class V (the lowest social class).

Another way of looking at this is to consider life expectancy; that is, the number of years that a person can expect to live, on average, at their birth. For men belonging to social classes I and II, life expectancy at birth increased by two years during the 1980s; yet for classes IV and V, the increase was only 1.4 years. Men could expect to live to 75 in the higher social classes, but only to 70 in the lower classes. Women could expect to live to 80 in the higher social classes, but to 77 in the lower classes.

If all males in England and Wales had the same death rates as those in the higher social classes, there would be 17 200 fewer ('premature') deaths each year. Death rates are particularly higher for heart disease, suicide and accidents in adulthood, but infant mortality rates are also noticeably different. At present, 5 out of every 1000 infants from parents in the two higher social classes die, but 7 out of every 1000 infants from parents in the two lower social classes die at birth.

Morbidity

Morbidity refers to levels of illness and disability in the population. Unlike death rates, there does not appear to be a decline in morbidity rates. However, we should bear in mind our earlier discussion about the subjective nature of health and illness. At present, for those aged 45–64, 17% of professional men reported a 'limited long-standing illness' (sometimes referred to as 'chronic illness'), compared to 48% of unskilled males. For women of the same age, 25% of professional and 45% of unskilled women workers disclosed such a condition.

A commonly used measure of poor health is obesity (linked, for example, to heart problems, one of the major killers in Britain): 25% of women in class V were obese compared to 14% in class I, while the relevant figures for men are 18% compared to 11%.

It's not just physical health that is linked to social class – so too is mental health. For women in particular, the chance of experiencing mental illness is much higher if they belong to one of the lower social classes. About 25% of all women in classes IV and V suffered from mental disorder of some kind, compared to about 15% of women from social classes I and II. (Before we move on, apart from the differences in social class, what is also striking is the high proportion of *all* women suffering from some form of mental health problem.)

Ethnicity and health inequalities

Despite the extent of research on differences in health amongst ethnic groups, our knowledge is much less accurate and clear than it is for gender and social class. The main reason is that the statistics are based on information obtained on 'country of birth'. In the statistics that we give here, only those people actually born in the Caribbean or on the Indian subcontinent actually are accurately recorded as belonging to an ethnic minority. This means that the health and illness experiences of people of African Caribbean origin who were born in Britain are not included in the 'ethnic minority' statistics.

Bearing this statistical drawback in mind, we should note that people from African, Caribbean and Indian backgrounds can be classified as having a higher than average chance of having a limited long-standing illness, and those from Bangladeshi and Pakistani backgrounds have the highest levels of long-term illness. In contrast, those of Chinese origin have the lowest levels of

long-standing illness in Britain. When we look at infant mortality rates, it appears that those children born to mothers from Caribbean and Pakistani places of birth have twice the average levels of infant mortality. These differences do not appear to have decreased over the past 20 years.

When looking at mortality statistics however, there is not as clear a pattern as for morbidity. Table 6.1 illustrates differences in causes of death for people born in different countries, but resident at the time of death in the UK. Clearly, certain causes of death are closely linked to certain 'ethnic groups'. People from Scotland are the most likely to die from lung cancer, but they are far less likely to die from strokes than people from a West African background. People born in the Caribbean are much less likely to die from coronary heart disease than those from East Africa, but they are significantly more likely than them to have strokes. So, unlike the statistics we have looked at for gender or for social class, a much more complex pattern appears to exist here.

Gender differences in health experience

Death rates for both sexes have been declining since the mid-19th century. More recently, since 1971, death rates have decreased by 29% for males and by 25% for females, although women continue to have a longer expectation of life than men. Causes of death vary too, with males more likely to die from cancer and heart disease. The pattern of mortality varies too. The age-specific mortality rates for males are higher throughout

Table 6.1 Standardised mortality ratios, by country of birth, selected causes, men and women aged 20–69, England and Wales, 1989–92

	All causes		Coronary heart disease		Stroke		Lung cancer		Breast cancer
	Men	Women	Men	Women	Men	Women	Men	Women	Women
All countries	100	100	100	100	100	100	100	100	100
Scotland	132	136	120	130	125	125	149	169	114
Ireland	139	120	124	120	138	123	151	147	92
East Africa	110	103	131	105	114	122	42	17	84
West Africa	113	126	56	62	271	181	62	51	125
Caribbean	77	91	46	71	168	157	49	31	75
South Asia	106	100	146	151	155	141	45	33	59

(Wild and McKeigue, 1997)

Table 6.2 Age-standardised mortality rates per 100 000 people, by social class, selected causes, men and women aged 35–64, England and Wales, 1976–92

	Women (35–64)			Men (35–64)		
	1976–81	1981–85	1986–92	1976–81	1981–85	1986–92
All causes						
I/II	338	344	270	621	539	455
IIIn	371	387	305	860	658	484
IIIm	467	396	356	802	691	624
IV/V	508	445	418	951	824	764
Ratio IV/V : I/II	1.50	1.29	1.55	1.53	1.53	1.68
Coronary heart disease						
I/II	39	34	29	246	185	160
IIIn	56	57	39	382	267	162
IIIm	85	67	59	309	269	231
IV/V	105	76	78	363	293	266
Ratio IV/V : I/II	2.69	1.69	2.69	1.48	1.58	1.66
Breast cancer						
I/II	52	74	52			
IIIn	75	71	49			
IIIm	61	57	46			
IV/V	47	50	54			
Ratio IV/V : I/II	0.90	0.68	1.04			

(Harding *et al.*, 1997)

life, but peak at certain ages – in particular between 15 and 22, with the higher rates of death as a result of motor vehicle accidents. In childhood, boys are far more likely than are girls to die from accidents.

However, the differences are not so clear when it comes to morbidity. Overall, once age is taken into account, there is little difference in the proportions of males and females reporting limiting long-standing illnesses (women live longer and are therefore more likely to report ill health in their final years). During the child-bearing years of women's lives, they report significantly higher levels of illness. More than two-thirds of people with disabilities in Britain are women – although this is likely to be partly due to the fact that women live longer than men and are therefore more likely to have disabilities.

Region and health

One final point to note about variations in health in the UK is that there are noticeable differences in morbidity and mortality levels between the regions. For example, Scotland and the North-East of England have higher morbidity and mortality rates than the South-East of England. Furthermore, research by Peter Townsend (1979) has demonstrated quite significant differences in morbidity between London boroughs. Ill health is more likely to be experienced by people who are poor (see Chapter 5, pp. 112–143). The poorer London boroughs therefore have higher morbidity rates.

Explanations for inequalities in health

The statistics described above indicate that there are clear relationships between health and illness experience and social factors such as social class and gender. But why should this be? There are a number of possible ways of explaining the social inequalities in health and illness experience that exist. These competing explanations have rather different implications for health policy and, indeed, for social policy in general.

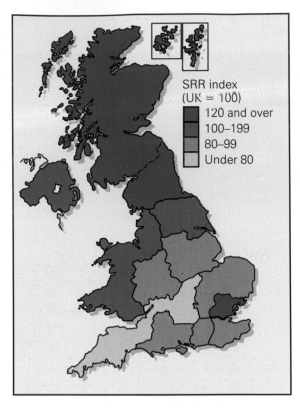

Lung cancer, by region, 1989

What we have uncovered so far is that ill health and early death are not randomly distributed across the population. There are patterns of health and illness that are linked to social class, gender, ethnicity and region. There have been a number of attempts to explain these inequalities. Two of the more significant explanations have been put forward by the Black Report (Townsend *et al.*, 1988) and the Acheson Inquiry (Acheson, 1998) into inequalities in health.

The Black Report

This report focused essentially on social class differences in health. Sir Douglas Black put forward four possible explanations for the relationship between health and social status:

- artefact
- social selection
- cultural
- material

The **artefact** approach challenges the statistics that link ill health to social class. The argument that there is a growing gap between the higher and lower social classes is seen to be a statistical quirk that is based upon a misreading of the statistics. The changing nature of employment in Britain over the past 30 years means that there are extremely few manual workers remaining – in other words, social class IV has shrunk to a very small proportion of the population. On the other hand, there have been very great increases in the middle and higher social classes. Although it is true that the gap in health may have increased between the lowest social class and the rest of society, the numbers remaining in social class V mean that actually there is only a very small number of people whose health is not improving at the rate of the majority of society.

The **social selection** explanation is simply that those people who are fitter and of better health have a better chance of achieving higher-status jobs. Conversely, those in poor health are more likely to be unemployed or in lower-paid occupations. The evidence that exists partly supports this explanation, in that those with long-term illnesses and disabilities are likely to have poorly paid occupations, or to be reliant on benefits. Poor health over a long period is partly related to downward social mobility. However, we also know that those in higher social classes have higher standards of health and less chance of mortality throughout their lives. Good health, however, is not a cause of *upward* social mobility.

Cultural explanations have until recently largely been the favoured explanations of governments. They stress that peoples' lifestyle choices are the key to health and illness. The choices made by individuals – which are the result of employment patterns, regional and class values, patterns of food purchase and consumption and level of exercise – are all linked to health. Government health campaigns have therefore suggested that lifestyle changes can lead to higher standards of health and lengthened life expectations.

A more radical and critical version of this is that advertising places immense pressure on people to undertake potentially unhealthy patterns of eating, such as relying on convenience foods, and to suffer a lack of exercise (through car use).

Materialist explanations are based upon the argument that it is not personal choice that determines lifestyle, but *necessity* – based upon differences in income and/or power. For example, a study by Marmot *et al.* (1991) found that the lower the grade of employees in the civil service, the greater the level of illness and higher the level of mortality. Indeed, civil servants in the lowest grades were three times more likely to die before pensionable age than those in the top grades. Marmot *et al.* (1991) argued that the most likely reason for this was the higher levels of stress found amongst the lower grades.

Poverty in the UK

Peter Townsend (1979) studied areas in the North-East of England and in London. He found that there was a close relationship between material deprivation – as indicated by high levels of unemployment, low car ownership levels and household overcrowding – and poor health, high levels of disability and low birthweight. Townsend argued that the living conditions and high levels of deprivation are not a lifestyle choice, but a state of life imposed on these people by the existence of extreme social inequality in the UK. Ill health and early death are the outcomes, therefore, of poverty and inequality, and there is little that can be done to change behaviour while these conditions exist.

The Acheson Report

The Acheson Report (1998) was very sympathetic to the two final explanations suggested by Sir Douglas Black; that is, the cultural explanation and the materialist one. The model chosen by Sir Donald Acheson was that a complex inter-weaving between individual biological factors, individual personalities, lifestyle choice and the necessities imposed by income and employment provided a fuller explanation for health levels than simply concentrating on the wider social or individual personality factors.

The model suggests that health inequalities are, in the words of the introduction to the report, 'the outcome of causal chains which run back into and from the basic structure of society'

(Acheson, 1998). The key point that the report makes is that individual health is the result of a complex set of wider cultural and economic factors that interact with a series of personal choices based on biological and psychological influences.

Intervention to change one part of this complex interaction process would in itself have little effect. What is needed is to try to alter the entire range of influences. Acheson's (1998) explanation is also useful for understanding gender differences, ethnic differences and even geographical ones.

'A policy which reduces inequalities in income and improves the income of the less well off, and one which provides pre-school education for all four year olds are examples of "upstream" policies which are likely to have range of consequences, including benefits to health. Policies such as providing nicotine replacement therapy on prescription, or making available better facilities for taking physical exercise, are "downstream" interventions which have a narrower range of benefits. We have therefore recommended both upstream and downstream policies – those which deal with wider influences on health inequalities such as income distribution, education, public safety, housing, work environment, employment, social networks, transport and pollution, as well as those which have narrower impacts, such as on healthy behaviours.'

(Acheson, 1998: 7–8)

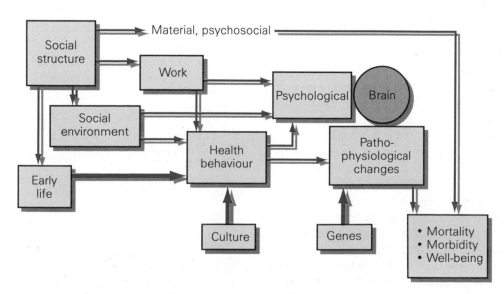

Social and economic influences – as well as biological ones – affect health

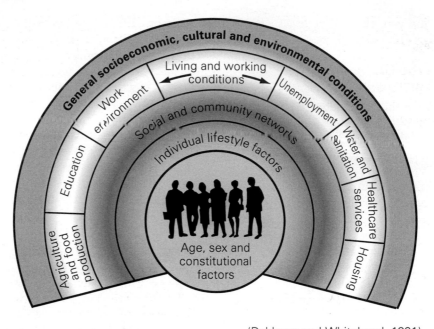

(Dahlgren and Whitehead, 1991)

Policies and factors

Policy approaches to reducing health inequalities

Historically, successive governments have been involved in a variety of different schemes to improve the health of the entire population – although whether the motives were altruistic or stemmed from a fear that the poor health of the working class might harm the rich is a matter of debate. Thus 19th-century urban regeneration, the provision of clean water and effective sewage systems all contributed to increasing standards of health in the British population (for further explanation, see pp. 38–41). However, the 20th century saw a move to defining health and illness in terms of the individual's biological status, and an acceptance of the view that the way to solve health problems was through the work of medical professionals working in hospitals, to cure people who were already ill. Medically dominated health services were the main focus of government health policy for most of the 20th century.

The NHS was an attempt to provide comprehensive, high-quality health care for all, regardless of social position or ability to pay. The mortality and morbidity statistics that have been collected over the life of the NHS suggest that it has had little impact in terms of changing the unequal social pattern of health experience. Does this support the view that 'health' experience and the likelihood of premature death are not biologically determined, but are more dependent on social factors? The present answer is both 'Yes' *and* 'No'!

Health and illness experience are currently thought to be the result of an interaction between an individual's biological make-up, the lifestyle choices that they make and external social factors. Mortality and morbidity are influenced by a number of factors:

- *genetic inheritance* – this affects longevity and the likelihood of acquiring certain diseases and conditions
- *lifestyle* – including diet, alcohol and smoking habits
- *environmental and housing conditions* – pollution, poor housing and traffic accidents
- *poverty and deprivation* – this often causes poor diet, poor housing and stress through low income and a low quality of life

Linking health to the third and fourth of these four elements is controversial, in that it implies that tackling health inequalities involves tackling wider social inequalities.

In 1992 a government White Paper, entitled *The Health of the Nation* (Department of Health, 1992), recognised some of these factors and began to set targets to achieve higher standards of 'health' in five key areas:

- cancer
- heart disease and stroke
- mental illness

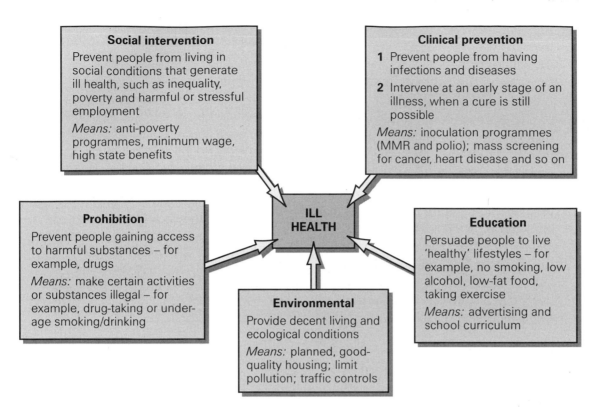

Types of policy intervention to prevent ill health

⊚ HIV/AIDS and sexual health

⊚ accidents

A series of *targets* were set out for each of the categories, and government departments were encouraged to coordinate their activities. A central theme of the approach was to have collaboration between the NHS, local authorities, voluntary agencies and the Health Education Authority. The general approach taken was that of education, influenced by the belief that poor health was caused by individuals making incorrect lifestyle choices. The White Paper chose to focus on standards of health and to set targets for reducing these, rather than on the attacking the social causes of ill health. This took the spotlight off inequality and poverty, and focused instead on combating illness.

Critics of the strategy pointed out that where there were clear examples of lifestyles impacting on health – such as excess alcohol consumption, obesity and a high level of smoking – the government was simply not prepared to take on the powerful industries that were linked to activities. The food lobby, the tobacco companies and the alcohol industry were all able to block any significant attempts by the government to introduce radical policies.

The policy approach of the new Labour government to health services and the reduction of health inequalities is outlined and discussed later in the chapter, on pp. 173–176.

⊚⊚⊚⊚⊚ REVIEW POINTS ⊚⊚⊚⊚⊚

⊚ The likelihood that a person will experience either health or illness is not simply the result of biology or 'chance'. Factors such as social class, ethnicity and gender play an important role in determining health and illness experience.

⊚ Mortality, or death, rate statistics show a clear social class pattern. The higher a person's social class group is, the less likely they are to die prematurely.

⊚ Morbidity, or illness, patterns also follow social class, ethnicity and gender patterns. It appears that these social features of a person's background affect their health and illness experience.

- ◎ Inequalities in health have been widely investigated and described in influential reports such as the Black Report and the Acheson Inquiry.

- ◎ Investigators have identified a number of possible explanations for the relationship between health and social factors. These are called the **artefact**, **social selection**, **cultural** and **materialist** explanations.

- ◎ Policies that attempt to reduce health inequalities, such as the *Health of the Nation* strategy, tend to be based on the idea that cultural and material factors interact with biological and psychological factors to influence health and illness experience.

REVIEW ACTIVITIES

1 What role does social class seem to play in health and illness experience?

2 How does a person's ethnic origin seem to affect his or her health experience?

3 Explain how the 'cultural' approach, referred to in the Black Report, can be used to explain inequalities in health and illness experience.

4 Which explanation of health inequalities suggests that factors such as poverty and stress play a key role in determining health and illness experience?

5 Identify the main policy aim and approach of the *Health of the Nation* strategy.

Medicine and the medical profession

The 'medical model' is the dominant approach to health in contemporary Western societies. The term is used to describe the approach to 'health' and the forms of knowledge that doctors typically use. Because the 'medical model' is so powerful and dominant in Western healthcare systems, it can be difficult to believe that it is a relatively recent way of thinking about and practising 'health' care, and that a range of credible alternatives also exist. In this section, we will explore the nature of the medical model and medical knowledge, considering how it has come to be so dominant. We will then look at how the complementary and public health models challenge the medical model of 'health', and examine their implications for health policy and the provision of health care.

The emergence of the medical profession

Ideas about 'health' and 'health care' practices have a very long history. The ways in which people have thought about 'health', and have used these ideas to try to influence life-cycle and disease processes, is sometimes presented as a linear process of 'improvement' and 'progress' from simple, unsophisticated beginnings until complex, 'scientific' medicine as we know it today emerged. While modern medicine does draw on earlier ideas about 'health', it is

important to clarify what its 'scientific' approach involves, and to locate its emergence in a broader social and historical context. Table 6.3 outlines how knowledge about blood has developed through historical time. Our current understanding of the composition and function of blood is based on relatively recent developments in scientific thought.

Chapter 2 outlines a number of the social changes that took place in Britain during the 18th and 19th centuries. As well as changes in the way in which people lived and worked, there was a significant shift in the way in which people thought about issues such as 'health'. Religion provided the dominant 'system of knowledge', or way of thinking about and explaining phenomena such as health and illness, in the pre-Enlightenment 17th century. People explained and understood the world, and their existence within it, in terms of the 'Will of God' and divine intervention. 'Scientific' thought emerged out of the Enlightenment, and gradually became the dominant 'system of knowledge' during the 18th and 19th centuries.

'Science', developed by people such as doctors, became the new source of 'truth', taking over from God. In the 18th and 19th centuries, 'medicine' was a new 'scientific' way of thinking about and dealing with 'health' matters. Doctors claimed that they could use the 'scientific method' objectively to identify and deal with 'ill-

Table 6.3 Knowledge about blood

Date	Name	Idea
AD190	Galen	Believed that blood moved in the veins and arteries, carrying 'spirits'. Claimed that it passed through holes in the 'septum' (a thick membrane in the heart)
1242	Ibn-an-Nafis	Argued that blood could not move through the 'septum', but believed that it circulated through the lungs instead
1543	Vesalius	Discovered that blood could not move through the 'septum'
1559	Columbo	Showed how blood circulates through the lungs
1579	Fabricius	Saw valves in the arteries
1628	Harvey	Developed a full theory of blood circulation
1661	Malpighi	Saw capillaries in the lungs
1733	Hales	Measured blood pressure
1800+	Various	Structure and chemical composition of the blood worked out
1909	Landsteiner	Discovered different blood groups
1910+	Various	Further knowledge of the complex chemistry of the blood and how it functions is discovered. Research continues to extend this knowledge through the medical speciality of haematology

(Scott and Culpin, 1996)

health'. They did this by developing techniques and procedures that applied positivist, 'scientific' thinking to the care of the sick individual's body. Medical knowledge is largely based on positivist assumptions (see box).

Basic assumptions of positivist thinking

Naturalism	This is the idea that it is possible to study 'health' using natural science methods.
Phenomenalism	This is the belief that 'scientific', valid knowledge can only be obtained through directly observed experience. If something cannot be observed, it is said to be metaphysical.
Scientific laws	Universal laws can be developed from making observations and establishing 'causal' relationships.

'Science' became the dominant 'system of knowledge' during the 19th century, and remained a very powerful and important way of thinking about the world throughout the 20th century. This has enabled doctors to establish and maintain control over the way in which 'health' and 'illness' are defined, and has strongly influenced the development of our present healthcare system. The 'medical model' used by doctors assumes that:

- health is the absence of biological abnormality in the body
- doctors can use special 'scientific' methods and knowledge to observe the body, and to identify whether or not there are symptoms of any biological abnormality
- the causes of ill health are located in the individual's malfunctioning biological system
- health can be restored by using surgery and drugs to correct the malfunctions that occur

Doctors have been very successful in establishing the 'medical model' as the dominant way of thinking about health. Until the 19th century, they were only one of a number of groups in Britain who were competing to be the dominant healthcare provider. Doctors were successful in introducing a 'curative' model of health and illness that took the human body as it's object of concern, and established the hospital as the context of its practice.

Acceptance of the 'medical model' and its assumptions about health ran through health policy during the 20th century. As far as its impact upon health provision is concerned, the importance and significance of this way of thinking cannot be overestimated. The structure of the National Health Service is based primarily upon the activities of specialist doctors, seeking to cure the diseases that they have identified. However, there is considerable doubt that this model actually reflects reality and, increasingly, the medical profession's claim to have a monopoly on health care is being challenged.

The questioning of medical knowledge and dominance

The validity and usefulness of medical knowledge has been questioned in a number of ways. Sarah Nettleton (1992) refers to these challenges to medicine as being part of a 'social constructivist' approach to health and illness. The 'social constructivist' approach refuses to accept that medical knowledge and practice is simply based on 'objective' techniques and pre-given 'facts' but, rather, sees bio-medicine as a socially created phenomenon.

Challenges to medical knowledge and practice

The 'medicalisation thesis' challenges the claims and legitimacy of orthodox bio-medicine in a number of ways. The key point of the medicalisation thesis is that medicine and medical practitioners claim expertise in areas that are not legitimately their concern. Feminist analyses, such as those of Barbara Ehrenreich and Dierdre English (1979) and Ann Oakley (1980), have challenged the legitimacy of the way in which male doctors have 'medicalised' the natural process of childbirth, and by so doing have gained control over women's lives and bodies.

Medical practice has been also challenged on grounds of effectiveness. The work of Thomas McKeown (1979) showed that public health interventions rather than medical practice was actually responsible for the decline in the mortality rate in the 19th century. Ivan Illich (1976) also questions the effectiveness of medicine, claiming that bio-medical doctors actually *create* forms of illness, and have an interest in doing so. Illich called this doctor-caused illness 'iatrogenesis', and identified three basic forms:

1 'Social iatrogenesis' is created when bio-medical doctors treat 'normal' human experiences, such as pregnancy, childbirth, unhappiness and dying, as 'medical' phenomena. Illich (1976) claims that doctors create illnesses and medical problems out of these phenomena, and provide opportunities for big business to produce drugs and equipment to enable them to deal with them.

2 Illich (1976) argues that the growth and dominance of the bio-medical profession has led to 'cultural iatrogenesis', whereby people are now dependent on doctors and their technological treatments, and have been robbed of their own ability to cope with their problems, pain and illnesses.

3 Illich also claims that bio-medical doctors create 'clinical iatrogenesis', in that their interventions and treatments often have side-effects that actually cause new health problems. For example, many of the drugs used to treat psychiatric problems have damaging side-effects that destroy features of their users' central nervous systems.

At the beginning of this chapter, we considered the difficulties of actually defining 'health' and 'illness'. One of the issues that we looked at was the way in which the meanings of both terms shift over time and between cultures. This is a problem for bio-medical doctors, because medicine claims to be able to identify the 'timeless' and 'culture-free' *biological* determinants of illness. Medicine's inability to establish timeless, independent 'truths' about 'health' leads to criticisms of its effectiveness. The medical approach to health and illness fails to accommodate the 'culturally relative' nature of what counts as 'health' and 'illness'.

The claim of medicine – and the expectation of the patient – is that a doctor can tell you what is causing your *illness*. Despite this, there are many situations in which people visit the doctor and, even though they are 'feeling unwell', they are told that medically (that is, biologically) there is nothing wrong with them. There have been a number of recent battles over whether or not the symptoms of 'ill health' that people report are actually evidence of underlying disease/disorder processes. A classic example is the debate over ME, many bio-medical doctors refusing to recognise the 'reality' of the condition in the absence of objective, biological evidence (see box).

ME: a disputed illness

ME or *Chronic Fatigue Syndrome*, is a complaint which, it is claimed, leads to a feeling of exhaustion and possible memory loss, amongst other symptoms. It can last for a number of years and profoundly affect the lives of its sufferers. However, whether or not there is actually any such thing as ME remains in dispute. Scientific tests can find no evidence for the 'disease' – in fact, in objective, scientific terms it simply does not exist.

Whether sympathetic treatment or support is obtained from medical practitioners depends upon the personal views of the doctors. During the early 1990s, the dismissive term 'yuppie flu' was used to describe the syndrome. This conveyed the message that it was a middle-class problem, with little substance to it. However, although still a disputed disease, a formal report from the combined Royal Colleges, representing doctors and psychiatrists, has argued that *Chronic Fatigue Syndrome* is a recognisable condition that could be classified as an 'illness', and that it is caused by a combination of social, psychological and psychiatric factors.

In addition to bio-medical doctors disputing whether or not symptoms exist, a number of studies have shown that even when doctors are able to identify and record physical symptoms, they don't always know what 'health' significance these measurements have. The problem is that the very nature and identification of what constitutes a disease or – at least an abnormality – is clearly linked to culture. Lynn Payer (1989), for example, points out that definitions of 'normal' levels of blood pressure vary across different countries, despite the fact that there are 'objective' ways of measuring it. Comaroff (1978) argues that medicine is, in fact, another belief system like religion. She suggests that Western medicine must be viewed 'as a problematic socio-cultural system whose substance cannot be taken for granted' (Comaroff, 1978: 247).

Payer and Comaroff are pointing out that in many cases the 'scientific' medical model is irrelevant and ineffective as a way of identifying and dealing with 'health' and 'illness' issues. It simply does not help people to understand their 'ill health', and cannot provide a 'cure' for many of their perceived problems. People frequently go to their bio-medical doctors with problems of 'stress', 'tiredness' and 'unhappiness'. Many of

the categories of 'illness' that 'lay people' define are re-categorised by bio-doctors under headings that are essentially meaningless in medical terms. So, if people complain that they are 'exhausted' and feeling 'tired all the time', but show no observable, physical symptoms of any clearly identifiable disease, then doctors may 'explain' this by saying that the person has an unspecified 'virus'. In effect, the doctor is saying that he or she does not know what causes the problem, and is managing the uncertainty of the situation by giving an empty, meaningless diagnosis to preserve his or her 'expert' credibility.

The contribution of the medical model

We have outlined a number of ways in which medical knowledge and power have been questioned. Clearly, there are grounds for doubting that 'medicine' can deliver 'health' for all in a simple curative, way. Nevertheless, given the power and importance of medicine, it is worth making the point that medical knowledge and medical practitioners do have an important role to play in developing physical treatments for identifiable biological 'diseases' and disorders. Pharmaceuticals and surgical interventions are now very sophisticated, and can improve and prolong a person's life in a situation in which – 100 years ago – they would have died or suffered much more. Clearly, medicine does have a very important role to play in 'fighting' disease and 'saving lives', but there are plenty of arguments and sources of evidence to show that it is useful only for a segment of the 'health' problems that people face, rather than for the entire range.

With our social policy interests in mind, it is important to restate the point that the UK's healthcare system has been developed to accommodate and support the dominant knowledge system and practices of the 'curative' medical profession. However, despite the power of the medical model and the medical profession, there is a growing interest in other ways of thinking about and providing 'health' care. The growth of interest in complementary therapies and public health has, for example, led to a shift towards 'social' theories of 'health' and 'illness', and new policy approaches to the provision of services.

Alternative approaches to the medical model

The medical model and the current hospital-based health system are not the only way of thinking about health and providing health care. The alternatives include public health medicine at one extreme and complementary therapies at the other. Both have recently begun to make a comeback in debates about health and how health care can be provided.

Public health medicine and the environment

During the 19th century, the tradition of public health medicine developed alongside, but separate from, the biological/individual focus of the medical model tradition. Both shared a negative definition of health as being the absence of illness. However, the public health model attempted, through preventive methods such as improving water supplies, and developing public housing programmes and health education campaigns, to prevent general ill health from occurring in society in the first place. The public health approach adopts a social model of health. The real causes and origins of ill health are seen as being located in the environment rather than the individual. For example, poor housing and poverty are environmental factors that contribute to respiratory problems. The 'public health' solution is better housing, and programmes to tackle inequality and poverty. The medical model solution consists of antibiotics to treat the pathology, or malfunctioning, that is occurring in the individual's respiratory system.

The public health tradition was very important in reducing ill health and premature death rates at the turn of the 20th century. Thomas McKeown (1976) has presented evidence to show that many infectious diseases declined as a result of public health interventions, rather than the new 'scientific' techniques of individual

medical practitioners (see figure). The social model informed the efforts of public health reformers at the end of 19th century, when better sanitation and clean water became social policy issues.

Despite its application in the 19th century, the public health approach was much less influential than the medical model in attracting the attentions and finances of health policy-makers in the 20th century.

Public awareness and acceptance of these alternative models of health and illness and the new methods of 'treatment' that they involve grew significantly in the last few decades of the 20th century. One of the consequences of this is that medical knowledge has been questioned and the dominance of the medical profession reduced to some degree. This shift in thinking about health and 'ill health' has led policy-makers to consider new ways of addressing 'health' needs and providing healthcare services.

Complementary health and therapy models

Alternative, or complementary, therapies involve ways of thinking about the nature of 'health' and 'ill health' that are significantly different to the medical model approach. Complementary therapies include practices such as homoopathy, which uses a range of herbal remedies in different strengths to stimulate the body's own 'defences', and acupuncture, which involves the insertion of needles at stimulus points in the body to effect 'cures'. Both these and most other forms of complementary practices have no 'scientific' basis – indeed, they may actually fly in the face of 'rational' thinking. An example of this is reflex-

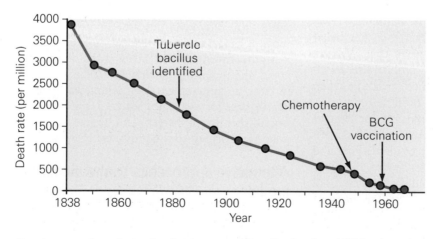

Respiratory tuberculosis: death rates per million, England and Wales   (McKeown, 1979)

Table 6.4 Complementary therapy ideas about 'health'

Type of treatment	Fundamental ideas
Acupuncture	This a form of alternative therapy that has its origins in Ancient China. It involves needles being inserted into the body to restore the 'energy flow' necessary for the Ying and Yang elements of chi to be in balance.
Herbal medicine	Uses various herbs to provoke the body's natural protective responses as a treatment for various illnesses.
Homeopathy	This is based on the principle that 'like is cured by like', and involves the patient being given a very small dose of a remedy that is vigorously shaken to increase its potency. The idea is that this then allows the body to build up a natural immunity to the substance (and cures the problem).
Reflexology	This therapy is based on the belief that different parts of the feet correspond to different organs and parts of the body. By applying pressure to thse different parts of the feet, the body can be treated for various problems.
Hypnotherapy	Patients are put into a trance-like state in which they are felt to be more receptive to suggestions about behaviour change (for example, stopping smoking or over-eating) or are more able to express repressed feelings. The idea is that they may retain these suggestions or benefit from the emotional release after the hypnosis is ended.

(adapted from Senior and Viveash, 1998)

ology. This therapy is based on the belief that by treating the foot all parts of the body can be healed. There is no medical evidence to suggest that this is possible, yet people claim that it works – as they do for the entire range of practices classified as 'complementary therapy'.

Practitioners of complementary therapies pursue a range of different beliefs about how their techniques work (see Table 6.4), but generally they agree that the division of the body into a separate mind and a mechanical body – the basis of the bio-mechanical model – is false. In complementary medicine, a remedy needs to involve both body and mind if it is to be effective.

The growth of complementary medicine has been so rapid that it is estimated that there are now over 100 000 therapists in the UK and that over 10% of the British population now use them. Until recently, the medical profession had been hostile to complementary therapies, but the British Medical Association (a very powerful pressure group that represents the medical profession) has begun to accept that there are a range of possible ways of combating ill health. Indeed, just under 50% of GPs are now providing, either directly or indirectly, complementary therapies, and 70% of health authorities are also purchasing complementary therapy services.

REVIEW POINTS

- Medicine is a scientific way of thinking about health and disease that first emerged in the 18th-century Enlightenment period.

- Medicine, as a part of scientific thought, has evolved into the most politically powerful approach to healthcare practice.

- The medical model is based on a negative definition of health, which concentrates on the absence of biological abnormality as evidence that a person is 'healthy'.

- The medical model is 'curative' and is based on the treatment of the individual's malfunctioning body in specialist hospital and clinic settings.

- Medicine has been challenged since the 1960s by feminists and alternative therapy practitioners, as a legitimate and effective way of thinking about and practising health care.

- Ivan Illich identifies various forms of **iatrogenesis**, or doctor-caused illness, as evidence of the ineffectiveness and failure of medicine to offer solutions to health problems that are often non–biological in nature.

- Non-medical, alternative approaches to health care include the public health model, which focuses on social and environmental factors and strategies, and a variety of complementary therapy models that look at health in terms of the positive functioning of the whole body and mind.

> ### REVIEW ACTIVITIES
>
> 1 What was the dominant system of thought that preceded the development of scientific thinking?
>
> 2 Outline the key features of the medical model of health.
>
> 3 To what does **social iatrogenesis** refer?
>
> 4 Describe some of the prevention strategies that you would expect a policy-maker using a public health model to incorporate in his or her health policies.
>
> 5 How do complementary therapy approaches to health differ from the approach taken by the medical model?

The development of healthcare provision

At the beginning of the 21st century, the United Kingdom has a complex and relatively highly developed healthcare system. The present system of health care has evolved gradually, from at least as early as the 14th century (see Chapter ?) The present structure of the health and social care system, the range of services offered, and the roles of health and social care practitioners have all evolved over this period in response to social, economic and political influences and events. The medical profession, and the 'scientific' medical model ideas on which their work is based, have played a particularly important role in shaping the present system.

The development of health and social care services in the UK can be divided into a number of distinct organisational periods, centring around the creation of a national health and social security system, commonly referred to as the 'welfare state':

- the system prior to 1947

- the welfare state between 1948 and 1978

- the changing direction between 1979 and 1989

- the new internal market from 1989

- the NHS reforms of New Labour from 1997 onwards

In the following discussion we will first look at the development of healthcare services and then consider the origins and development of the social care/social work system.

Health and social care services in the pre-NHS period

The most important development in state intervention in healthcare provision in the pre-NHS period was the enactment of public health legislation at the end of the 19th century and the beginning of the 20th century. These measures put in place a public health infrastucture that was the main reason for the decline in infectious diseases. The development of public and environmental health services occurred before the development of large-scale personal medical and social services.

During the pre-NHS period, health services were haphazardly divided between public and private sectors. Rob Baggott (1997) describes the pre-NHS private sector as consisting of voluntary hospitals, private practitioners and a range of voluntary and private organisations. The pre-NHS public sector was made up of municipal hospitals and community health services that were provided through local authorities.

The pre-NHS private sector

Voluntary hospitals were funded through philanthropy and public subscriptions. Many voluntary hospitals were founded in the first two decades of the 20th century. The initial aim of voluntary hospitals was to provide free treatment for those unable to pay. Services were generally provided free of charge for people who could not afford to

The Royal Infirmary, Glasgow – an example of a voluntary hospital founded to serve the needs of the poor

pay for private treatment, although not everyone could gain access to their services. According to Brian Abel-Smith (1960), people who were very poor or who had an infectious disease were often not admitted. Gradually, the voluntary hospitals introduced charges for their services. By the 1930s they had evolved into fee-charging institutions, which received funding from insurance companies and subscription plans. Many patients took out health insurance or joined subscription schemes to cover these costs.

General practitioner (GP) care was another area for which, in the pre-NHS period, people had to make some payment. Originally, GPs charged fees to their affluent patients, but gradually, with the development of friendly societies and later insurance companies, they were contracted by these to look after the health care of their members. The **National Insurance Act 1911** was a key piece of legislation in enabling employed working-class people to gain 'free' GP care in the pre-NHS era. In 1939, at the beginning of the Second World War, over 40% of the population was covered by compulsory national health insurance, and nine out of ten GPs were members of the scheme.

However, the system was heavily flawed, as it did not cover the unemployed and the dependants of the employed – generally women and children. The argument behind providing health care for employees only was that if they were out of work then the entire family would be thrown into poverty. However, if the employee was fit and well, then he could make the payments for health care for the rest of the family. A problem with this argument was that it relied upon there being adequate numbers of jobs to employ people – in the Depression of the 1930s this was challenged forcefully, and more than 200 000 workers (and of course their families) lost health coverage.

The pre-NHS public sector

In the early part of the 20th century, local authorities took over a range of specialist hospitals and Poor law institutions, and became involved in providing health care. In the pre-NHS era, **municipal hospitals** run by local authorities provided most in-patient healthcare services. The municipal system included hospitals that provided services for specific categories of patients, such as 'isolation hospitals' for infectious diseases and maternity hospitals, as well as former workhouses and Poor Law infirmaries.

As well as hospital services, the pre-NHS public sector included environmental and public health, community health services and child welfare clinics, all provided through local authorities. Local authority Medical Officers of Health had wide-ranging powers over water supplies, sanitation, food and hygiene and certain community health services – for example, for children. However, there was a clear distinction between the local authorities' roles as providers of hospitals and that of ensuring public health. This division between preventive public health and curative hospital-based health care continues to some extent today.

Despite the range of public-sector services, there were significant problems that affected the provision of health service in the pre-NHS period. These problems included:

- a shortage of facilities and trained manpower
- inequitably distributed services, both geographically and functionally
- the uneconomic use of services arising from poorly thought out organisation
- a lack of adequate funds, which made any significant expansion impossible

Rob Baggott (1997) describes how the pre-NHS public sector was the subject of various criticisms from the end of the First World War onwards. This gradually led to calls for national planning to coordinate service provision, and to ensure that what was offered matched 'need', or what was required.

REVIEW POINTS

The pre-NHS era

- Modern healthcare services have their origins in a mixed system of private, voluntary and municipal services that existed from the mid-19th century.
- The private and voluntary sectors were more important in the pre-NHS

period than they were after the emergence of the NHS.

- The inequalities and inefficiency of the pre-NHS system led to calls for greater government involvement in the provision and funding of health care in the 1930s and 1940s.
- The emergence of the National Health Service (NHS) in the 1940s was a watershed in healthcare provision. It introduced a nationalised system of health care that was free to all.

REVIEW ACTIVITIES

1 Which organisations had responsibility for **municipal hospitals** in the pre-NHS era?
2 Explain how voluntary hospitals funded their healthcare services in the pre-NHS era.
3 What is the significance of the **National Insurance Act 1911** in relation to GP care?
4 Identify the main weaknesses in the insurance-based system of health care that existed before the NHS emerged in the 1940s.
5 Why was the pre-NHS system generally unable to provide adequate, effective health care for the British population?

The development of the National Health Service

The intervention of the state into health and social care during the Second World War, through the creation of the Emergency Medical Service, is seen as a major influence on the development of a national system of health and social care provision. During the Second World War, it was necessary to coordinate the activities of most of the hospitals and healthcare professionals in the Emergency Medical Service. This system showed that it was possible to have a coordinated system of health care; that this system was efficient and effective; and, finally, that the previous system had serious shortcomings in its coverage of the population.

Various alternatives for a new system to be introduced after the war were discussed. These included a Ministry of Health plan to develop a system based solely on local authorities, in which GPs would be local authority employees; while an alternative British Medical Association report argued for independently salaried GPs. The main conflicting interest groups that the government had to deal with were the local authorities, who wanted to be in control of the system, and the doctors (particularly the GPs), who wished to retain as much autonomy as possible. Aneurin Bevan, the Minister for Health, managed to split the doctors, by winning over the consultants and eventually isolating the GPs, who were represented by the British Medical Association. The local authorities were pacified by the retention of a range of community and public health functions.

The social and political conditions were also right for the development of a national system of health provision. Prior to and during the Second World War, consideration had been given to the idea of a national health and social security system. The first major policy statement of these ideas came in the Beveridge Report (1942). It drew attention to the necessity for a national system of health care and social security provision, a 'welfare state' (although Beveridge did not use this term himself) for postwar Britain. The concept of the welfare state established a new interventionist role for the state in funding and providing health and social care, that would last until 1989 before any major revisions took place.

The Beveridge Committee's investigation and report is outlined in some detail in Chapter 2. One of the most significant outcomes of the report was the setting up of a comprehensive National Health Service (the NHS). The proposals of the Beveridge Report were revised several times before the first Minister for Health, Aneurin Bevan, a Labour Party politician, created a national health and social security system that began in 1948. The resulting system was rather cumbersome, but was national, effective and allowed planning, while at the same time bringing all the key players together in agreement. A 'tripartite' system was created in 1948, and lasted until 1974. The system was composed, first, of the hospitals; second, of the family practitioner services, including GPs, dentists and opticians; and, third, of the local authority-run community and public health services.

Following the National Health Service Act 1946, the structure of the health service was as shown in the accompanying figure.

The improvements offered by the new NHS system included:

- a comprehensive system of health care for all
- a service that was free 'at the point of delivery'
- the possibility of nationally high standards of health care
- an integrated system within which it was possible to plan for the healthcare needs of the nation

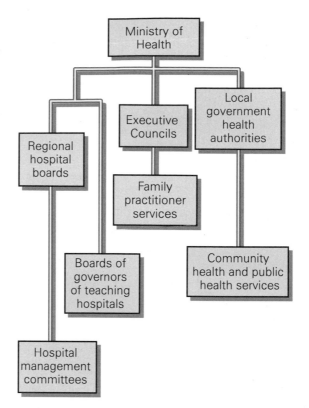

The structure of the NHS, 1948–1974

The new NHS system was paid for through a combination of compulsory National Insurance and general taxation, and led to a belief that it was 'equitable' (fair) and just. Indeed, it could be claimed that the NHS took on a major symbolic role in Britain, such that politicians who have opposed the NHS in later years – including Mrs Thatcher – have been unable to dismantle it, or even generate discussion about the possibility of its replacement by a privatised system. This can be compared with housing, public amenities and transport, which were privatised with little public opposition.

The pattern of healthcare provision, 1948–1979

Health and social care services evolved and developed between 1948 and 1970. The new National Health Service offered all British citizens a comprehensive, free, accessible healthcare system for the first time. The system was planned, funded and coordinated by government, and delivered through local 'nationalised' services. The NHS was very popular in its early years and was seen, very optimistically, as a means through which the health of the British nation could be dramatically improved. During the postwar

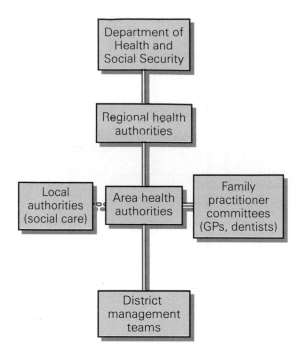

The structure of the NHS, 1974–1979

consensus era, all political parties supported the development and continued public funding of the NHS. Despite this, and the optimism that was initially associated with it, the NHS faced a number of problems between 1948 and 1979, when significant reforms began.

Structural problems

The problems that emerged concerned overlap, duplication of services and lack of coordination between family practitioner services, local authority community health and social services, and the nationalised hospital service. The structure was eventually changed in 1974 (see the above diagram) but the problems remained. While community health services were integrated into the NHS, three separate agencies (the NHS, local authorities and family practitioner committees) remained. Excessive bureaucracy and management were also seen to be a problem.

Accountability, control and planning problems

Health and social care policy-making was the domain of health ministers. Day-to-day running and service development happened at a local level, and was mainly controlled by the medical profession. Together with local authorities, who ran social services, the medical profession were

able effectively to veto the implementation of national policies that affected their own priorities (Baggott, 1997).

Equity and resource allocation

As we have mentioned on pages 103–104, the NHS has always faced very significant pressures on its finances, partly because of the enormous amounts of money involved in providing a national healthcare system. When the Conservative government set up the Guillebaud Committee in the early 1950s, in the hope that it would recommend cost-cutting measures, the Committee commented in its 1956 report that, if anything, more finance was needed.

However, it became apparent by the 1970s that if the system was efficient in terms of expenditure, it was not equitable (for a discussion of 'equity', see p. 63) in terms of providing health care where and to whom it was most needed. Certain groups, particularly the chronically ill, older people and those with long-term mental illness, were receiving less funding than the average patient, while NHS regions were receiving and spending very different amounts of money on their populations.

In an attempt to iron out healthcare funding inequalities, the then Labour government introduced the RAWP formula in 1976. RAWP stands for the Resource Allocation Working Party that devised a formula to assess each region's healthcare needs. On the basis of this formula, funding was to be gradually shifted to those regions with the greatest need, based upon indicators of levels of illness, expectation of life, and population size and characteristics.

RAWP was ultimately unsuccessful, because of the slow pace of change in the funding allocated to each region, and the fact that the formula had to be altered to take into account the different costs of providing care in different regions. Arguably, RAWP could also be criticised for ignoring the fact that many of the reasons for differences in mortality and morbidity were linked to lifestyles, use of medical services and non-financial barriers, such as ethnic minority ignorance of the provision of appropriate services – or, indeed, the lack of specialist services for them in some areas.

Despite the problems that occurred during this period, there were also some identifiably positive developments as national health provision evolved. Myfanwy Morgan (1985) suggests that these included:

Table 6.5 The growth in health spending

Year	£ billion
1978/9	23.5
1982/3	27.1
1983/4	27.4
1984/5	28.0
1985/6	28.1
1986/7	29.2
1987/8	30.4
1988/9	31.4
1989/90	31.8
1990/1	33.0
1991/2	35.2
1992/3	37.2
1993/4	37.4
1994/5	38.7
1995/6	39.5
1996/7	40.2

(HM Treasury)

- an initial decade of reconstruction, re-equipment and consolidation
- from 1960 until 1974, a period of innovation, expansion and strategic planning
- addressing the problem of the uneven distribution of GPs and services – GPs began to work in practices, to which other health professionals were attached
- the movement into the hospitals of some services (for example, midwifery) that had been provided outside of the hospital – also, community services took on a preventive role
- sowing the seeds of the community movement, particularly in respect of mental health care
- centralisation of resources and services, usually around a district hospital

The NHS 1979–1989

The period between 1979 and 1989 saw decisive changes in the character of the NHS and the services that it provided. The return to government of the Conservative Party in 1979 saw a programme of public expenditure curbs in order to defeat inflation, and to enable the depressed economy to pay its own way. These two aims led to a watershed in the provision of health services. The nature of these changes is outlined on pages 170–173. Following their election to government in May 1997, the New Labour government embarked on a new phase of NHS 'reforms'. These are outlined and discussed on pages 173–176.

REVIEW POINTS

The development of the NHS

- The Emergency Medical Service and the Beveridge Report (1942) were two key influences in the emergence of a national system of healthcare provision in the UK.
- The National Health Service Act 1946 brought the National Health Service into being. It was based on the principles of comprehensive provision, 'free' services and access being based on clinical need.
- The NHS was initially funded through National Insurance and general taxation. It quickly became apparent that comprehensive, national health care would be costly to provide.
- The period 1948–1979 was characterised by growth and development of healthcare facilities and services throughout the UK. There was general agreement between politicians that a national system, based on public funding and provision, was a good thing.
- The NHS was reorganised in 1974, to deal with organisational and funding problems that had emerged over the previous 26 years.
- During the 1970s the principle of state funding and provision of services, and the high costs of healthcare provision, became topics of significant political

debate. The Conservative Party wished to reform the NHS to curb the ever-increasing cost of providing public health care.

The origins and development of the social care system

The present social care and social work system has its roots in the 19th century. Social work as we know it today is a relatively recent development and, like health care, has gradually evolved into its present form. The voluntary sector plays a more significant role in providing social care – as opposed to health care – in the UK. By contrast, the private social care sector is relatively small in comparison to the private healthcare sector. However, as in health care, responsibility for, and funding of, social care and social work services falls on statutory or government bodies.

The era before the welfare state

In Chapter 2 we looked at the impact of industrialisation and urbanisation on living conditions in 19th-century Britain. For many people, living conditions were terrible. Poverty and ill health were widespread. It was in this context that social work developed, out of the various attempts that were made to deal with the problems that people faced. Self-help organisations in the form of friendly societies and trades unions worked to reduce the impact of poverty on members, and to improve their working conditions. Middle-class Victorians also engaged in a great deal of philanthropic work and developed charitable organisations to address what they saw as the key social

problems of the time. Middle-class women, such as Octavia Hill, were particularly prominent in these early attempts to improve the social conditions and behaviour of people who were experiencing poverty and ill health.

During the early part of the 20th century, support grew for some form of statutory social work provision for people in need. Following the 'welfare state' reforms of the 1940s, social work – and the present statutory social care system – began to develop. Historically, the client groups who have been provided with social care by local authorities have been children and families, people with disabilities, older people and people with mental health problems. There have also been significant social class differences in the use of statutory social care services throughout their history.

The welfare state era

Local authority 'children's departments' were set up on the recommendations of the **Curtis Report** (1946). The Curtis Report was the culmination of an inquiry into an incidence of child abuse that resulted in the death of a child. The inquiry and report led to the **Children Act 1948** being passed. Under the Act, local authorities took over responsibility for child welfare and protection services from voluntary-sector organisations. Local authorities took on responsibility for adoption, fostering, children's homes and family casework. Their powers were gradually extended to include the investigation of child abuse and child protection work. Until the early 1970s, local authorities also provided some healthcare services. Hospital social workers, occupational therapists and mental welfare officers all worked in hospitals or other healthcare settings, but were employed by local authorities. In addition, local authorities had developed more general 'welfare departments'. These took on responsibility for the residential care of older people, homeless families and disability services. The range of social care and social work responsibilities of local authorities was gradually extended to include day care and community support services.

Despite the growth of a welfare state in the postwar years, social care and social work services developed without the creation of a social care equivalent of the NHS. During this period, local authorities throughout the UK worked along basically the same lines, but there was no overarching, centralised organisation to plan and control their development of social care services. The result was a more complicated and less integrated social care system of structures and responsibilities. The overlap and coordination problems that this caused led to a review, in the late 1960s, of the way in which social care services were organised and delivered.

The **Seebohm Committee** (1968) proposed that a single 'social services department' – that would merge the children's, health and welfare departments into one – should be established by all local authorities. These were developed after the **Local Authority Social Services Act 1970** was passed. At this time, local authorities lost their health responsibilities, which were handed back to the NHS. New personal social services departments integrated statutory social care and social work provision within local authority organisations.

The next landmark in the development of social work and social care provision was the **Barclay Report** (1980). This proposed a new 'community approach' to social work and care provision, based around more accessible local offices and the development of partnerships with communities. The report pointed to the signif-

icant efforts of, and reliance on, informal carers in providing social care. It argued that social workers should support and develop members of the community, so that people could care more effectively for their own.

The development of social care

- Social care services have their origins in the self-help and voluntary organisations that developed in the late 19th century to protect people from the effects of poverty.

- Statutory social care and social work services have evolved through the work of local authorities. These have generally developed along the same lines, but have never been part of a broader organisation such as the National Health Service.

- Present-day local authority social services departments began in the 1970s, when a number of health and social care departments were merged within local authorities.

- Social services departments now focus on purchasing and providing personal social care and social work services in community settings.

REVIEW ACTIVITIES

1 Which client groups have social care services traditionally been provided for?
2 What role did charity and philanthropy play in the development of social care?
3 What was the reason for, and outcome of, the Curtis Report in 1946?
4 What did the Local Authority Social Services Act 1970 create?

The introduction of 'marketisation' strategies in health and social care provision

The 1980s saw significant reform of the state system of health and social care provision. While various administrative reforms took place in the 1980s, the really radical change took place in 1990 with the introduction of the 'internal market', following the passage of the **NHS and Community Care Act 1990**.

The New Right Conservative governments of the 1980s and early 1990s were influenced by monetarist ideas and pursued a goal of public spending reduction. Whether Thatcherism was a planned strategy or a series of *ad hoc* reforms, driven by this key goal, is a matter of debate (see pp. 51–53). What is clear is that **'marketisation'** (the introduction of 'market forces') was a key strategy in changing the largely state-funded and state-provided health and welfare system.

Marketisation of the health and social care system happened gradually throughout the 1980s and early 1990s. The NHS was first subjected, in 1983, to a major review by Roy Griffiths, a managing director of the Sainsbury's supermarket chain. The first Griffiths Report (1983) recommended making NHS services operate in a more businesslike way, through:

◎ giving health and social care organisations their own budgets, which they would then be held accountable for

◎ linking NHS funding to 'service productivity' – that is, more money for treating more patients

◎ creating competition between various health and social care providers, including state, voluntary and private-sector organisations

A second review of the NHS took place in 1987. The NHS was struggling to cope with bed reductions, financial restrictions and pressure for services. The review focused on two issues:

◎ possible alternative sources (rather than taxation) of funding health care

◎ new ways of allocating existing public funding and resources

While several different possibilities for private funding, social insurance and 'earmarked' taxes were considered, the tax-funded healthcare system was felt to represent the best and cheapest way of funding health and social care services at that time.

The main outcome of the review was the development of a new way of allocating resources within the public health system. This was outlined in a White Paper called *Working for Patients* (Department of Health, 1989b). The key proposal of *Working for Patients* was that an 'internal market', based on a system of purchaser/provider contracts, should be developed. The internal market was a product of the New Right, which argued that constantly changing the administrative structure of the health service would have little real impact on quality, efficiency and equity of services. New Right thinkers believed that the only way to achieve these objectives was to introduce a 'market economy' into health care.

The 'market economy' idea

A market economy of health care is a fairly simple idea. In an ideal world, each individual has the right – and the income – to choose which doctor and hospital he or she wishes to attend for treatment. It follows that the 'ideal' individual would choose the best, most effective service providers to deliver the health care that they need. These successful healthcare institutions would then blossom, and the other less effective ones would have to close down. In the process, quality would be rewarded and incompetence punished. However, there were two major problems in this scenario that needed to be faced. First, that there was no competition within the NHS – this was crucial if quality was to be driven up and prices driven down. Second, it was not possible to give individuals the funds to seek out their own health care – both for reasons of knowledge (How would the average person know what is appropriate treatment?) and for reasons of finance (it would just be too expensive, and some form of rationing would be needed).

The 'internal market' solution

According to the US health economist Allan Enthoven (1985), the answer to these problems lay in creating an **'internal market'**. That is, both hospitals and community-based healthcare organisations would be expected to compete between themselves to provide health care. The decision as to where the patients should be sent would be determined by health authorities (on

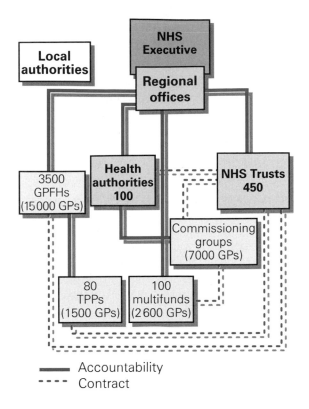

— Accountability
---- Contract

The structure of the 'internal market'

behalf of the smaller GP practices) and a certain type of large GP practice called a 'fundholding practice', both of which would seek contracts for medical care.

How did the 'internal market' work?

The 'internal market' changed the way in which the funds for healthcare services were allocated. The system was based on what became known as the 'purchaser/provider' split. This simply meant that local health authorities and GP fundholders purchased care, while hospital 'trusts' or community care 'trusts' would bid to provide these services. All of the funding was provided by central government on the basis of a formula that was similar in some ways to the abandoned RAWP system. This model was strongly influenced by the Health Maintenance Organisations that are characteristic of US health care. The organisations compete to obtain contracts to provide all medical care to a specific population. The 'internal market' introduced a significant change in the British system of organising statutory health care, and led to a powerful debate about the appropriateness of using market economics in a healthcare system that was originally devised to care for people on the basis of need.

The structure of the NHS during the initial 'internal market' period is described in the accompanying box. The functions of the different parts of the structure are also outlined.

The structure and functions of the NHS during the 'internal market' period

- **Central government**, in the form of the Secretary of State and the Department of Health, determines overall health and social care policy. It also reviews and monitors the performance of NHS authorities and allocates resources to them.

- The **NHS Policy Board** is responsible for overall policy and strategy.

- The **NHS Management Executive** implements policies and strategies formulated by the NHS Policy Board.

- **Regional health authorities** (RHAs) have a strategic role, planning services within their areas and allocating resources to 'purchasing' district health authorities (DHAs) and GP fundholders. They also monitor the work of DHAs and family health service authorities (FHSAs).

- **District health authorities** (DHAs) have to assess the needs of people living in their area and then purchase services to meet these needs, with the exception of GP services. GP services are purchased by family health service authorities (FHSAs). DHAs merged with FHSAs in 1996 to form 'commissioning health authorities' that are responsible for all healthcare commissioning/purchasing.

- **Family health service authorities** (FHSAs) initially manage family practitioner services (GPs, dentists) and complaints against practitioners.

- **GP fundholders** receive budgets from FHSAs to run their services and buy non-emergency care for their patients from a range of providers. Non-fundholding GPs have to place their patients on a waiting list for DHA-funded services.

- **NHS Trusts** are self-governing organisations that operate within the National Health Service. They are run by a board of directors, and are involved in the delivery of direct care. NHS Trusts must prepare and operate a business plan.

The advantages and disadvantages of the internal market

The 'internal market' in health care was the subject of continuous political debate during the early 1990s, and raised a number of important issues about the purpose and funding of statutory healthcare provision. The supporters of the internal market argued that:

◎ the internal market improved efficiency as Trusts competed for patients, and this was shown by an improvement of 2% per year in the amount of health care provided in the first two years for the same resources

◎ before the internal market, no one knew how much many medical treatments actually cost, whereas the reforms led to the Trusts having accurate cost figures

◎ the internal market was far more flexible, and was more responsive to the demands of patients than the centrally planned provider-led services

◎ increased choice for patients was created by the new market economy, as hospitals and community services lost their local monopolies

◎ GP fundholder practices allowed GPs to ensure that they obtained the best possible service for their patients – by negotiating directly with Trusts

Criticisms of the 1990–1999 internal market system

The internal market in health and social care was a very contentious development. It has been subjected to a number of criticisms:

◎ *Increased administrative and managerial costs.* The number of administrators and managers needed to run the 'internal market' increased significantly during the early 1990s. This, it is claimed, led to a diversion of money away from patient care in to simply running the system. Management costs rose by £½ billion each year, and the system cost £2 billion to set up. In total, it is claimed that management costs rose by 28%.

◎ *Winners and losers – a two-tier system.* Competition between provider organisations led to some NHS Trusts doing better than others. By the same token, some patients benefited more than others. There was a lot of controversy over the 'two-tier system' and the 'queue-jumping' that was possible within the internal market.

◎ *Negative effects of competition.* The internal market created competition for patients, with some GPs (fundholders) getting better service for their patients. Competition also prevented the sharing of best practice, as this would reduce a Trust's commercial advantage.

◎ *Fragmentation and unrepresentative management.* There was little strategic coordination within the overall NHS system, as it was fragmented into many individually managed NHS Trusts. The planning of services was split between 100 health authorities, 3500 GP fundholders and 400 different NHS Trusts. Furthermore, NHS Trusts had unrepresentative management boards and were run as companies, not as public services. In general, they were not in the business of co-operating with each other.

◎ *Loss of 'choice'.* In reality, patients had little or no 'choice' about the kind of services that they wished to receive; and, in reality, they did not have the freedom to choose between different service providers. The decision on where a particular patient was sent for treatment depended upon the contracts agreed between the Trusts, the local health authorities and GP fundholders. GP fundholders did achieve good 'deals' for their patients, but at the expense of other non–fundholding GPs. Trusts would give priority to fundholders in order to get the additional income from them.

The era of marketisation and change in social care

The introduction of a 'marketisation' policy by the Conservative governments of the 1980s and early 1990s affected both the structure of local authorities and their function with regard to social care and social work provision. Changes in both of these areas occurred as a result of the passing of a number of important pieces of legislation.

The **Children Act 1989** had a major impact on the way in which local authority social services departments dealt with and delivered children's services. As a result of the Act, local authorities focused on the inspection and registration of child care and early education services for under-eights, and on child protection work. The **NHS and Community Care Act 1990** further altered the structure and role of local authority social services departments. Their new role, as 'enablers' and purchasers of care rather than large-scale providers, is discussed in more detail on pp. 176–177.

pp. 176–177

care and led to new 'contract' relationships.

- The internal market was politically contentious, with supporters claiming that it brought efficiency gains, cost control and choice. Critics of the internal market identified increased management costs, a two-tier system of 'winners and losers', and a fragmentation of the NHS into competing 'NHS Trust' organisations.

REVIEW POINTS

The 'marketisation' of care

- The 'marketisation' of health care during the 1980s and 1990s involved the introduction of 'market forces' and business strategies into the management and operation of the statutory healthcare system.

- The Conservative governments of the 1980s, led by Margaret Thatcher, used various marketisation strategies to control public expenditure on health, and to change the character of the NHS.

- The key strategy used in the marketisation process was the introduction of the 'internal market', which created a distinction between 'purchasers' and 'providers' of health

REVIEW ACTIVITIES

1 What does the term '**marketisation**' mean in relation to the NHS?
2 Explain how the 'internal market' in health care worked.
3 What role did the district health authorities and NHS Trusts each have in the internal market?
4 Identify the benefits for patients that, according to its supporters, the internal market introduced.
5 What criticism can be made of the claim that the 'internal market' was an efficient and equitable (fair) system of providing health care?

The NHS from 1997

In late 1997, the newly elected Labour government published a White Paper called *The New NHS: Modern, Dependable* (Department of Health, 1997), which introduced a further set of significant reforms to the NHS. The aims were further to loosen central planning, to reform the internal market and to give greater power to Primary Care Groups. It was accepted that the internal market had distorted healthcare provision and planning, by attempting to introduce a market-based system in place of a needs-based one. However, a return to central planning was also ruled out, as the division between planning for health needs and providing health care that the 'purchaser/provider' split introduced was viewed as a success.

It was also felt that the general principal of giving GPs greater choice and power through

budget-holding had considerable merit, but that a division, and inequality, had developed between budget-holding GPs and non-budget-holders. The answer to these problems, according to the government has been to abolish fundholding GPs, and to create 'Primary Care Groups' in their place.

The structure of the new NHS

The 'new NHS', as the Labour government call it, has a number of key organisational elements. Some of these *are* new, while others have been retained from the previous 'internal market' structure. The way in which many of the retained elements, such as NHS Trusts, function has been modified to reduce competition and encourage co-operation and integration within the NHS.

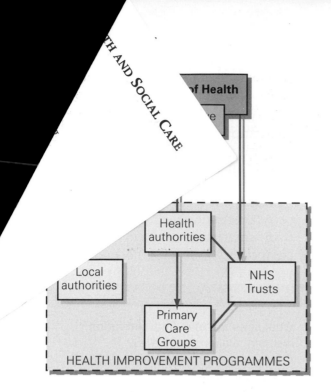

The present structure of statutory healthcare services in the UK

NHS Executive regional offices

Regional offices are required to ensure that NHS Trusts, Primary Care Groups, local authorities and health authorities all work together efficiently and in partnership. There are eight NHS Executive regional offices covering England, with one each for Scotland, Wales and Northern Ireland.

The NHS regions in England

Health authorities

The 1997 reforms didn't significantly change the role of health authorities in England and Wales. As a result of the reforms, however, health authorities have become smaller bodies that cover wider areas, and they will have stronger powers to oversee the effectiveness of the local NHS. They will lead the development of Health Improvement Plans for their areas, based on an assessment of health needs, which will guide all health care for the following three years. They will gradually withdraw from commissioning work as the new 'Primary Care Groups' develop. They are still responsible for assessing the health needs of the local population and making arrangements for services to be provided by NHS Trusts and other agencies.

NHS Trusts

These will continue to provide patient services both in hospitals and in the community, and to negotiate long-term service agreements that will be based upon treatment for particular groups of patients (such as children) or disease areas (such as heart disease). The White Paper stresses that doctors and nurses – as opposed to managers – will be closely involved in the design of service agreement and standards. The Trusts will be legally obliged to work in co-operation with other organisations, rather than in competition as before.

NHS Trusts are the key providers of secondary-level health care through hospitals and via community-based services. However, NHS Trusts now have to establish formal, co-operative links with 'Primary Care Groups' through long-term service agreements. These three-year agreements set out what services will be provided at what cost, and have to incorporate national and local health targets and standards.

Primary Care Groups

The reformed NHS is based on it being 'primary care-led'. The development of Primary Care Groups is therefore a very significant feature of the new NHS. Primary Care Groups comprise all GPs in an area plus community nurses, and are run by these professionals. Primary Care Groups will gradually develop responsibility for commissioning services, and may eventually take over the role of health authorities altogether. If they take on full responsibility, they will be known as primary health care Trusts. The White Paper envisages a flexible range of groups, with some going for full Trust status while others take less responsibility.

The Primary Care Groups will replace GP fundholders. The specific roles of Primary Care Groups will be to work within the Health Improvement Programme by commissioning services from the relevant NHS Trusts and then monitoring the performance, and by integrating primary and community health services wherever possible. As far as the commissioning of secondary care from the primary care sector is concerned, the introduction of Primary Care Groups represents a modification of the 'internal market' rather than a total abolition. Basically, all GPs are now part of larger fundholding groups.

Policy initiatives in the new NHS

The policy initiatives developed by the Labour government and incorporated into the new NHS health strategy follow three themes: integrating care, raising standards and improving access. Several policy initiatives have been developed, and are now being implemented in each of these areas.

Integrating care

Health Improvement Programmes (HIPs) are a key feature of the government's attempt to integrate the work of different health and social care providers, so as to avoid duplication and make the most effective use of funding. Integrated care, based on co-operation between service providers, is an alternative to the competitive internal market system.

The first Health Improvement Programmes were started in April 1999. HIPs are to be drawn up every three years by a consortium of groups led by the health authorities. Membership of the consortium involves NHS Trusts, Primary Care Groups, local authorities and representatives of the local voluntary sector. The HIPs identify local health needs and then, on the basis of these needs, will determine the range and alignment of services.

One of the main purposes of Health Improvement Programmes is to encourage the formation of partnerships within the community, to achieve the targets laid down by the government in the policy document *Our Healthier Nation*. Other major functions are to help address any inequalities in health in local communities, and to ensure that effort goes into planning specific programmes to bring about improvements in their area.

The **Health Action Zones** were launched in June 1997, with the aim of specially targeting effort and funds on a number of areas in which, it was believed, the health of local people could be improved by better integrated arrangements for treatment and care.

The first wave of 11 Health Action Zones was announced on 31 March 1998. These were areas thought to have the greatest need. The funding for Health Action Zones will be available for up to three years, but projects with a shorter timescale can also be undertaken. Their purpose will be to bring together all the local bodies that can affect health, and to put into action an agreed, coordinated strategy for improving the health of the people in that area. It is hoped that new innovations will emerge.

Raising standards

National Service Frameworks (NSFs) set national standards in a particular area of health care. They also define the way in which the services for a particular care group should be delivered. The first two National Service Frameworks, produced in 1999, were for coronary heart disease and mental health. A NSF for older people is due in Spring 2000, and for diabetes in Spring 2001. Like many of the other initiatives, National Service Frameworks are designed to improve quality and reduce variations in standards of care and treatment.

National Service Frameworks will require partnerships with a wide range of organisations. This will not only include Primary Care Groups, NHS Trusts and health authorities, but also social care providers, local authorities, voluntary organisations, business and industry. Users and carers are also to be involved.

The **Commission for Health Improvement (CHImp)** is a new statutory but independent body, which has been set up to ensure that high-quality service standards are being met by statutory health and social care organisations. It starts its first full year of operation in 2000. The Commission for Health Improvement has the job of reviewing the performance and effectiveness of local health organisations every three or four years. It will play a key role in implementing the government's 'standards' and quality assurance policies.

Improving access

NHS Direct is a 24-hour telephone confidential advice line staffed by nurses, who use their skills,

Official reports that stimulated the focus on community care

◎ *Audit Commission Report, 1986.* This report pointed out the 'perverse incentive' of local authority funding working against community care (see Audit Commission for England and Wales, 1986).

◎ *The Griffiths Report, 1988.* This reviewed the funding of community care. It argued that overall responsibility for community care should lie with local authorities (see Department of Health, 1988). The Griffiths Report led to the NHS and Community Care Act 1990.

◎ *The Wagner Report, 1988.* This investigated residential (institutional) care and recommended that a variety of types of care should be provided by local authorities, including care at home (see National Institute for Social Work, 1988).

◎ *Caring for People, 1989.* This was a White Paper that adopted many of the recommendations of the Griffiths Report (see Department of Health, 1989a). The White Paper outlined six objectives:
  – the promotion of domiciliary day and respite care, to permit independent living at home
  – that support for informal carers was a 'priority'
  – proper assessment of need, and good 'case management'
  – promotion of the independent sector
  – clarification of responsibility between NHS and local authority organisations
  – the introduction of a new way of funding care, to remove the bias towards institutional care

The impact of community care on informal carers and community well-being

Informal carers are people who provide care for a friend, relative or partner, usually in the cared-for person's home, on a voluntary, unpaid basis. There are a large number of informal carers in the UK – about 6.8 million according to the 1990 General Household Survey – who provide a broad range of care services. Indeed, in the UK, most people who receive care are cared for at home by an informal carer. The majority of informal carers (just 'carers' from this point on) are not professionally trained and, in many cases, receive little support from formal care workers or organisations.

Community care, in the form of care by the community, has had a significant impact on informal carers. The community care policy assumes that families and/or relatives will provide care at home. Nevertheless, the NHS and Community Care Act 1990 did not include any special provisions regarding support for carers.

Feminist analysis and critique of community care policy

Claire Ungerson (1998) argues that the informal sector was previously referred to as 'the family' or 'the community', and was renamed as part of 'second wave feminism' in the late 1960s and 1970s. At this time, feminists questioned the 'expected role' of women as housewives and

Table 6.9 The effect on the immediate family of caring for a mentally ill adult at home

Aspect of family life	Percentage of families	
	Some disturbance (%)	Severe disturbance (%)
Health of closest relatives:		
Mental	40	20
Physical	28	–
Bringing up children	24	10
Domestic routine	13	16
Income	14	9
Employment (other than mentally ill person)	17	6

(Sainsbury and Grad de Alarcon, 1974)

mothers, and began to analyse 'caring'. They concluded that 'community care' as a policy rested on the assumption that, as 'natural' carers, women would replace paid carers in institutional centres.

> 'Care in the community equals care by the family equals care by women'
>
> (Finch and Groves, 1980)

The feminist critique of community care as being exploitative of women led to the development of carers' lobbies, including the Carers National Association. The policy responses were focused on providing social services support for carers. Claire Ungerson (1990: 171) states that 'it is probably the case that second wave feminism's greatest triumph, as far as British social policy is concerned, is the successful identification of informal care as a legitimate issue for public discussion and as part of the policy agenda'.

The Invalid Care Allowance is an example of policy action as a result of the feminist critique. The Carers (Recognition and Services) Act 1995 also now gives carers the right to an assessment of their needs when their relative is being assessed, although it doesn't give them rights to services themselves.

Criticisms of community care

A number of criticisms of community care have been identified, including the following:

1 *The ideal doesn't match the reality*. The ideal of providing high-quality, individualised care for people in their own homes is one that most people agree with. The reality of the 1980s and 1990s has been that this is expensive, difficult to achieve and largely hasn't happened.

2 *Cost*. Community care has turned out to be more expensive than institutional care, and no extra funding has been made available to ease the transition from one to another. Community care has, as a result, been extremely under-funded.

3 *Inequality of provision*. There are significant differences in community care provision across the country, and even within the same region. Different local authorities and NHS Trusts allocate differing amounts of funding to community care provision. There are no spending guidelines (especially

with regard to a minimum amount) and thus standards of care may vary considerably. This can result in 'revolving door' care.

4 *Lack of coordination*. Community care requires co-operation between a range of different care providers, and considerable coordination of different inputs between GPs, community health units and Local Authority social service departments. This often doesn't happen very effectively.

5 *Community apathy and resistance*. 'Community' only exists in the limited sense of 'family' (that is, female) carers. People receive little help or support from the broader community. There is a lot of 'community' rhetoric, but there is also significant NIMBY (Not In My Back Yard) resistance to providing community-based residential care, particularly for people with mental health problems and learning disabilities.

The outcome – community care in reality

Whether or not community care has been a success depends on the perspective from which it is viewed – it is probably still too early to judge. However, the effect that it had on local authority social services departments was to change their organisations quite dramatically. Departments were reorganised into separate teams – those that commissioned and purchased care and those teams that provided care.

Purchasers and providers

Community care has changed the function of social services departments. Rather then being major providers of care, as they used to be, they are now principally planners and purchasers of care. Care coordinators or social workers whose job it is to assess and arrange care for people are on the purchasing side. Those services such as day centres or residential homes that actually perform the caring tasks are known as provider units.

User groups

As far as the different user groups are concerned, adults with learning disabilities have probably gained most. They now are more likely to live in the community and lead 'normalised' lives than remain in long-term institutional care. People with mental illness have had a more mixed experience.

The closure of many large mental hospitals has not always gone hand in hand with the creation of adequate facilities in the community. Older people have also probably gained, in the sense that more older people have the opportunity to remain in their own homes for longer. Older people can get 'lost' between the health services and the social care services, which is one of the reasons why the government launched a two-year research programme in June 1998, called Better Government for Older People. The idea is to develop strategies for providing a seamless and more user-friendly service for older people.

Community care

- ◎ 'Community care' is a term that has a wide range of meanings. It has come to be associated with the policy objective of providing care in non-institutional settings.

- ◎ Current community care policies have their origins in the 1950s, when attempts were first made to close down, or de-institutionalise, large Victorian asylums, children's homes and long–stay hospitals.

- ◎ The 'community care' movement is influenced by sociological, financial and ideological arguments that see institutional care as ineffective and inappropriate for individuals with long–term social problems.

- ◎ The main groups affected by community care policies have been people with mental health problems, people with learning disabilities and older people in need of long-term care.

- ◎ Care in the community became associated with 'care by the community' in the 1980s, as an ideological shift and a need to reduce

public expenditure saw the government attempt to increase the care role of families and partners of people with long-term care needs.

- ◎ Informal, or family, carers provide a large volume of care in the community. In reality, these carers are usually female relatives of the person in need of care. Feminists argue that the whole 'community care' policy has been based on the belief that women would, and should, be the 'natural' providers of care for family members.

- ◎ Community care has been justified on ideological, economic and sociological grounds as being a more appropriate and effective way of providing care for people with long-term needs.

- ◎ Community care is criticised on the grounds that it has offered recipients poor-quality, under–funded and uncoordinated provision.

REVIEW ACTIVITIES

1 What's the difference between 'care in the community' and 'care by the community'?

2 What sociological evidence is there to suggest that 'institutional' care may have a negative effect on people?

3 Why was 'community care' slow to develop in the 1960s and 1970s? What happened in the 1980s to change this?

4 Explain why feminist policy analysts criticise the assumptions of the 'community care' policy.

5 Outline three criticisms of the policy of providing care in the community.

6 Using the data in Table 6.9, explain how caring for a mentally ill relative at home affects family members.

References

Abel-Smith, B. (1960) *A History of the Nursing Profession*. Heinemann, London.

Acheson, Sir Donald (1998) *Independent Inquiry into Inequalities in Health: Report*. HMSO, London.

Audit Commission for England and Wales (1986) *Making Community Care a Reality*. HMSO, London.

Baggott, R. (1997) *Health and Healthcare in Britain*, 2nd edn. Macmillan, Basingstoke.

Comaroff, J. (1978) Medicine and culture: some anthropological perspectives. *Social Science and Medicine*, **12B**, 247–254.

Dahlgren, G. and Whitehead, M. (1991) *Policies and Strategies to Promote Social Equity in Health*. Institute of Future Studies, Stockholm.

Department of Health (1988) *Community Care: an Agenda for Action* (The Griffiths Report). HMSO, London.

Department of Health (1989a) *Caring for People: Community Care in the Next Decade and Beyond*. HMSO, London.

Department of Health (1989b) *Working for Patients*. Cm 555. HMSO, London.

Department of Health (1992) *The Health of the Nation*. London, HMSO.

Department of Health (1997) *The New NHS: Modern, Dependable*. HMSO, London.

Ehrenreich, B. and English, D. (1979) *For Her Own Good: 150 Years of Experts' Advice to Women*. Pluto Press, London.

Enthoven, A. C. (1985) *Reflections on the Management of the National Health Service*. Nuffield Provincial Hospitals Trust, London.

Finch, J. and Groves, D. (eds) (1980) *A Labour of Love: Work and Caring*. Routledge and Kegan Paul, London.

Goffman, E. (1961) *Asylum*. Penguin, Harmondsworth.

Harding, S., Bethune, A., Maxwell, R. and Brown, J. (1997) Mortality trends using the longitudinal study. In: *Health Inequalities: Decennial Supplement* (ed. Drever, F. and Whitehead, M.). DS Series no.15. The Stationery Office, London.

Illich, I. (1976) *Limits to Medicine: Medical Nemesis*. Penguin, Harmondsworth.

Jones, K., Brown, J. and Bradshaw, J. (1978) *Issues in Social Policy*. Routledge and Kegan Paul, London.

Leadbetter, P. (1990) *Partners in Health: the NHS and the Independent Sector*. National Association of Health Authorities and Trusts, Birmingham.

Marmot, M., Davey-Smith, G., Stansfield, S., Patel, C., North, F. and Head, J. (1991) Health inequalities among British civil servants: the Whitehall Study II. *Lancet*, 337.

Mays, N. (1991) Community care. In: *Sociology as Applied to Medicine* (ed. Scambler, G.). Baillière Tindall, London.

McKeown, T. (1979) *The Role of Medicine: Dream, Mirage or Nemesis?* Basil Blackwell, Oxford.

Ministry of Health (1962) *A Hospital Plan for England and Wales*. Cmnd 1604. HMSO, London.

Ministry of Health (1963) *Health and Welfare: the Development of Community Care*. HMSO, London.

Morgan, M. (1985) *Sociological Approaches to Health and Illness*. Croom Helm, London.

Morris, P. (1969) *Put Away: a Sociological Study of Institutions for the Mentally Retarded*. Routledge and Kegan Paul, London.

National Institute for Social Work (1988) *Residential Care: a Positive Choice*. Report of the Independent Review of Residential Care (The Wagner Report). HMSO, London.

Nettleton, S. (1992) *Power, Pain and Dentistry*. Open University Press, Buckingham.

Oakley, A. (1980) *Women Confined*. Martin Robertson, Oxford.

Office of Population Censuses and Surveys, Social Survey Division (1987) *General Household Survey, 1985: an Inter-departmental Survey Sponsored by the Central Statistical Office/Office of Population Censuses and Surveys, Social Survey Division*. HMSO, London.

Payer, L. (1989) *Medicine and Culture: Notions of Health and Sickness in Britain, the US, France and West Germany*. Victor Gollancz, London.

Sainsbury, P. and Grad de Alarcon, J. (1974) The cost of community care and the burden on the family of treating the mentally ill at home. In: *Impairment, Disability and Handicap* (ed. Lees, D. and Shaw, S.). Heinemann, London.

Scott, J. and Culpin, C. (1996) *Medicine Through Time*. Collins Educational, London.

Senior, M. and Viveash, B. (1998) *Health and Illness*. Macmillan, Basingstoke.

Townsend, P. (1962) *The Last Refuge*. Routledge and Kegan Paul, London.

Townsend, P. (1979) *Poverty in the United Kingdom*. Penguin, Harmondsworth.

Townsend, P., Davidson, N. and Whitehead, M. (eds) (1988) *Inequalities in Health: the Black Report and the Health Divide*. Penguin, Harmondsworth.

Ungerson, C. (1998) The informal sector. In: *The Student's Companion to Social Policy* (ed. Alcock, P., Erskine, A. and May, M.). Blackwell, Oxford, pp. 169–173.

Wild, S. and McKeigue, P. (1997) Cross-sectional analysis of mortality by country of birth in England and Wales, 1970–92. *British Medical Journal*, **314**, 705–710.

World Health Organisation (1946) *Constitution: Basic Documents*. WHO, Geneva.

Young, P. (1995) *Mastering Social Welfare*, 2nd edn. Macmillan, Basingstoke.

7 | Family and Community

By the end of this chapter you should be able to:

- ◎ Identify the various forms of the family.
- ◎ Appreciate the diversity of family types.
- ◎ Provide explanations for the changes in family types and the development of diversity.
- ◎ Discuss the implications of these changes for social policy.
- ◎ Distinguish between families and households, and examine the relationship between them.
- ◎ Identify and explain the changes in marriage and divorce, and their implications for social policy.
- ◎ Identify and debate ideologies of the family and apply them to the lone-parent debate.
- ◎ Provide examples of policy changes on the family since 1944.
- ◎ Discuss the changing roles of family members and the policy implications.

The family is certainly *the* most important institution when it comes to issues of health and welfare. On the one hand, the family provides a wide range of *informal* emotional, physical and caring services to its members, and on the other hand it represents the channel through which much of government financial aid, in the form of welfare benefits, is channelled. These can be said to be the positive aspects of the family. However, there is another side to the family, in that it is the source of many of the social problems that the welfare state attempts to combat. The family is the arena in which social services departments operate, for example, in their attempts to prevent abuse and neglect of children, and in which the police are forced to intervene to prevent violence against women.

'Families are private institutions but private institutions that have public effects. Our children are the next generation. How they grow up will decide society's future. "We are not in the business of telling people how to lead their lives ... [but] families need government policies that nurture them rather than damage them by neglect and carelessness".'

(*The Guardian*, 24 July 1998; leading article reporting on a speech by the Home Secretary about the family)

The significance of the family to society – both as a provider of welfare and very often a focus of social problems – has to some extent led to a conflict with the belief in British society that the family is a 'private' institution, and that what goes on 'inside' it is only the business of family members. For many people, the state has no right to intervene in the running of the family. Therefore, we can find, throughout our discussion on the family and the welfare state, a division between those who regard it as important that the state actively involves itself in determining what family relationships are like, and those who say that the state should leave the family alone to get on with caring for and disciplining its own members.

In this chapter, we provide all of the information needed fully to understand these debates on the nature of the family. We begin by sorting out the confusion that surrounds the very term 'the family', as this has often led to debates being based on misunderstandings. What we discover is that there are a number of different forms of the family in the contemporary United Kingdom, and that only by accepting that a diversity of types exist is it possible to understand the relationship between the health and welfare systems and 'the family'. We note that the contemporary family is characterised by 'diversity', in terms of such things as economic and social status, ethnicity, location and sexual orientation. We also distinguish the family – as a set of relationships – from the household (a living arrangement), as this too has caused some misunderstanding.

Having clarified the structure of the family and explored its diversity, we then move on to explore the dynamic nature of the family. By 'dynamic', we mean that any one family is in a constant process of change, as members age, die and divorce. The result of these changes is a shift in the relationships between the family members. So, for example, parents change from being providers and educators to (eventually) being dependent grandparents.

The 'facts' about the family, which we explore in the early part of the chapter, can be interpreted in many different ways, and the implications for policy towards the family is also affected by the differing interpretations. Two examples of different approaches to the family that we explore in this chapter are the 'New Right' and the feminist positions. For the New Right, the family is a place of love and affection and an important provider of informal welfare, while for feminists the family represents a 'site of patriarchy' – that is, an institution that benefits men rather than women or children. We will illustrate this debate by using policy examples, both historical and recent.

Finally, and bearing all of this in mind, we examine the specific impact of policy on the roles of all members of the family, from children to grandparents.

Types of family: forms of diversity

Defining the family

It should be easy to start our discussion with a definition of the family – after all, it is something that virtually all of us have lived in at some time in our lives. However, standard definitions are either vague or inaccurate. Giddens (1993), for example, defines the family as 'a group of people directly linked by kin connection, where the adult members take responsibility for caring for children'.

This is helpful, but we then need to go on to define 'kin'. Where does marriage or cohabitation appear in the definition? The plural term 'adult members' seems to suggest that there need be more than one adult, which rules out the family headed by a single person.

A classic definition of the family that is often quoted in textbooks, produced by George Murdock (1949), is less vague but, as a result, much more problematic. Murdock defines the family as:

> 'a social group characterised by common residence, economic co-operation and reproduction. It includes adults of both sexes, at least two of whom maintain a socially approved sexual relationship, and one or more children, own or adopted of the sexually cohabiting adults.'

Why common residence? What about grandparents or grown-up children? Surely they are members of the same family as the parents. The definition also fails to include gay and lesbian couples, and people who become lone parents as a result of divorce, or because they never marry or cohabit with a partner.

It has been so difficult to construct an accurate definition because the family has many different *structures*, and these different structures are characterised by *diversity*. Gittins (1985) points out that it is better to talk about 'families' rather than 'the family', as this allows us to see that there are a number of different groupings, all of which fall – in one way or another – under the umbrella term 'family'. For the purposes of our discussion in this chapter, we can examine the variation in families that Gittins refers to under two headings – as set out in the box on page 190.

In the discussion that follows, we shall also be referring to 'households' quite frequently. It is important to realise that families and households are different things. A **household** is simply one or more people living in the same dwelling, whereas a family – however we define it – will, as a minimum, be a group of people, related by ceremonial and/or blood ties, who live together or

	Focus	Examples
1 Variations in structure	The different arrangements of people generally regarded as comprising the family	• The nuclear family • The extended family • The lone-parent family • The reconstituted family
2 The diverse forms of the family	Social factors that affect the form of family and the relationships between them	• Social class • Ethnicity or culture • Sexual orientation • Location

are in contact. As we shall see, household statistics can provide a useful picture of life in the United Kingdom, and will help us to understand both the family and the community.

Differing family structures

The nuclear family

The **nuclear family** was regarded as the norm in the UK and most of Western Europe during most of the 20th century. It is defined as consisting of a heterosexual couple (who engage in a sexual relationship) plus their dependent children. However, it is declining quite markedly. If we look at households by family type, then we can see (as shown in Table 7.1), that the 'traditional' family of a couple with dependent children comprises approximately 23% of all households, a drop of 15% compared to 30 years ago. Indeed, this model actually only represents about 1 in every 20 households in the UK at any one time. This decline is important to note, as the traditional nuclear family is still the model that politicians refer to as the 'ideal' – the model that helps to drive social policy. When politicians refer to the need to support the family, this is the form of family that they are usually referring to.

The extended family

The **extended family** consists of more than one generation of nuclear families, living together or in close proximity. In Britain, this form developed in the early period of industrialisation, at which time it provided a range of services to its members. As the state began to take on some of these services, it became economically possible for nuclear families to gain some independence, and by the 1950s the extended family had largely given way to the nuclear family – although, as we will see in our discussion on diversity, this is not

true for all ethnic groups living in the UK. However, the idea that this means that the majority of families are 'isolated' is not born out by surveys. for example, Janet Finch and Jennifer Mason (1993) found that 72% of (adult) respondents lived within one hour of their mother, and over half saw their mother at least once a week.

The lone-parent family

The **lone-parent family** is almost always headed by a female: about one-third of all families with only one child are lone-parent families. The numbers of lone parents has increased by 30% during the 1990s. By the end of the 20th century, there were over 1.5 million one-parent families in the UK, and about 2.8 million children lived in such families, an increase of one-third in ten years. Single and divorced lone mothers now form 72% of all lone mothers. About 14% of lone mothers have never married or lived with a partner. A further 14% have cohabited once, and 48% have married once.

However, lone parenthood is not a static state in which women remain. Each year, about 12% find a partner and will marry or cohabit. This pattern of entering new relationships with children leads us to the final structural version of the family in the contemporary UK.

The reconstituted family

This term refers to families that are composed of individuals who have formed new relationships, and who have brought with them dependent children from previous relationships. The family situation may be further complicated when the new partners have their own 'joint' children. In the UK today, about 6 million people live in reconstituted families, and about one in ten children live with their step-parents. The growth in divorce rates, which shows that 15% of all marriages are second or subsequent marriages (see p. 196), does not provide a full picture of the extent of the reconfiguring of families, as we have to include the numbers of people who move into and out of cohabitation. In 1997 for example, of the 27% of women cohabiting, 17% of women entering a cohabitation relationship were single, 5% were previously divorced and 4% were previously separated, with the final 1% widowed.

The National Child Development Programme, a longitudinal study of young people, reported in 1998 that step-families were likely to be poorer than average, and that the parents were found to express greater unhappiness over relationships than those in first families. The highest levels of unhappiness (18% of step-fathers and 20% of partners) occurred when they had both step-children and their own joint offspring.

Family diversity

This discussion of the main family structures in the UK needs to be seen alongside what we might call the 'diversity' of family types. As mentioned earlier, by **diversity** we mean factors that influence each of the structural types that we have just looked at, and fragment them further. For example, the experience of extended families may vary greatly depending upon aspects such as social class background, cultural background, the ages of the various members of the family and the relationships between the members.

Social class

The experience of family life is linked heavily to sets of values and financial differences that are themselves a reflection of social class. The early work of Michael Young and Peter Willmott, in the 1950s, showed the existence of a functioning extended family network amongst working-class people (Young and Willmott, 1962). Willmott's later work in North London, in the late 1980s, pointed to the continuing existence of a working-class extended family, albeit with greater flexibility and greater distances between members' households (Willmott, 1988).

The middle-class family is still more heavily characterised by the nuclear unit, with less direct contact between members. Social class differences in forms of family structure are largely caused by a rather greater emphasis on geographical mobility amongst the middle classes, in their search for career advancement.

Ethnicity and cultural belief

It is important not to stereotype families and individuals by ethnic background. However, the first thing to note is that the image, or perhaps the stereotype, of the family is essentially a white, Christian one. Yet a range of alternative models exist. According to the Office for National Statistics, for example, in their statistical breakdown of families in the UK:

> 'South Asian families, that is those of Indian, Pakistani or Bangladeshi origin, tend to be larger and more likely than those from other ethnic groups to live in households of two or more families.'
>
> (*Social Trends* 29, 1999)

People from Indian, Pakistani and Bangladeshi backgrounds are far less likely to live in lone-parent households than those classified by the Office for National Statistics as 'white' or 'black'. Whereas 22% of white families comprised lone parents, the figure was only 9% for Indians and 17% for Pakistani/Bangladeshi families. The figures for those classified as 'black' indicate that 55% of their families are headed by lone parents. According to Jon Bernandes (1997), the differences between the groups should be seen less in terms of a problem associated with 'race' – that is, women of African-Caribbean origin are more likely to be lone parents – than in terms of cultural diversity. He suggests that:

> 'African-Caribbean men are discriminated against in harsh ways in the UK, most clearly seen in poverty, unemployment and education. Whereas 38% of single mothers in the general population earn an income, 59% of Black single mothers do. This suggests that Black single mothers are vigorous and economically active rather than passive victims of Black men. It is likely that Black single motherhood is far from being a "problem" when taking account of employment, income and social class. Perhaps the plight of Black single motherhood should suggest the need for supportive social policies.'
>
> (Bernandes, 1997: 152)

Whatever views are held about morality, or whether lone parents are a social problem, the point that emerges is that cultural differences impact upon the structure and life experiences of families.

Sexual orientation

In many ways, this has been one of the most challenging aspects of the changing conceptions of what constitutes a family. Gay and lesbian partners have increasingly demanded the right to undergo 'marriage' ceremonies, claiming that the law ought to be altered to enable them to do so. Although there is limited public resistance to this, what has created greater discussion has been the increase (although still only tiny) of lesbian-headed families, caused when one lesbian partner had previously had a heterosexual relationship that had resulted in the birth of children. The newly 'reconstituted' family headed by two lesbians has therefore become a 'family'. A further twist to the debate has taken place, with gay and lesbian couples seeking to have their own families through adoption and artificial insemination. Whatever society's views on these changes, they do represent a strong challenge to the traditional expectation and definition of families being based on heterosexual marriage.

Location

Relatively little research has been carried out to examine the significance of location for the family, but where a person lives is an important influence on his or her life, and family types do vary by region , depending partially upon ethnic mix, social class and regional values. Some examples of this are the larger size of families in the Midlands; the higher proportion of lone parents in London and the lower proportion of cohabitation in the North of England.

Dynamic families

As we have seen in the previous section, there are numerous variations on the family. This is partially caused by the different formations affected by social and economic factors, but the complexity of understanding the family does not finish here. We need to understand that the family is a *dynamic* institution. Indeed, one can see the family as being just as much a *process* as a *structure* – any one individual family is constantly in a state of change. In the majority of families, couples come together and children are born. The children are initially dependent, but then leave home, become independent and form their own families. In turn, the original parents eventually move to a position of dependency.

This is known as the **family life-cycle** and is illustrated in the accompanying diagram. The family life-cycle is certainly as significant for

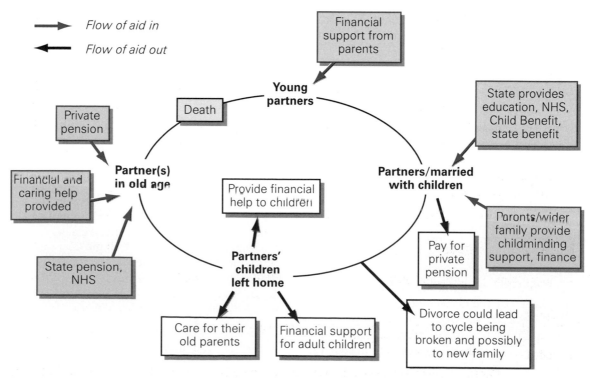

The family life-cycle and social policy

social policy as the structure of the family in general. At each 'stage' in the cycle, family members have different needs, and varying abilities to provide for themselves. Social policy is often targeted at situations in which the family is seen as having 'failed' to provide for their needs at the appropriate time. For example, the state might have increasingly stepped in to support older people, as their younger relatives may be unable or unwilling to do so.

Families and households in the United Kingdom today

This section provides some of the essential information regarding contemporary change in the composition of families, relationships and households in the modern United Kingdom. Government policies are based on careful analyses of these changes.

Households

Most people in the UK live in households comprising two or more people – in 1998, this amounted to 72% of British households. Although this leaves 28% of the population living alone, the statistics do not paint a picture of isolated individuals. Half of these single-person households are formed by people under pensionable age, who may enter a stable 'couple' relationship at some later point. The average size of households had almost halved since the beginning of the 20th century with, on average, 2.4 people per household in 2000. At the start of 2000, there were approximately 58.4 million people living in private households in the UK. One in ten lived alone and seven in ten lived in a household headed by a couple.

Table 7.1 Households: by type of household and family, Great Britain (percentages)

	1961	1971	1981	1991	1998[1]
One person					
Under pensionable age	4	6	8	11	14
Over pensionable age	7	12	14	16	14
Two or more unrelated adults	5	4	5	3	3
Single-family households					
Couple[2]					
No children	26	27	26	28	28
One or two dependent children[3]	30	26	25	20	19
Three or more dependent children[3]	8	9	6	5	4
Non-dependent children only	10	8	8	8	7
Lone parent[2]					
Dependent children[3]	2	3	5	6	7
Non-dependent children only	4	4	4	4	3
Multi-family households	3	1	1	1	1
All households[4] (=100%)(millions)	16.3	18.6	20.2	22.4	23.6

[1] At Spring 1998.
[2] Other individuals who were not family members may also be included.
[3] May also include non-dependent children.
[4] Includes couples of the same gender in 1998.

(Census, General Household Survey, Labour Force Survey and Office for National Statistics: Department of the Environment, Transport and the Regions)

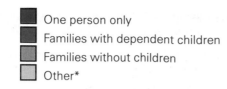

One person only
Families with dependent children
Families without children
Other*

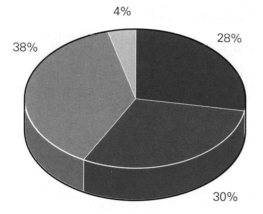

4%

38%

28%

30%

*Other includes households containing two or more
unrelated adults (3%) and those containing two or
more families (1%)

*Recent data demonstrates that there is a variety of
family types in the UK*

Family size

The size of family varies according to family type. At the start of 2000, married couples had 1.9 children on average, lone parents 1.7 children, cohabiting couples 1.5 children and step-families (or 'reconstituted' families) 2.3 children.

REVIEW POINTS

◎ It is inaccurate to talk about 'the family' as an homogenous entity as this fails to reflect the range of family structures and diversity.

◎ The most commonly identified types are the **nuclear family**, the **extended family**, the **lone-parent family** and the **reconstituted family**.

◎ The nuclear family is the most common type in the UK today, but the fastest growing types are the lone-parent family and the reconstituted family.

Table 7.2 The percentage of dependent children living in different family types, Great Britain (percentages)

	1972	1981	1986	1991–1992	1998[1]
Couple families					
One child	16	18	18	17	17
Two children	35	41	41	37	37
Three or more children	41	29	28	28	25
Lone-mother families					
One child	2	3	4	5	6
Two children	2	4	5	7	7
Three or more children	2	3	3	6	6
Lone-father familes					
One child	–	1	1	–	1
Two or more children	1	1	1	1	1
All dependent children[2]	100	100	100	100	100

[1] At Spring 1998.

[2] Includes cases where the dependent child is a family unit, e.g. a foster child, for Spring 1998 Labour Force Survey.

(General Household Survey, 1998)

◎ These family structures are further diversified by a range of factors that include, amongst others, social class, ethnicity, religious beliefs, sexual orientation and location.

◎ It is important to remember that each family is a dynamic institution that is constantly changing. Families pass through a number of different periods in what has been termed a **family life-cycle**.

Marriage, cohabitation and divorce

Marriage

Statistics show that fewer women and men are marrying than was the case 20 years ago. Despite this, the majority of the British population (according to current trends, 75–80%) will marry at some point, and 60% of adults are currently married. In 1996 there were 309 200 marriages, a decline of over 85 000 compared with 20 years earlier but even this is misleading, for there were only 178 000 first marriages, while the remainder were remarriages. There appear to be two, linked factors that affect the decrease in first marriages. Since 1971, the average age of first marriage has increased by approximately five years: today, the average age of marriage is 28 for men and 26 for women. This delay is partially linked to a longer participation in education and, consequently, later entry into work, but a much more important factor has been the increase in cohabitation amongst the British population.

Of those couples involved in remarriage (for at least one partner), there does not seem to be a rejection of marriage, as approximately 22% of individuals who separate from their partners marry again within three years (General Household Survey). This popularity may not be as high for the never-married. At present in the UK, cohabitation appears to be a precursor to marriage, but if the trends in the Scandinavian countries are followed here, it may well develop into an alternative. Historically, patterns of marriage have had a significant impact on the provision of welfare, through its allocation of women into married and non-married categories.

Often unmarried women were expected to undertake caring roles within the family, or undertake low-paid care work.

In the first half of the 20th century, for example, women outnumbered men, as a result of wars and higher male child mortality. It was therefore impossible for all women to marry, and many of these single women were allocated a caring role, looking after elderly or ill family members. This ensured a cheap and ready supply of unpaid carers for the family, and relieved the obligation of the state to provide. Today, with a more even balance between the numbers of men and women in the population and changing attitudes, the *relative* lack of unpaid women carers has helped contribute to the crisis of care.

Cohabitation

Cohabitation, in which non-married couples live together, with or without children, has increased dramatically over the past 25 years. Today, 10% of British adults are cohabiting, but for those aged under 35 the figure is as high as 30%. In 1979, just 3% of all women aged 18–49 were cohabiting. However, cohabitation has not yet replaced marriage as the normal form of permanent relationship. It is now normal for cohabitation to be a period that precedes marriage, with over 60% of couples cohabiting – the majority either break up or convert to marriage within an average time of two years. However, there is considerable evidence that cohabitation as a state in itself is increasing in popularity, and there is a noticeable shift to longer periods of cohabitation.

If cohabitation is less stable than marriage, the implications of cohabitation for social policy are great; while they are of limited significance if it is as stable as marriage has traditionally been. The main concern of legislators at present is to ensure that fathers in long-term cohabiting relationships have legal rights that are equivalent to those of married fathers (for instance, in the event of the relationship breaking up), that they also have equal legal obligations (under the law for the conduct of their children) and, finally, that they experience no tax or benefit advantages or disadvantages.

However, in terms of moral debates in recent years, those who argue in favour of a state that supports the traditional notions of marriage and family have been set against those who argue that the state must respond to social changes, including cohabitation. There has been a dispute over the extent to which taxation and state benefits should support marriage rather than put cohabitation on an equal footing. The result has been a clear victory for those who wish to respond to social change. The abolition of the married tax allowance, the move towards independent taxation of partners, and legislation that gives fathers equal rights compared to mothers, where the partners are not married, have really given cohabiting families exactly the same status as married couples.

Divorce

In 1998, there were 145 200 divorces, a rate of approximately 12.9 per 1000 of the married population. For every divorce in 1998, approxi-mately two marriages took place. However, approximately 40% of those marriages will end in divorce. Between 1970 and 1998, the number of divorces more than doubled. Although divorce is possibly a tragedy for those involved, about one-third of the couples who divorce are childless. More important in terms of consequences are those divorces where children are involved. Approximately one in four of all children will experience the divorce of their parents before reaching the age of 16 (*Social Trends* 29, 1999). One interesting point is that those whose parents divorce have a significantly higher chance of getting divorced themselves in later life.

Changes in divorce levels do have implications for government policy. High rates of divorce lead to increases in the numbers of lone-parent families, which are more likely than two-parent families to receive state benefits. Furthermore, divorcing families need two homes to live in, and so this can increase the demand for social housing. Divorcing families also lead to the situation of reconstituted families, with the problems that we discussed earlier of lower levels of emotional satisfaction than amongst single married families (those where each partner has only been married once).

A report published by the Joseph Rowntree Foundation (Rodgers and Pryor, 1998) reviewed 200 studies on the effects of divorce on children. The report concluded that the children of divorced parents run twice the risk of suffering social problems, ranging from poor performance at school to psychiatric disorders in later life, compared to children from non-divorcing families. They are more likely to drink and smoke

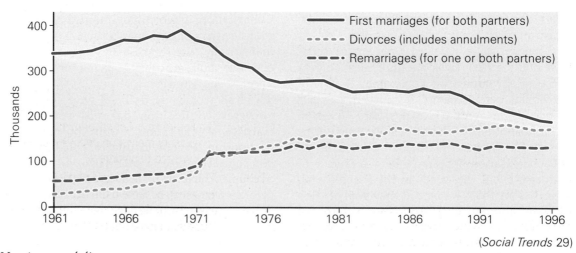

(*Social Trends* 29)

Marriages and divorces

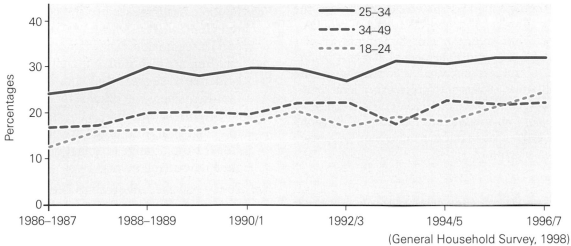

(General Household Survey, 1998)

The percentage of non-married women cohabiting, by age (calendar years to 1988; fiscal years thereafter)

heavily, and to take drugs. The authors claim that it is not necessarily divorce itself that leads to these problems, but the antagonism and disputes which may lead up to it.

The growth in divorce first began after the **Divorce Reform Act 1969**, which allowed divorce after a minimum of two years if both parties agreed, and after five years if only one wished for divorce. The Act both reflected and helped to create changing attitudes towards marriage. The pressure for divorce reform had come from a higher proportion of people who wanted separation, as a result of the 1960s trend towards early marriage. One of the most important factors that affect divorce is, in fact, marrying young. But the desire to divorce also reflects a change in marriage, from a contract between two people – which had to be adhered to 'for the sake of the children' – to an agreement to stay together as long as a decent relationship remains between the partners. The move towards independent households and looser family connections has also meant that the pressures from wider kin to stay together are less strong. The Act has influenced the actions of the succeeding generations, as it formalised a new form of contract that emphasised the importance of the emotional contentment of both partners.

The continuing rise in divorce – with its impact upon children, the resulting growth in lone-parent and reconstituted families, the legal costs to the parents and the potential welfare costs to the state – led to the **Family Law Act 1996**, Part 2 of which allows 'no-fault' divorces. The intention was that such divorces could only take place after a period of mediation (or 'infor-

The development of divorce legislation

1857	Divorce became available for the first time.
1878	A dual system of cheap 'separation' and expensive divorce was introduced.
1937	Divorce was made much simpler and cheaper. One partner was required to prove the fault of the other, on grounds such as adultery and cruelty.
1950	Financial help (legal aid) was made available for divorce. This greatly helped non-earning women, who were previously unable to afford a divorce.
1969	The concept of fault, as the reason for divorce, was largely overturned. The irretrievable breakdown of marriage became the sole ground for divorce. If one partner wanted a divorce, it was necessary to wait for five years. If both agreed, then divorce took place after two years. This led to a very significant rise in the divorce rate.
1984	The law was altered to allow divorce after one year, if both partners agreed.
1996	The Family Law Act introduced compulsory mediation between couples who wished to divorce.
1999	As a result of the failure of pilot mediation schemes, the Labour government decided that compulsory mediation would not be introduced.

mation meetings', as they were called under the law). However, in 1999, the Labour government decided not to implement the reforms, as pilot schemes indicated that mediation was a failure: 40% of couples indicated that they were *more* likely to see a solicitor to protect their legal rights. However, one piece of legislation that has gone forward – in the **Welfare Reform and Pensions Act 1999** – has been the requirement for spouses to share pensions.

- There has been a significant decline in first marriages over the past 20 years.
- The numbers of second, or subsequent, marriages for one or both partners have increased, but the total number of marriages is still in decline. This has implications for care of children and the stability of relationships.
- Cohabitation has increased, to the point at which it is now a normal stage in couples' lives, and currently is a stage before marriage. However, trends indicate that it may, in the longer term, become a normal alternative to marriage, perhaps even supplanting it. Government benefits and taxation patterns have been adjusted to take the growth of cohabitation into account.

- Divorce has increased to the point at which 40% of marriages are likely to end in separation. The effects on children are disputed, but there is evidence to suggest that children in families where the divorce is acrimonious (or where a continuing marriage is acrimonious) are likely to suffer from a range of social problems throughout their lives.
- Policy towards divorce has been to attempt to make it easier to obtain, to move away from blaming one partner and, finally, if separation really is wanted, to attempt some form of mediation or counselling before final divorce.

REVIEW ACTIVITIES

1 How can the decline in the number of first marriages over the past 20 years be explained?
2 Describe some of the implications that the increase in cohabitation may have for social policy.
3 Identify the social policy implications of the changes in divorce rates for social policy-makers.
4 What effect, according to research, does divorce have on the children in the family?
5 What did the Family Law Act (1996) aim to introduce into divorce proceedings?

Ideological approaches to the family

The family has become the 'site' of a great – and, at times, bitter – debate initiated by the New Right on the moral structure of society. The two major opposing groups are the New Right and the Women's Movement. For the New Right, the family represents all that is good about society – affection, sharing, caring and interdependency. For the Women's Movement, the family is the major site of oppression for women, who are physically and sexually abused, and are denied status and recognition of their contribution to household life.

The New Right

The New Right have argued that the family is under threat due to the different structures and diversity of forms that have emerged in the later part of the 20th century. In essence, their argument is that the decline in the family is both the result of and, in turn, a cause of, a general collapse in shared values. The result is increased crime, an increase in 'incivility' (rudeness, and a lack of consideration or care for others), the growth of an underclass of people who do not want to work but prefer to live off the state – and virtually any other social problem that you care to mention. New Right commentators target their venom particularly on families headed by a never-married, single mother.

The New Right relies upon traditional views of the family drawn from 'functionalist' sociologists, who argue that – throughout history, and across a wide range of societies – the family has performed a number of key roles for both its members and society in general. For example, Murdock (1949) argued that these roles were sexual, reproductive, economic and educational. The adult couple received sexual gratification, children were conceived and cared for, the family worked together as an economic unit – producing and consuming – and, finally, the children were socialised by their parents into society. Writers such as Ronald Fletcher (1973) then argued that the family had lost some of these functions to other agencies; for example, the schools had taken over education, while health and caring had been taken over by the welfare state.

The outcome of this loss of functions has been a decline in the family. The consequence of this decline is that the wider social role played by the family, of **social integration** – that is, of pulling people together through bonds of kinship, and creating in them a sense of responsibility to others – has also been lost. What has replaced it is a sense of individual freedom and of self-centredness. The individual has replaced the family as the basic building block of society. This decline in functions, and the stress in society on individual satisfaction, have also had important effects on relationships between family members.

For married couples, if the family no longer provides adequate personal satisfaction, then either partner would feel it to be their right to leave the marriage – unlike the traditional family, where obligations to the institution of marriage and to other family members held relationships together. The result has been the huge increase in divorce rates. Furthermore, the increasing emphasis on equality between partners, as opposed to the dominance of the male, has led to a confusion over the role of men in society; whereas, in fact, the male is naturally suited to the role of provider and defender. As Green and Webster-Gardiner (1988) put it:

> 'We believe that men and women are biologically suited to their different roles, that these are God-given and that it is within the family where fathers provide and mothers care that children are given the best, most stable and most fulfilling start to life.'
>
> (Green and Webster-Gardiner, 1988; quoted in Abbott and Wallace, 1992)

Amongst young people, individualism and the emphasis on sexual satisfaction has led to increasing numbers of children born out of marriage, or even settled relationships, which has created the 'problem' of lone motherhood. For children, the growth of rights over obligations has meant that they are less likely to obey their parents when young, and to be unclear about morality, and about the appropriate roles that men and women should play. As they grow up, they also feel less obliged to provide support and assistance for their ageing parents. Instead, they regard this as the role of the state. What the New right want, therefore, is:

> '... a return to what they see as the traditional family form: an independent, mutually self-supporting family with the husband/father as the bread-winner and the wife/mother as the home-maker, both providing for dependent children; a family where parents take responsibility for the moral, social and economic support of their children and the father is clearly respected as the head. They perceive this "natural" family as having been undermined by feminism and the welfare state. The family is seen to be the foundation of a strong, moral society and to be essential for the maintenance of capitalism. This view of family and family life is central to New Right thought.'
>
> (Abbott and Wallace, 1992)

So, the New Right point primarily to a moral decline in society, which then has real implications for the welfare state, as it has to support and care for older people, those with disabilities, and lone mothers and their children. Much of the anger of the New Right has been directed at lone parents (and their absent partners), who are seen as the clearest example of the decline in traditional values.

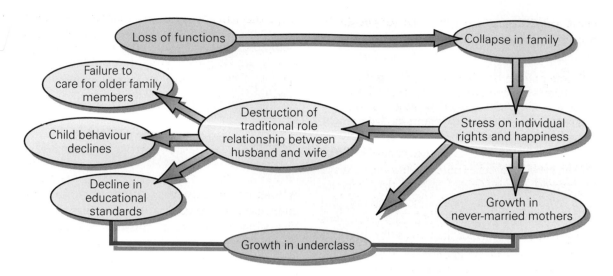

A view of the contemporary family from a New Right perspective

Feminist approaches to the family

The influence of feminist writers and their demands for equality of treatment for men and women in society was one of the reasons for the development of the New Right. Feminist writers had centred many of their attacks on the family because, for them, it represented the very foundation of male power over females. Feminist writers have criticised the family on a number of grounds, including:

- ◎ the physical control of women
- ◎ the economic control of women
- ◎ the ideology that 'women's place is in the home'

The feminist view is that for women to be free, the family as we understand it has to be radically changed, if not abolished.

The physical control of women

Women are maltreated in marriage. This is demonstrated by the rates of domestic violence, with one in five women claiming to have been subject to violence at some time in their lives. They were also, until recently, subjected to sexual attacks. It was not until 1991 that it became possible to charge a husband with the rape of his wife.

The economic control of women

Women are economically exploited by men, in that they have to give up careers in favour of housework and caring for the children. They therefore become economically dependent upon men and thus subordinate to them. The majority of women are therefore confined to part-time employment when their children are young – indeed, nine out of ten part-time jobs are performed by women.

A woman's place is in the home

Finally, the family perpetuates an ideology that says the domestic role (or the 'private sphere') is the one most appropriate for women – 'a woman's place is in the home'. This implies that it is the natural role of women to care for family members (and others), while men carry on with economic matters. Thus caring in its widest sense becomes the prerogative of woman. This ideology of the caring women underpinned many of the ideas in the 1989 Griffiths Report and the subsequent **NHS and Community Care Act 1990**. This assumed that the majority of caring would be carried out at home and by women. Under the terms of this Act, mental hospitals and long-term hospital wards for older people were closed down, and people decanted into the community where – it was claimed – they would find better levels of care. But, in fact, for many the family became the care providers, and within the family the women.

Lone parenthood: an area of ideological dispute

'Single parenthood has become a central political issue here and in the US ... There is a fundamental division of views about single parenthood, morality and the state. We can divide the camps into the "moral re-armers" and the "responders". The first see it as the state's duty to reassert the role of the traditional family and penalise those who transgress. The state is making things works by accepting and supporting these lifestyle changes. Others say the world has changed, and the risk of single parenthood is so great that meeting that risk is one job of a welfare state. We have a fundamental conflict here. It is no use blaming politicians or the Child Support Agency.'

(Glennerster, 1998)

The New Right and the lone-parent family

As we saw earlier, lone parenthood has arguably been the single greatest change in the structure of the family in recent times. This change has coincided with a resurgence of new right-wing political views in the early 1980s in the USA, which were closely linked with the right-wing administration of Ronald Reagan.

New Right thinking sought to lower government spending and government 'interference' in general as much as possible, but also it wanted to reconstruct traditional values and institutions such as the family, so that it could take back many of its functions. This would, it argued, cut taxes and help recreate a sense of 'community' that had been lost by the excessive emphasis on individual satisfaction and individual rights in contemporary US and British societies. This clearly involved bringing the family centre-stage.

Writers such as Charles Murray (1990), amongst others, began to argue that, by having state funding of lone mothers, any responsibility for the welfare of the mother – and for the child – was removed from the father. This, he argued, encouraged young men to act irresponsibly. In particular, as there was no incentive for the male to work – he was less likely to seek employment – because he too would be eligible for state benefits. The lack of a father figure within the home, and the example given by adult males in refusing to take on their responsibilities, were helping to

shape the attitudes of a new generation – which were likely to be anti-work and reliant on state welfare, often supplemented by crime. According to Murray, this helped in the creation of an 'underclass' in US cities, consisting of people who were reliant upon welfare. Children from lone-parent families were also shown to have higher levels of criminality and truancy – and, indeed, most other social problems. For the New Right, therefore, the answer to many social problems was to attack the lone mother and her family – as well as the absent fathers – because these social problems were caused by lone parenthood. The answer was to force absent fathers into taking responsibility for their children, and to show them that there were costs involved in parenting.

These views reached Britain in the mid-1980s, and immediately provided moral and academic support for the government's desire to cut social security spending. In 1982/3, the costs of lone-parent family benefits were £1.4 billion, and were set to rise to £7.1 billion by 1992/3. The New Right analysts (see Dennis, 1993) took over many of the US arguments and suggested that much of the cause of inner-city disturbances and high crime rates could be attributed to the growth in lone motherhood. In particular, they attacked the fact that different categories of lone mothers were treated equally. For them, there was a moral distinction between widows at one extreme, divorced women in the middle and 'single mothers' at the other extreme. They argued that the concept of *deserving* and *undeserving* was appropriate here and that different benefit levels ought to apply. This argument influenced the Conservative government, so that in 1995 it phased out 'premiums' or special higher rates of benefit for lone parents. A further result of the right-wing argument was the passing of the **Child Support Act 1991** (see p. 205). The Act introduced the Child Support Agency, whose job it was to track down fathers of lone parents, and ensure that they contributed to the costs of the upkeep of their child. At the time the Act was passed, four out of five lone mothers received no maintenance from the fathers of the children. Therefore, the aim was to 'attack' both mothers and fathers through benefits, so that they were forced to realise the costs of their actions.

Feminist approaches to the lone-parent family

Feminist and liberal writers responded by pointing out that there was actually no evidence to support the causal link made between lone-parent families and crime, truancy and the growth of an underclass with a set of values stressing dependency on the state. An equally strong case could be made that these problems were caused by poverty and social exclusion, rather than lone parenthood. There was also no evidence that the people identified by Dennis (1993) in the UK actually had values that differed significantly from those of the majority of the population.

Second, according to Jane Millar and Jonathon Bradshaw (1987), the majority of lone mothers (92%) claimed not to have become pregnant deliberately. It would seem an unforgiving society that sought to punish them and their children by witholding state benefits.

Finally, feminist writers pointed out that for many young women, the lone-parent family was more likely to provide safety and security than the two-person household, given the rates of violence and abuse by men against women and children.

REVIEW POINTS

- The family is the centre of much ideological debate. In particular, the views of the New Right and feminists are the most extreme.

- New Right commentators argue that the functions that the family has traditionally performed have been taken over by the state and by other specialist agencies. This has weakened the family.

- The effect of the weakened family is to undermine the bonds that hold society together. This has resulted in a decline in moral standards and an increase in crime.

- The feminist analysis opposes this, by arguing that the family is the place where women's oppression is based.

- Women have been put under the power of men through their lack of economic power, which is caused by the expectation that they will stay at home to look after children.

- Linked to their lack of economic power is the belief that it is the role of women to care for others. This includes not just children, but also the infirm and the old. Even female patterns of employment reflect this.

- For feminist writers, the new forms of the family reflect greater freedom for women.

- One example of their very different approaches is the lone-parent family.

- The New Right argue that this is a good example of how individual selfishness has helped to undermine traditional values and has placed an enormous burden on the taxpayer.

- Feminist writers reply that the lone-parent family represents the rejection by women of their dependency on men.

REVIEW ACTIVITIES

1 What specific concerns do the New Right have over the changes in the family?
2 What three key issues have feminists identified in their critique of the family?
3 Why do the feminist writers see the caring role in a negative light?
4 What is wrong, according to the New Right, with the state providing financial assistance to lone mothers?
5 What criticisms have been made of the New Right approach to lone parents?

Policy, ideology and the family

The complexity of the family has already been demonstrated in a previous section. A number of authors have suggested that the family is more of an *ideology* than anything else. Tied up with the structure of the family is a whole ideological baggage of values and ideas about what family life *ought* to be about.

In this section we will explore, first, the way in which family policy over time has *reflected* beliefs about what the family ought to be and, second, the way in which policy has actually *influenced* family life. Women (married and unmarried), fathers and children and lone mothers have been seen in different ways by policy-makers, and the results of their policies have had clear and very different impacts upon each of them.

We begin by looking at the assumptions about the family when the welfare state was being constructed in the 1940s, explore the implications of the policies for various members of the family, and then – using the same framework of analysis – move forward in time to examine other more recent policies.

Family policy and the Beveridge Report

As we have seen elsewhere in this book, the Beveridge Report (1942) led to the introduction of what we now call the welfare state. The main reforms included:

- **The National Health Service Act 1946**, which provided free and universal health care
- **The Family Allowances Act 1945**, which provided universal benefits for families with two or more children
- **The National Insurance Act 1946**, which provided a wide range of unemployment and sickness benefits
- **The Children Act 1948**, which gave local authorities the power to set up social work for children
- Allied to these was the **Education Act 1944**, which provided free secondary education for all children

Now, underlying all these reforms were a number of assumptions about the family. The first of these was that the family would be headed by a married couple, who would most probably stay together until one partner died. Therefore the adults could be treated as a unit. It was not necessary to think of the man and woman as possibly having separate lives. Therefore, pensions, tax and benefits could be based upon a married (for life) couple.

Second, there were clear gender roles within the family. Men worked full-time and were responsible for bringing home a 'family wage'. It was the role of the state to ensure that there was full employment to enable this.

Third, the role of the wife was to be a full-time mother and housewife. Employment for women was not considered essential, or desirable. This

ensured that children received care, as did the older generation. The role of the wife was strengthened by extremely influential academic research carried out at that time by John Bowlby (1953), who claimed that children suffered from a variety of behavioural problems if they were not cared for by their mothers.

State benefits – the example of National Insurance

Some of these assumptions about the family can be seen in the **National Insurance Scheme**, which was an attempt to guarantee a minimum standard of living for all British citizens. A weekly contribution towards an 'insurance stamp' would give the person the right to receive income-linked state benefits if they were sick, had suffered an industrial injury or had become unemployed, and would provide a pension on retirement. However, these benefits were aimed almost entirely at men, on the assumption that it was the man who was the main earner, and that it was up to him to provide for his family. As the Beveridge Report says:

> '... it [the state insurance scheme] should leave room and encouragement for voluntary action by each individual to provide more than a minimum for *himself* and *his* family.'
>
> (Beveridge, 1942; italics added)

This clearly demonstrates that the man was supposed to look after the family, and that the welfare of the women and children was based upon *his* employment and *his* health. When the national insurance system began, women were given a separate insurance class, on the argument that marriage was their main occupation, and that it was the role of women to 'ensure the adequate continuance of the British race and of British ideals in the world' (Beveridge, 1942).

The Beveridge Report contains other, similar statements: '[On marriage the woman] gains a legal right to maintenance by her husband' and 'During marriage most women will not be gainfully employed.'

This 'ideology of the family' had a crucial impact upon women's place in the benefit system. Under the 1946 Act, women did not receive National Insurance benefits. This was bad enough for married women who were caring for children. However, it was far worse for unmarried women or those in full-time informal caring, who did not receive a wage. These women were excluded from receipt of National Insurance (the higher level of benefit, obtained as a right) and were made to apply for National Assistance (today's Income Support), which offered much lower levels of benefit.

The report had little to say about lone mothers, either divorced or never married. These women were particularly hard hit and had to rely upon a range of means-tested benefits. As there was no government help with childcare, lone mothers were prevented from working full-time, and were therefore kept in poverty by their reliance upon the lowest levels of state benefits.

Taxation

Right up to the 1990s, taxation policies continued to benefit married couples through higher tax allowances. Furthermore, it was not until the mid-1970s that the tax allowance for children was replaced by specific child allowances. Tax allowances go into the pay packet of the main earner – usually the male – and, therefore, the amount that would be provided for the upkeep of the children was left to the discretion of the father, as the wage-earner. On the other hand, the child allowances that were eventually introduced were to be collected from Post Offices by mothers, on behalf of their children. This method of payment was intended to emphasise that the money was intended for the children. Evidence suggested that children were far more likely to receive the benefit if the mother was given the responsibility than if it was left to the father.

Deserving and undeserving families

The image of the nuclear family, which consisted of a heterosexual couple plus their dependent children, provided the norm against which benefits and state welfare policies were based from the late 1940s to the late 1970s. But by the 1980s, a rise in single-parent families and teenage pregnancies, and an increase in the divorce rate all demonstrated the inaccuracy of the image. Rather than welfare policies being modified to accommodate these changes, the emerging influence of the New Right (which we discussed in the previous section) began to push government policy in a different direction.

The New Right argued for much *greater targeting* of benefits for the 'genuinely' needy, to 'crack down' on the 'sponging' families and to help *normal* families to take back some of their

powers and responsibilities. A much more moral view of 'normal' and 'abnormal' families emerged at this time, with the result that government policies emphasised the need to 'crack down' on those who were abusing welfare. Dysfunctional and abnormal families therefore began to be *blamed* for social problems, rather than being seen as being *caused* by them:

> ... to a large extent poverty and unemployment and even the largely psychological condition of 'unemployability' are chiefly reflections of family deterioration ... Nothing is so destructive to all those male values as the growing ... recognition that when all is said and done [a man's] wife and children are better off without him.'
>
> (Gilder, 1982; quoted in Abbott and Wallace, 1992)

Policy at this time reinforced the role of the family in caring for its members, and tried to replace state services and benefits with support by family members. In the 1980 budget, for example – the first under the Conservative administration that had taken office in 1979 – child benefit was cut, along with some of the income-related National Insurance benefits we discussed earlier. The aim here was primarily to lower government spending, but linked to that was the desire to encourage the family to look after its own rather than the state having to 'interfere'. This move back to the 'caring family' appears later, in the 1990 community care legislation, which we look at below.

A series of reforms passed in the **Social Security Act 1986** attempted to reconstruct a 'responsible' family that looked after its own. Changes in Income Support, Family Credit and maternity benefits under the various Conservative governments all limited state responsibility, and were designed to encourage – or even force – families to be responsible for the well-being of their members. An example of this is the cutting of benefits for 16- and 17-year-olds, who were then made to be reliant upon their parents rather than on the state. The targeting of maternity benefits to the less well off and the freezing of child benefits (a universal benefit paid to all parents) once again carried the message that the state should not be providing where the family is able to do so. State funds would only be targeted at the poorest.

Community care

The **NHS and Community Care Act 1990** was very much based on the belief that the family had to take responsibility for 'its own'. The Act included provisions for closing long-stay care institutions, and wherever possible providing support at home for the ill or disabled person. This aim was supported by all political parties and most academic commentators, but there was a sting in the tail. The funding was not available to give adequate support at home for all of these people and, as a result, their families were expected to provide the care that the state had previously provided. And, of course, it was not generally the families, but the women in the families who ended up providing the majority of the care. Writing at the time, Janet Finch (1989) commented that the belief in the decline in the family and its failure to help its members:

'produces a commitment to "support the family" to enable it to care for its members better, a commitment characteristic of all recent governments of whatever political party. It has found its most obvious expression in the development of policies for the so-called community care of various groups, which actually means that female relatives carry the major burden, with limited support – if any – from outside the family.'

The Child Support Agency

The Child Support Agency (CSA) was set up in 1993, as a result of the **Child Support Act 1991**. The idea behind the Act was that too many lone-parent families were being funded by the state, while no financial support was being provided by the father. This had resulted in about 75% of lone parents living on Income Support. Each year, about 900 000 single parents received funding by the Department of Social Security, because they received inadequate or no maintenance payments from the absent parent. By looking back at our comments on the 'ideology of the family', you can see that the belief that the father had a duty to look after his children had remained relatively intact from as far back as the Beveridge Report. Furthermore, the Act clearly reflected the view that lone-parent families were a 'problem' for society, in that they were a financial burden on the state. They also represented a 'moral' burden,

in that it was believed that – for many young people – lone parenthood was becoming a normal way of life, one that allowed women to live off state benefits, permitted the fathers to 'drift' on to a new relationship at no cost to themselves, and also ensured that the normal values of society were not passed on to their children. This was supported with a range of surveys that showed higher rates of school failure, higher levels of truancy and greater involvement in anti-social behaviour by children from lone-parent families.

The previous system of child maintenance had been fairly flexible. It had been based upon the absent parent contributing amounts as set out by the courts, or agreed between the two estranged parents. The new system was assessed using a single, set formula. Maintenance was to be assessed, collected and enforced by the CSA. Mothers who refused to give information about the father of the children could be subject to loss of benefits. When the money was collected and distributed by the Agency, the amount of benefits was reduced by exactly the same amount. This shows that the Agency was not interested in improving the lot of the children and the lone parent but, instead, was engaged in saving the taxpayer's money and enforcing the moral policy that the traditional family was better. By 1995, faced with critical reviews by both parents who were clients of the Agency and by MPs who had scrutinised its activities, the operation of the Agency was amended, but greater changes were introduced in 1999. The criticisms included the following:

- there were huge delays in setting payment levels – this was taking a minimum of six months
- there was a failure to enforce – 90% of the CSA's time was spent working out payments, while only 10% was devoted to enforcement
- harm being done to children – only 250 000 children were benefiting, compared with the 1.8 million who should have
- there was no incentive for lone parents to co-operate, especially if a lone mother was frightened of the father, as the money collected went directly to the Treasury if the woman was on benefit

The 1999 changes included:

- a simplified formula for payments, that would allow the CSA to act with much greater speed

The negative side of the family

So far, we have looked at the way in which the family benefits both society and its own members. We have seen that it has modified its structure over time in ways that have allowed its members to benefit most from changes in wider economic and social structures.

We have also seen that many writers have been very concerned that recent changes in the family in particular, the development of the lone-parent family – have irreparably harmed society. The argument was that the family headed by a lone parent was one in which, amongst other social problems, poverty, crime and low educational attainment were much more common. The lack of a father figure in particular was seen as contributing to the decline of traditional values, and helping to undermine local communities. The underlying assumption of arguments such as these is that the nuclear family must be a good thing, and that alternatives – particularly lone-parent families – must be bad. However, as always in the social sciences, there are many writers who are very critical of this point of view. For these writers, the family has many negative elements and can actually be harmful to its members.

Domestic violence

'The home is, in fact, the most dangerous place in modern society. In statistical terms, a person of any age or of either sex is far more likely to be subject to physical attack in the home than on the street at night. One in four murders in the UK is committed by one family member against another.'

(Giddens, 1993)

Domestic violence refers to violence within the household, usually violence by the male partner against the female. The extent of domestic violence is not known for certain , but research by Jane Mooney (1993) suggested that as many as 10% of the women in her survey had undergone some form of serious physical attack. Mooney also claimed that, over their lifetimes, about 25% of the women in their survey had been subjected to some form of violence by family members. In Mooney's survey in Islington in the early 1990s, about 22% of victims reported the assaults to the police, although the latest British Crime Survey (1999) suggests that the overall figure of reporting

is now about 50%, a huge increase compared with the figure of 20% for the early 1980s. Despite this increase, many women do not report attacks because of fear, embarrassment or the belief that, in some way, they may be to blame for their partner's violence.

Policy responses to domestic violence

Over the past 15 years, there has been a sea change in attitudes by the police and the judiciary towards domestic violence. Studies in the 1980s (Pahl, 1985) showed that police officers were reluctant to view domestic violence in the same way as stranger violence. The family was regarded as a 'private place', in which activities were seen as being outside the domain of the law unless the actions were extreme. Therefore, quite considerable violence had to take place for the police to intervene. A further complication at that time was the high rate of withdrawal of complaints by female victims: the majority of women actually withdrew their complaints before prosecution took place. The feelings of guilt and partial blame that have been mentioned above prevented women from reporting violence, and were a major factor in the later withdrawal of complaints.

However, in the 1990s a number of initiatives took place which have changed both women's attitudes and the role of the police. The police introduced Domestic Violence Units, staffed by sympathetic officers whose role was to monitor, advise and support the victims of domestic violence and, where necessary, to ensure the arrest of the offenders. Police officers were also instructed to regard domestic violence in just the same way as other forms of violence.

These changes in policing practice were just one aspect of the new approach. Legal changes were also made. The **Family Law Act 1996** and the **Protection from Harassment Act 1997** contained provisions for excluding a violent partner from the home and giving powers for non-molestation orders. The **Crime and Youth Justice Act 1999** speeded up the prosecution process and gave witnesses protection from intimidation.

Support was also made available, via a 24-hour helpline and a grant of £1 million (in 1998) for victim support. Finally, there was additional funding for women's refuges – places where they could escape from male violence.

Explaining domestic violence

Three types of explanation have been suggested for domestic violence: individual, subcultural and feminist:

- *Individual explanations* are based on the idea that men who use violence against women have certain personality characteristics that make them different from most 'normal' men. For example, researchers have suggested that these men may well have suffered violence themselves, or have had other negative experiences in childhood . Others have pointed to the role of alcohol in violence. For example, Jan Pahl suggested that over half of her sample of violent husbands 'drank to excess' (Pahl, 1985).

- *Subcultural explanations* locate violence amongst poorer men, with fewer educational qualifications, who have been brought up with a belief in the use of violence as a normal way of resolving difficulties. This suggests that violence against women is part of a general use of violence in their dealings with others (Wolfgang and Ferracuti, 1967). However, there is some dispute about the accuracy of this, as a report by a House of Commons Select Committee on Domestic Violence has stated that violence in the home occurs in all social classes and social groups. In short, domestic violence is normal in the UK. Just to illustrate this, according to the British Crime Survey (1999), 43% of all violence against women is committed by their partners!

- *Feminist explanations*, as set out by writers such as Goldner *et al.* (1990) contend that there are a number of assumptions about the roles of males and females in relationships that can lead to violence in certain circumstances. Historically, they claim, men are viewed as being the dominant partners in relationships, whereas women should be subordinate. Men use a variety of techniques to maintain this domination, such as financial control, emotional control and – in some cases – violence.

Child abuse

Abuse against children takes four main forms – physical, emotional and sexual abuse, and neglect. Clearly they overlap, as any one type can accompany the others. The National Society for the Prevention of Cruelty to Children (NSPCC) has suggested that there may be as many as 1.5 million children in the UK who are suffering from one or more types of abuse. However, only about 220 000 children are on the 'at risk' register (a list of all children considered to be at risk of abuse) each year, which leaves a staggeringly high number of children who may have been harmed in some way by family members, and yet receive no support or help.

The protection of children from abuse and neglect can be traced back to the first prevention of cruelty act in 1889, which enabled children to be taken away from their parents and cared for under the Poor Law. Usually, children were housed in residential homes for their protection. In 1948, local authorities were given the duty to take children into care if they should become orphaned, if their parents were unable to look after them, or if they were victims of abuse. However, it was not until 1952 that local authority 'child welfare departments' (the forerunners of social services departments) were required by law to investigate cases of possible abuse. Similarly, it was not until 1963 that they were required to work with families to prevent abuse. We can see, then, that although there has always been rhetoric about the importance of children and their safety, it is only in the relatively recent past that abuse has been taken seriously and responded to.

Paramountcy

It took the death of Maria Colwell in 1973, as the result of prolonged abuse (at the level of torture) by her stepfather, to bring the physical abuse of children to the direct attention of the public. The consequent outcry led to very greatly increased activity by social work departments. Partially as a result of this, **The Children Act 1989** was introduced. This was perhaps the most significant piece of legislation regarding children in the latter half of the 20th century. The Act laid out the responsibilities and rights of parents, local authorities and children themselves. The actual provisions are probably less important than the underlying principles, the main one of which – the principle of **paramountcy** – is that any decision taken must be in the interests of the child. Here, it is clear that children are finally being viewed as people in their own right, who should be able to make decisions in their individual interests, rather than having their parents or social services make decisions for them.

The Act enables children to initiate proceedings on their own behalf, and there have been well publicised cases of children seeking to 'divorce their parents'.

The social construction of abuse

It would appear that the response to abuse depends to some extent on how it is defined by society. David Archard argues that:

> What has been 'discovered' is a certain kind of abuse, and this has helped to determine the ways in which 'abuse' is defined, explained, and dealt with.
>
> (Archard, 1993)

Archard goes on to argue that in the 1960s and 1970s abuse was defined in terms of physical violence, but by the 1980s it had become much more likely to be defined in terms of sexual abuse as well. Yet what constitutes 'abuse' varies over time, with no fixed standard. The **Human Rights Act 1998**, for example, may well be interpreted as banning all physical punishment, including the slapping of children. In 1999, a Scottish sheriff's court ruled that a father used 'excessive' force when he slapped his daughter after she refused to be injected during a visit to a dentist. It seems clear that the use of physical punishment by parents – which was acceptable, within limits, until a relatively short time ago – is now under threat as it becomes defined and categorised as abuse. So, Archard's point about the nature of 'abuse' is demonstrated by this shift over time. However, a second point that Archard makes is that the definition of abuse is still very restricted, and by thinking in much wider terms about what harms children, other things can be defined as abuse. Therefore, it could be regarded as abuse that some children are allowed by society to be brought up in poverty, or with poor housing conditions, inadequate educational facilities and so on.

Sexual abuse

Janet Hadley (1987) suggests that 'four million adults in Britain have experienced some form of sexual abuse as children', but – quite frankly – the true figure is not known. The majority of sexual abuse is carried out by male relatives or family friends, although about 30% of abuse is believed to be by those aged under 21.

Explanations for sexual abuse of children are generally based on psychological theories that suggest that the adult may have had poor socialisation in childhood, which makes it difficult for him to engage in an adult sexual relationship, or that he may have himself been abused in childhood. Feminist writers have pointed out that there are close similarities between this and the sexual abuse of women by men, in that both relate to the need of males to control and dominate others.

The numbers of those abused have increased significantly from the late 1980s up to the present day. The reason for this is not necessarily that there is an increase in the numbers of young people being abused, but that there is a greater awareness of this abuse amongst children and adults, and acts that would previously have been hidden are more likely to be reported.

In the 1980s, when cases of sexual abuse of children were beginning to be reported, the response from the public was largely sceptical. People found it hard to believe that sexual abuse existed on so large a scale as social services departments and hospitals claimed. Indeed, in 1987, when doctors diagnosed 121 cases of sexual abuse amongst children brought into the Accident and Emergency Unit of Cleveland General Hospital, the public responded by criticising the social services staff and the doctors rather than the families. In an official inquiry into the occurrence, the judge criticised the social workers for 'excessive zeal and over-confidence'. Since then, however, sexual abuse has gained a much higher profile amongst both the public and social work departments.

Abuse of older people

Life expectancy at birth has risen from 45.5 years for men and 49 years for women in 1901 to 75 years and 80 years respectively in 2000 (*Social Trends 29*, 1999), and with it has emerged a range of new problems not faced by previous generations. Although older people are fitter than ever before, there is also a higher proportion of older people who need care. Despite much publicity, the role of the state is still only marginal, as the majority of older people are cared for by (female) relatives. It is estimated that there are currently about 6.8 million carers in total, who spend more than 20 hours each week caring for relatives, while about 1 million carers contribute over 45 hours each week. If the state had to bear the cost, it would face a bill in the region of £28 billion. In the UK today, approximately 25% of single women aged over 80 live with one of their children (*Social Trends* 17, 1987). For many carers, the result is disastrous:

> 'Caring has made me a physical and mental wreck, totally unable to relax and without a clue how to even try to think of myself'
>
> (Pitkeathley, 1989, quoting the words of an interviewee)

One of the outcomes of this pressure has been an increase in abuse of older people. This can take a wide range of forms. According to Frank Glendenning (1993), it can include not only the obvious act of physical violence, but also the withholding of care or medicine, psychological abuse such as threats, fear and isolation, the extensive use of drugs to sedate the older person and even theft of the older person's property.

REVIEW POINTS

◎ The family has been portrayed, particularly by right-wing commentators, as a place of affection and care. However, it has become increasingly apparent that the family is also a place of harm.

◎ Violence against women by partners or ex-partners is extremely common, and exists across all social groups. Only recently have higher levels of violence become apparent, as women were previously often too frightened to report it.

◎ The development of legislation and the changing attitudes of the police have gradually improved the provision of places of safety, and the possibility of obtaining a legal order to exclude the violent partner from the household.

◎ Abuse is not limited to women, but is also common against children and older people.

REVIEW ACTIVITIES

1 What is meant by domestic violence?
2 How does it challenge New Right conceptions of the family and their policies?
3 What explanations have feminists provided for domestic violence?
4 What is the principle of **paramountcy**? How does it influence the way in which decisions on families are made?
5 Why is the term 'abuse' still a matter of great debate? How might this impact on policy?
6 What explanations have been offered for the abuse of older people? Therefore, what could be done to combat this abuse?

Changing family roles

In the same way that the structure of the family has altered over time and become more diversified, so the relationships and roles of family members have altered too. In this section, we will examine the changes in the roles of men, women and children, as well as exploring the changing role of grandparents.

As we saw in the earlier section on changes in the family, the extended family that developed out of industrialisation had clear gender roles. These were graphically described by Michael Young and Peter Willmott, in their studies of family life amongst white, working-class people in the 1950s (Young and Willmott, 1962). There was a clear division of labour between the parents,

with the mother having responsibility for the 'caring' activities as well as for all housework. The male role was primarily that of the breadwinner, who remained at a slight distance from the children and was a figure of authority. According to John and Elizabeth Newson (1976), who conducted studies in Nottingham at a slightly later date, parenting was generally strict, and physical punishment for children who misbehaved was common amongst working-class families. In these same families, grandparents – or at least grandmothers – provided very important childcare help, as well as retaining a role in keeping the wider kin network together.

Studies of middle-class family life showed

some degree of similarity. In the second half of the 20th century, the roles of husband and wife were still largely 'segregated' into those of providers and carers, respectively, although the very sharp division noted in working-class homes was less evident. As the family was more mobile, the help offered by grandparents tended to be more financial than direct.

In both middle- and working-class families, most studies indicated that power was largely held by men, and that most major decisions – particularly regarding finance – were made by men.

As we will see later, these images – of male breadwinner, and female carer with dependent children – had a very strong influence on the health, welfare and social security provision of the welfare state. It was assumed that the role of men was to look after their families: therefore National Insurance benefits were targeted at supporting men in full-time employment. It was assumed that women were carers, and that the role of social services and the health service was to step in only when this 'natural' caring arrangement broke down.

However, the picture that we have described above was only a 'snapshot' of the family in the early to middle 20th century, and it failed to recognise the dynamic nature of family relationships. If we had stepped back 200 years to construct our picture of males and females, we would have found a very different – probably more equal – relationship. Similarly, as society moved towards the later part of the 20th century, family relationships altered. Whether the changes that we are about to explore are good or bad is not the key issue. It is more important to consider whether the health, welfare and social security systems have acknowledged these changes, and have responded by altering their services and benefits.

The discussion that follows is necessarily based primarily on white, 'Christian-tradition' families. The overwhelming bulk of research has been on these families, and so these will consequently provide us with most of the material for our review.

The role of women in the family

The most commonly noted change in the family has been the decline in male dominance – or **patriarchy**, as it is known. Traditionally, the man was the undisputed head of the family, with the woman playing a subservient role. However,

most studies have pointed to a shift towards greater equality between partners. There are several reasons for this move towards greater equality.

The decline in numbers of children

The average number of children in completed families is now 1.9, compared to double this figure in the earlier part of the 20th century. Therefore, the time that women spend in childbearing and child-raising has declined. Not only has the total time declined, but the 'spread' of time has also declined. Women now tend to have children at a later age, and complete childbearing within a shorter period. A typical woman will now have her first child at 28 years of age, and will leave a gap of two years between her first and second children. This shortening of the time spent bearing children allows women much greater opportunities for employment.

The increase in women working

Today, women form approximately half the workforce, and it is normal for women to be employed. Indeed, the expansion of the workforce in the past 20 years has largely been a result of increases in women working. This changing role of women has been recognised in related changes in the law and in welfare provision. The state now provides nursery education, assistance with child-minding costs for the lowest paid, maternity benefits, and legal rights to paid leave from work during pregnancy and in the period immediately after birth. The passing of equal rights legislation for wages and job opportunities has also benefited women, particularly the extension of legal rights associated with full-time employment to part-time workers, who are overwhelmingly female.

It is still important to remember that women's working patterns are quite distinctive from those of men. According to Brannen and Moss (1992), there are 'high levels of employment before child-birth and for older women whose children [are] at school or grown up, but low levels for women with "pre-school" children.'

Changing values

Neither employment nor the decline in the number of children can in themselves change the role of women. The crucial factor has been the changing attitudes of women themselves and of society in general. The critique of women's position in society in general, and in the family in particular, came from feminist writers who, first of all, pointed to the way in which decisions were made in the family (more important decisions made by men); how money was spent within households (less on women, more on men); and who had to undertake the bulk of the caring work for children, the sick or disabled and grandparents (women). Feminist writers began to challenge these assumptions, and argued that it was equally the role of males to engage in household tasks. By the 1970s some evidence of growing equality had begun to emerge. Michael Young and Peter Willmott claimed to have uncovered a new form of relationship between the spouses – the *symmetrical* family – in which males and females were more likely to co-operate in child care and household tasks (Young and Willmott, 1975).

But, even if we accept that there has been a move towards greater equality, we need to remember that there is considerable dispute over just how far towards equality the family has moved. The argument for the symmetrical family was based on a question posed by Young and Willmott, that asked how much the husband or partner 'helped' to undertake the household tasks. The term 'helped' still indicates an assumption that these tasks remain the primary responsibility of the female, and that a good partner is one who offers 'help' rather than 'shares' (Young and Willmott, 1975).

Despite considerable evidence that men now do share in child care and housework, more recent studies still suggest that gender roles continue to exist, with women having the ultimate responsibility for caring and housework, even if male partners now play a much more important role in the family.

The role of men in the family

Jon Bernardes (1997) has argued that, in most Western societies, when compared to motherhood, fatherhood is best described as a *status* rather than an *activity*. So the statement 'I am a father' indicates more the fact of having children, and possibly having the duty to ensure that they have sufficient income, than the primary responsibility to *care* for children.

In the 1980s and 1990s, the argument developed that a 'new man' was emerging, who was capable of caring for children and committed to sharing housework. However, according to Christine Delphy and Diana Leonard (1992), it remains a fact that the new man still expects the woman to have the *primary responsibility* for caring and housework – despite actively sharing it. This is reflected in society's values. For example, if a child attending school is dirty and unkempt, this is regarded by teachers and other parents as reflecting the failure of the *mother* to look after her child, rather than the failure of the *father*. In terms of social policy, these assumptions are reflected, for example, in opposition to paternity leave for fathers to look after young children, whereas maternity leave is available to all mothers.

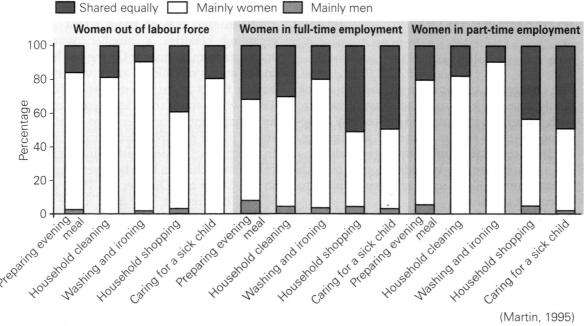

Division of labour by women's economic activity

(Martin, 1995)

and acceptance as full citizens is against disability being treated a medical issue or problem. Many social policy-makers and care professionals feel that they have a political, professional or ethical responsibility to identify and provide care services that meet the 'needs' of disabled people. However, the recipients of these services are increasingly complaining about and challenging the ways in which such professionals and policy-makers make them dependent on forms of welfare that effectively limit their lives. Debates about the consequences of welfare provision for disabled people are now putting disability issues, and the struggle of disabled people for full citizenship, higher up the social policy agenda.

Ideas about disability

At the outset, all of us – both the writer of this chapter and you, the readers – have some specific ideas about what 'disability' means. It is important to think of these ideas as starting points from which to develop an understanding of disability issues and their links to social policy, and to be prepared to question and revise them. Language and terminology are important in the 'disability' field. The way in which disabled people are seen and described is a sensitive and hotly contested issue. Language is important because, as we said earlier, language defines, or sets out, possibilities. The struggle over how to define disability – a theme that we will keep touching on throughout the chapter – is not just about finding the correct words. It is really a political struggle, an issue to do with how the meaning of the 'disability' words and ideas that we use empower or diminish the people that they refer to:

'I've been chronically ill for twelve years. Stroke. Paralysis. That's what I'm dealing with now. I've gone to rehab program after rehab program. I may be one of the most rehabilitated people on the face of the earth. I should be President. I've worked with a lot of people. I've seen many types and attitudes. People try very hard to help me do my best on my own. They understand the importance of self-sufficiency and so do I. They're positive and optimistic. I admire them for their perseverance. My body is broke but they still work very hard with it. They're very dedicated. I have nothing but respect for them. But I must say this: I have never, ever, met someone who sees me as a whole ...

'Can you understand this? Can you? No one sees me and helps me see myself as being complete, as is. No one really sees how that's true at the deepest level. Now I understand that this is what I've got to see for myself, my own wholeness. But when you're talking about what really hurts, and about what I'm really not getting from those who're trying to help me ... that's it: that feeling of not being seen as a whole.'

(Dass, Ram and Gorman, 1985: 27; quoted by Pardo, n.d.)

Disability is a term that has negative connotations in British society. Robert Drake (1999) suggests that it conjures up images of the 'paraphernalia of disability', such as wheelchairs, white sticks and charity boxes. Disabled people are often seen as a group who are in constant need of medical help. Social policy-makers have subscribed to this view for a long time. However, in the recent literature, and in the 'language' debate about the nature of disability, it is common to find a distinction being made between *impairment* and *disability*. These terms describe distinctly different dimensions of the human experience of disabled people.

The accompanying box may present the first challenge to your ideas about 'disability'. It is a commonly held view that a person's disability is the same thing as their impairment. Many disabled people, and an increasing number of care practitioners, would not agree. In fact, they'd disagree strongly, on the grounds that impairments involve physical or mental difference, and sometimes medical problems, whereas the causes of disability lie outside of the person and are social rather than medical. The idea that disability and

Impairment versus disability

An **impairment** is any loss or abnormality of psychological, physiological or anatomical structure or function. For example, a person who loses the use of a limb as the result of an accident could be said to have a physical impairment. A person who is born without the ability to hear will have a permanent hearing impairment.

By contrast, a person with an impairment is only **disabled** if his or her opportunities to participate equally in the normal life and activities of their community are restricted by the creation and maintenance of physical, social or attitudinal 'barriers'. For example, people who have physical impairments that prevent them from using their legs to walk may overcome their mobility problems by using wheelchairs. They are able to mobilise provided that the environment is suitable for wheelchairs. But in buildings that have no wheelchair access, stairs but not lifts, or door frames and corridors that are too narrow to manoeuvre a wheelchair in, they are disabled by the environment. It is physical, environmental barriers – not their physical impairments – that disable them.

An inaccessible environment will contribute to the disabled person's experience of feeling excluded

impairment are the same thing reflects what is known as the **medical model** approach to disability. This is described in more detail below. The alternative **social model** approach suggests that disability is widely experienced and suffered by people with various forms of impairment. However, people who prefer the social model of disability argue that it's not a person's impairment that causes them to be disabled but, rather, physical environments and social attitudes that refuse to accommodate or adapt to the individual's difference and particular needs.

Despite seeing them as whole and capable individuals, those who adopt the social model also refer to people who have various forms of impairment as **disabled people**. The term is used to acknowledge the regular, and sometimes continuous, experience that is endured by people who have some form of impairment – one of being excluded, frustrated and undermined by the physical environment and social attitudes of the world in which they live.

The medical model of disability

The medical model of disability was a very influential way of defining and explaining disability

throughout the 20th century. The acceptance by both social policy-makers and the general public of the medical approach to disability has had profound effects on the lives and opportunities of disabled people. We will explore some of the implications of the medical model in this and several other parts of the chapter. As well as being called the 'medical model', this approach to defining and understanding disability is also known as the 'personal tragedy' – and, conversely, the 'personal heroism' – approach.

The essence of the medical model is outlined and explained in Chapter 6 (see pp. 157–159). Just as medicine looks for evidence of health and illness in the biological functioning of the human body, the medical approach to disability primarily focuses on *abnormalities* in the structure and functioning of the human body. Medicine as a discipline represents human beings as biologically similar and predictable entities. Human beings are seen as having a specific and expected biological structure, physiological processes that operate in predictable and definite ways, and a level of intel-

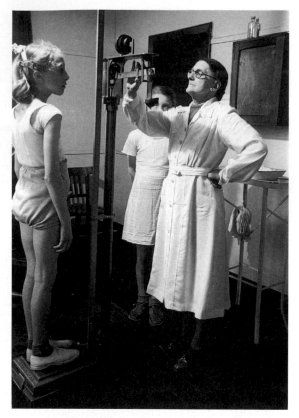

The medical approach to disability looks for abnormalities in the structure and functioning of the human body

lectual ability within an expected range. Implicit within the medical approach, then, is the idea of a 'normal' human being – someone who has all the expected parts and features, all of which operate in the expected way and within 'normal' ranges. By defining and constructing the idea of the 'normal' human being, and identifying people with physical or mental differences as being disabled *because of* their abnormal structure or functioning, the medical definition effectively locates disability *within* the individual. According to the medical model, having an impairment makes an individual disabled.

Medical explanations of disability are supported by 'science', especially the science of **genetics**. The **Human Genome Project** is a major, international scientific effort that has set out to map all of the genes in human DNA. Part of the project has involved the development of techniques to identify 'faulty' genes that cause disease and impairment. A wide range of tests is now available to identify whether a foetus has any unusual or 'undesirable' features. The medical model of disability is integral to this project. Drake (1999) argues that science 'geneticises' *difference*, and

explains physiological and cognitive impairment as a kind of fundamental 'abnormality'. In the new world of geneticised medicine, there is a danger is that different values may be associated with embryos, foetuses and whole people depending on their genetics and bodily make-up. As a result, the future direction of medicine is a source of concern to some disabled people. One reason for this is that *medical* definitions of disability are integral to much of the social policy (or lack of it) that affects the lives of disabled people.

Social models of disability

Social models of disablement locate the causes of disability in the physical and social environment rather than in the individual. In contrast to the medical model approach, social explanations do not see the individual as *possessing* a disability. 'Disability' is defined and explained, from a 'social' perspective, as being a *consequence* rather than the cause of *difference* between people. Those who are in some way physically or mentally different from the majority may have all kinds of potential skills and abilities. But these are often ignored, undermined or left undeveloped, because of the inability or unwillingness of the majority to accommodate diversity. In effect, such people are 'disabled' by the social and physical environment in which they live.

In the medical model, the onus is on the disabled person to adapt to society – not vice versa. The disabled person is encouraged to 'make the best' of his or her situation, and to accept his or her limitations. In the social model, the onus is reversed. Society is seen as having a responsibility to adapt to and accommodate the needs of people who have impairments. The social model does not see impairment as a 'personal tragedy', or disabled people as somehow lesser human beings than 'able-bodied' people. The social model places emphasis on social policy-makers, and requires that they do something about the disabling environments and attitudes that restrict the lives of people who have various forms of impairment.

REVIEW POINTS

◎ In the field of disability, language and terminology are hotly contested. The various ways of defining terms such as 'disability' result from differences in the personal, political and professional agendas of disability interest groups.

◎ Welfare and medical professionals have tended to see disability as resulting directly from individual physical, intellectual or sensory impairment.

◎ Alternatively, those who adopt a **social model** distinguish **disability** from **impairment**.

◎ In the social model, disability is seen as being caused by physical, social and attitudinal barriers in society, which have a 'dis-abling' effect on those with impairments.

◎ The term **disabled people** is used by disability activists to acknowledge and draw attention to the shared experience of disablement that is faced by those with impairments.

◎ The **medical model** of disability locates the causes of disablement in the individual. Impairments are seen as being the direct cause of disability.

◎ The medical model defines impairment/disability as abnormality, and draws on scientific theories of normal human anatomy and functioning to justify this view.

◎ The medical model of disability has been accepted and used by social policy-makers and welfare professionals since the beginning of the 20th century, to design and deliver policy and welfare solutions to the 'problem' of disability.

REVIEW ACTIVITIES

1 Why is the medical model of disability also known as the 'personal tragedy' model?

2 Explain, using a social model approach, the difference between impairment and disability.

3 Why is the way in which disability is defined so important to disabled people?

4 Explain why developments in the science of genetics are a cause of concern to some disabled people.

5 Using ideas from the social model approach, explain how the disablement of people with impairments could be reduced.

Understanding disability as a 'situated' phenomenon

Cross-cultural and historical evidence suggests that current Western perceptions, and the medical model approach to understanding disability, are historically and culturally **situated**. That is, the medically based perception of disability, which is widely held in Western society at the present time, is not simply a neutral, logical description of 'given', natural phenomenon.

Colin Barnes, Geof Mercer and Tom Shakespeare (1999) give a number of examples of archaeological evidence to support the claim that, in pre-industrial Britain and Europe, people with impairments were accepted, supported and integrated into social groups. Michael Oliver and Colin Barnes (1998) also cite examples of anthropological evidence from non-Western, traditional societies, to make the point that people with impairments are not always excluded from family and social groups, or seen as having less value than the non-impaired members of a social

community. Robert Drake (1999: 9) explains how present-day Western societies have constructed a particular view of 'disability' when he says that 'our understanding of, and everyday response to, phenomena such as "disability" or "poverty" is profoundly shaped by values and beliefs brought to general acceptance by powerful social groups and actors'.

In the previous section, we tried to make it clear that the individualised medical model currently provides the dominant explanation of disability that is accepted by powerful groups in British society, such as politicians and policy-makers. How did this happen if, as proponents of the social model argue, the medicalised concept of 'disability' is a social construction? In order to understand how social attitudes, and policy, towards disability and people with impairments have developed, it is necessary to 'situate' the development of attitudes to disability and impairment in an appropriate historical and social context.

Situating the development of 'disability': the historical and cultural context

> 'A sociological approach suggests that the common meanings associated with impairment and disability emerge out of specific social and cultural contexts.'
>
> (Barnes *et al.*, 1999: 14)

Ideas about disability are not fixed, or even similar, across cultures or history. Some cultures have no word for 'disability', and the way in which 'disability' and impairment has been perceived appears to have evolved over time. Social attitudes to disabled people can be identified as falling into three distinct phases (Finkelstein, 1981):

- ◎ pre-industrial integration
- ◎ 'segregation' under industrialisation
- ◎ equality of opportunity, or 'equal rights'

Pre-industrial Integration

Historical evidence about the existence and treatment of disabled people is sparse and difficult to interpret. There is archaeological evidence that people with impairments existed – surviving birth and subsequently not being put to death – as far back as the Neanderthal period, and that they formed part of social groups (see Oliver and Barnes, 1998: 25). This suggests that people with impairments were of value to their social groups, although it is impossible to use archaeological evidence to tell how prevalent impairment was. It was not until the 5th century BC, with the emergence of the **Hippocratic Oath**, that medicine was first differentiated from superstition and religion as a system of thought. Medicine gradually evolved into a way of diagnosing and treating physical and mental difference. Progress towards more enlightened thinking about impairment came to a halt during the so-called 'Dark Ages' (5th–10th centuries). Explanations about disabled people reverted to thinking that was founded on beliefs in spirits, demons and witchcraft. Nevertheless, during the Middle Ages (10th–15th centuries), people with impairments were provided for in informal, customary ways, without any special institutions being created.

In the pre-industrial period, British society was primarily based on small rural communities and agriculture was the main form of production (for more explanation, see p. 30). There was little specialist division of labour, and little or no requirement for individuals to seek employment away from their families. People with impairments were therefore likely to be absorbed into the family – or household – economy, where they would perform whatever tasks they could manage. During the pre-industrial phase, people with impairments were treated and thought of as being a part of their communities.

'Segregation' under industrialisation

The industrialisation of Britain occurred from the beginning of the 18th century, and had a profound effect on the structure and organisation of British society. This is outlined and discussed in more general terms in Chapter 2 (see pp. 30–33). For those with impairments, one of the key consequences of industrialisation was that production processes became more specialised, and an individual's level of skill and speed of work became important to potential employers. While the development of more complex occupational structures and competitive labour markets presented greater difficulties to those with impairments who wanted to find work, the pressure on their families was also increased when they were unable to do so. As families began to depend on large employers for work and became less self-sufficient, they were less likely to be able to absorb and support family members whose impairments made them less economically productive.

Michael Oliver and Colin Barnes (1998) identify industrialisation as a key factor in stimulating the separation, and gradual segregation, of people with impairments from their families and communities. The growing economic pressure on families, combined with a changing attitude to people with impairments as medical explanations grew in influence, stimulated the emergence of separate provision for disabled people. For example, early industrialisation saw the growth of large institutions such as hospitals, asylums and workhouses, in addition to factory-based production. These institutions were based on medicine, and on the creation of a system of identifying, assessing and defining a broad range of medically based disabilities.

Specialist institutions became the physical means of segregating people with impairments from their communities. The changes in attitude towards people with disabilities resulted from the growth in influence of medical 'expertise' about impairment, and enabled the enforcement of the 'personal tragedy' explanation in institutions. As a result, so-called 'sufferers' were seen as being incapable of caring for themselves, and as being in need of specialist forms of protection and care. Consequently, large-scale incarceration of disabled people on the basis of medical impairment rendered them socially inactive and largely invisible, and so prevented them from being responsible for their own actions.

The 20th century marked the beginning of new therapy and rehabilitation industries. A variety of professions developed that specialised in particular aspects of the 'needs' of disabled people. The 'needs' of people with impairments, as identified by the new disability professionals, became a rationale for the employment of a class of health and welfare professionals that developed rapidly in numbers. Arguably, the development of the medical and rehabilitation professions, using forms of 'specialist' medical knowledge and insight, has been instrumental in shaping social attitudes towards people with impairments.

It is now argued by supporters of the Disability Rights Movement, for example, that care professionals have to bear at least some of the blame for the 'disablement' of people with impairments. Acceptance of the medical model of disability by both these professionals and the general public has provided – and continues to provide – some justification for the exclusion of people who have a form of impairment from full participation in society as equal citizens. To some extent, people with impairments have been 'disabled' and segregated by specialised care services, and their opportunities for participation in mainstream society have thereby been reduced. The impact of care professionals and welfare services on the lives of disabled people is discussed in more detail later in this chapter, on pp. 236–240.

Equality of opportunity

The third, and latest, phase in the history of 'disability' involves a move by disabled people towards seeking equal rights, full citizenship and independent living in the community. This is also a new phase in terms of attitudinal changes by social policy-makers, welfare professionals and the general public towards impairment and 'disability'.

Disabled people have now organised themselves into effective lobbying and campaign groups

The present struggle for independent living, equal legal rights and protection from discrimination can be traced through the political lobbying and challenges of the Disability Rights Movement (see p. 239). Since the mid-1970s, disabled people have gradually organised themselves into effective lobbying and campaign groups. Disability organisations, such as Disabled People's International and the Disability Alliance, want policy-makers, and society in general, to see and treat disabled people as citizens with equal rights and protection from discrimination and segregation – not as clients of health and social services. Disabled people are seeking to be defined in terms of their skills, abilities and potential – not in terms of differences that result from their apparent impairments. This does not mean that the existence and effects of impairment should not be taken into account. However, disabled people do not wish to be defined simply in terms of being impaired.

The position of the Disability Rights Movement is straightforward – they want to ensure that disabled people have the opportunity to participate fully in society. The barriers to this are physical, attitudinal and political. However, the movement is now a powerful force in policy debates, because of the effective way in which its members have developed and applied the social model to redefine our general understanding of the causes and effects of 'disability'.

◎ Situating disability historically and culturally is a way of understanding how disability is a socially constructed concept. It is also a way of drawing attention to alternative possibilities for disabled people.

◎ Archaeological and anthropological evidence has been put forward to show that people with impairments have been perceived and treated in inclusive ways in earlier periods of history and in non-Western cultures.

◎ In Western societies, the concept of disability and the policy response to disabled people has evolved through a pre-industrial 'integration' phase, a segregation phase during industrialisation and then into the latest 'equal opportunities' phase.

◎ Industrialisation had a profound effect on the lives of people with impairments. It resulted in their exclusion from the workplace and their gradual separation from their families and communities. The policy response of the industrialisation period was to segregate disabled people in large, state-run institutions.

◎ The most recent phase in the perception of disability and the treatment of disabled people has involved a demand for rights and full citizenship, and the redefinition of disablement as a social process rather than a medical problem.

REVIEW ACTIVITIES

1 How does historical and anthropological evidence help to show that concepts of 'disability' are a culturally specific phenomenon?

2 What factors enabled people with impairments to be included in, rather than segregated from, their families and communities during the pre-industrial period?

3 How did industrialisation 'dis-able' people with impairments?

4 During industrialisation, which growing system of thought was applied to 'disability' in the new institutions that grew up to house people with impairments?

5 Identify and explain what disabled people are seeking from policy-makers, welfare professionals and society as a whole in the new 'equality of opportunity' phase.

Who are disabled people?

In the previous sections of this chapter, we've tried to make it clear that there are a number of ways of thinking about 'disability', and that definitions are contested and seen as problematic, especially by disabled people. One of the things implied by our discussion is that there is an identifiable group of disabled people 'out there' in society. To what extent is this true? Academics, writers and campaigners who focus on disability issues, especially those who are disabled people themselves, frequently make the point that disabled people are a very diverse population and shouldn't necessarily be thought of as a discrete social group. Disability activists reject the idea that impairment is the same thing as 'disability', and also make the point that while a broad range of impairments exist, they are experienced in unique ways. Not everybody is disabled by their apparent impairment. Taking this into account, it's clear that we need to think critically about the assumptions of, and be wary about, figures that claim to be accurate indicators of the prevalence of disability.

Policy-makers and population figures

Politicians often present carefully chosen statistics to support their social policy ideas

Statistics are a common feature of social policy literature, and appear to be something that social policy-makers are keen on producing and using.

One reason why government policy-makers like to quantify the problems that they perceive is that they want to know how much specific policy interventions might cost in financial terms. If, for example, it was proposed that all adults who were wheelchair users should be given a pass that allowed them to use public transport for free, the costing of the policy would need to be based on an estimate of how many adults are wheelchair users.

Oliver and Barnes (1998) identify the 1851 Census as the first of several attempts to gather statistics about disabled people. Legislation such as the **Disabled Persons (Employment) Act 1944** and the **Chronically Sick and Disabled Persons Act 1970** has also required registers of disabled people to be kept. Government surveys on the prevalence of disability that were carried out by the Office of Population, Censuses and Surveys (now called the Office for National Statistics), in the mid-1980s are the most recent attempt to produce official statistical information on the prevalence of 'disability' (see Table 8.1). The study revealed that there were 6.2 million disabled adults in the British population (note that the figures do not include children).

More recent figures have been compiled by aggregating (bringing together) the official

Table 8.1 Estimates of the numbers of disabled adults in Great Britain by age and severity category, for men and women (thousands), 1988[1]

Severity category	Men				Women				Total population
	16–59	60–74	75 +	All	16–59	60–74	75 +	All	
10	23	17	24	64	22	18	105	146	(210)
9	31	42	52	125	47	59	135	240	(365)
8	49	52	50	151	62	59	125	245	(396)
7	59	53	51	163	77	81	165	322	(485)
6	73	58	49	179	103	101	163	367	(546)
5	96	90	69	255	134	139	180	453	(708)
4	105	108	70	283	140	133	147	420	(703)
3	117	134	70	320	124	154	151	429	(746)
2	121	187	85	393	112	179	155	447	(840)
1	231	273	107	612	203	218	166	587	(1189)
Total	904	1104	627	2544	1023	1139	1494	3656	(6200)

[1] Figures do not always add across the columns because of rounding for each age group. 10 = highest severity.

(from Martin *et al.*, 1988; adapted by Barnes *et al.*, 1999: 24)

Disability protest and rights campaigns are reshaping the 'disability' thinking of welfare professionals and policy-makers, and thereby providing the 'conditions of possibility' for new policy developments regarding work and living arrangements. 'Independent living' for disabled people is a major focus of the Disability Rights Movement. As a policy goal, it is likely to redefine the problem of disability in ways that contrast with the medical rehabilitation model. Policy-makers are now beginning to listen to disability activists, and are starting to consider how they can promote the goals of citizenship and social inclusion.

The goal of citizenship

A **citizen** is 'a member of a state or nation' (*Collins Dictionary*). In political and policy terms, this definition is extended to mean a person who is 'able to take part in decisions that create or recreate the contours of a society, and (is) able to participate in key functions such as work, leisure, political debate… .' (Drake, 1999: 41). People who do not enjoy full citizenship experience **social exclusion**. Because disabled people are currently unable to participate fully in social and economic activity, changes are needed to remove physical and attitudinal barriers and strengthen their legal rights. Disablist prejudice and unfair discrimination must be challenged and eradicated before inclusion can be achieved. Only social policies that challenge these barriers to inclusion are likely to bring about full citizenship.

There is still some way to go to achieve full citizenship for all disabled people. Where governments have developed policies to address the deprivation and disadvantage experienced by disabled people, they have tended to involve professionals identifying individual 'needs', coupled with a strategy to persuade members of society to remove disabling barriers and change restrictive environments. While rights and anti-discrimination measures are now on the political and policy agenda, the policy outcomes that disabled people seek (equal citizenship and self-determination) are likely to require the support of strong legislation and a significant change in attitudes. Disability is no longer an issue of managed care. It has now become one of civil rights.

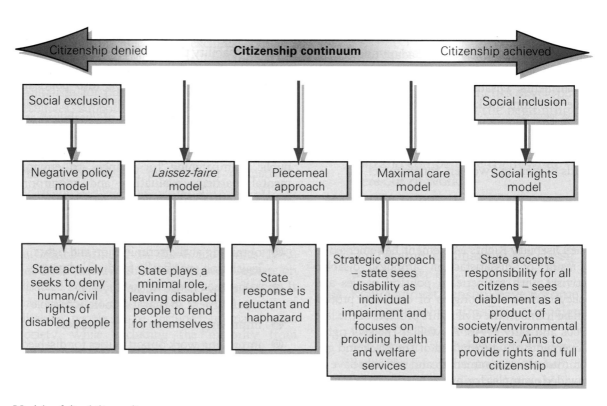

Models of disability policy

◎ The Disability Rights Movement emerged in the late 1960s and early 1970s, as a result of the dissatisfaction of disabled people with mainstream politics and policy-makers.

◎ The Disability Rights Movement has protested about disabled people's lack of power, influence and legal protection in UK society. The protests and campaigns for equality have provided opportunities for disabled people to organise themselves politically and to campaign for change on self-defined policy issues.

◎ The fundamental goals of the Disability Rights Movement are to achieve equal rights and full citizenship for all disabled people.

◎ The emergence of citizenship as the key policy goal for disabled people has forced social policy-makers and welfare professionals to redefine their understanding of the causes and consequences of disability.

◎ Disability is increasingly seen as having social causes, and as being a rights issue.

REVIEW ACTIVITIES

1 What factors stimulated the development of the Disability Rights Movement?
2 Name three changes that the Disability Rights Movement has campaigned for.
3 Which model of disability does the Disability Rights Movement use to inform its thinking and policy stance?
4 In what ways are disabled people denied full citizenship?
5 Explain what disability activists mean when they state that 'disability is now an issue of civil rights'.

References

Barnes, C., Mercer, G. and Shakespeare, T. (1999) *Exploring Disability – a Sociological Introduction*. Polity Press, Cambridge.

CSIE (1997) *Inclusive Education: a Framework for Change*. Centre for Studies on Inclusive Education, Bristol.

Dass, Ram and Gorman, P. (1985) *How Can I Help? Stories and Reflections on Service*. Alfred A. Knopf, New York.

Drake, R. F. (1999) *Understanding Disability Policies*. Macmillan, Basingstoke.

Finkelstein, V. (1981) Disability and the helper/helped relationship. An historical view. In: *Handicap in a Social World* (ed. Brechin, A., Liddiard, P. and Swain, J.). Hodder and Stoughton, London.

Martin, J., Meltzer, H. and Elliot, D. (1988) *OPCS Surveys of Disability in Great Britain: Report 1 – The Prevalence of Disability among Adults*. HMSO, London.

Nolan, P. (1993) *A History of Mental Health Nursing*. Stanley Thornes, Cheltenham.

Oliver, M. (1990) *The Politics of Disablement*. Macmillan, Basingstoke.

Oliver, M. (1998) Disabled people. In: *The Student's Companion to Social Policy* (ed. Alcock, P., Erskine, A. and May, M.). Blackwell, Oxford, pp. 257–262.

Oliver, M. and Barnes, C. (1998) *Disabled People and Social Policy – from Exclusion to Inclusion*. Longman, London.

Ramon, S. (1985) *Psychiatry in Britain – Meaning and Policy*. Croom Helm, London.

Warnock, Lady Mary (1978) *Report of the Committee of Enquiry into the Education of Handicapped Children and Young People*. HMSO, London.

Internet source

Pardo, P. (n.d.) *Portraits or Pity or Possibility? Images of People with a Disability from Around the World*. Canadian Centre on Disability Studies (CCDS), Online Electronic Texts: http://www.escape.ca/~ccds/article4.html

9 Crime and Penal Policy

By the end of this chapter you should be able to:

- Provide an overview of the main legal processes and institutions in the British criminal justice and penal systems.
- Discuss explanations for criminal behaviour.
- Evaluate the different methods used to obtain and construct crime statistics.
- Outline and explain the changing nature of policing.
- Evaluate the different forms of punishment given by the courts.
- Detail the relationship between sentencing and issues of race and gender.
- Describe and evaluate the role of the prison service.

In this chapter, we explore the criminal justice system of England and Wales. The role of a fair and honest criminal justice system is crucial in maintaining a democratic society. The starting point for citizenship is being treated equally under the law. Furthermore, a functioning criminal justice system helps to foster the sense of community and belonging that is necessary for a welfare system to exist. By believing that the law applies equally to all, and that the laws themselves are honest and just, members of society are prepared to put faith in that society and trust it to reward them. Societies in which members have little confidence in the law have great difficulty persuading citizens to pay taxes that are necessary to run the range of governmental functions – the foremost of which is spending on welfare and health.

The chapter begins with a discussion of the variations that have occurred in crime rates and the factors that have influenced these variations. Following on from this, we examine the victims of crime, and the changing views about who the victims are, and the role that they should play in the criminal justice system.

We then examine why people commit crime. But explanations of crime are of little use in the real world unless they can be turned into practical policies. We therefore explore the way in which these explanations are linked to policies.

Having explored explanations for crime,

we need to turn to the criminal justice system itself. There are three elements to be considered: policing, judging and punishing. Each of these areas is explored in turn.

The role of the police is to maintain law and order in society, and to do so in a just manner. In our examination of the culture and models of policing, we explore whether the ideal is also the reality. However, police forces cannot function unless they are managed well, and they cannot represent the rule of law unless they are democratically responsible. Both of these issues are examined. The courts have the unenviable job of judging alleged offenders and of sentencing them. This chapter investigates the nature of the judiciary and the role that they play in administering justice. We will pay particular attention to issues of gender and race.

Punishment in the United Kingdom usually takes two forms – custodial penalties (imprisonment) and community sentencing. Despite the increase in the use of community sentencing, British prisons have recently seen a huge increase in numbers. The currently accepted way of describing the prison service is that it is 'in crisis', with increasing numbers of inmates and restricted resources. We will look at the conditions within prisons and the steps being taken to improve them, including the introduction of privately owned and operated prisons. We will also explore the growth in community sentencing and its usefulness.

Crime statistics

Official statistics, which are fairly reliable from the late 19th century to the present day, show that crime levels remained relatively low from 1876 until the 1920s, and that a gradual increase in crime levels then followed until the late 1950s. From the late 1950s to the mid-1990s, crime levels rose at an increasingly sharp rate, but then they stabilised – even declining slightly in the very last years of the 20th century, before beginning to rise again.

In recent years, crime statistics have taken on a very great importance for the government in power. There are two reasons for this: one has to do with *symbolism* and the other with *policy*:

- *Symbolism*. Crime statistics have become a battleground for politicians, who wish to use them to prove to the public that they are 'winning the war' on crime. If the crime figures are decreasing, then the government claims that its policies are working. Similarly, if the figures are increasing, then the opposition attacks the government for its incompetence. Symbolically, then, low crime rates represent 'success'. Social surveys indicate that crime and personal safety are amongst the highest concerns of the electorate, and any government that failed to respond to these concerns would be committing electoral suicide.

- *Policy*. Statistics are also important to governments because, if collected accurately, they can point to areas of concern and indicate where resources ought to be directed. In the **Crime and Disorder Act 1998**, for example, local authorities and the police were required to collect statistics on local crime and disorder issues and, on the basis of these statistics, to devise strategies in order to combat crime.

As we shall see in the statistics that we discuss below, certain groups of people – usually the poorest and least powerful in society – have a particularly high chance of becoming victims. This contrasts with the stereotypical view that the rich are the main victims of crime.

The cost of crime

Not only is it important to look at the *extent* of crime, but we also need to consider the cost to society. Crime Concern – a charitable organisation that receives government funding – has authoritatively estimated that crime cost society approximately £25 billion each year in the mid-1990s. This figure was made up of:

- £9 billion government expenditure on the criminal justice system
- £1.6 billion on private security companies
- £1 billion in burglary losses
- £1.9 billion in losses from theft
- £500 million due to arson
- £500 million due to vandalism against local authority property (no estimates were made for private or commercial property)
- £10 billion (maximum) as the cost to British business due to credit card fraud, business fraud and computer-based crime

Counting crime

We have just seen how important it is for policy-makers to gauge crime accurately, but the measurement of crime is not as simple as it appears. Researchers are faced with many methodological problems, and so there is some dispute about the very best way of collecting information. The three methods that are most commonly used are as follows:

- *official statistics* – provided by the police and criminal justice agencies
- *victim surveys* – in which people are asked what crimes they have experienced being committed against them (the best known is the **British Crime Survey**)
- *self-report surveys* – in which people are asked what offences they have committed

The first two methods are generally regarded as the most reliable. This is mainly because they cover much larger numbers and draw upon more representative sample of people than the self-report surveys. However, virtually all studies on drug dependency make use of self-report studies.

The British Crime Survey, police statistics and self-report studies all have their strengths and weaknesses, as shown in Table 9.1.

Table 9.1 A comparison of crime statistics

The British Crime Survey	Police-recorded crime	Self-report study

• Collected since 1982
• Measures both reported and unreported crime. Not affected by changes in reporting, or changes in police recording rules or practices
• Survey conducted every two years
• Includes some offences that the police are not required to notify to the Home Office
• Based on estimates from a *sample* of the population, and therefore possibly subject to sampling error
• Because it is a national survey it has weaknesses in measuring crime at the local area level
• Does not include crimes against:
  – those under 16
  – commercial and public-sector establishments
  – those in institutions
• Does not provide a measure of:
  – victimless crimes (e.g. drug, alcohol misuse)
  – crimes where a victim is no longer available for interview
  – fraud
• Collects information on what happens in crime (e.g. when crimes occur, and effects in terms of injury and property loss)
• Provides information about how the risks of crime vary for different groups
	• Collected since 1857
	• Measures offences that are both reported to and recorded by the police, so they are influenced by changes in reporting behaviour and recording rules and practices
	• The police provide monthly crime returns, and the figures are published every six months
	• Only includes 'notifiable' offences which the police are required to notify to the Home Office for statistical purposes. So, some crimes omitted
	• Provides an indicator of the workload of the police
	• Provides data at the level of 43 police force areas
	• Includes crime against:
	  – those under 16
	  – commercial and public-sector establishments
	  – those living in institutions
	• Measures:
	  – victimless crimes
	  – murder and manslaughter
	  – fraud
	• Collects information about the number of arrests, who is arrested, the number of crimes detected, and by what method
	• Does not show which groups of the population are most at risk of victimisation
		Strengths:
		• Reveals hidden criminality
		• Gives backgrounds to offenders such as age, gender etc.
		• Gives information on 'victimless' crimes
		
		Disadvantages:
		• Respondents may lie
		• May exaggerate or minimise extent of criminality
		• Concerned usually with trivial crime as dependent upon population studied, which is usually young people

(based on page 2 of *British Crime Survey*, 1998, HMSO)

Patterns of offending

The majority of crimes are most easily classified as either *crimes against property* or *crimes of violence*, and in Table 9.2 we present a brief picture of the extent of crimes within each of these categories.

Crimes against property

According to the 1998 British Crime Survey, 62% of crime was accounted for by *theft* and 18% by *vandalism*. The government's response to property theft has mainly been to finance publicity campaigns that urge people to mark their property, to fit adequate locks to doors and windows, and to secure their garden sheds and outbuildings. The development of **neighbourhood watch schemes**, which now cover approximately 20 million people in the UK, has also been encouraged. These schemes, which were first set up in 1982, are coordinated by a local neighbourhood volunteer and are meant to provide an informal network of people who keep an eye on each other's property.

Table 9.2 The number of crimes estimated by the BCS in 1997[1]

	Number of crimes, in thousands
Vandalism (against vehicles and other private property)	2917
All property thefts	10134
Burglary (actual and attempted)	1639
Vehicle-related thefts (thefts of, from and attempts)	3483
Bicycle thefts	549
Other household thefts	2067
Other personal thefts (including stealth thefts)	2397
All violence	3381
Mugging (robbery and snatch thefts)	390
Wounding	714
Common assault	2276
All BCS crime	16437

(*British Crime Survey*, 1997)

Crimes of violence

All forms of violence account for approximately 20% of the crimes reported by the British Crime Survey in 1998. The majority of these acts of violence – about 68% – had only a very minor physical impact ('at most, slight bruising'). Only 714 000 acts of violence out of a total of 3 400 000 involved 'more than trivial injury'. A more interesting breakdown is provided by looking at the victims:

- *Acquaintance*. The most common pattern – which occurred in about 50% of cases – was where the victim and offender knew each other.

- *Domestic*. In about 28% of cases, the offender was a partner, ex-partner, household member or other relative.

- *Stranger violence*. this occurs in only about 22% of cases, which suggests that random violence is comparatively uncommon, compared to the majority of cases where the offender is known by or extremely close to the victim.

These figures on violence have led to a shift in police activity away from an emphasis on stranger violence and increasingly into neighbourhood and family violence. All police forces now have Domestic Violence Units that offer support and counselling to women who are subjected to violence.

REVIEW POINTS

- The level of crime that is perceived by the public does have a significant impact on confidence in the government and on the continuing existence of democracy. When crime is seen as 'out of control', demands are made for a restriction of civil liberties and the imposition of more authoritarian government.

- Crime statistics influence government policy on crime. Their importance is both symbolic and factual.

- Since crime statistics were first gathered 150 years ago, they have indicated an overall rise. The increase has been most rapid in the past 20 years, although more recently there has been some fluctuation.

- When 'reading' crime statistics, we must exercise caution, since – like all statistics – they reflect the methodology that was used to collect them.

- Despite this need for caution, we must realise that crime is a major problem to society, both in terms of the economic cost and in the distress and hurt caused.

◎ Attempts to measure crime accurately, so that sensible policy choices can be made, are based on the British Crime Survey, police statistics and self-report studies.

Victims of crime

According to the 1998 British Crime Survey, 35% of the adult population reported being a victim of a crime in that year:

◎ 5.6% of households had undergone a burglary or attempted burglary that year

◎ 15.7% had experienced a vehicle-related theft

◎ 4.7% had experienced violence during the year

However, these figures mask very great variations between groups and localities. The accompanying figure indicates the highest and lowest chances of being the victim of crime.

Repeat victimisation

Not only are victims more likely to be found amongst certain social groups than others, and in certain localities, but the chance of becoming a victim more than once – 'repeat victimisation' – also varies. Those who are most at risk of repeat victimisation are the victims of domestic violence, although younger people living in single-parent households, in social housing and in areas with 'high levels of physical disorder' are most at risk from other forms of repeat victimisation. Just to give an idea of the impact of repeat victimisation, in the 1998 British Crime Survey, 0.4% of all those interviewed had experienced 21.4% of all burglaries in the survey.

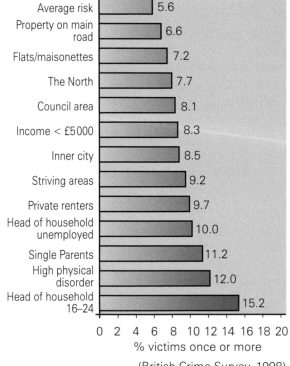

Category	% victims once or more
Average risk	5.6
Property on main road	6.6
Flats/maisonettes	7.2
The North	7.7
Council area	8.1
Income < £5000	8.3
Inner city	8.5
Striving areas	9.2
Private renters	9.7
Head of household unemployed	10.0
Single Parents	11.2
High physical disorder	12.0
Head of household 16–24	15.2

(British Crime Survey, 1998)

Households most at risk of burglary

Policy and victims

Traditionally, the victim played little or no *active* role in the criminal justice system. After reporting the offence, he or she was excluded completely from the process of trial and sentencing. The victim's own trauma was not considered to be of any relevance to the work of the system. It has taken a long time to acknowledge the rights of victims, and the emotional and economic consequences of offences. Nor was there any support from the police regarding fears that offenders might want to take revenge against those who had given evidence for the prosecution. In the UK, the banner of victims' rights was first taken up by the organisation Victim Support, which was founded in 1974, although it was not until 1987 that full funding was received from the Home Office. In 1990 a Victims' Charter that emphasised the rights of victims was published. However, the 1996 Victims' Charter, drawn up by the Home Office, truly represented a watershed with regard to the way in which the criminal justice system treated victims. The charter recognised the key work of Victim Support and required the probation service, amongst other agencies, to work with the organisation. Probation officers are now required to contact victims after serious offenders have been sentenced, to find out whether they wish to be informed and consulted about the conditions under which the offender is released. Pre-sentence reports (which are required by courts before a guilty person is sentenced) need to include some consideration of the position of the victim. The growing importance of victims in the criminal justice system is demonstrated by the provisions of the **Crime and Disorder Act 1998**, which has introduced the concept of reparation for young offenders.

The **Young Offenders and Criminal Evidence Act 1999** further strengthened the position of victims in the criminal justice system. This Act incorporates new rights for more vulnerable victims, including victims of sexual offences, child victims, those with learning difficulties and, finally, those who are at risk of intimidation. The provisions include giving evidence by video,

having someone to communicate on behalf of the victim and – in cases that involve sexual offences – limiting some of the powers of the defence to cross-examine. Overall, in the criminal justice system, there has been a move towards the idea of **restorative justice** – the belief that the offender ought to repay or compensate the victim for the offence committed.

REVIEW POINTS

◎ The chance of becoming a victim of crime is not random, but is affected by a number of factors that include age, place of residence and type of housing.

◎ A similar pattern holds for 'repeat victimisation' – some people and some households are more likely, compared to the majority, to become victims on more than one occasion.

◎ The ways in which victims have been responded to have changed over time, and there is a lively debate over the role of victims in the criminal justice system.

REVIEW ACTIVITIES

1 Are the chances of becoming a victim of crime simply random?
2 What is the significance of 'repeat victimisation'?
3 What is meant by **restorative justice**?
4 What changes in policy have taken place in order to take account of the role of victims?

Explanations for crime

There is a bewildering plethora of theories to explain crime, and it would take a whole textbook to cover them. However, we can shed some light on this by squeezing these competing explanations into a few broad categories:

◎ explanations centred on the individual
◎ explanations based on values and culture
◎ structural explanations, based on economic factors

Explanations centred on the individual

Theories that explain crime by reference to the individual usually search for reasons why those who commit crimes differ – either biologically or psychologically – from those who do not:

◎ *Biological explanations* are based on the idea that criminal behaviour is caused by some physical abnormality within the offender. A good example of this is the work of Price

(1966), for example, who claimed that males with *abnormal chromosomes* were more likely to commit crime.

◎ *Psychological explanations* are more likely to place greater emphasis on parental socialisation, although biological factors are also accepted as being important.

Implications for criminal justice policy

These biological and psychological explanations do not generally find much favour with policy-makers, except for their ability to explain the actions of a few particularly disturbed people, such as sex offenders or psychopaths.

Explanations based on values and culture

These approaches suggest that certain groups of people are likely to be socialised by their families, friends or neighbourhood groups into believing that it is acceptable to commit crime. That is, their values and culture predispose them to criminal activity. One study of 411 working-class males, begun over 30 years ago by Donald West and David Farrington (1970), found a close association between family background and criminality. The study found that fewer than 6% of the families in the survey accounted for more than 50% of all the criminal convictions of every family member of all 400 families included in the survey!

Other writers, such as Howard Parker (1974), argue that it is not so much the family as the neighbourhood values that are important. Therefore, young people living in certain areas are more likely to be socialised by their friends with values that support crime and disorder.

Implications for criminal justice policy

These theories based on values and culture have been extremely influential in policy terms, and much direct intervention work takes place on the premise that family background plays a key role in forming attitudes towards committal of crime. The Audit Commission (a government monitoring agency) in particular has been keen to urge governments to support approaches based on intervening with families. Examples of this sort of work include:

◎ interventions to help parents whose parenting techniques are inadequate

◎ interventions in schools, to support truants and offenders

◎ interventions with offenders, to help them to change their behaviour

◎ employment programmes

Structural explanations

Structural theories do not dismiss the importance of friendship groups or the family, but argue that both of these are dependent upon wider factors, such as the economy of the country or the nature of urban society.

According to environmental explanations, there needs to be a major re-shaping of housing and possibly urban planning; while theories based on economics point to tackling social exclusion. One particularly influential approach that is derived from this is **Left realism**. This approach argues that social inequality is one of the main causes of crime, and that it is important over the long term to combat poverty and inequality. But it also notes that those most likely to be victims live in the poorer areas of cities and have little faith in the police. So, alongside attempts to eradicate poverty and inequality, there need also to be other crime prevention strategies.

The policy implications of Left realism

The implications of this argument for policy are very significant, because they point to the need to make much wider – and possibly radical – changes in society before crime can truly be tackled. Thus policies to tackle social exclusion are at the top of the agenda for both local and central government, coupled with measures to ensure that those who live in areas with high crime rates can have greater faith in the police.

REVIEW POINTS

◎ Explanations of crime can be grouped into three broad groups that emphasise the individual, values and culture, and structural factors.

◎ These have very different implications for policy to combat crime. Individual factors generally imply some form of psychiatric help and/or punishment; values and cultural explanations suggest educational programmes; while structural explanations require significant government expenditure on employment and social reconstruction.

⊚ The most influential theoretical approach currently is Left realism, in which crime is linked to a broader range of policies to tackle social exclusion.

REVIEW ACTIVITIES

1 Explain what sorts of theories are to be found in the general category of explanations centred on the individual.

2 What implications can individual-focused theories have for policy?

3 How has the family been used to understand and explain offenders' actions?

4 Some criminologists have suggested that the values that a group shares may lead them to commit crimes and acts of violence and crime. Drawing upon the text you have read, give an example of a set of values that can do this.

5 Explain the term **Left realism**. Give an example of a policy that draws upon it.

Policing and police strategies

Policing and democracy in the United Kingdom

The importance of policing in a democratic society is often overlooked. The police force is the main authority through which the government can impose its will upon its own population (the army plays a similar role in foreign affairs). An undemocratic government could potentially use the police to maintain itself in power. Therefore, it has been regarded as crucial that the police maintain a degree of **autonomy** from central government. This has been done by making sure that there is no national police force that is directly accountable to the Home Office but, instead, a series of 'independent' police forces that are largely answerable to local police authorities, which in turn are partially controlled by democratically elected members of local authorities.

There are two further aspects:

⊚ *Impartiality*. The police need to enforce the law in a way that is **impartial**, so that all groups in the population can feel confident that the law is upheld in a way that ensures that all citizens are equal. The police have come under increasing criticism for their apparent oppression of ethnic minorities (more aggressive policing methods and higher arrest rates).

⊚ *Legitimacy*. The implications for democracy of the centralisation of policing and of biased policing practices are very important. As the representatives of the law and the state, if the police lose the confidence of the public and their **legitimacy**, then there may also be a loss of confidence in the political system itself.

The development of policing

Before 1829, there were no police forces as we now understand the term. In fact, policing as a concept was still vague and unclear. The roles that we expect of the police today (see below) were performed by a variety of people, such as watchmen, local 'constables' employed by parishes or boroughs, gamekeepers and even private guardians for the rich.

These arrangements were disturbed by the process of industrialisation and its associated urbanisation of British society (see p. 30). The older *ad hoc* arrangements were inadequate to cope with the increase in population and the greater complexity of urban life. An early private attempt at law enforcement was initiated at the end of the 18th century, in the form of the Bow Street Runners. But the modern policing began with the introduction of the Metropolitan Police in 1829, and by 1859 there were 239 police forces in England and Wales. However, the authority of the police was opposed by large sections of the working class – and even the middle class – throughout the 19th century and, according to Robert Reiner (1992), it was not until the end of the Second World War that the police became the established force that we know today.

The roles of the police

We can distinguish four main roles that the police undertake:

- ◎ *law enforcement* – investigating crimes, arresting suspects and advising the Crown Prosecution Service on prosecution of suspects
- ◎ *maintenance of order* – monitoring public gatherings and demonstrations
- ◎ *road traffic policing* – ensuring that traffic flows smoothly, and dealing with traffic accidents and disruption
- ◎ *a social role* – dealing with other accidents and emergencies, and giving advice

Note that a significant proportion of this does not involving investigating crime. Indeed, Rod Morgan and Tim Newburn (1997) found that 53% of calls to the police involved crimes, 20% involved social disorder, 18% had to do with information and a variety of services, and 8% concerned road traffic issues.

We should appreciate, therefore, that any discussion on policing must be seen in the context of the police as an organisation that *penetrates* British society. The police are probably the most diffused 'arm of the state' in the UK and can be said to play a major role in maintaining social cohesion. They also represent the state – 'symbolically' as well as practically.

Controlling the police

PACE

Concern about the way in which the prevailing culture within police forces was influencing the interrogation and arrest of suspects led in 1981 to a Royal Commission on Criminal Procedure, the findings of which formed the basis of the **Police and Criminal Evidence Act 1981** – or 'PACE', as it has become known. The Act both extended police powers and introduced a number of procedural safeguards. Although the Act extended police powers of arrest and stop and search, it also controlled these powers to a far greater extent than previously, and introduced the tape recording of interrogations. The significance of PACE only emerged much later, in the appeals and re-trials of a number of high-profile cases – particularly of convicted IRA 'terrorists' such as the Birmingham Six. It became clear that, in the desperate desire to appease public opinion and gain convictions against a group of unknown terrorists who had placed a bomb in a crowded pub in 1974, the police had fabricated evidence against innocent people. It is likely that the PACE regulations would have prevented this from happening.

The tape recording of interviews by the police, as opposed to the previous reliance on officers' written notes, is probably the best known innovation of PACE. The attempt here was to control bullying and harassment of suspects, and to prevent false confessions from being devised. The results of the tape recording process have changed the practice of interviewing, and this has been seen as being successful overall. On the other hand, research by Michael McConville, Andrew Sanders and Roger Leng (1991) has shown that officers were having informal 'chats' outside the interview room or at the scene of the offence, where no tape recording took place. Although the rules were revised in 1991, critics still argue that investigating officers can avoid them. On the other hand, the police have argued that they are hampered in their investigations by the PACE regulations, which are bureaucratic and supportive of offenders, particularly professional criminals. Partially as a result of police complaints, the **Criminal Justice and Public Order Act 1994** limited the rights of suspects to remain silent, and allowed courts to draw unfavourable inferences from their continuing silence.

The practice of 'stop and search' in the street was also protected by certain rules, with police officers having to note down each instance. This allowed monitoring to be carried out which might demonstrate that certain groups in the population were being stopped and searched more often than others – one of the most frequent complaints of young men from African Caribbean backgrounds. However, it would appear that police officers have subsequently found means of manipulating the statistics by 'agreeing' informal searches with suspects, thus avoiding the need to note them down.

Complaints against the police

PACE introduced the Police Complaints Authority, or PCA, which is an independent body that has the power to investigate any serious complaint against the police. Other complaints are routinely handled by the police themselves. However, police culture, with its emphasis on mutual support and suspicion of outsiders – even if they are other police officers, on secondment to the PCA – tends to frustrate PCA investigations, and it is rare that either the complainants or the officers are satisfied with the outcome.

Local accountability

The Police Act 1964 set up police authorities, composed of two-thirds councillors and one-third magistrates, who were required to oversee the running of the local police. Their powers included the appointment of the Chief Constable and if necessary, his or her retirement (a polite way of saying 'the sack'). The decisions of the police authorities were always subject to the approval of the Home Secretary and, crucially, 'operational independence' was given to Chief Constables, including the right to appoint all lower ranks. The result of this structure was that Chief Constables effectively had complete independence, since they could define all issues relating to policing as 'operational independence' and therefore ignore the police authority. During the 1980s, the resentment of democratically elected councillors in Labour-controlled local authorities in particular, boiled over. The police were perceived as being beyond local control, and the decisions as to which crimes to concentrate on, which areas should receive higher levels of policing and police attitudes to certain groups (gays, blacks, and so

The McPherson Report: police culture, racism and policy

On the evening of 22 April 1993, two young, black youths were waiting for a bus when they were approached by five young white men who stabbed one of them, Stephen Lawrence, to death. This was inexcusable, but the police response was almost beyond belief. On arriving at the scene, the police officers gave no medical help to Stephen Lawrence, and they treated the incidence with a considerable degree of disinterest. During the later investigation, the police ignored information given to them on the probable identity of the murderers, and consistently insulted the parents of the murdered young man through their attitude and conduct. The five who are presumed to be the murderers remain free today.

As a result of the persistence of Stephen Lawrence's parents, a judicial inquiry was set up in 1998, under Lord Justice McPherson, to investigate the police actions. His report accused the police of institutional racism, which he defined as

'the collective failure of an organisation to provide an appropriate and professional service to people because of their colour or ethnic origin. It can be seen or detected in processes, attitudes and behaviour which amount to discrimination through unwitting prejudice, ignorance, thoughtlessness and racist stereotyping which disadvantages minority ethnic people.'

Perhaps a simpler definition of **institutional racism** would be that it describes a situation in which the normal, everyday activities of police officers subconsciously incorporate racist thinking and actions. This does not necessarily mean that they deliberately express racist ideas, or that they consciously set out to 'pick on' black youths but, rather, that it is normal – *a part of the job* – to behave in such a way. This way of thinking and acting partially reflects the racism of British society in general, and partly what Simon Holdaway (1997) calls *routine policing*, which is derived from the necessity faced by police officers of making rapid decisions about their actions in situations of conflict or stress. In other words, in order to cope with their work, police officers learn – as a 'stock-in-trade' – the stereotyping of a wide range of groups in the population. These popular stereotypes include a belief in high rates of crime amongst young black youths.

The McPherson Report resulted in the Home Office instigating a vigorous campaign against racism in the police. Measures included each local force being allocated quotas for recruiting more police officers from the ethnic minorities and – just as important – retaining and promoting them. Furthermore, any police officer acting in a 'racist manner' will now face dismissal.

on) were all considered to be beyond the remit of local councillors.

In 1992, the Sheehy Inquiry was instituted to examine the rank structure, pay and conditions of service of the police. When it reported in 1993, it recommended significant changes to the pay levels, including performance-related pay for senior officers and the abolition of certain more senior ranks. Also, in 1993, a White Paper was published, which later formed the basis of the **Police and Magistrates' Courts Act 1994**.

Rather than tackling the lack of democratic accountability, the Act reflected concerns about poor management within the police. The accompanying diagram shows the current structure of the police authorities. The democratic element consists of the five 'local people', who are chosen by a very complex system to ensure a balance between local wishes and those of the Home Secretary. Management issues are more to the fore, with\the authority having to publish yearly plans, including its policing priorities for the year, and the availability and allocation of resources. Financially, the majority of the police budget comes from central government, but a proportion must be raised locally. However, the local policing priorities and the funding must be consistent with the priorities and guidelines laid down nationally by the Home Secretary.

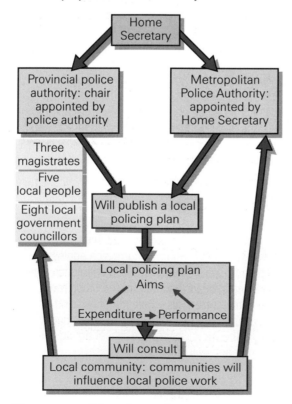

The structure of the police authorities

Styles of police work

If the police represent the state both physically and symbolically, then how they go about policing also gives us clues as to the way in which the state sees its citizens. Five models of police work have been distinguished:

- ◎ beat policing
- ◎ fire-brigade policing
- ◎ saturation, or military, policing
- ◎ community policing
- ◎ proactive policing

In practice, all of these are likely to occur, but there may be differences in the extent and support given to one model at the expense of the others.

Beat policing

The traditional method of policing, beat policing is often looked back on as the 'golden age' of police work, but police officers rarely came across law breakers, and were more symbolic than effective in combating crime. Beat policing was much disliked by police officers. However, although it was unlikely that offenders would be caught, the police officers had close links with members of the community, and the symbolic role may have helped to maintain the community's confidence in the police force.

Fire-brigade policing

This was introduced in the 1970s, as a reaction against traditional beat policing, which was regarded as inefficient. The widespread use of cars and individual mobile radios allowed police officers to react quickly to events, and to mobilise relatively large numbers of officers to attend any incident. This model of policing had a number of disadvantages compared to its predecessor, which had not been foreseen. In particular, it removed police officers from the community and isolated them – thus leading to the lack of information that brought about saturation policing. Second, police officers only ever arrived *after* an incident had taken place.

Saturation policing

This model is based on the principle that the local community is essentially hostile to the police, and that the only way to control the local population is use large numbers of police officers to stop people at random, in order to obtain information. This form of policing has been used successfully within very limited areas, such as a road noted for drug dealing or prostitution. However, when used on a wider scale, or routinely, against particular neighbourhoods, it has helped to cause anti-police riots by resentful communities, angered by the implication of blanket criminalisation. This form of policing was common in large urban areas in the 1980s, but was reduced during the 1990s.

Community policing

This approach was introduced as a response to the failure of saturation policing in the inner cities, and specifically as a result of the Scarman Report (1982), which followed the inner-city riots of 1981. Lord Scarman argued that since the police could not make much impact on law and order by themselves, the community must also be actively involved. Scarman argued for the active *consent*, *trust* and *participation* of the community in its policing. In order to achieve these aims, police forces were required to liaise with community organisations and local authorities, and support the victims of crime. This approach is associated with Left realism.

Proactive policing

This relatively new approach has been drawn from US experience. Traditionally, the police have *responded* to crime and have then sought to solve it. This model isolates a particular problem – burglary, for example – and then puts resources into obtaining intelligence on suspects. Then, in a series of specific, targeted arrests, the main perpetrators are arrested.

What factors influence changes in styles of policing?

- *Ideology* – the values of the government, and the role they perceive that the police should play. For example, the introduction of more military-style policing in the early 1980s reflected the views of the then Conservative government, which saw industrial unrest – such as the 1984 miners' strike – as a sign of political unrest. The crackdown on young males at this time, particularly those of African Caribbean origin, was also driven as much by fear of social disorder as much as by fear of criminal activity.

- *Social differentiation* – the belief that the various sections of the community are seen as needing different methods of policing, in order to maintain control. This is very closely linked to the previous point about ideology. The police have always operated differently against different sections of the community. According to Phil Scraton (1987), for example, the police have always adopted a more rigorous and confrontational style in working-class areas, where both the police and the government believe that the threat of crime is higher and the acceptance of police legitimacy is lower.

Table 9.3 The relationship between styles of policing and public attitudes: initial situation of high crime levels

Reactive policing	Consultation or community-driven policing
• Failing to consult public	• Police consult community
• Police create list of priorities to police	• Prioritise policing based on community wishes
• Loss of confidence by public in police and sense of 'distance' between them and the police	• Receive support of the majority of the public
• Police come to be seen as an outside 'oppressing' or insensitive force	• Receive information from community
• Lack of information coming to police	• Carefully targeted arrests
• Police forced into stop and search or 'swamp' methods of policing due to lack of information	• Support of the community allows police to create neighbourhood watch and other crime prevention initiatives
• Increases public's mistrust, increases resentment from those stopped	• Lower crime levels and better relationships between police and public
• Continuing high crime levels	

◎ *Technology* – the technological methods that are available to enforce control over the population. For example, the move away from beat policing reflected the greater availability of patrol cars. The shift to proactive policing has really only become possible through the use of surveillance technology.

The culture of policing

Although the police, like most other professions, would claim that the rules are applied fairly and honestly, the reality is that laws are generally only guidelines, which the police use as rules of thumb. When dealing with the public, police officers routinely use their discretion. This use of discretion is developed through a complex series of interactions with other police officers of similar rank, and with senior officers. The learning process begins when a new officer is taught the 'real world' of policing, and the informal *working rules* that all police officers follow. The culture teaches them appropriate attitudes towards the criminal justice system, provides explanations for criminality and how to deal with it, and also distinguishes between 'real' police work and 'rubbish', the latter consisting of the administrative work (Holdaway, 1983).

Fairly rapidly, officers learn how to distinguish criminal types from law-abiding people, and also to recognise what could be defined as a 'crime' (in the sense of something interesting), compared to a similar activity that can be ignored, because either the action or the offender is not worth bothering with. In order to bond new officers into the fraternity of the police, the officer is put through various tests and rites of passage, in order to see whether he – or, to a much lesser degree, she – is really 'one of them'. Because of working hours and public attitudes, police officers tend to become isolated by their job, and they develop a suspicion of the public, which serves to isolate them further. The job of policing is difficult, sometimes dangerous and, because of the particular nature of the work, susceptible to charges of impropriety. All of this strengthens the bonds between police officers, and reinforces the belief that they are separate from the public and have a particular role to ensure that justice is done, even if the rules (made by outsiders) place obstacles in their way. This culture is closely linked to the miscarriages of justice that have taken place, as the police have sought to ensure that the 'real' culprits are punished even if the procedural rules have to be ignored (Reiner, 1992).

REVIEW POINTS

◎ The police play an important role in maintaining democracy. However, this can only be done by a democratically accountable police force, which is regarded as 'legitimate' by the bulk of the population.

◎ Policing as we know it developed alongside the urbanisation of society.

◎ The police play a number of very different roles in society, including law enforcement, maintenance of order, road traffic policing and a social role.

◎ The police force has operated in a number of different ways, depending upon: the ideology of the government; the attitude of police officers to certain sections of the population, linked to the 'legitimacy' given to it by that population group; and the available technology.

◎ These approaches include beat policing, fire-brigade policing, saturation policing, community policing and proactive policing.

◎ Concern about policing methods and miscarriages of justice led to the PACE reforms.

◎ The problem of making police forces democratically accountable has led to a number of changes in the way they are controlled.

REVIEW ACTIVITIES

1 Explain why it is important that the police have 'legitimacy' in the eyes of the public.
2 What key elements of policing emerged in order to gain this legitimacy? Do you think that those principles still apply today?
3 Identify and explain any three 'styles of police work'. In your opinion, which is the more preferable?
4 What is PACE? What is it meant to ensure?
5 What is meant by 'police culture' and what are the implications for police activities?

The courts and the judiciary

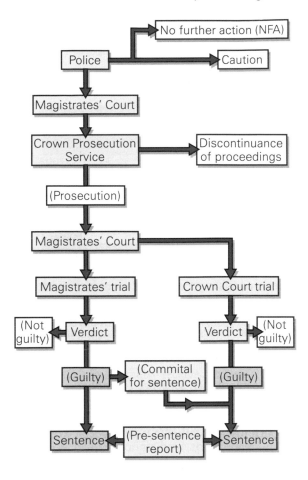

The criminal justice process

Arrest and committal

Once the police have decided that there is sufficient evidence to put a person on trial, they will do one of two things:

◎ Issue the person with a warning. This is an official warning delivered by a senior police officer. No punishment follows the caution, but it does go down as part of a criminal record. About 40% of all offenders are 'diverted' (from prosecution) through the use of warnings.

◎ Charge a suspected person with an offence. This information is then 'laid before' a magistrate, and at that point the prosecution is taken on by the **Crown Prosecution Service (CPS)**. The CPS is an independent agency that prosecutes defendants on behalf of the state.

The person who is charged may then be granted 'bail' (conditional release before the trial), or he or she may be remanded in custody.

Criminal offences are of three types:

◎ **Indictable**. These more serious crimes – for example, armed robbery or murder – are always tried in a **Crown Court**.

◎ **Summary**. These less serious offences – such as the majority of motoring offences – are always tried in a **Magistrates' Court**.

◎ **Triable either way**. These offences – such as burglary and theft – can fall into either category. The magistrate will decide whether the accused must stand trial in a Crown Court, or will offer the accused person a choice of Crown or Magistrates' Courts. As there are strict limits on the maximum sentence that the magistrates can apply, the majority of defendants – about 80% – of defendants opt for the Magistrates' Court.

Types of court

◎ *Magistrates' Court*. This consists of either three 'lay' magistrates or one 'stipendiary' magistrate. The maximum sentence of the court is six months' imprisonment or a fine of £5000. The court hears summary offences.

◎ *Crown Court*. This is presided over by a judge. Serious cases are dealt with, and guilt is determined by jury. The judge is able to impose the maximum penalties as allowed by the law.

The trial

In court, the defendant – or the *accused* – can plead guilty or not guilty. If he or she pleads not guilty, then it is the responsibility of the CPS to prove 'beyond reasonable doubt' that the defendant is guilty of the offence. In other words, it is not up to the defendant to prove his or her innocence: the defendant is presumed to be innocent until proven guilty. However, over 90% of defendants in Magistrates' Courts and 70% of men, while others receive more lenient sentences. Factors that influence judges and magistrates include the following:

- Different motivations are ascribed to offending women, ranging from hormonal abnormalities to marital problems. These explanations are rarely used or accepted for men.
- Judges are likely to distinguish between women by family responsibility, marital status and 'moral background'.

Legal aid

In 1998, the government published a consultation paper entitled *Access to Justice*, which provoked a bitter argument between the majority of the legal profession and the Lord Chancellor's Office. The debate concerned the introduction of strict controls over legal aid. First introduced in 1949, legal aid is the system of providing financial assistance to the less affluent in order to pay legal fees. The government argues that it needs to reform legal aid because it is now an outdated concept that actually hinders justice. The cost of legal aid in 1998 was £1477 million, and yet the number of cases taken has been declining year on year. The decline is caused by the fact that the means test for legal aid is pitched so low that only the poorest in society are funded. Because of the extremely high costs of law, this excludes the vast majority of less well off, or even middle-income, people from having recourse to law. Furthermore, the cases that receive legal aid may not be those that are the most serious, but simply those where the solicitor has a good chance of obtaining legal aid. The government argues, therefore, that 'good' cases are not funded because of the high costs to potential litigants, while weaker cases may be put forward simply because they are funded. At present, there is no way of stopping these weaker cases.

The proposals put forward by the government include the following:

- *Conditional fee arrangements* (better known as 'no win, no pay litigation'). In future, for the majority of cases, the solicitor must decide whether or not there is a decent chance of winning. If the case is won, then the solicitor will receive his or her costs, plus a proportion of any damages that the client wins. If the case is lost, then there is no fee. This puts pressure on the solicitor to make sure that the case is strong.

- *Contracting*. Only solicitors who have a contract with the new Legal Aid Board (see below) will have the right to claim legal aid for cases. The contracts will be won on quality and price agreements.
- *Legal Aid Board*. This will be a central government organisation to fund the contracted solicitors.
- *Community Legal Service*. This will vary from area to area, but will consist of a organisation that will provide 'effective mechanisms' to allow the socially excluded to enforce legal their rights over housing, welfare, consumer and employment issues.

Criticisms of the proposals

Critics of the new proposals have suggested that they will exclude large numbers of people from recourse to law, because solicitors will now only take on cases that they are bound to win. Those with a good chance – as opposed to near certainty – will be excluded from obtaining a solicitor.

Solicitors will lose a huge amount of income, and may have to recover this by putting up fees in other areas, thus making the use of their services prohibitive in general.

Critics argue that the idea of contracting was not successful in the National Health Service, so why – they ask – should it work in the law? The quality of work may well decline: the various solicitors' practices will have to compete for the contract, and therefore they may wish to lower their costs and perhaps the quality of their services.

REVIEW POINTS

- The police and the judiciary apply the law and criminal justice policy in dealing with people who are accused of committing criminal offences.
- An accused person can be given a formal warning by the police or charged with an offence.
- Once charged, the person will have to appear in court.
- The type of court that a person is tried in largely depends on the seriousness of his or her offence. Indictable offences are always tried in a Crown Court, before a judge and jury.

- Magistrate's Courts hear less serious cases and impose less severe punishments.

- Courts can impose custodial or non-custodial sentences. The first involves being detained in prison or a young offenders institution, while the second usually involves a form of fine, community service or tagging restriction.

- Research suggests that women and people from minority ethnic groups are treated differently to white male defendants by the courts, in terms of the severity of charges and sentences imposed on them. There is evidence that they are both discriminated against in some circumstances and treated more leniently in others.

- Many defendants in criminal cases rely on legal aid, or financial assistance, to pay their legal fees. There has been much recent debate about the adequacy and impact of legal aid on the criminal justice process. The government's policy is to impose limits on the extent of legal aid available through conditional fee arrangements.

REVIEW ACTIVITIES

1 Does a formal warning by the police lead to an individual having a criminal record?
2 Explain the difference between an indictable and a summary offence.
3 Is there evidence to support the belief that people from minority ethnic groups are unfairly discriminated against by the courts?
4 Explain how women tend to be treated differently by the courts when sentencing decisions are made.
5 What does the conditional fee arrangement involve?

Punishment

The role of the courts is to decide on guilt and to punish the guilty. But what is the aim of punishment? When a court sends someone to be punished, what is it trying to achieve? Surprisingly enough, there is considerable debate about this, and the answer is not at all clear! Criminologists have suggested five possible (and sometimes contradictory) aims:

- deterrence
- retribution
- rehabilitation
- incapacitation
- reparation

Deterrence

This refers to the approach to punishment that believes that it that it is possible to stop law-breakers repeating their actions and to make other potential criminals think twice before committing an illegal act, because the penalties will always outweigh the benefits.

There are three problems with deterrence. The first point concerns the level of punishment that is acceptable to society and appropriate to the crime. For example, in order to deter someone from parking on a double yellow line, it would be possible to introduce an extreme penalty – such as being burned to death! This might have a deterrent effect, but most people would regard it as unjust and extreme.

Second, the punishment is based on the idea that a 'rational person' weighs up the 'pros and cons' and then decides that committing the crime is to his or her benefit. But, in reality, crimes are often carried out on impulse. In these circumstances, deterrence would be unlikely to work.

Indeed, the question that needs to be asked is: Does deterrence work at all? The answer might be provided by the use of the death penalty. Capital punishment has been re-introduced in the USA and is 'routinely' used in China, yet – looking at the levels of murder and crime in these countries – there is no conclusive argument that the death penalty acts as a noticeable deterrent.

of people found guilty of offences actually declined during this period. Whereas, in 1992, one in six people found guilty of more serious (indictable) offences went to prison, by 1997 the figure was one in four.

Costs

Despite overcrowding and poor conditions, the costs of running prisons are enormous. In the late 1990s, prisons cost the government approximately £1.6 billion per year.

The sheer scale of the costs, allied to the increase in the numbers of people being sent to prison, has persuaded the last two governments to innovate. Two initiatives in particular have been followed – private prisons and electronic monitoring of offenders. Both of these options provide cheaper alternatives to state prisons.

Types of prisons

- *Dispersal* – for long-term prisoners, who are regarded as posing a security threat.
- *Local prisons* – for shorter-term prisoners.
- *Remand centres* – usually attached to larger prisons, where those awaiting trial are kept.
- *Open prisons* – for those nearing the ends of their sentences.
- *Young offenders institutions* – for those under 21.

Limiting numbers in prisons

In order to limit the growth in the prison population, four policies have been introduced:

- *Diversion*. Courts have been encouraged to keep offenders out of prison wherever possible and to impose community penalties. This is based on the belief that as many people as possible should be 'diverted' from prisons, which are no more effective in preventing minor crimes than community sanctions, yet cost much more.
- *Bifurcation*. Sometimes, a prison sentence is unavoidable. Where this is the case, those who have committed relatively less serious crimes are likely to receive shorter periods of incarceration than previously, but those who have committed more serious crimes or are repeat offenders are likely to receive even longer sentences. The result is that the prison population has become increasingly

segmented into two groups, with very different experiences of prison and attitudes towards it.

The result of these first two policies is that 40% of those given custodial sentences are serving four years or more, compared to only 12% in 1974.

- *Electronic monitoring*. Offenders are given an electronically controlled 'curfew' instead of a custodial sentence. We will discuss this later.
- *Parole*. Prisoners are released early in their sentence, and have to report regularly to a probation officer.

The purpose of prisons

When we explored the approaches to punishment (pp. 259–260), we saw that there is some debate over what the purpose of punishment is. Similarly, there is some debate over exactly what prisons set out to achieve.

Rehabilitation

From 1895 until 1979, the aim of the British prisons system was to 'encourage and assist [prisoners] to lead a good and useful life'. This has become known as the *rehabilitation model*. However, the very high rates of **recidivism** (people returning to crime after release) meant that by the 1970s this aim had been abandoned.

Positive custody and human warehousing

In 1979, the May Committee, which was set up to clarify the aims of prisons, recognised that prisons simply did not achieve the aim of rehabilitation, and proposed instead the aim of *positive custody*, which would 'preserve and promote prisoners' self-respect'.

This was supposed to take account realistically of what happened to prisoners, and was meant to avoid the alternative of simply storing offenders in buildings with no particular aim in mind – an approach known as *human warehousing*.

Managerialism

According to its critics, in the 1990s the prison service largely turned away from having a clear vision of what it was meant to achieve and, instead, followed a policy of *managerialism*. This meant that rather than having any clear purpose, the prison system merely set out to be efficient and economical in looking after inmates. It was

Table 9.4 The prison population by ethnic mix and gender, England and Wales, 30 June 1997. Prisons reflect the higher numbers of black people processed by the criminal justice system

Sex of prisoner	Total Number	%	White Number	%	Black[2] Number	%	South Asian[3] Number	%	Chinese and other[4] Number	%	Unrecorded Number	%
Males and females	61 467	100	50 000	81	7658	12	1920	3	1887	3	2	–
Males	58 795	100	47 966	82	7152	12	1895	3	1780	3	2	–
Females	2672	100	2034	76	506	19	25	1	107	4	–	–

[1] Prior to 1993, coding of ethnic origin was similar to that used in the EC Labour Force Survey. In 1993 a new ethnic classification system was adopted in prisons, which is congruent with that used for the Census of Population. The change in coding means that figures for 1992 and 1993–97 are not directly comparable.

[2] In 1992, ethnic origin classification was 'West Indian, Guyanese, African'. These categories comprise approximately 6% of the population of England & Wales.

[3] In 1992, ethnic origin classification was 'Indian, Pakistani, Bangladeshi'.

[4] In 1992, ethnic origin classification was 'Chinese, Arab, Mixed origin'.

(White and Woodbridge, 1998)

set targets by the government in terms of costs, quality of care and security of inmates, and had to meet them. Quite *why* was rarely discussed.

Inside prisons

Conditions

Until the mid-1990s, prison conditions were awful. They are still poor. Until 1996, the majority of prisoners had to 'slop out'; that is, there were no toilets in the cells and so prisoners had to use covered pails, which were then left all night. Prisoners normally have to share cells with one or two others. This may not seem a terrible hardship, but being locked in a room for 12 hours or more (in some local prisons, inmates can be expected to be locked up for 23 hours each day) can place an intolerable strain on some inmates. The suicide rate is seven times higher than in the outside community, with remand prisoners (those being held before trial) having a three times higher rate than prisoners as a whole. The suicide rate has risen consistently since the 1970s.

Apart from the poor physical conditions, the general quality of life that inmates experience can also be damaging. For example, in most prisons boredom is a major problem. Although there are regulations that limit maximum hours of work, there are no regulations that impose minimum hours, or that insist on the provision of suitable

work. Inmates may typically work for less than 20 hours a week, and the work that they do is extremely poorly paid, repetitive and uninteresting. This lack of money prevents them from saving for their release, or being able to provide anything for their families. Indeed, the lack of contact with family and friends remains a major complaint of prisoners. Limited visiting rights exist, but these are often disrupted by security measures and staffing shortages.

Prisons have a specified number of inmates that they are supposed to be able to take. This is known as the certified normal accommodation, or CNA. During the 1980s and early 1990s, prisons routinely exceeded their CNA, sometimes by up to 70%.

Discipline in prison

Because of their very purpose – that of holding people against their will – all prisons suffer problems of discipline and order. There need to be effective measures by which inmates can be kept under control. Historically, control was maintained by physical force – until 1962, flogging was used if it was regarded as necessary.

Long-term prisoners in dispersal prisons pose particularly high risks. Until the 1980s, 'MUFTI squads' – specially trained riot control squads – were used in extreme cases of indiscipline. However, after complaints about extreme violence they were disbanded, and now officers

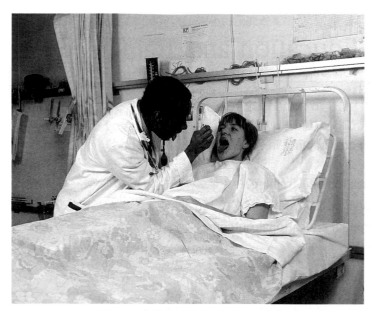

This doctor's professional skills rest upon academic knowledge and vocational expertise

practical tasks. Politicians like the word 'training' because it implies helping practitioners to work competently using tried and tested procedures. An educated person is a thinker and a trained person a doer, so to speak.

But can't they do both? Of course they can. Who wants to be taught by an educated teacher who knows the theory of teaching but is uninspiring in the classroom? Or what do we make of a teacher who has first-rate IT skills but doesn't understand how pupils learn? Ideally, we need teachers who possess theoretical knowledge that underpins and supports their classroom practice.

There is, however, a long-standing tradition in the UK, that the educated person is thought of as being somehow superior to the trained person. In part, this dates from the notion – identified by the German sociologist Max Weber – that the goal of a 'gentleman's' education is to cultivate rather than to impart practical know-how. The principle is exemplified in Bertrand Russell's quip that the gentleman doesn't use his hands except in war or when a duel advances a reputation. Such images seem outdated today, but they still endure in modified form.

The British habit of judging vocational education against an academic 'gold standard', for example, invariably results in vocational learning and qualifications being devalued. However, this isn't the case in Norway where, amongst other differences, 16-year-olds have a choice of 13 courses in Senior High School. Ten of these are vocational and three academic. Somewhat more than half of young Norwegians opt for vocational courses, not because these are second best, but because they carry status and access to well-paid jobs.

Similar trends are beckoning in the UK, where new AS- and A-levels can be mixed and matched with Advanced vocational qualifications.

Overstated distinctions between education as a mind-broadening affair and training as a skill-building process don't hold as much sway now as they did before. Today's workers need analytical ability as well as vocational competence. To suggest that education provides the former and training the latter is hair-splitting. What really matters is effective learning. And it's just as important to analyse when faced with a practical task as it is to consider real-life applications when pondering a theory.

In a society (such as that of the UK) that is on the threshold of a new learning age – where jobs are changing and, with them, the skills needed for flexible employability – people need to be astute thinkers and good operators. The capacity to cope with change is producing a new enthusiasm for learning, not as a one-off experience but as a lifetime venture.

Lifelong learning

For most of the 20th century, a higher education was the preserve of an elite minority, for whom periodical 'brushing up' was deemed helpful but not essential after graduation. The majority of school-leavers went straight into work, where they received 'on-the-job training', which was often patchy and variable in quality and length.

How things are changing! The 21st century will be characterised by its emphasis on lifelong learning, from the cradle to the grave. Qualifications acquired in youthful years no longer carry the 'now or never' cachet that they once did. Once, education gave you a start in life. Today, learning is for life.

In this climate, distinctions between education and training make little sense. Instead, the onus is on learning, whether this involves logical thinking or practical skills – or, as is more likely, both. The consequence of successive careers instead of a 'job for life' means that we all have to become 'eternal students'. The need to keep pace with rapidly changing technology (consider, for example, the continuous upgrading of televisions and computers) requires updateable solution-focused learning rather than yesterday's qualifications.

In its 1998 Green Paper, *The Learning Age*, the Labour government set out its vision of a knowledge-based economy, with learning throughout life at the forefront. The government wants to see higher education playing a key role here by:

- increasing and widening access, particularly from groups who are under-represented in higher education, including disabled people and people from low-income households
- providing educational and training opportunities later in life to people who missed out first time round
- using new technology to make courses more easily accessible

Policy-makers are keen to point out that lifelong learners needn't be tied to particular locations. 'Perpetual students' will be able to study at home, at work, or in a local library or shopping mall, as well as in colleges and universities. In that context, the University for Industry (founded in 1999) has the task of stimulating mass demand for learning, acting as the hub of a brand new learning network by connecting those who want to learn with ways of doing so.

The ultimate goal of policy-makers is to help people to plan and manage their own learning and to be able to make timely transitions between education, training and working life as and when the need arises.

The functions of education and training

Although education and training are lifelong processes, the task of preparing the young for the knowledge and skills expected of them as they mature into adulthood rests heavily upon schools. In England and Wales, parents or guardians of all children of compulsory school age (from 5 to 16) are legally responsible for ensuring that their children receive a proper full-time education, either by registering the child at a school or by making other arrangements that provide a sound education.

Schools allegedly serve two main functions:

1 The formal transmission of knowledge and skills from teachers to pupils.
2 The socialisation of children into mainstream adult values.

You might wonder why we have used the word 'allegedly'. This is because some commentators don't agree that schools do (or should) carry out the above functions. For example, a number of Old Left thinkers contend that, far from conveying mainstream values, schools promote

Schools pass knowledge, skills and values from one generation to the next

an upper-class ideology. This ideology is claimed to reproduce existing power relations, turning the children of the middle and upper classes into managers and leaders and the children of the working class into subservient employees.

You might reasonably object that this idea – of schoolteachers 'conspiring' with the ruling class to make sure that some children are primed for leadership and others for servitude – seems a little conspiratorial! Many teachers, of course, would rebut the assertion that they collude with the powerful in order to provide different learning cultures for future leaders and servants. However, a number of sociologists, while accepting that the majority of teachers don't consciously intend to do the will of the dominant class(es), point out that teachers' actions can have unintended consequences. As the sociologist Stuart Hall remarks:

> 'Change in education takes place because the Capitalist system "requires" it, not as a consequence of the "activity of men [*sic*] in pursuit of their ends".'
>
> (cited in Blackledge and Hunt, 1985: 159)

Thus, for example, teachers are sorters of different children's abilities, because politicians insist that they set and assess government-prescribed tests. Whether or not teachers like this, the resultant scores have consequences for pupils' job prospects. It's on this macro level that Old Left commentators have a strong case. For education does indeed place students on different tracks, even though many individual teachers conscientiously strive to help all of their pupils to obtain good life chances.

at that time, ushered in a work ethic where economic success was seen as the just reward of educational achievement. A more meritocratic society was on the march. Planned schooling was to play a major role in rooting out habits of dependent poverty and providing the type of minimal instruction that an industrialising nation required.

In this setting, the principle of education's accountability to government and the state was finally and irreversibly established. From 1833 onwards (when Parliament voted public finds to 'popular education'), the question was no longer whether there should be state intervention in mass schooling but what form the instruction should take and how extensive it should be.

Every vote of confidence in educational reform – from the successful passage of the Parochial Schools Bill in the Commons in 1807 to the school buildings' grant in 1833, to compulsory education in 1880 for those aged between 5 and 10 years old, to the raising of the school-leaving age to 14 in 1918, right up to the Education Act 1944 (which raised the leaving age to 15, as well as introducing other important measures) – involved a move towards more statism.

The Education Act 1944 and its aftermath

The **Education Act 1944**, passed one year before the end of the Second World War, raised the school-leaving age to 15, and made it incumbent upon LEAs to provide education appropriate to a pupil's age, aptitude and ability. The Act also established separate primary and secondary schools. In the secondary school sector, a so-called **tripartite** (three-pronged) system of education was set up, with grammar schools catering for 'academic children', secondary modern schools attending to 'practical children' and technical schools (of which there were very few indeed) looking after 'technical children'.

From the outset, grammar schools were seen as premier division academic establishments and secondary moderns as second-rate institutions, whose metal- and woodwork shops often signalled a training ethos. As indicated, very few technical schools were built, and one imagines that they held an intermediate status between the grammar schools and secondary moderns.

Transfer from primary to secondary education was at age 11, with children mainly being sifted into grammar or secondary modern schools. An IQ test, known as the '11-plus' (taken by children

at the age of 11) determined their educational fate. A minority of pupils passed, and they went to grammar school. Most failed and they attended secondary moderns. A very small proportion of 11-year-olds went to so-called technical schools.

In general, pupils who were selected for grammar school were from the middle and upper classes, as well as the 'brightest' among the working class. Some parents opted out of the tri-partite system altogether and sent their children to fee-paying schools. For historical reasons, fee-paying schools in the secondary sector were (and still are) commonly called 'public schools'. Among the more famous are Eton, Harrow and Winchester, but there are many others and they vary widely in quality and standards. The most prestigious public schools recruit almost exclusively from very able middle- and upper-class families. That said, a grammar school tie, particularly if worn by a boy pupil, can rival a public school tie in terms of status.

The tripartite system was stoutly defended by Conservative politicians, but came under heavy attack in the 1960s from Labour MPs, many of whom argued that the system was elitist and divisive. A Labour government, elected in 1964, decided to promote an inclusive form of secondary education, and its vehicle for doing so was the **comprehensive school**. 'Comprehensive' means all encompassing, and this was the educational ideal of the new schools for all.

Today, most secondary school pupils in England and Wales attend comprehensive schools. There are, however, as the saying goes, 'comprehensive schools and comprehensive schools'. Comprehensive schools in leafy suburbs resemble the old grammar schools insofar as pupil intake and resources are concerned, whereas those in poor neighbourhoods are more like the old secondary moderns. It is equally worrying that, in some comprehensive schools, it's still not uncommon for 'bright' pupils (who tend to be middle class) to be hived off into fast track streams of subject bands and for 'less bright' pupils (who tend to be working class) to end up in 'remedial classes'.

The 1970s 'great debate'

The postwar period saw many debates among policy-makers on the role of education and training. One of these was so important that it became known as the 'great debate'.

In 1976, the then Labour Prime Minister Jim Callaghan launched a national debate at Ruskin

Some politicians want to turn the clock back to Victorian whole-class teaching. Many teachers see things differently

College, Oxford, about the relationship between schools and industry. 'I am concerned', he said during his lecture, 'to find complaints from industry that new recruits from the schools sometimes do not have the basic tools to do the job'. The 'tools' that Callaghan referred to weren't, of course, machines but educational 'know-how' – being able to read and write fluently, understanding basic mathematical operations and so forth.

At the heart of the then Prime Minister's concern was an alleged lack of match – of relevance – between school and work. Callaghan blamed this, in part, on the wide prevalence of progressive teaching methods which, according to him, 'seem to produce excellent results when they are in well-qualified hands but are much more dubious when they are not'.

This charge laid down the gauntlet to progressive educationists and placed the 'rediscovery' of traditional methods high on the political agenda, which is where it's been ever since. Importantly, the 'Ruskin Lecture' opened up the possibility – eagerly seized upon by Margaret Thatcher when she became Conservative Prime Minister in 1979 – that politicians might 'know better' than teachers about how to teach children.

There followed a massive politicisation of the educational debate, with schools attracting more intervention than almost any other area of government. A series of major reforms were fired off – among them, a National Curriculum, league tables of school results and Ofsted 'quality control' inspections – which were used to make teachers more accountable to Whitehall and to parents.

This sounds reasonable enough. But hold on a moment. By pinpointing teachers and their alleged progressive methods (not to mention their supposed left-wing leanings) as being largely to blame for the lack of fit between school and industry (as industry defines that gap), the job of government becomes one of hunting down failing schools and identifying the usual suspects – incompetent teachers. This approach neatly sidelines the impact of poverty on educational outcomes, let alone the effects of policies shamelessly based on market forces rather than on hard empirical evidence.

How do politicians know that the 'Three R's' and whole-class teaching (peppered with a bit of teacher-led interaction) produce better results than discovery methods and project work? The truth is that they don't know, because not enough research has been carried out into what works well in classrooms. What the research does tell us is that teachers need to be 'situational experts' (that is, able to respond to a variety of situations as they arise) rather than dogmatic exponents of one teaching approach or another. Different classrooms create their own rules of engagement. Five-year-olds respond well to play-based learning, and 12-year-olds to project work.

But, even here, there are variations – and good teachers know this.

Policy-makers who claim that schools are out of touch with the world of work believe that the content of education and training in the classroom doesn't sufficiently serve the knowledge and skill needs of the labour market. This isn't a new idea. As far back as the 19th century, MPs (some of them 'landed gentlemen') were arguing that working-class education should connect more with industry, and they supported British Society schools for the poor that provided vocational training. The Bolton British School, for example, taught mechanical engineering, while the Circus Street British School in Liverpool offered instruction in printing.

Vocationalism

As we can see, a vocational role for schooling isn't something new. Strangely, however, the 1980s witnessed a lot of discussion in policy circles about the so-called 'new vocationalism'. Was this just old wine in new bottles, or did the 1980s debate really foster a different and original outlook?

In some respects, the old themes of training versus education were revisited and reconsidered. There was nothing really new here. However, there was, among policy-makers, a resolve to 'talk up' the status of vocational subjects in the post-16 school curriculum. The late 1980s and early 1990s saw the introduction of a raft of new vocational qualifications, since streamlined into two main courses – GNVQs and NVQs.

GNVQs are school- or college-based courses in subjects such as health and social care, leisure and tourism, engineering, science, and art and design, with an emphasis on work-related knowledge and skills. They offer a vocational alternative to the more academic GCSEs and A-levels. **NVQs** are largely work-based courses on the knowledge and skills that people need to be able to perform effectively at work. The areas of study are all related to major sectors of industry or commerce, and include, for example, communications and manufacturing.

With around three-quarters of 16-year-olds now opting for further study, the demand for a vocational alternative to the traditional GCSE and A-level is high. GNVQs and NVQs provide this alternative, and echo Jim Callaghan's call in 1976 to bring schooling more in step with the needs of industry. Therein lies a dilemma. There's still a habit among some teachers to regard vocational courses as offering low-level, low-prestige skills to poorly motivated, low-achieving students. By contrast, A-levels are still widely perceived as the gold standard benchmarks of academic scholarship, offering ready access to a university education, and even (and this is ironical) to vocational courses such as dentistry, law and medicine.

Although it is outmoded, the quintessentially English notion that students can be placed into the either/or categories of 'hands' who toil and 'heads' who think still holds sway in some high places – not least among educational elites who climbed the ladder by taking A-levels themselves. There's also opposition to an over-vocationalisation of the school curriculum by commentators on the Left, who fear that schools are being asked to produce 'factory fodder'. Such critics wryly note that A-levels are typically favoured by those who later obtain the best jobs.

As things now stand, the academic path still leads to better university and career prospects. However, the new vocational alternatives to GCSEs (Foundation GNVQs) are becoming increasingly popular – a trend that, if it continues, could signal the beginning of the end for the blue chip status of academic courses. Perhaps, in the future, people (and, importantly, universities and employers) will see vocational qualifications as different rather than as inferior. From 2002, for example, UCAS will award the same number of points for a grade A in Advanced GNVQ as for a grade A in an A-level. There are also clear signs of a 'mix and match' approach to subject choice, with students selecting from an 'à la carte' menu of academic and vocational modules.

The Education Reform Act 1988 and its aftermath

The implementation of the **Education Reform Act 1988 (ERA)** brought about the promise of a National Curriculum, opted-out schools and national tests. According to its architect, Lord Baker (then Conservative Education Secretary Kenneth Baker), this Act was 'the biggest single measure of social reform which was undertaken in the Thatcher years'. In support of that claim, Baker cites recent improvements in reading and numeracy scores, in GCSEs and in 'staying-on' rates. This is, of course, the talk of a politician, and Baker would be hard pressed to prove that there's a cause and effect relationship between his Act and these progress indicators.

The legislation, enacted during an era when enthusiasm for a competitive market in education was high, implemented four main measures: a National Curriculum for children aged from 5 to 16 in state schools; more parental choice about which schools to send children to; local management of schools; and grant maintained schools.

The National Curriculum

The Big Idea in the 1988 ERA was the **National Curriculum**. This measure required that all children in England and Wales should have a right and an obligation to a common curriculum (with some discretionary departures) between the ages of 5 to 16. Compulsory schooling has been on English statute books since 1880. But it wasn't until 1988 that the law had something to say about what pupils should be taught – with the exception of religious education.

Jim Callaghan's Ruskin speech in 1976 (see above) had earlier called for a core curriculum of basic knowledge for all pupils, and must therefore be seen as an important prelude to the ERA. It fell to Kenneth Baker to implement this call in 1988.

Current National Curriculum specifications apply to most pupils aged between 5 and 16 in state schools in England and Wales. As at 2000, the National Curriculum consists of the following subjects: English, mathematics, science, design and technology, information technology, history, geography, music, art, physical education and a modern foreign language. Pupils also have to study religious education, and secondary schools must provide sex education. Unlike National Curriculum subjects, the content of these two subjects is decided (within lawful limits) locally. Secondary schools are obliged to provide careers education.

In order to standardise testing procedures on a nationwide basis, the ERA also provided for formal end-of-course (so-called 'key stage') assessments of pupils at ages 7, 11, 14 and 16.

It seems paradoxical that a Conservative government (the one led by Thatcher when the ERA was passed), whose stated aim was to roll back the state, should allow Whitehall to decide what our children should be taught. But that's what happened. One might argue – and some commentators have – that the then government saw its chance to use schools as vehicles of ideological indoctrination. Thus, for example, the prescribed content for history, since revised, seemed to foster a very Anglocentric (even jingoistic) view of the world.

Some teachers have serious misgivings about politicians in London telling them what to teach

the nation's children. It's almost tantamount to instructing priests on the content of their sermons, lawyers on how to address a jury or doctors on which diagnostic tests to use. On the other hand, argue the supporters of the National Curriculum, what this offers is a common learning entitlement for all – no more 'domestic science' just for the girls and 'woodwork' just for the boys!

Parental choice

Over the past decade, parents have (at least, in theory) been given the right to send their children to the school of their choice, unless it was full. This system of open enrolment has proved to be froth rather than substance. Today, good schools are more over-subscribed than ever, and many parents have to make do with second or third choices.

In 1996, an Audit Commission Report (*Trading Places*) on school enrolment found that nearly one in five parents failed to get a place for their child in their first-choice school. The threefold rise in parental appeals during the mid-1990s against schools that wouldn't admit their children tells its own story.

Unpopular schools, of course, weren't always able to fill their quotas, costing the taxpayer some 100 million pounds a year for surplus places. Ministers hoped that parental choice – a vivid example of market principles – would lead to good schools expanding and bad ones closing. Yet widespread closures didn't happen. Indeed, some schools that were threatened with closure simply opted out of LEA control.

Having raised parental expectations without always being able to meet them, the policy-makers have bequeathed the present government with a challenging legacy. Parent power is the big slogan, and politicians will ignore it at their peril.

Local management of schools

This measure, which continues to pick up pace today, gave schools control of about 85% of their budget, with LEAs keeping the remainder. In practical terms, this means that responsibility for expenditure on books, equipment, staff and minor repairs was delegated to schools. Overnight, head teachers became financial managers, with responsibility for most of the school budget. For example, if a school needs new computers, the decision can be made on site, without having to call the town hall.

Prior to **local management of schools (LMS)**, LEAs received the full budget and then decided how to cut the cake between the different schools in the district, also exercising some control over how each school might spend its share. By giving schools considerably more say over how to spend their money, the ERA also conferred a high degree of control by schools over their own internal affairs, empowering head teachers and governing bodies in a manner that was unthinkable prior to the legislation.

Educational professionals at school level could now take decisions once taken by local councillors. By shifting areas previously in the domain of the LEAs over to schools, Whitehall politicians argued that head teachers and governors would be much more responsive to their school's particular needs. But where does this leave the LEAs? Do they still have a role to play, or have they become absent landlords?

The current debate here involves finding ways to combine maximum self-government for schools with effective central support services (for example, advisory and educational psychology services) from the LEAs. If schools are given 100% control of their budgets – a situation that some policy-makers would like to see – there's a risk that some ('eccentric') heads might, for example, choose not to buy in educational psychologists from central services, and use on-site 'non-experts' instead.

Grant maintained schools

These 'opted out' schools were introduced in order to strengthen school control, and thus weaken LEA control, over education. By opting out of LEA control, **grant maintained (GM) schools** took LMS one step further, transforming schools into independent educational enterprises. For example, 'Oil Drum Lane County Comprehensive' might become 'Urban Lane College, plc' – an exaggeration, perhaps, but not too wide of the mark in some cases!

While grant maintained schools were introduced amid much fanfare by the then Conservative government, the current Labour government is in the process of scrapping them, and replacing them with so-called **foundation schools**. The supporters of GM schools argued that, by opting out of LEA control, schools were enabled to become the arbiters of their own fortunes. Opponents countered with the assertion that GM schools unjustly received more money than schools that remained within LEA control. Audenshaw, the first school to become grant maintained, set the tone for the debate.

About half of its staff, including a deputy head, resigned as a result of the decision to leave the LEA. Audenshaw, of course, represents one extreme. Other GM schools have kept their staff and have been successful.

The post-Dearing era

So named after Sir Ron Dearing's brief from government in the early 1990s to slim down the National Curriculum, the post-Dearing era witnessed the consolidation of the ERA, as well as a range of other policy initiatives.

In its day, the ERA was controversial. Today, many of its ideas have become, in modified form, social policy orthodoxies that few politicians would want to (or dare to) challenge. Much of the current preoccupation with measuring standards and publishing the results in league tables has its roots in the 1988 Act, as does the trend towards autonomy in school management.

In so far as the provisions of the ERA are concerned, where the present Labour government and previous Conservative governments differ is more a matter of degree than of substance. Indeed, Kenneth Baker, the architect of the Act, is on record as saying that some of the present Labour Education Secretary's speeches sound like some of his old scripts.

These days, politicians across the political spectrum favour the retention of a National Curriculum, but in a more streamlined form. Dearing set the tone here. His recommendations (Dearing, 1993), which were accepted in full by the then Conservative government, included the following measures:

◎ making the National Curriculum for pupils aged between 5 and 14 (particularly, subjects outside the core of English, mathematics and science) less all-embracing, and giving teachers more professional discretion

◎ reducing the number of attainment targets (essentially, the content to be covered in National Curriculum subjects)

◎ providing more scope for pupils aged between 14 and 16 to study subjects (such as sociology) that were not part of the National Curriculum, and allowing them to select from a wider choice of vocational subjects

Wisely, Dearing insisted that – following the implementation of the revised National Curriculum for pupils aged between 5 and 14, in

September 1995 – there should be no further major changes for the next five years. This proved a major relief to teachers, who needed to know that, in an era of radical and swift educational reform, the dust was going to settle for at least a while.

Effective schools

For as long as there have been schools, policy-makers have sought to find ways of making them effective. During the past 20 years or so, successive governments have shown an interest in research into school effectiveness, but have steadfastly refused to see any necessary policy implications in the findings. Now, according to Peter Mortimore, Director of London University's Institute of Education and a leading light in effectiveness research, politicians are keen to use research findings in order to raise educational standards.

Mortimore is worried that there's an element of zealotry in the government's approach here. Some policy-makers seem to have adopted the approach that 'if it moves, measure it'. We have league tables for all sorts of things these days, from reading scores to truancy rates. By 2002, the government wants 80% of 11-year-old children to be at the 'right reading level', and 75% to have the maths skills expected of pupils that age.

Before becoming Labour Prime Minister in 1997, Tony Blair had made it clear that the quality of education mattered and deserved public scrutiny. Nobody disagreed with that. The debate is about what needs to be done and how to measure progress. According to school effectiveness researchers such as David Reynolds (1997) – a professor of education and adviser to the government – we need to learn from effective schools. If there is a body of good practice in schools that leads to positive educational outcomes, how can we make sure that all teachers possess it?

This is a central question for Reynolds. He doesn't, however, advocate 'one size fits all' solutions but, rather, a bespoke approach, with different school policies in different contexts. Lists of the factors that make *all* schools effective tend to produce simplistic remedies, and assume that schools are all alike – which they're not. Reynolds favours 'cherry picking'. If, for example, in school A, whole-class teaching of maths – combining teacher talk and teacher–pupil interaction – produces an encouraging outcome, why not try it in school B and see if it works?

Like other school effectiveness researchers, Reynolds accepts that any measurement of in-school outcomes must take account of outside-school factors. The most important consideration here is the entry-level profile of a school's pupil intake. If, for example, in school A, most 11-year-olds start their secondary education with below-average reading scores, it makes little sense to expect them to produce the same 'raw' results as in school B, where most pupils start with excellent reading scores.

To get around this measurement problem, researchers use what are called 'value-added calculations'. The crucial question becomes: 'What has this school added to a benchmark starting point?' If school C has upped its pupils' average reading age from 8 to 16, this represents a lot more progress than school D's improvement from 14 to 18.

Value-added measurements of educational progress make it possible for low 'raw' scores to be regarded as relatively successful outcomes, if the pupils' starting point is relatively low. However, it would be wrong not to have high expectations of such pupils. If value-added approaches are used as an excuse for schools in disadvantaged neighbourhoods to try to avoid attempts to improve 'raw' scores, that doesn't help working-class children one bit.

Value-added judgements about a school's performance add the important dimension of social background to the overall equation, but this dimension is captured in rather crude statistical terms (for example, numbers of pupils on free school dinners). What happens, however, when we try to account for the achievement of a middle-class pupil who normally performs very well, but who fails an exam because of a recent death in the family, or because his or her father has just become unemployed. When working with large samples, it is very difficult indeed to eliminate the influence of factors such as these.

Even when value-added measurements provide policy-makers with more background information than they otherwise would have, it's the actual level of achievement that employers and universities are mainly interested in. A student who has gained triple As at A-level is more likely to get a job than one who has achieved three grade E passes, but started on a lower baseline!

Reynolds and other school effectiveness researchers want to see all pupils doing well. A high-end result for everyone is the goal. The only way to do this in practice, argues Reynolds (1997), is to introduce massive programmes of 'positive discrimination', of which he identifies two main types:

1   Schools with more disadvantaged children should get more money. This happens, for example, in Holland, where school intakes are 'weighted' in terms of social composition to increase the budgets of those with the most disadvantaged pupils. The extra money, says Reynolds, should be 'ring-fenced' for spending on effective learning programmes (for example, Reading Recovery).

2   Schools whose pupils perform badly, even though pupil intakes aren't disadvantaged, need support and guidance. Reynolds expresses his concern over the failure of some schools in more advantaged areas to develop children' talents, but isn't very specific about how to tackle this problem. One imagines that he would approve of money being spent on effective learning schemes and, perhaps, on improving teaching skills.

The challenge to educational policy is to use the findings of school effectiveness research in order to assess the impact of social disadvantage and other problems on pupil achievement without accepting that such an impact is inevitable. By looking at what works in schools with good educational outcomes, and by trying out their successful remedies in underachieving schools, the hoped-for outcome is better results all round.

Ofsted

In the present climate of testing, league tables and quality control, governments are keen to ensure that schools and other educational institutions are accountable to society. One way of keeping check that educationists are doing a good job is to inspect them. That's the task of Ofsted, or to use its unwieldy full title, the Office for Standards in Education.

Set up on 1 September 1992, Ofsted is a non-ministerial government department (independent of the Department for Education and Employment) and is headed by Her Majesty's Chief Inspector of Schools in England. Ofsted's main role is to improve standards of educational achievement and quality of educational provision through regular independent inspection, and to report on its findings and offer informed advice.

Her Majesty's Inspectors (HMIs) were established in 1839 and are the permanent inspection staff of Ofsted. As well as visiting schools, HMIs regulate the inspection service, analyse educa-

tional trends, evaluate the effects of educational policies, and follow up issues to which inspection findings have drawn attention. HMIs also inspect independent schools on behalf of the DfEE, teacher education departments, LEA central services and LEA-funded further education establishments.

Ofsted compiles a national database from inspection reports and uses this to provide policy-makers with advice on standards in English schools and on other relevant matters. The reports are intended to be objective. However, in recent years, Ofsted has been accused of being less than rigorous in its collection and interpretation of data.

Leading the attack in 1998, Professor Tim Brighouse (1998), Birmingham's chief education officer, wondered, with a strong pinch of irony, if Ofsted had become the first fault-free 100% reliability organisation. If not, added Brighouse, it was time to consider the consequences of Osted's fallibility.

Specifically, Brighouse referred to a big secondary school on a poor Birmingham estate which, over a period of 18 months, went from serious weaknesses through very favourable comment from HMIs to being strongly criticised by an Ofsted team. Called to give evidence at a 1998 Commons select committee on education, Brighouse maintained that the school and its outstanding head teacher had been 'damaged by an act of great misjudgement and injustice'. Ofsted final draft reports, said Brighouse, often bring to mind a game of poker, with Ofsted staff 'unwilling to reveal their hand of evidence even when called'.

One might assert that Brighouse would say this, because one of his own Birmingham schools was in the firing line. However, Ofsted, at least in its early days, was bound to invite attacks on the credibility of its evidence. Instead of using the tried and tested year-long 'apprenticeship' for beginning school inspectors, Ofsted trained thousands of inspectors in a matter of days. Lack of rigour and inconsistency of judgement were therefore inevitable. Brighouse's colleagues think that Ofsted's margin of error is as high as 15%. If this estimate is accurate, perhaps it's time to inquire more about the people who are checking the people who are checking the schools, the Office for Standards in Inspection (OFSTIN)!

Citizenship education

Schools have long sought to raise 'good citizens'. This is an ancient concern (but not Plato's – he was appalled by uncritical, well-socialised citizens) that schools now tackle on a more systematic basis. Mass schooling, 'invented' in its English form in the 1800s, was intended (by policy-makers) to infuse the working class with a new and socially desirable moral and religious outlook, and to bring about a marked reduction in crime (Holland, 1807; Whitbread, 1807). Against the crudely deterrent mechanism of the hanging tree, a number of MPs saw education as a better way of 'socialising' the potentially rebellious poor.

There were also a number of voluntary educational bodies in existence, whose board members (usually, 'gentlemen of high station') endorsed the view that the right kind of schooling would 'help' the poor to adjust to *their* station in life. One such body, the Society for Bettering the Condition and Increasing the Comforts of the Poor (founded in 1796), proudly recorded the visit of its secretary, Sir Thomas Bernard (1890: 130–131), to one of a number of girls' schools:

'I was present at their breakfast today (10th of August, 1801), when abundance of very good milk porridge was served up, and partaken of by all the children, in a cleanly and decent manner. The object, which has been attained by providing the breakfasts, is the punctual attendance of the children in the morning ... It is proposed that they [the pupils] shall ... be encouraged to bring oatmeal and flour from home; so as to make bread and oak cake at the schools, for their respective families. This will not only be very useful to servants, but will also supply most essential qualifications for the wife of the cottager; so as to enable her to fill properly and *economically*, the duties of her station in life.'

Nineteenth-century 'citizenship education' was rooted in the Bible and moral tales. The moral tales of the writer Sarah Trimmer, in particular, were endorsed by Anglican bishops as sound literature for use in church schools. Her books reflected the orthodox Anglican view that society was headed by country folk, with the squire and his wife figuring prominently. In descending order, came the parson, the farmer, the publican, the schoolteacher and the nurse. Below them were the poor, separated into the 'respectable' (devout and hard-working) and the 'not-so-respectable', who lacked these virtues (see Goldstrom, 1972).

Trimmer's tales were designed to keep the poor in their place with, of course, an expectation of a modest degree of social improvement for those at the bottom of the pile – but not too much, mind! For example, Trimmer was critical of the system of merit adopted in more 'progressive' schools, because:

'Boys accustomed to consider themselves the nobles of the school may, in their future lives, form a conceit of their own merits, (unless they have very sound principles) aspire to be nobles of the land, and to take (*sic*) place of the hereditary nobility.'

(cited by Smith, 1806: 182)

Today, policy-makers have different designs on citizenship, but they're still keen to use schools to socialise pupils into adult compliance with contemporary norms and values. This is spelled out no more clearly than in the government's proposals on compulsory citizenship lessons. For example, from ages five to seven, pupils will learn how to make and keep rules; from ages 7 to 11 they will study the consequences of anti-social behaviour (including bullying); from 11 to 14, legal and human rights and responsibilities; and, from 14 to 16, the need for mutual respect and understanding.

Such citizenship values are a far cry from knowing one's place in a rural 19th-century society, but they nevertheless represent a deliberate attempt by government to turn pupils into law-abiding citizens who uphold British values and show respect for human rights. Whatever you or I think about how morally just these aims are, it's important, from a social policy standpoint, to recognise that politicians are explicitly using schools to impart a citizenship ideology.

There are, however, problems with this strategy. What happens, for example, if a different government imposes a citizenship curriculum that some groups in society don't agree with, or which omits areas that they believe should be included? Few people would disagree with citizenship lessons that seek to tackle bullying, but some disabled people might reasonably argue that too little is being done to promote a more inclusive society.

There's also the issue of practising social justice in the classroom. It makes little sense to teach children to have respect for teachers if some teachers behave badly. Principled teachers who relate to their pupils with a generosity of spirit are not only good instructors but citizenship models worthy of imitation. Teachers who – by example as well as instruction – manage to replace racism, sexism, disablism and other negative '-isms' with an enlightened outlook, hearsay judgements with critical awareness, and half-truths with honest scholarship are doing their job well.

To the extent that schools are part of a democratic society, it seems reasonable that they should encourage the young not only to value freedom but also to exercise it. If this means 'allowing' their pupils to stand by what they believe in even if doing so runs contrary to a government edict, then – provided that such beliefs don't injure others – it's important that a citizenship curriculum can handle this. Otherwise, we run the risk of placing obedience before freedom.

The Greek sage and philosopher, Plato, recognised this in ancient times when he concluded that citizens who accepted dominant beliefs without a strong measure of scepticism were gullible. This theme was taken up in English elite public schools, where the children of the governing class were encouraged to think independently.

© In 1976, the then Labour Prime Minister Jim Callaghan launched a national debate about an alleged lack of match between school and work. There followed a massive politicisation of the educational debate, with schools attracting huge state intervention.

© The most important piece of legislation in this period was the Education Reform Act 1988 with its National Curriculum, more parental choice, local management of schools, and grant maintained schools.

© During the past 20 years or so, successive governments have shown an interest in school effectiveness research, and are now keener than ever before to use research findings in order to raise educational standards.

© Policy-makers also have designs on using schools to promote good citizenship.

REVIEW POINTS

© The Education Act 1944 raised the school-leaving age to 15, and made LEAs provide education appropriate to a pupil's age, aptitude and ability. The Act also established separate primary and secondary schools. In the secondary school sector, the tripartite system of education was set up, with grammar schools catering for 'academic children', secondary modern schools attending to 'practical children' and technical schools looking after 'technical children'.

© Labour MPs attacked the tripartite system in the 1960s, and a Labour government, elected in 1964, promoted an inclusive form of secondary education through comprehensive schools. Today, most secondary school pupils attend comprehensive schools.

REVIEW ACTIVITIES

1 What is the 'tripartite system'?

2 What was Jim Callaghan's main concern, as expressed in the 'Great Debate' of 1976?

3 Is it right that the government decides (mainly through the National Curriculum) what our children should learn in schools?

4 What evidence is there that market principles have had a strong influence on educational policy over the past two decades?

5 What are the debates surrounding school effectiveness research?

6 How would you assess Professor Brighouse's judgement of Ofsted?

7 What are the advantages and challenges of citizenship education in schools?

Educational outcomes

Access to state education between the ages of 5 and 16 is guaranteed for all children in England and Wales. Over 90% of pupils attend publicly funded state schools. These schools make no charge to parents. In most areas, pupils aged between five and ten go to primary schools, and transfer to secondary schools at 11, for education up to the age of 16 or beyond. More and more young people are entering further and higher education.

Since the early 1970s, the proportion of 15-year-old pupils gaining one or more higher-grade GCSEs (or previous GCE O-level equivalents) has risen from 42% to 70%. The proportion of 17-year-old pupils gaining one or more A-levels has also increased significantly. Entry to higher education is disproportionately over-represented in the higher social classes. However, once in university, students of working-class background generally do just as well as those from middle- and upper-class homes.

Educational achievement in school remains stubbornly class-based and is also influenced by gender, ethnicity and disability. In particular, child poverty and educational achievement are strongly linked, which is why the government's goal of eliminating child poverty within a generation makes excellent educational sense.

Sociology provides compelling evidence on the extent to which educational success in British society is strongly affected by social class, gender, ethnicity and disability.

Social class

In the 1950s, 1960s and 1970s, the link between social class and educational achievement dominated research in educational sociology. Study after study (Glass, 1954; Floud, Halsey and Martin, 1957; Hargreaves, 1967; Douglas, 1968; Keddie, 1971; Bernstein, 1973; Willis, 1978; Corrigan, 1979) confirmed that middle-class pupils outperformed working-class pupils.

Differences in educational achievement mirror, in part, differential access to different kinds of school. Middle-class and upper-class pupils were (and still are) more likely to attend state schools in prosperous neighbourhoods, and to be among the 7% of the school population who go to private schools. Working-class pupils were (and still are) more likely to attend 'run-down' state schools in poorer neighbourhoods.

It's important to emphasise the words 'still are'. Some politicians seem to think that the 1980s and 1990s witnessed the death of social class. This isn't the case. Social class, as Mairtin Mac an Ghail (1996) points out, is still alive and kicking. It remains a powerful predictor of educational outcomes.

Working-class students, reports the Policy Studies Institute (1997), encounter obstacles at every stage:

Once at university, students from very diverse backgrounds do well

- fewer stay on at school
- more choose vocational rather than A-level courses
- those who do take A-levels have poorer results
- they're less likely to apply to university
- those who do apply are less likely to be admitted

For working-class children, educational disadvantage begins early. By the same token, children from middle- and upper-class backgrounds begin their schooling with a head start. Economic and cultural factors are both implicated. For example, middle- and upper-class children are more likely to live in homes where facilities for doing homework are better, and to have the language skills that schools prize.

One of the most important social scientific indicators for determining if a child comes from a low income household is whether he or she is eligible for free school dinners. As eligibility for free school meals increases, average GCSE score tends to decrease. The more disadvantaged the pupil intake is, the lower is the average score (Ofsted, 1998).

Access to university has also long been the preserve of the better-off. In 1962, for example, the Robbins Committee found that 45% of 21-year-olds with fathers in professional jobs entered full-time higher education, compared with 4% of those whose fathers had skilled manual jobs and 2% of the children of semi-skilled and unskilled manual workers.

Disparities in class-linked access to a higher education are still apparent, with people from low-income backgrounds woefully under-represented. The Committee of Vice-Chancellors and Principals (see Mendick, 1998) reported that while 16 out of 20 teenagers from high-income families go on to university, 17 out of 20 from low-income families don't. The overall figure for university attendance in the UK was just over one-third. According to the Vice-Chancellors, universities have neglected schoolchildren from the poorest families, leaving a large pool of educational talent untapped. Interestingly, working-class students who did get to university were found to be just as high achievers as students from wealthier backgrounds.

Although the 1980s and 1990s have witnessed a shift of interest by some sociologists to the relationship between educational achievement and gender, ethnicity and disability, class still remains a very powerful (probably, the most important) predictor of educational outcomes. As David Gillborn and Caroline Gipps (1996: 17) point out:

'Social class is strongly associated with achievement regardless of gender and ethnic background: whatever the pupils' gender or ethnic origin, those from the higher social class backgrounds do better on average.'

The relative educational 'disadvantages' of working-class pupils start long before they might contemplate going to university. Thus, for example, Pamela Sammons's (1995) research confirms that class has a profound influence on the reading progress of primary school children in the UK. Children from semi- or unskilled manual backgrounds made 'less progress, attaining poorer results than predicted, given their prior reading attainment and taking account of the impact of other factors' (Sammons, 1995: 473).

Educational researchers often use eligibility for free school dinners as a proxy for a 'low working-class' position, and then use this information to plot the percentage of poor pupils against the performance of all pupils in national tests. This is illustrated in the figure on page 290, which provides an indication of how pupils in different LEAs scored in English, maths and science tests in primary schools.

In the page 290 figure, for example, in LEAs where 10% of primary school pupils were eligible for free school meals, the aggregate of percentages scoring level 4 in the tests is clustered around 225, whereas in LEAs where between 30% and 55% of pupils were eligible, the clusters are often below 200. It's important to note, however, that the scattergraph shows considerable variation in performance among LEAs who have relatively high numbers of pupils on free school meals.

While it would be an exaggeration to portray England as a nation divided by state school 'oiks' and public school 'toffs', the educational system still helps those at the top to maintain their class advantage. Elite self-recruitment, whereby 'old boys' assist their 'own kind' in the job market, is also fostered by an Oxbridge education, with graduates from Oxford and Cambridge dominating among generals and judges. This pattern is perhaps less apparent in the new sectors of employment that have resulted from the boom in communications technology.

Social class and educational achievement

Countless sociological studies have confirmed that middle-class students outperform and/or attend better schools than their working-class counterparts. Among the more important of these studies – many of which, regrettably, have only focused on males – were those of the following researchers.

D. V. Glass
Glass led a team of social scientists at the London School of Economics and Political Science in the 1950s. He reported that, for the sons of skilled manual and routine non-manual workers who attended grammar schools or their equivalent, there was a rise from 2.2% for boys born before 1890 to 10.7% for boys born in the period 1920–1929.

However, referring to the 1950s, Glass (1963: 21) wrote that 'the general picture so far is of a rather stable social structure, and one in which social status [here referring to occupational ranking] has tended to operate within, so to speak, a closed circuit. Social origins have conditioned educational level, and both have conditioned achieved social status.'

J. E. Floud, A. H. Halsey and F. M. Martin
Floud, Halsey and Martin investigated the link between class and educational opportunities in England in the 1950s. They discovered that the chances of boys getting into grammar schools at that time were more closely related to measured ability than to social origins. Nevertheless, they (Floud et al. 1957: 142–143) noted that 'the probability that a working-class boy will get to a grammar school is not strikingly different from what it was before 1945, and there are still marked differences in the chances which boys of different social origins have of obtaining a place.'

In 1953, the proportion of working-class boys who entered grammar school in one Yorkshire borough was 12%, and in a Hertfordshire district the figure was 14%. Importantly, however, Floud et al. (1957: 87) found that 'what are often taken to be characteristically "middle-class" attitudes and ambitions in the matter of education are, in fact, widespread among parents much lower in the occupational scale.' They also drew attention to the material plight of children of 'poor but educationally well-disposed parents' (Floud et al., 1957: 145).

David Hargreaves
Case study research carried out by Hargreaves in a boys' secondary modern school revealed that the teachers 'constantly under-estimated or were ignorant of the power of the peer group in regulating the behaviour of pupils' (Hargreaves, 1967: 183). Boys placed in low-ability streams were associated with a sense of status deprivation at school. But boys in these streams often had no desire to be promoted into a higher stream, and sometimes actively avoided this. High-stream boys, by contrast, had a fear of demotion. Thus, as Hargreaves put it, 'One of the most important results of the segregation of the pupils into streams at Lumley School was ... that the boys in one subculture perceive the other subculture as a major negative reference group' (Hargreaves, 1967: 186).

A similar stand-off between academic and anti-academic school subcultures was documented by Paul Willis, in his study, Learning to Labour: how Working-class Kids Get Working-class Jobs (1978).

J. W. B. Douglas
Douglas carried out a longitudinal study – which began in 1946 – of a large representative sample of children living in England, Wales and Scotland. He found that, for middle-class children, primary school and family environments tended to support each other, whereas the opposite often happened for working-class children. Douglas found that parental encouragement was an important predictor of children's success in picture, reading, vocabulary and arithmetic tests. In that respect, middle-class parents were generally found to take more interest in their children's progress at school than working-class parents.

However, Douglas also noted that some working-class parents had 'middle-class standards ... in their expectations of grammar school awards' (Douglas, 1968: 84).

Nell Keddie
Through observation, questionnaire and discussion, Keddie discovered that teachers in the humanities department of a mixed comprehensive school were inclined to see pupils from the top stream as displaying middle-class, conforming behaviours, and pupils from the bottom stream as having working-class, noisy behaviours. Says Keddie, 'Clearly, A stream pupils' definition of appropriate behaviour in the situation was taken over from or coincided with that of the teachers' (Keddie, 1971: 143). By contrast, 'C stream pupils are often seen to lack those qualities which are deemed by teachers desirable in themselves and appropriate to school.' The B stream pupils were left in the middle and tended to shift around in the teachers' perceptions.

Basil Bernstein
Bernstein's research revealed that working-class speech was less valued by teachers than middle-class speech, thus placing working-class children at an educational ▶

disadvantage. When working-class children hear their teachers speaking middle-class English, the pupils are sometimes left puzzled, because 'The working-class child has to translate and thus mediate middle-class language structure through the logically simpler language structure of his [sic] own class to make it personally meaningful' (Bernstein, 1973: 47). Failure to do this leads to confusion and misunderstanding.

In making these observations, Bernstein isn't forming a personal judgement about working-class language. Rather, he's documenting society's judgement on speech.

Paul Willis

Willis (1978) conducted interviews with working-class boys – the 'lads' – in a Midlands secondary school, and exposed a subculture that rejected academic values and subverted the authority of teachers. The 'lads' equated manual work with success and intellectual work with failure. For them, achievement was measured in terms of winning the battle with teachers and ridiculing 'ear'ole' swots.

While they may have won the battle in the classroom, these working-class rebels lost the war by ending up in low-paid, dead-end jobs.

Paul Corrigan

Corrigan's study of working-class boys in Sunderland revealed that they experienced secondary school as oppressive and rallied together against its power. Seeing teachers as 'big-heads' who pushed them around, the boys played up, 'to continue their normal way of life despite the occupying army of the teachers and the power of the school' (Corrigan, 1979: 58). School for these pupils was an imposition, and therefore something to be vigorously challenged.

Stephen Ball, Richard Bowe and Sharon Gewirtz

Ball, Bowe and Gewirtz (1995) conducted research into parental choice of school, and found that working-class parents often subordinated the selection of secondary school to considerations of family and local constraints. Deciding on a school was sometimes seen as a matter of 'getting by'. Among middle-class families, these sociologists discovered that it was much more common for parents to prioritise the school above household considerations.

This research doesn't suggest that working-class parents care less about their children's schooling, but just that they often face more difficult life circumstances and can't easily adapt. It's important to add that a child's chances of doing well in exams improves considerably if he or she attends a good school.

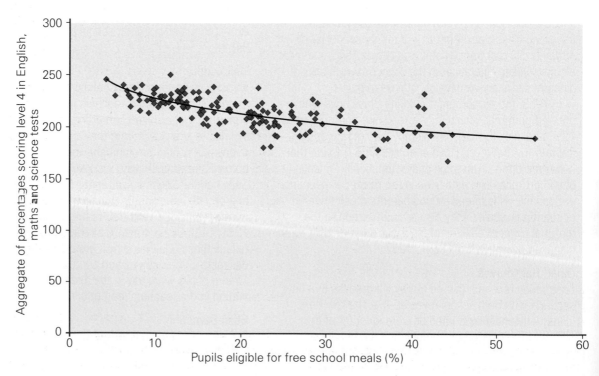

LEA key stage 2 aggregate test scores and the percentage of primary school pupils eligible for free school meals

Gender

Because social class interacts with gender, working-class girls are less likely to have equal access to educational advantages than middle- and upper-class girls and middle- and upper-class boys. However, gender plays an important role in its own right.

These days, girls generally do better at school than boys from pre-school to post-16. However, it's important to understand that rising achievement among girls isn't the same as girls having equality of opportunity. Post-school achievements and jobs indicate that girls are still making stereotypical 'choices', and are failing to maximise their career potential. Moreover, in the workforce, women are still over-represented among the low paid and under-represented among the top earners.

Female life chances are decidedly better in the educational sphere than in the world of work. While boys are making little significant progress at school, girls are performing a lot better. Even so, when subject 'choice' enters the fray, old habits die hard. We've placed inverted commas around 'choice' to indicate that what girls study isn't really about free choice but more about prevailing stereotypes. Girls still do the 'soft', arty and creative subjects, while boys predominate in the sciences, except for biology. At university degree level, more women obtain upper seconds, and men are over-represented at the top and bottom – more of them get firsts, thirds and passes.

Evidence points to three main areas of gender differences in educational performance (National Foundation for Educational Research, 1998):

1 Boys lag behind in literacy skills when they first start school and in English throughout primary and secondary school.

2 Boys perform less well than girls in GCSE exams.

3 Even though they are on a par with boys in terms of number of entries and performance in GCSE maths and science, girls continue to opt out of maths and science in post-16 education.

It's also interesting and relevant to point out that girls in single-sex comprehensive schools achieve better exam results than equivalent boys' or mixed institutions. This is despite the fact that girls' single-sex comprehensive schools have more pupils from traditionally disadvantaged groups (poor families, pupils whose first language isn't English, and so on).

In the public school sector, girls romp home ahead of boys at GCSE, but at A-levels boys get more top grades.

Despite clear differences in girls' and boys' educational achievement, a surge in the performance of 11-year-old boys in English tests in 1999 is beginning to narrow the literacy gap in this age group. In 1998, only 56% of boys passed English, whereas 73% of girls passed. In 1999, although boys trailed behind girls on average by about 11 points, the gap had narrowed from about 16 points in the previous year. In maths and science, the sexes remained roughly equal, with girls narrowing the slight lead of boys. But, lest policy-makers rest on their laurels, they should remember that it took ten years to get girls' achievement at GCSE on a par with that of boys.

It's likely that improved educational outcomes for females will translate into better life chances in the workplace, and it's surely significant that women now constitute the majority of applicants to higher education. That said, the subject 'choices' that teenage girls make at school might make it more difficult for them to enter scientific and technological professions, even if they excel in subjects such as, say, English and history.

Once women leave school and university and enter employment, there's nothing inevitable about gender or inequality. In Sweden, for example, one half of the Cabinet is made up of women, much of the caring done by women in other societies is provided by local councils, and both mothers and fathers can get time off from work to look after young children.

While it's wrong to imagine that recent efforts to raise girls' achievement have led to a neglect of boys' potential, policy-makers are very concerned with the relative underachievement of boys. Even though boys sometimes have access to more teacher time than girls (by 'demanding' more attention), the Qualifications and Curriculum Authority (1998) concludes that an obstacle to boys' achievement is a 'boy culture', or 'laddish culture', that deters hard work and enthusiasm. This same theme was taken up by Paul Willis 20 years earlier (Willis, 1978).

Ethnicity

The relationship between ethnicity and educational achievement is complex. In primary schools, African Caribbean pupils seem to achieve less well than white pupils, but the situation is sometimes reversed. A more consistent pattern of

SOCIAL POLICY AND WELFARE

lower than average achievement in early primary school is evident among Bangladeshi and Pakistani pupils (Gillborn and Gipps, 1996). This may be linked to levels of fluency in English and insufficient access to extra support in the subject.

At the end of secondary school, GCSE results at age 16 show that, regardless of ethnic origin, pupils from well-to-do backgrounds achieve the highest average scores. Indian pupils consistently seem to achieve more highly, on average, than pupils from other South Asian backgrounds, and they sometimes outperform white pupils. Bangladeshi pupils often achieve relatively less well than pupils from other ethnic backgrounds and, in many LEAs, African Caribbean pupils achieve significantly less than other ethnic groups (Gillborn and Gipps, 1996).

More recently, Ofsted (1999) has noted that the educational achievement of minority ethnic groups as a whole is improving. However, some groups continue to underachieve. Ofsted has summarised the position in these terms:

◎ 'Gypsy' Traveller pupils are the minority ethnic group most at risk in the educational stakes. Although some of them make a quite promising start in primary school, by the time they enter secondary school, their generally low attainment is a matter of serious concern.

◎ The early years' performance of Bangladeshi and Pakistani pupils remains below par. But, once they become proficient in English, things take a decisive turn for the better, with the attainment of these pupils often matching, or even surpassing, native English speakers in similar circumstances. However, the generally low representation of Bangladeshi and Pakistani pupils among the higher grades at GCSE remains a worry.

◎ Black Caribbean pupils make a good start in primary schools, but their performance shows a marked slide at secondary school level.

◎ Generally, girls from minority ethnic groups attain more highly than boys.

The proportion of young people from minority ethnic groups in full-time education (post-16) is higher than that for young white people. For example, in the 16–19 age group, in spring 1997, 81% of those from minority ethnic groups were in education and training, compared to 67% of the white population. In higher education, 13% of students entering courses in 1996–1997 were

from minority ethnic groups, more than double the 6% that such groups represent nationally.

In other respects, however, as Francis Beckett (1999) points out, the statistics are less encouraging. Minority ethnic students have a harder time, for example, getting on to the most popular higher education courses, such as medicine. According to Professor I. C. McManus and his research team at St Mary's Hospital Medical School, having a European surname predicts acceptance better than ethnic origin itself, which suggests direct discrimination. Ethnic origin is, of course, guessed from the candidates' surnames.

Another concern – this time in schools – is the over-representation of African Caribbean pupils (especially, boys) among excluded pupils. Nearly six times as many African Caribbean pupils are excluded as white pupils. Reporting on the characteristics of black pupils who had been excluded, David Gillborn (1996) noted that:

◎ they had more educational ability than other excluded pupils, but were seen as underachieving

◎ they had less deep-seated trauma

◎ they had less of a history of disruptive behaviour – while other pupils had often been excluded from primary school, there was an indication that black pupils' problems began in secondary school

The most significant access issue in relation to exclusion is that, once permanently excluded, there's only a slim chance that pupils will get back into mainstream education. In the case of black pupils, Gillborn (1996) believes that exclusion operates in a racist way.

Another area of concern in relation to black pupils is the school curriculum. The black journalist Trevor Phillips (1999) eloquently notes that:

'there seems little reflection of that ebony thread in the tapestry of pre-20th century British history as it is taught in schools, nor is there recognition of how tightly woven that thread is to Britons' national and personal histories.'

The place of black people in Britain's history is easily overlooked. Yet the nation has long been a mixed society, a place inhabited by migrants – from the Bronze Age and Neolithic peoples who journeyed to north-west Europe 40 000 years ago to the refugees from Eastern Europe and Africa who are arriving today.

The UK has gained much from its ethnic diversity, but this isn't proudly proclaimed to the extent that it ought to be in the National Curriculum which, in large measure, effectively excludes black role models, thereby demotivating already underachieving black children. How, asks Phillips, can black pupils be enthusiastic about their studies when the curriculum essentially ignores their existence? Sure, 'Black peoples of the Americas' shows up, but you'll search in vain for a black contribution to British history, which has been deftly airbrushed out of the curriculum.

As Sir Herman Ouseley prepared to step down from his job as chairman of the Commission for Racial Equality in January 2000, he expressed his disappointment that he hadn't landed the 'knock-out blow' that could have established cultural diversity as a core value in British schools. In the light of the McPherson Report on Stephen Lawrence (see p. 251), Ouseley wanted a much more forthright approach in the National Curriculum to expressing the value of a non-racist society.

Importantly, Ouseley favours a balanced curriculum. He doesn't want a curriculum that offers black children everything they need to know about black history at the expense of knowing less about English, maths and science. Equally, he adds, he doesn't want well-educated pupils going around beating up others because they're Asian, black or white.

Sir Herman Ouseley, former Chairman of the Commission for Racial Equality, thinks that the government could do much more to make cultural diversity a core value in all schools

Disability and impairment

It's estimated that between 2% and 3% of the population have a learning difficulty ranging from mild to profound. According to David Denney (1998), there are about 30 000 children under age 16 in the UK with severe or profound learning difficulties.

Learning difficulties aren't, of course, always synonymous with physical disabilities. Some children who have physically impairments are high achievers, and some children who have no physical impairment are low achievers. Nevertheless, a child with cerebral palsy in a school that fails to give him or her the special 'writing tools' that are needed is clearly at an educational disadvantage. Such a child might, for example, lag a couple of years behind a non-impaired classmate in English tests because of this problem rather than the physical one.

Although special schools are sometimes well resourced to help children with learning difficulties, being placed in them involves a degree of social exclusion from the mainstream (see Chapter 8). The learning of mathematics might improve, but perhaps at the expense of broader social skills. Moreover, if a child attends a special school that does not have the range of subject teachers normally found in ordinary schools, he or she is dis-*abled* by not getting the best teaching in certain subjects. Non-disabled children in mainstream schools also lose out by having fewer chances to socialise with disabled children in special schools.

The best model offers an inclusive education, in which all pupils attend the same school, but special support is provided for those with learning difficulties.

Yet, despite the rhetoric of an inclusive education for all, pupils with impairments are often segregated from so-called 'normal' pupils. In 1978, the Warnock Report on *Special Educational Needs* argued that pupils with special educational needs (for example, disabled children, and children with emotional and behavioural difficulties) should be educated in mainstream schools if at all possible. But successive governments have done little to implement an inclusive philosophy of education.

This dismal picture is evident at all levels of the educational system, from primary schools through to universities. Consequently, many pupils and students with learning difficulties don't receive an education of as high a quality as that experienced by other pupils and students.

11 Employment and Unemployment

By the end of this chapter you should be able to:

◎ Understand ways of defining employment and unemployment.

◎ Consider the functions of employment and unemployment.

◎ Take account of employment and unemployment trends.

◎ Outline employment and unemployment life chances in relation to social class, gender, ethnicity, age and disability.

◎ Contemplate the economic, social and psychological effects of employment and unemployment.

◎ Discuss social policy initiatives on employment.

Employment takes up a large part of most adults' working lives. It gives them an income, a status and, if they're lucky, a great deal of pleasure. In some cases, income, status and enjoyment levels are low; in other cases not. Being unemployed, however, almost always leads to reduced income and status, and often to considerable personal suffering.

There are, of course, some people who don't want a job. In social scientific language, such people belong to a group called the **inactive**, a category that also includes people who want to work but can't. Some inactive people don't need to work because of inherited wealth, good fortune, early retirement and so forth. Others lack the qualifications and skills to enter employment, or are unable to work owing to disability or illness.

One of the significant trends of the late-modern world is the gradual eclipse of the 'job for life'. Companies and public-sector employers are assigning short-term contracts to temporary employees more than previously, a trend that looks set to continue in the flexible employment practices of an information-based economy, with its 'just-in-time' workforce.

When you finish full-time education, the setting in which you work is more likely than that of your parents to be one in which workers will be doing different things for different people without being able to describe everything under the heading of 'one job'. Some jobs for life will continue for a while, but those who are able to 'hang on in there' will probably be middle-aged people and those approaching retirement age, with a long track record in one or a few workplaces.

The future of work for you, the reader, needn't be a bleak one. Provided that you ride the wave of change by seizing the opportunity of lifelong learning and training, you'll do well and prosper. On the other hand, young people who enter – or don't enter – the labour market without good qualifications and flexible skills will have poorer prospects.

This chapter examines employment, unemployment and variations on these themes (such as inactivity and underemployment) in relation to concepts, social functions, trends, life chances, effects and social policies. While the main focus is on current issues, the section on trends necessarily looks back at recent history.

Defining employment and unemployment

This is not as easy as it might first seem! Not even policy-makers are in full agreement as to what counts as employment and unemployment. For example, some commentators regard the unemployed as people in receipt of unemployment benefits, while others extend the net wider, to include all those who are actively seeking a job, even if they're not on benefits.

In sociological terms, we can say that employment and unemployment statistics are to some extent socially constructed – that is, they reflect, in part, the ways in which the government chooses to categorise these states. This doesn't mean that employment and unemployment, as experienced by real, breathing human beings, are simply what policy-makers say they are. Experiences are one thing, but documentation is another. If, for example, you lose your job but don't apply for unemployment benefit, you 'know' that you're unemployed even if the statisticians think otherwise. You may not be on the benefit claimant count, but you'll be reminded of your jobless status (with a jolt!) when you're taken off the payroll.

Here we have a dilemma. Claimant count officials say that I'm not unemployed. I say that I am. Where do we go from here? The short answer is that, in different ways, we're both right. The officials are correct in saying that, according to their criteria, I'm not *officially* unemployed. I'm right in saying that I'm *personally* unemployed But now we have another problem. Which version is more accurate? If we're looking at the bigger picture, the official version is objectively valid, because it's widely accepted in social policy circles and its legitimation has consequences – my right to benefits. When we consider the unofficial position, my individual version is subjectively valid, because it correctly describes my felt perceptions.

In this book, we're largely concerned with the employment and unemployment statistics that affect government policies. We accept that these figures don't tell the whole truth and nothing but the truth, and may have little or nothing to do with some individual personal realities. In that context, it's fair and reasonable to consider whether policy-makers are actually asking the right questions. But, for now, we have to consider how they define and measure employment and unemployment – because their decisions have important outcomes for society as a whole.

Employment, unemployment and inactivity

In the United Kingdom, policy-makers often divide the adult population into three main labour market categories (Joseph Rowntree Foundation, 1998):

1 The **employed** – people in paid work in an employee or self-employed capacity, or who are on government-backed training and employment programmes.

2 The **unemployed** – people without paid work, but who are available to take up a job.

3 The **inactive** – all remaining members of the adult population, some of whom may want a job, while some others don't.

These rather tight categories shouldn't be overstated. In the real world, there's a continuum from *complete employment* to *complete non-employment*, with unemployment lying in between these two extremes.

Internationally agreed definitions of **employment** and **unemployment** are generally based on *people in paid work* and *people not in paid work who are looking for a job*, respectively. There are, however, nuances. For example, some statisticians include people who work without pay in a family business or on a farm for at least one hour each day as among the employed. As for unemployment, since 1979, successive governments have changed the method of 'counting' the unemployed about 35 times or more.

Employment

In official (and even public) eyes, employment is often considered to be synonymous with work. However, this is an over-simplification, because some work isn't employment. When, for example, I fix a rickety armchair at home, I am working – but not as an employee. For some commentators, the defining feature of employment is *doing work for pay or profit*. But even this definition doesn't always stand up to scrutiny.

Thus, for example, the Labour Force Survey, conducted every month since September 1946, counts as employed not only people who work for pay or profit but also unpaid family workers. The Labour Force Survey defines those in employment as:

'people aged 16 or over who did some paid work in the reference week (whether as an employee or self-employed); those who had a job that they were temporarily away from (on holiday, for example); those on government-supported training and employment programmes; and those doing unpaid family work.'

(adapted from Biz/ed, 1997)

This definition is essentially in line with the one adopted by the International Labour Organization (ILO).

In general terms, the **employment rate** can be defined as the number of employed people as a percentage of the working-age population. In most cases, 15 is the beginning of the working-age population, but this varies from country to country. In the UK, the working age runs from the minimum school-leaving age (16) to the start of the state retirement age (59 for women, and 64 for men).

Let's say that we want to calculate the employment rate in the UK. The working-age population is the sum of those employed and unemployed people who are aged between 16 and either 59 or 61. That percentage of people in the working-age population who have a job, or who otherwise qualify (for example, are on a government training scheme), are the employed.

Such figures can easily become confusing, so let's consider an imaginary island of 150 inhabitants. On this island, 100 people are of working age, of whom:

- ◎ 95 have a job, or are on an official training course
- ◎ five are unemployed

Thus the percentage of employed people is 95% and the percentage of unemployed people is 5%. The same simple mathematics applies to countries such as the UK, even though the scale is much larger.

Unemployment

Unemployment refers to the number of people who are out of work in a particular society or area. In the UK, it's usually expressed monthly, as a percentage of jobless people in the total workforce.

However, there are a number of ways of measuring unemployment. UK governments have traditionally used the number of jobless people who are claiming unemployment benefit.

This is called the **claimant count**. It omits people who aren't eligible for unemployment benefit but who nevertheless may be looking for work. It also leaves out unemployed people who are on special training programmes.

In April 1998, the Labour government decided to take more explicit account of the Labour Force Survey unemployment figures, as well as the claimant count. The Labour Force Survey takes account of all jobless people who are looking for work, not just those on benefit. The Labour Force Survey count is recommended by the International Labour Organization, because it provides more internationally comparable data on unemployment.

Unsurprisingly, the Labour Force Survey figures show that more people are unemployed than the claimant count might suggest. This is because the Labour Force Survey count (known as the **ILO count** – see the figure opposite) doesn't just include those out of work who are claiming unemployment benefit, but all unemployed people who are seeking jobs.

In general terms, the unemployment rate can be defined as the number of unemployed people who are available for work as a percentage of the working-age population. This doesn't include, for example, full-time students.

Let's say that we want to calculate the unemployment rate in the UK. The working-age population is the sum of employed and unemployed people who are between the ages of 16 and either 59 or 64. The percentage of people in the working-age population who don't have a job or who don't otherwise qualify (for example, are not on a government training scheme), are the unemployed.

The factors that affect how many people are officially defined as unemployed are of four main types:

1 *Statistical changes*, such as only counting people on benefits.

2 *Benefit rule changes*, which then automatically translate into changes in the numbers of people who are officially considered unemployed.

3 *Administrative changes*, such as making people accept work that they're not suited to, by tightening up the 'availability for work' rules.

4 *Temporary work* and training schemes, which can create short-lived 'employment blips'.

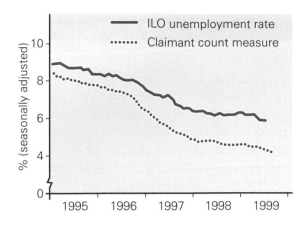

(Office for National Statistics)

Unemployment rates

In official terms, to be unemployed in the UK today is to be either:

- registered for unemployment benefit, and both available for and actively seeking work – persons in this category constitute the **claimant count** – *or*

- without a job, but available to start work in the two weeks following a Labour Force Survey interview, and having either looked for work in the four weeks before the interview, or having been waiting to start a job that has already been obtained – people in this category constitute the **International Labour Organization (ILO) count**

The *Financial Times* newspaper uses both claimant count and ILO count in its documentation of unemployment trends, as illustrated in the accompanying figure.

Labour market statistics are very complex, and in a book of this kind it's entirely appropriate to concentrate on the bold outlines, as provided, for example in the Joseph Rowntree Foundation (1998) definitions on page 297. That said, we will at times refer to nuances as and when they arise in particular contexts.

Economic inactivity

In official terms, economically inactive people are those who are neither in employment nor unemployed. The category includes, for example, people aged under 16 and retired people. It's important to emphasise that this is an official rather than a literal categorisation. Thus, for example, teenagers aged under 16 who babysit

their younger brothers and sisters are clearly working, even though this doesn't officially count as employment. This doesn't mean that those aged under 16 are officially unemployed. They're not, because they're too young to be included in the working-age population.

Definitions of employment as a condition of being in paid work, and of unemployment and inactivity as forms of unpaid 'non-work', beg a number of questions: What is work? What is 'non-work'? And, while we're at it, what is leisure?

Work, non-work and leisure

Once again, we find ourselves in difficult conceptual territory. What you call work mightn't be how a friend sees it – and, of course, vice versa. The same applies to non-work and leisure. Let's say that your friend is a professional musician. Is he or she working while playing in a band for money – but not while just playing for fun, with no financial recompense? Is the second category leisure? And even if your friend considers playing for money a form of leisure, is it really work?

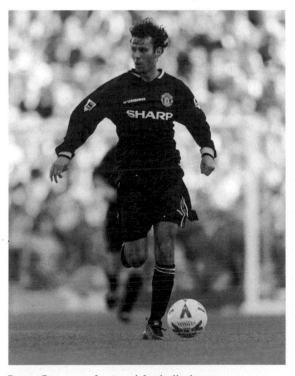

Ryan Giggs, professional football player (Manchester United). Is this work or leisure, or a bit of both?

These are difficult questions. They serve to remind us that social scientists, in the spirit of social constructivism, must take account of people's socially constructed perceptions. Allowing for this, we know also that some meanings are more prevalent than others. For example, many people see leisure as a recreational slot, during non-work time, when they're not preoccupied with mundane, routine activities (such as making a pot of tea).

Allowing for different interpretations, the following definitions capture, at least, for most Britons, the essential qualities of work, non-work and leisure:

◎ **work** is an activity that produces goods and services (for example, building roads and parenting)

◎ **non-work** is activity or non-activity that occurs before work is undertaken (for example, in childhood), during the time that remains when work is completed (for example, relaxing after a hard day at the office) and after work is no longer undertaken (for example, in retirement)

◎ **leisure** is recreational activity that typically occurs during non-work time (for example, going to the movies at the weekend)

These three spheres impinge upon each other. For example, ship-builders do work that's at risk of being replaced by non-work (through early retirement or unemployment) as shipyards shut down. Firefighters often spend their leisure time together, because their work creates strong social bonds based on supporting each other during tough, dangerous work. Influences can also flow from what people do during non-work time to what they do at work. For example, some people choose to work in music stores because listening to music is their favourite form of leisure activity.

REVIEW POINTS

◎ In the UK, policy-makers often divide the adult population into three main labour market categories: the **employed**, the **unemployed** and the **inactive**.

◎ The **employment rate** is the number of employed people as a percentage of the working-age population.

◎ The **unemployment rate** is the number of unemployed people who are available for work as a percentage of the working-age population.

◎ The factors that affect how many people are officially defined as unemployed are of four main types: statistical changes, benefit rule changes, administrative changes, and temporary work and training schemes.

◎ There are two official ways of being unemployed in the UK. These are the **claimant count** and the **International Labour Organization count**.

REVIEW ACTIVITIES

1 Why is it difficult to define **employment** and **unemployment**?
2 What is the difference between being unemployed and economically inactive?
3 When is work not employment?
4 What factors influence how many people are officially classified as unemployed?
5 What is leisure?

The functions of employment and unemployment

People usually work in order to live. In ancient societies, work was largely centred around hunting, harvesting and building. Physical labour met basic survival needs – food in the belly and a roof over the head. This isn't to say that everyone worked. In slave societies, for example, slave owners had plenty of time for leisure and 'amateur' politics, because slaves did the menial tasks.

So what's changed? People still hunt, harvest and build homes. But fewer of them do this, and machines do much of the physical activity. Indeed, one of the great achievements of the 20th century was, with the help of advanced technology, to reduce the importance of manual work to such an extent that only a minority need do it. In the late-modern age, work increasingly provides products and services that people don't need for survival but want for fulfilment. Societies have functioned without organised educational and healthcare systems for most of history, but Britons today couldn't imagine living in a society without schools and hospitals.

When we consider the functions of employment and unemployment, we need to take account of space and time, and of whose views are in the ascendancy. In the British government's view, a key function of employment is to help provide the goods and services that society needs. For example, bridges are necessary when rivers run through the middle of towns. Therefore society must ensure that enough civil engineers are employed to carry out the construction work.

Two other important functions of employment, say the politicians, are to provide working adults and their dependants with economic security, and to raise taxes from earnings in order to fund investment in public services, such as education and health. Central planning isn't, however, the whole story. Some goods and services (possibly, most) are provided through the mechanism of the market. When enough people demand a particular product, suppliers provide it. Often, the suppliers are private capitalists, such as large commercial companies.

In societies such as the UK, where production, income and investment are inextricably bound up with paid employment, to be unemployed through one's 'own fault' is considered 'dysfunctional'. Put simply, unemployment is a problem, not a function. Some commentators on the Left, as we shall see, contest this argument, but theirs is a voice that has little sway in the corridors of power.

The motivation to work in a paid capacity within a clearly defined time span (for example, five days a week for 47 weeks a year) is, in historical terms, a recent phenomenon. When factories and machines began to take over from field work and farm horses during the English Industrial Revolution (very roughly, from the middle of the 18th century to the mid-to-late 19th century), people stopped *doing jobs* and *got a job*. Instead of work 'ceasing' when the harvest was in, factories provided continuous employment, week in, week out.

Seasonal tasks in agriculture, punctuated with quite long periods of non-work, gradually yielded to regular work in factories with short periods of recuperative rest. To be sure, all of this didn't happen overnight, and pockets of rural life and work existed alongside each other in some parts of the country. Nevertheless, industrialisation and factories represented a distinct 'march of history'.

Sociological theories of employment

The providers of goods and services in society, whether public or private, are usually employers. This places them in a particular relationship with those whom they employ. Some sociologists, those known as **functionalists** (see Chapter 13, p. 350), maintain that a harmonious relationship between employers and employees helps to ensure that the production process runs smoothly. This doesn't mean that functionalist sociologists approve of harmony, but they note that its presence in the workplace usually increases productivity.

Out of this perspective (even though it wasn't always couched in explicitly functionalist terms) arose so-called **human relations theory**. Most closely associated with the work of the early 20th century thinker, Elton Mayo (an Australian who settled in the USA), human relations theory assumes that when a 'hand' is hired, the whole person comes with it. Mayo argued that workers required more than wage incentives. They also needed to like their jobs.

Human relations theory is therefore based on the assumption that bosses and their managers should offer non-manager employees intrinsic rewards – notably, enjoyable working conditions – as well as decent pay, because happy workers are productive workers. 'Coaxing' rather than 'carrot and stick' becomes the main management tool. In that respect, argues the Marxist sociologist, Harry Braverman, 'the practitioners of "human relations" and "industrial psychology" are the maintenance crew for the human machinery' (Braverman, 1974: 87). They're 'indulgent persuaders' rather than 'sergeant majors'.

Employers who adopt a human relations outlook are, of course, interested in control. But instead of forcing unwilling and often resented obedience, they seek the co-operation of those over whom they exercise authority. Commentators of a left-wing persuasion, including a number of Marxist sociologists, seize upon the control issue. According to **Marxist theory** (see Chapter 13, p. 350), whatever their strategy, bosses and managers are in the business of controlling. Human relations hasn't, say the Marxists, removed an underlying conflict between the 'suits' and the 'overalls', but has kept discord at bay by 'humanising' the relations between the controller and the controlled.

The root of this conflict is the unequal distribution of goods and services in society. Marxists contend that upper-class bosses employ workers on low wages, but make vast amounts of money on the employee-produced goods and services that they sell. This means that employees are exploited by a capitalist upper class, because they only get a very small portion of the value of the goods and services that they produce. The rest – the so-called **surplus value** – goes to the upper class who, even allowing for their expenditure on factories, machines and the like, make huge profits.

Although, according to Marxists, relationships between employers and employees are more openly exploitative in private institutions, power differentials and conflict within public institutions aren't overlooked. In theory, public concerns are 'owned' by the public, as represented by government. In practice, well-paid managers exercise considerable operational control over less well paid junior employees. Consider the pay and control gap, for example, between NHS managers and NHS nurses. That said, in the public sector, managers are more accountable to the public at large than to individual owners (typically, large shareholders).

Both functionalists and Marxists accept that employment serves societal needs, irrespective of how such needs are defined and by whom. The main difference between the two approaches is that, whereas functionalist theory emphasises the importance of employers and employees as joint stakeholders in the productive process, Marxists stress the real and potential conflict of interests between these different groups. It was in this latter context that workers formed trades unions to protect themselves from being exploited by bosses. However, in functionalist (and Blairite) terms, trades unions are now increasingly seen as partners, alongside owners and their own employer organisations, each committed to promoting enterprise and investment and enjoying the returns.

Trades unions

We've already referred to Marx's claim that capitalists and workers have different and conflicting interests. Capitalists want to maximise their profits and therefore try to keep wages down. Workers want decent pay, so they seek to keep wages up. It was during the 19th century that Marx put forward his argument, and that workers began to get increasingly organised through trades unions in their bid for better pay and conditions.

Marx hoped that once the working class, through the collective power of trades unions, had improved their material position, they would continue the war against capitalist oppression through revolutionary politics. He was to be disappointed, at least in so far as England was concerned. From the first enfranchisement of the working class in 1867, the Left waited for the day when the sleeping giant would sweep socialism into Parliament. This didn't happen. After scrutinising the results of the first general election that followed in 1868, Engels expressed his exasperation in a letter to Marx:

> 'What do you say to the elections in the factory districts? Once again the proletariat has discredited itself terribly ... It cannot be denied that the increase of working class voters has brought the Tories more than their simple percentage increase; it has improved their relative position.'
>
> (cited by McKenzie and Silver, 1968: 14)

Ninety years and 23 elections on, a section of the 'big battalions of the poor and unprivileged' – as Peter Short (1952, cited by McKenzie and Silver, 1968: 14) called them – were still 'discrediting' themselves. Labour (a more left-wing party then than it is today) was ejected from office in 1951, confounding the Left's hope that socialism would become the natural creed of government.

After Marx's death in 1883, his friend and co-writer, Friedrich Engels, bemoaned the 'bourgeois' inclinations of British workers, some of who struck a deal with capitalism in exchange for better wages. But other commentators still believed that workers and their trades unions embodied the potential for socialist politics. History has proven them right in only an episodic sense, with occasional strikes turning into political battles against right-wing politicians.

Coal-miners, in particular, have a reputation for taking on the status quo. C. Kerr and A. Siegal (1954; cited by Hirszowicz, 1981) suggest that coal-miners display a strong united front during strikes because of their deep immersion in working-class communities. The relative isolation of miners from mainstream society and their socialisation into remote but tightly cohesive communities foster an *esprit de corps*. When conflict erupts between miners and bosses, the issue isn't just about pay and conditions. It's also rebellion against people at the top in society – an 'us' and 'them' struggle. In that respect, it embraces the Marxist concept of class struggle. Here, there's a theoretical and an empirical meeting. Marxists theorise that the root cause of conflict is between the working and ruling classes.

Historically, strikes have been particularly concentrated in mining, the metal industries and transport. In the case of the first two sectors, it's likely that the occupational communities one finds in pit villages and steel towns help to develop the resolve to react to common problems through collective action. However, while physically tough elemental work embodies the potential for militant trade unionism, pit villages and steel towns are now in decline. In the absence of a social setting characterised by an epic tradition of heroism and struggle between workers and bosses, Third Way politics are latching on to the more moderate union instincts that Marx lamented.

New Labour politicians increasingly speak of 'workplace stakeholders', in an effort to distance themselves from the 'bad old days' of industrial relations during the 1960s and 1970s when trade union militancy (although probably less commonplace than tabloid media reports suggested) was nevertheless resorted to in well publicised stand-offs between workers and bosses.

Given the close historical links between the Labour Party and the trade union movement, trade union leaders had hoped that the new government would tip the balance of industrial relations in their favour. However, while recognising that people should be free to choose whether or not to join a trade union, the government extended an olive leaf to employer groups by making it amply clear that the UK, under New Labour, still had the toughest labour laws in the Western world.

Tough laws or otherwise, for the first time in about 20 years, Trades Union Congress (TUC) membership is up as the trade union cause turns the corner. Full-time male membership in manufacturing is in decline, but the TUC has become better at recruiting women, black and other ethnic minority members and part-timers. Moreover, trades unions are signing more new recognition deals than ever before (Trades Union Congress, 2000). Taking advantage of a new right to union recognition in companies where 50% of the workforce are trade union members, union chiefs are more positive than ever before about the prospects of recognition.

In language that clearly echoes an affinity with New Labour politics, the TUC General Secretary, John Monks (Trades Union Congress, 2000) reports that:

> '... unions are taking full advantage of the new legal climate. Employers are losing the instinctive hostility to trade unions as they look across the economy and see partnership employers leading so many market sectors. The old scare stories cut little ice with today's sensible employers.'

In similar vein, Monks (Trades Union Congress, 1999a) has welcomed the proposal that the TUC, the Confederation of British Industry (CBI) and the British Chamber of Commerce 'should put their heads together to draw up a statement of principles for how the UK training revolution is to proceed', adding that this initiative 'is a welcome endorsement of the value of *partnership* in the workplace' (italics added).

'Tomorrow's union as partner', is the clarion call of the TUC, with a clear cold shoulder given to the old militant tactics of the past. Employment rights, say the union chiefs, are as important for white-collar and professional employees as they are for blue-collar workers. The message seems to be working in so far as union membership is concerned.

Even the Old Left is warming to the new positive mood towards trades unions today, and has applauded union efforts to gain wider recognition in the wake of new employment rights. However, this hasn't stopped Old Left commentators criticising the government for leaving most of the anti-union legislation from the Thatcher years intact – including ballots and notices before strikes, and the abolition of the closed shop, secondary action and mass picketing.

New Labour and employment

As indicated in Chapter 13, although he probably wouldn't call himself a functionalist, Tony Blair adopts a functionalist view of things. Thus, for example, he believes in a society based on rules and order, where the battle isn't between capitalism and socialism but between progress and conservatism. In 'Blair's Britain', as the Prime Minister envisages it, economic efficiency and social justice are finally working in partnership, with private capital alongside public investment.

New Labour is very pro-employment. The government wants to make work pay for the

around 20% in 1981. This trend looks set to continue.

- ◎ *Flexible hours*. More than 50% of all employees in the UK, compared to about 3% in 1984, work flexible hours, either because their basic hours are variable or because they work varying amounts of overtime.

- ◎ *Temporary employment*. The number of employees in temporary work increased by a massive 43% from 1990 to 1997. This includes people who are on fixed-term contracts, seasonal, casual or agency work. The extent to which this might be part of a long-term trend is uncertain. That said, at just over 6% of employees, the extent of temporary work in the UK is well below the EU average of 11%.

- ◎ *Self-employment*. The number of self-employed people has increased significantly, from about 1.9 million in

1979 to over 3.3 million in 1997. The self-employed now account for around 13% of employed people. Self-employment is a hallmark feature of a flexible labour market, offering a route out of unemployment for some people, and a source of new jobs for others.

Only 10% of employees work a 'standard 40 hour week', reports HM Treasury (1997), a fairly long-standing statistical trend and a defining feature of the early 21st century UK labour market. Things look set to continue that way, with a flexible job market enabling more individuals to match their working hours to their (and their employers') needs.

In some respects, flexibility offers new and exciting prospects. Flexible working hours, for example, have made it easier for more women to enter the labour market. Today, women account for about half of the workforce, compared to 36% in 1971 – and the proportion continues to rise. New technology has freed some workers from the drudgery of work, leaving them to concentrate on creative and intellectually satisfying job roles. And a shorter working week allows people the opportunity to be more active in leisure.

On the other hand, we've already referred to Fleetwood's (1999) fear that, in a flexible age, less unemployment can mean more bad employment. There's a sharp and growing division between employees with a sophisticated knowledge of new technology, who have well-paid, creative jobs, and less computer-literate employees, who have low-paid, unskilled and repetitive jobs.

Consider, for example, the mushrooming growth in call centres (armchair banks, telesales, railway enquiries and the like): 'Good morning. This is David. How may I help you?' One wonders if David really likes his job or if he's confined to a routine, scripted task, devoid of all initiative. Has he become a white-collar worker in a white-collar factory where burnout and stress abound?

Flexible jobs can also lead to blighted long-term job prospects, a problem identified by the Policy Studies Institute (1998). Using data from a national sample of over 850 people who were unemployed during 1990–1992, Policy Studies Institute researchers found that three-quarters of the jobs that they eventually took were temporary, part-time, self-employed or required a substantially lower skill level than their previous job.

Following the same sample through to 1995, it was found that:

Do call centres such as BT's in Newcastle run the risk of becoming the new sweatshops of the post-industrial age?

- Less than a quarter of those who had taken part-time jobs were in full-time employment.

- The majority of those who had become self-employed remained so.

- There were few signs of career progress among those who had taken jobs below their previous skill level.

- While 38% of those who entered temporary employment were now on permanent contracts, 25% remained on temporary contracts and 36% were, again, unemployed.

- In spite of the growth in flexible jobs, one-fifth of the sample remained out of work throughout the period of the study. By 1995, most of them had stopped actively looking for work. Women with young children and older men faced special problems finding work, as did single people of either sex.

The researchers concluded that more needs to be done to help people in part-time and temporary employment, to improve their job status and earnings, and to tackle the particular problems encountered by women (Policy Studies Institute, 1998). Among the policy initiatives that they suggest might improve the employment prospects of these people are the following:

- training programmes to help people in flexible jobs to acquire new skills and improve their longer- term employability

- more childcare provision and childcare subsidies to enable more women to enter employment or increase their hours of work

Employment and unemployment life chances

The prospect of having a well-paid job falls unevenly on different sections of the population, as does the risk of unemployment. Take gender, for example. Globally, women provide some 38% of the economically active population, but only receive about 26% of earned income. Consider ethnicity. In Britain during the mid-1990s, roughly 19% of the white population were in the bottom fifth of the distribution of disposable income – and 27% of the black and Indian population and 64% of the Bangladeshi and Pakistani population were in the same position.

Take a look at unemployment. Unemployment rates for men are particularly high in mining and industrial areas. The shift from heavy industry to service jobs has favoured women in general, but growing numbers of lone mothers often find it difficult to take or retain jobs. The unemployment rate for people from 'non-white' ethnic minorities is more than twice that for white people. Among disabled people, not only is the rate of unemployment also high but, additionally, they're likely to be out of work longer than other unemployed workers. As with the unemployed from ethnic minority communities, discrimination is implicated.

Although being unemployed and poor is usually more stressful than having a job, it would be wrong to suggest that employment is stress-free. A nationwide survey conducted by the University of Cambridge and reported by the Joseph Rowntree Foundation (1999a) found that work has become more intense, with more than 60% of employees saying that the pace of work and effort had increased over the previous five years.

More than 40% of employees thought that managers could be trusted 'only a little' or 'not at all'. Three-quarters claimed that management and 'employees' weren't 'on the same side', re-awakening images of the 'us and them' dichotomies between bosses and workers reported by sociologists in the 1960s.

The researchers concluded that the root cause of work intensification lay with the reduced staffing levels pursued by senior managers, in response to market pressures from competitors and powerful stakeholders.

The study also highlighted a gradual rise in perceived job insecurity between 1966 and 1986, this being most apparent among 'blue-collar' workers during the late 1970s and early 1980s. Given the heavy losses in manufacturing during this period, such 'blue-collar' blues aren't surprising. More unexpected was the fact that feelings of job insecurity in the late 1990s, when the economy had 'recovered', were higher than at any point in the postwar period. Non-manual workers, in particular, reported a significant increase in job insecurity during the mid-1990s, and a large number of manual workers were worried too.

This kind of research, important though it is, doesn't tell the whole story. The subjective experience of employment and the objective material returns do vary markedly between different groups in society. The same applies to unemployment, but here we are much more likely to encounter a preponderance of vulnerable groups, such as lone-parent mothers, older men, disabled people, 'lower' class people, less qualified people and so on. It is true to say that the fortunes of the unemployed vary, but few of them enjoy good life chances.

Social class and employment

Some sociologists, notably those of Marxist leanings, contend that job satisfaction can never be fully realised in a society where one class of people – employees – are exploited by another class of people – employers. Based on this argument, capitalism fosters an illusion of happiness by giving workers token concessions, 'under the banner of job enlargement [i.e. swapping job tasks to relieve tedium] and the humanization of work' (Braverman, 1974: 37).

According to Marxists, conflict always exists between workers and capitalists, even if the former are lulled into thinking that this isn't the case. Non-Marxist sociologists regard this allegation as unproven, arguing that harmonious industrial relations have more to do with job satisfaction than with whether one works in a capitalist society.

Robert Blauner (1964), for example, found that workers on a car assembly line found their job exceptionally tedious and dissatisfying, whereas workers in a chemical plant obtained satisfaction from the control that they had over complex automatic machinery. Both factories were in the USA, a strongly capitalist society. Yet it was the technology they used that affected workers' levels of job satisfaction, rather than who owned the factory.

Job satisfaction and economic rewards differ quite markedly between different kinds of employee. Put simply, non-manual 'middle-class' employees usually enjoy their jobs more (or, at least, dislike them less) and earn more money than manual 'working-class' employees. As for the upper class, their income comes mainly from capital assets and shares, which means that some of them don't 'work' in the commonly understood meaning of the term.

Upper-class employment

Upper-class people are more likely to be employers than employees and to have sources of wealth that, through investment or via business, produce a significant independent income. The employer position of upper-class people tends to bring advantageous life chances and, because of the greater power and independence that being a relatively wealthy employer affords, minimal risk of unemployment.

Middle-class employment

The life chances within middle-class employment vary considerably. Those at the higher level – top lawyers and other elite professionals, politicians, senior managers, generals and ambassadors – are located in what John Westergaard (1995: 128) calls 'the foothills surrounding peak privilege and power'. They earn a lot of money, often obtain creative satisfaction from work, and enjoy life chances similar to those of the upper class. The middle section of the middle class – intermediate professionals, less senior managers, and so on – have decent salaries, good to excellent job conditions, good health and education, and relatively long lives, and participate in an affluent culture. However, the lower middle class do considerably less well in income terms, often earning no more than manual workers.

Working-class employment

Like the classes 'above' them, working-class people belong to a stratum that contains various subgroups. Manual workers are still a large (but declining) group within the working class, and are often concentrated in skilled/semi-skilled (for example, electrician/'postman') or unskilled occupations (for example, road sweeper). Job satisfaction levels tend to be relatively higher in skilled/semi-skilled work, as do earnings, with drudgery and poor pay (and the consequent diminished life chances) more common among the unskilled. There are echoes here of Blauner's (1964) thesis that more autonomy equates with more enjoyment at the workplace.

However, autonomy isn't just the preserve of middle-class occupations. Even in jobs where the assembly line remains a part of the production process, automation can perform the dull and dreary stuff. Car workers, for example, now push buttons and watch finished fuel tanks, welded by automatic machines, roll off the conveyor belt. This contrasts sharply with the days when workers were hunched over assembly lines, stifled by the heat and smoke of heavy welding torches. In the most modern car factories today, workers wear crisp, clean uniforms, maintain and repair their own machines, set and monitor their own quality control, and switch jobs regularly to avoid boredom.

Because of a shrinking (but still quite vibrant) manufacturing sector and a burgeoning service sector, routine 'white collar' employment (for example, retailing and office work) also figures prominently among working-class people of the 'post-industrial' age. This job market features lots of women, many of whom work part-time or on flexible terms. Routine non-manual work tends to have a low boredom threshold, and 'white collar woes' aren't compensated in money terms, with employees in the job sector sometimes earning less than manual workers.

Upper-class unemployment

In the 18th and 19th centuries, upper-class 'landed gentlemen' often belonged to a leisured elite, with any involvement in entrepreneurial activities kept to a low profile. In conventional upper-class circles, it was considered vulgar to engage in direct business transactions. W. D. Rubinstein (1977: 115) argued that, in English landed society:

> 'the number of aristocrats, or even minor landed gentry, who were directly concerned with industry or manufacturing (apart from membership on boards of companies exploiting the minerals on their own land) was surely nil.'

Today, of course, the upper class isn't just composed of 'landed gents'. They're still around, but their ranks also include an exceedingly prosperous business elite.

As for those hereditary peers for whom sitting in the House of Lords was a main occupation, many of them are now 'out of work'. This source of work finally ended in 1999, when the government decreed that no more seats in Parliament would be acquired through accident of birth. Notwithstanding this constitutional reform, 100 hereditaries look set to be allowed to continue to sit on the claret-coloured benches as a result of a deal brokered between the government and the Lords.

Middle-class unemployment

According to a report published by the Joseph Rowntree Foundation (1999a), perceived job insecurity has hit professional people badly during the 1990s, with many such employees reporting concerns. While fear of redundancy is one aspect of job insecurity, even employees who aren't unduly worried about actually losing their jobs are nevertheless concerned about the loss of valued job features, such as, for example, opportunities for promotion.

Perception of job insecurity isn't, however, necessarily borne out by real events. In that respect, middle-class employees generally enjoy better job prospects than less skilled workers. Moreover, unemployed people who previously had 'white-collar' jobs are more likely than unskilled workers to get back into work after a spell of unemployment.

Working-class unemployment

A dwindling demand for low-skilled workers, coupled with a shift away from industrial and manual work, poses a general problem for the working class, and a particular problem for its least qualified members. Men with few educational qualifications, and with craft skills that are specific to a declining industry (for example, mining or steel) are very vulnerable to unemployment.

In the 1960s, manufacturing output made up more than 33% of Gross Domestic Product. In the late 1990s, it accounted for about 20%. Over that period, employment in manufacturing fell from about 33% of overall employment to about 15%. The message is clear: working-class people who possess 'out-of-date' manual skills and limited qualifications find it more difficult to obtain work in an economy that's replacing muscle labour with knowledge labour.

Another reason why low-skilled labour is more at risk of unemployment is that global markets are taking routine work to cheaper low-skilled labour in poor countries. Next time you buy a pair of trainers or a casual jacket, check the label to see where they were made – more likely than not, its a non-UK country with an abundant supply of low-paid, low-skilled labour.

Gender and employment

Gender-based inequalities are apparent in the labour market. Since the 1970s, legislation – in the form of the **Equal Pay Act 1970** and the **Sex Discrimination Act 1975** – has required equal pay and treatment for women and men at work. Yet, in spite of this, and at almost all ages, on average women earn less than men.

The gap between average female and male earnings is narrowing, in part as a result of the minimum wage (most of the low paid are women), but is still – say women's campaigners – unfair, unjust and unacceptable. The largest

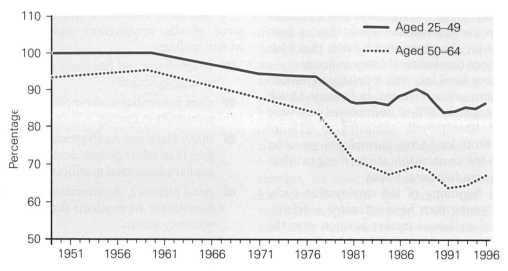

(Department for Education and Employment, 1999)

The employment rate of those aged between 50 and 59/64, Great Britain

dropped in 1999 for white employees, but had gone up for black and Asian workers, despite some 75 000 new jobs being created in the capital.

The TUC (1999b) concludes that 'Racism is rife in the jobs market and has got worse during the 1990s, despite growing employment opportunities.'

Recognising that experiences of unemployment vary between different ethnic minority groups, Richard Berhoud, of the Institute for Social and Economic Research at the University of Essex, used 11 years of the Labour Force Survey to hone in on the experiences of one group with an exceptionally high risk of unemployment – young Caribbean men (Joseph Rowntree Foundation, 1999c). He found that:

◎ young Caribbean men were more than twice as likely to be out of work as young white men, and they also earned less

◎ on average, Bangladeshi and Pakistani men were more likely to be unemployed than Caribbeans

Berhoud also discovered that African men suffered severe disadvantage in spite of educational success, with an African graduate being seven times more likely to be unemployed than a white graduate. His overall analysis revealed three broad groups:

1 White people and Indians, with a fairly consistent and relatively low risk of unemployment.

2 Bangladeshis and Pakistanis, with a consistently high risk of unemployment.

3 Africans and Caribbeans, with a high

average risk of unemployment, but with a notably strong variation within the group, depending on individual characteristics.

Age and employment

Employment rates vary considerably by age group. Among older male workers (those aged 50–64) participation in the labour market has fallen from about 95% in the 1950s and 1960s to about 65% in the late 1990s. If 1951 employment rates were to be reproduced today, there would be around 1.2 million more older men at work. For older women, employment rates haven't fallen, with more women of pre-retirement age now in work.

The above figure shows the overall decline in employment rates of those aged 50–64 from 1951.

Age and unemployment

Unemployment is particularly high among young people, often as a result of high relative inflows into, rather than long spells of, unemployment. However, the later job prospects of those young people who do become long-term unemployed are likely to be adversely affected. Moreover, and worryingly so, youth unemployment is linked to crime.

The prospect of becoming unemployed generally reduces with age, but when older workers lose their jobs, they can be particularly vulnerable to long-term unemployment, with the over-50s spending, on average, twice as long out of work as the under-25s. Around 80% of

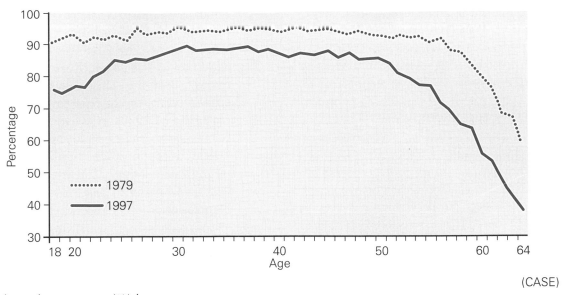

Male employment rates (%) by age

unemployed under-25s eventually get a job, and most of the rest enter training. For the unemployed over-50s, only about 60% get back into work, with a fifth or so moving on to other benefits.

The above figure shows that while, between 1979 and 1997, employment fell substantially for men of all ages, older people were especially affected.

One of the reasons for a sharp increase in the proportion of men aged 55–64 out of work (this rose from 14% in 1977 to 37% in 1997), is the growth in the numbers on long-term sickness and disability benefits. Whether more people are getting sick and disabled, or whether the criteria for describing these conditions have widened, is open to interpretation. One thing, however, seems clear. Much of the non-participation by older men in the labour market is 'voluntary' and is a response to the availability of early retirement packages. Limited skills and displacement from declining industries are important predictors of later-age unemployment, with only about 54% of men over 50 who have no qualifications in a job.

Although income generally declines in old age, inequalities experienced in working life are often taken through to later years. Thus, for example, women (who make up around two-thirds of the older population) are more likely to be poor pensioners because of lower previous earnings and interrupted employment. The fact that women live longer than men also means that they remain poor longer.

Disability and employment

Disabled people account for nearly one-fifth of the working-age population of the UK. They're only half as likely as non-disabled people to be employed, and are more likely to work part-time or to be self-employed (Department for Education and Employment, 1999).

A survey conducted by the Institute of Employment Studies in conjunction with NOP Social and Political (Meager *et al.*, 1998) on disabled people's participation in the workforce discovered a range of diminished life chances. The study, based on a national interview survey of 2000 disabled people of working age (women aged 16–59, and men aged 16–64) who had a long-term disability or health problem, found that:

- one in six disabled people (16%) who were or had been economically active said they had experienced discrimination or unfair treatment in a work-related context

- disabled people in employment were more likely to work in manual and lower-skilled jobs

- at £196 per week, the average take-home pay of disabled employees was lower than that of non-disabled employees (£212)

- more than one-quarter of disabled people who left their job because of their disability said that adaptations would have enabled them to stay in work, but fewer than one

315

in five of this group reported that they were offered such changes

◉ disabled people from ethnic minorities were more likely to be jobless than their white counterparts

Disability and unemployment

The unemployment rate for disabled people in the UK is almost double that of non-disabled people, at 10.7% compared with 5.7% for non-disabled people. Moreover, 38% of unemployed disabled people have been out of work for a year or more, compared with 25% of non-disabled unemployed people (Department for Education and Employment, 1999).

Opportunities to improve employability are held back by a number of factors. For example, disabled people are less well qualified than the non-disabled, being more than twice as likely to have no formal qualifications – 31% of disabled people, compared with 14% of non-disabled people (Department for Education and Employment, 1999). Access to transport and to the built environment also hampers the disabled, making it difficult for them to get to and from work, and also to move around in the workplace.

Despite the difficulties that they face, Meager et al. (1998) found that unemployed disabled people generally have a positive outlook on getting work. The great majority want a job and continue to keep looking for one.

REVIEW POINTS

◉ A job for life is becoming increasingly rare in the UK. Workers are expected to be quick on their feet and to perform multiple tasks. The government is upbeat about the flexible age, claiming that it can help individuals to match their working practices to their needs. Critics argue that flexible labour markets can generate poor quality jobs and, possibly, new kinds of under-employment.

◉ Official statistics indicate that, between 1855 and 1914, male unemployment fluctuated between 2% and 10% of the (then defined) male workforce, averaging around 4–5% –

what some policy-makers would probably consider as 'full' employment. The First World War added to an already buoyant labour market, bringing (almost literally) full employment for the first time in history. The 1920s, however, witnessed mass unemployment, with official unemployment figures never falling much below 10% in the 'best' years, and rising to 23% in the 1930s Depression.

◉ The impact of mass unemployment in terms of human misery and economic waste led policy-makers to look for radical solutions. The catalyst of war in the 1940s was to help them in this undertaking, and the 'full' employment that came in 1940 endured for three decades – and, arguably, longer (Glynn, 1999). Not only did 'full' employment reduce the extent of poverty in the country, but it also, claimed Beveridge, made the welfare state possible.

◉ The return of unemployment in the 1970s, fuelled in part by a world oil crisis in 1973 and later by Margaret Thatcher's rejection of full employment policies, led to massive job losses. Unemployment rose from about 1 million in 1979 and peaked at 3 million in the middle of the decade, before falling to less than 2 million in 1990. It rose again to over 2.8 million in 1993, declining steadily thereafter, a trend that's still continuing.

◉ In today's world of work, more people are working part-time, and more than half of all employees are working flexible hours. Temporary employment is also up, as is self-employment.

◉ Flexible working hours have made it easier for more women to enter the labour market, and new technology has freed some workers from the drudgery of work. On the other hand, there's a growing division between employees with well-paid creative jobs and others who have low-paid, unskilled and repetitive jobs. Flexible jobs can also lead to blighted long-term job prospects.

◎ The prospect of having a well-paid job falls unevenly on different sections of the population, as does the risk of unemployment. In both contexts, white, middle-aged, non-disabled men generally fare much better than other groups.

REVIEW ACTIVITIES

1 What is 'full' employment'?
2 According to Beveridge, 'full' employment made the welfare state possible. What do you think he meant by this?
3 What are the pros and cons of a flexible job market?
4 What explanations are there for an overall trend towards lower levels of unemployment?
5 In what ways does the prospect of having a well-paid job, as well as the risk of unemployment, fall unevenly in relation to any *two* of these categories: social class, gender, ethnicity, age and disability?

The effects of unemployment

While employment has increased in the United Kingdom over the past couple of decades, it hasn't kept pace with the numbers of people who want to work. Virtually all the proceeds of economic growth in the past two decades or so have gone, in the form of higher earnings, to people with jobs.

In general, people in work are better off in economic terms than those who aren't. This isn't to say that some people's 'non-work' incomes (for example, profits from shares, occupational pensions and so on) don't give them a high standard of living. But, for the majority of us, the most direct route to economic security is to be employed.

Psychological and sociological studies point to a clear connection between unemployment and deteriorating mental well-being and motivation (HM Treasury, 1997). There's also evidence that lack of a recent work history is used by many employers to sift out applicants. For these and other reasons, the long-term unemployed find it much harder to get a job, and those who do find work often have to make do with wages far lower than in their previous occupation (HM Treasury, 1997).

The effects that unemployment has on people's lives are directly related to how societies define and respond to the role of work. In the UK, under present government policy, paid work is construed as the main source of rights during working-age adult life. This means that being out of work is very likely to have damaging economic effects, as well as an increased sense of marginalisation.

Although the following categories overlap, it's helpful to consider the effects of unemployment under three separate headings: economic, social and psychological.

Economic effects of unemployment

'In relation to hardship, the financial consequences of unemployment are often instant and dramatic', notes Sir Donald Acheson in his 1998 *Independent Inquiry into Inequalities in Health Report*. Cohort studies of people becoming unemployed show that, for many people, income is cut by half as they switch from wages to social security benefits (Acheson, 1998). Families with an unemployed head are particularly at risk of poverty, and unemployed households with dependent children are hit hard.

Lone-parent households fare very badly in the unemployment and poverty stakes. The UK has one of the lowest employment rates for lone parents among industrial nations, with just over 40% of them in work. Given the relatively low levels of benefit in the UK, unemployed lone parents and their children are often poor.

Local authority housing and the underclass

The debate about the priority given to single mothers became closely linked to the idea of an underclass – a group of people who preferred to live on benefits, characterised by single motherhood and early pregnancy on the part of women, of sexual promiscuity and petty crime on the part of men. According to Charles Murray:

'... cohabiting mothers are poorly educated (43% have no educational qualifications, compared to 25% of married mothers) and *are two and a half times as likely as married mothers to be living in council housing*, almost five times more likely than married mothers to have an unemployed partner, and are somewhat less likely than married mothers to be working themselves. Given all this it may come as a surprise to learn that the average gross weekly income of cohabiting mothers is 86% that of married mothers – £283 compared to £328. The main difference is that cohabiting mothers are almost four times as likely as married women to report gross weekly incomes of £100 or less.'

(Murray, 1994; italics added)

to re-house themselves; otherwise, the local authority would be under no obligation to provide continuing accommodation. Further-more, the accommodation that the local authorities would provide on a temporary basis was largely to be outside the local authority housing stock. The homeless were therefore to be housed in the private for-rent market – if that was possible – or in hostels, or in housing association properties. This strategy was intended to free up the local authority housing stock for the families who were on the waiting list and who were not homeless.

Single people and homelessness

Over the past ten years, there has been a constant increase in the numbers of young people who are homeless. In a Department of the Environment study (Anderson, 1993) that focused on the single homeless, it was estimated that young people aged between 16 and 24 were considerably over-represented, and that they accounted for 30% of all people living in hostels and bed and breakfast accommodation. By the mid-1990s, there were approximately 250 000 young, single, homeless people.

Why should this be so? The reasons include the following:

◎ *A decline in the availability of rented accommodation.* The private sector has traditionally soaked up those young people who have left home. The decline in this sector has had a greater impact upon young people than on other groups, as young people are rarely eligible for social housing.

Table 12.3 Households in temporary accommodation, 30 June 1998, by region

	B&B	Hostels	Other	Total
North East	90	200	540	830
Yorkshire and Humberside	50	480	640	1170
East Midlands	10	350	1020	1380
Eastern	120	1170	1930	3220
Greater London	3360	3460	18880	25700
Rest of South East	770	1580	5780	8130
South West	410	570	2510	3490
West Midlands	80	510	1150	1740
North West	70	760	940	1770
Merseyside	10	230	220	460
England	4970	9310	33610	47890
Wales	140	134	540	814
Scotland	476	157	3387	4020

(Shelter)

◎ *Levels of unemployment*. Young people have a higher than average level of unemployment. In the late 1990s, young people were twice as likely to be unemployed than the average for the population as a whole. This means that they may well have to rely upon state benefits which, as we will see later, have been cut back since 1988.

◎ *Exclusion from the minimum wage*. Young people are excluded from the minimum wage, so they are more likely to be on low incomes. This and the high unemployment levels means that they are unable to afford higher rents in the private sector and are therefore restricted to the poorest-quality accommodation.

◎ *Abuse*. Although figures are difficult to come by, it appears that there is either an increase in physical and sexual abuse against young people in their homes, or that they are less likely to accept this than in the past. But an increasing number of young people are homeless because of some form of abuse in the family. One Scottish study has suggested that as many as 17% of the young homeless leave home specifically because of abuse. This is likely to be a considerable under-estimate.

◎ *Leaving care*. Fewer than 1% of children go into the care of local authorities, and yet this 1% forms 25% of all young, single homeless.

◎ *Leaving custody*. Over 30% of all young people leaving custody are homeless on release or are 'at risk of becoming homeless'.

◎ *Benefit changes*. Young people have been affected by benefit cuts to a greater extenet than the majority of the population (see below).

The **Social Security Act 1988** cut the Income Support Allowance (now the Jobseekers' Allowance) to a maximum of 80% of the level of those over 25, which gave them an average cut of £10 in their benefit payments. Benefits of any kind were stopped for those under 18, except in certain circumstances – generally when young people had left home for reasons of abuse, or were 'vulnerable' in some way. Also in 1988, the introduction of the Social Fund, which relied upon discretionary loans rather than the previous system of grants, created great problems for those young people who did not have savings to provide the initial deposit that many landlords require for private rented accommodation. In 1989, changes were introduced in the regulations concerning Housing Benefit and what it could be used for. The result was that 'bed and breakfast' accommodation often became too expensive for many young people.

Housing Benefit was further restricted by the introduction, for those aged under 25, of 'single room rent' (SRR), which limited the maximum rent that Housing Benefit would pay for to the average price of a single room in a shared house with basic amenities. SRR does not apply to some categories of people aged under 25, such as lone parents, young couples with children, and those aged under 22 who have left care. However, according to research by Kemp and Rugg (1998), the overall effect has been to make it more difficult for them to afford private-sector rents.

◎◎◎◎◎ REVIEW POINTS ◎◎◎◎◎

◎ Explanations of homelessness fall into two categories: the immediate and the structural.

◎ Immediate explanations look at the problems, or the 'faults', of the individuals and families who are homeless.

◎ Structural explanations stress the wider social and economic context within which these individual problems occur.

◎ Until 1977, only limited help for homeless families was provided by the welfare state. Usually, wider kin were expected to help in periods of difficulty. The government did not see it as the role of the state to become involved. Underlying this attitude was a belief that people were homeless through their own fault.

◎ The 1977 Act gave certain priority groups of homeless people, such as families with young children, and vulnerable people, the right to permanent accommodation.

◎ There were many critics of the Act, who claimed that the priority system was being manipulated by certain sorts of people – particularly lone mothers – to put them ahead of other 'ordinary' families who were already on housing waiting lists.

◉ By the mid-1990s, 40% of all new tenants in local authority housing were lone mothers, or non-married couples with young children, who were housed on the basis of their priority need.

◉ The 1996 Act removed their right to permanent housing. Instead, they were to be given temporary accommodation for two years.

REVIEW ACTIVITIES

1 Why is it both inadequate and inaccurate to explain homelessness by looking at the 'immediate causes'?

2 Which groups are most likely to become homeless, and why?

3 What criticisms were made of the Housing Act 1977, and which ones led to the Housing Act 1996?

4 Where in the UK is the highest concentration of homeless people?

5 Why are young people more likely than others to find themselves homeless?

The rough sleeper initiative

The most common perception of homelessness is that of a single person sleeping rough in the streets of one of the major towns or cities. Although this is actually a very small part of the problem of homelessness, it is nevertheless something that has changed very significantly over the past ten years.

Traditionally, 'rough sleepers' were known as 'tramps' and were typically older males who suffered from alcohol or mental health problems. However, during the 1980s there was a growth in younger rough sleepers. It has proved very difficult to measure the numbers of people sleeping rough with any accuracy, but counts made by voluntary organisations during 1999 suggested that there were probably about 2000 people sleeping rough each night in England, which means that possibly 10 000 are sleeping rough over the course of a year. The main concentration of rough sleepers in is London, where about 400 sleep outdoors each night, and about 2400 sleep rough at any one time in London.

According to the government's Social Exclusion Unit (1999), there are 'very few' rough sleepers aged 18 or under; around 25% are between 18 and 25 and 6% are aged over 60; 90% of rough sleepers are male. The research showed that about 5% of rough sleepers were from ethnic minorities, and yet a disproportionately high percentage of males sleeping in hostels are from ethnic minorities. The most common reason for rough sleeping is a relationship breakdown – either with family or a partner – with 86% claiming to have been forced to leave home rather than choosing to do so. Approximately 40% of the young women who left home had done so for reasons connected with sexual abuse.

What is particularly noticeable is the frequency of institutional life in the backgrounds of rough sleepers. For example, about one-third of them have been looked after by local authorities as children, and around half of the UK's rough sleepers have been in prison or on remand at some time. Older rough sleepers are eight times more likely to be unmarried than the average person and five times more likely to be divorced. Also, 20% of rough sleepers have been in the armed forces at some time.

Rough sleepers are more likely than the average population to be suffering from mental health and drug or alcohol problems. Approximately 35% suffer from mental health problems, and over 50% of rough sleepers have a serious alcohol problem: 20% misuse drugs, and the figure for those aged under 25 is as high as 40%.

Dealing with rough sleeping

Attempts to deal with rough sleeping have generally been made by voluntary organisations. However, since the early 1990s there have been a series of 'rough sleeper initiatives'. These have been government-funded attempts to provide hostels and winter shelters for rough sleepers, and to provide healthcare and accommodation advice.

- ◎ *Hostels* are available for those without accommodation, but according to the Social Exclusion Unit these are oversubscribed and there are very few vacancies. This is despite the fact that hostels are not popular with rough sleepers because of theft and violence.
- ◎ *Winter shelters* are provided by the DETR (Department of the Environment, Transport and the Regions) throughout the winter months.
- ◎ *Day centres* have been initiated to provide a range of services – some of direct practical use (food and clothing changes) and other of longer-term benefit (advice and education).

Foyers

Foyers are places where young, single homeless people can live under a controlled regime and receive training and counselling, with the aim that they should obtain permanent employment and their own accommodation. The concept was borrowed from France, where there are about 450 foyers. The idea was first introduced into the UK in 1992, and the number of foyers has grown consistently since then. In 1999 there were 93 such establishments in the UK, catering for those aged between 16 and 24, and there are plans to expand the number to 200 in total. They have mainly been funded by The Housing Corporation, which oversees the housing associations, and by the Single Regeneration Budget, which is a European Union fund to help areas in social need. The results seem to have been very successful, with high rates of employment being attained by the those who live in foyers. To give just one example, the foyer in Newham, London – which is the poorest borough in the UK – has managed to help 75% of its first group of homeless young people obtain employment.

REVIEW POINTS

- ◎ The growing problem of single homeless people has traditionally been ignored.
- ◎ Because of the costs of rent and difficulty in obtaining accommodation, there has been a rapid increase in homelessness amongst the young.
- ◎ This has been made worse by changes in Housing Benefit, which discriminate against young people aged under 25.
- ◎ There has been a great increase in the numbers of young people who are sleeping rough.
- ◎ Sleeping rough is often linked to childhood problems, to previous care in an institution of some kind or to abuse in childhood.
- ◎ Rough sleepers have high levels of mental illness, and of drug and alcohol abuse.
- ◎ Attempts to combat single homelessness include shelters, hostels and, most recently, 'foyers'.
- ◎ Foyers are special hostels for young homeless people, where they can live while also studying and seeking employment

REVIEW ACTIVITIES

1 What are the specific causes of single homelessness?
2 Explain what is meant by the 'rough sleeper initiative'?
3 In what way can 'foyers' be seen to tackle the causes of homelessness?

Housing and gender

At first, housing appears to be an issue that is 'gender blind': there seems to be no obvious connection between types of tenure or housing status and gender. However, there are crucial differences between the housing standards of males and females, which are caused by a number of factors, primarily those of income and marital status.

Women are less likely than men to be owner occupiers, as their generally lower income levels will prevent some of them from being able to purchase properties. The most likely route through into owner occupancy is by divorce or separation, when women are more likely to retain the marital home as a result of having custody of the children. However, according to McCarthy and Simpson (1991), when women obtain the marital home after divorce, their income drop may still be so great that they are unable to maintain the mortgage repayments and have to move into local authority housing. On the other hand, divorced men are more likely to remain in owner occupancy tenure.

For example, of women who were unemployed at the time of divorce, 17% dropped out of owner occupation, compared to only 9% of unemployed men, and it should be born in mind that women are over twice as likely to be 'economically inactive' at the time of divorce than men, because of their childcaring role.

The result of all this is that 44% of single women are owner occupiers compared to 54% of single males, and 46% of divorced women are owner occupiers compared to 54% of divorced males. The impact of the declining number of local authority rented homes, linked to the increase in families headed by lone mothers – plus the inability of divorced or separated women to maintain payments of mortgages – has resulted in a very significant growth in the numbers of lone-parent families in local authority accommodation. In the mid-1990s, approximately 45% of all female-headed households lived in local authority accommodation. The Housing Act 1996 has had a very significant impact on lone mothers, as they no longer receive the guarantee of local authority housing.

Ethnicity and housing

Housing tenure varies widely amongst the different ethnic groups in the United Kingdom, as the accompanying figure illustrates. Those of Indian and Pakistani origin are the most likely of all ethnic groups, including whites, in the UK to be owner occupiers. Those of African Caribbean and Bangladeshi origin are the least likely, along with 'Africans', to own their own homes. The quality of the housing is difficult to measure, but according to the Commission for Racial Equality (1999) '35% of the worst housing in the owner occupied sector was occupied by black and Asian groups, compared to only 7% occupied by white groups'.

When it comes to living in local authority or housing association rented property, the positions are reversed, with those of Indian, Pakistani or Chinese origin the least likely to live in these properties and those of African Caribbean, African or Bangladeshi origin most likely. There is some evidence that within local authority tenure, those of Bangladeshi or African Caribbean origin are most likely to have the poorer quality accommodation – for example, they are more likely to live in flats rather than houses. In terms of levels of overcrowding, even if they have high ownership rates, Pakistani households have the second highest levels of overcrowding (30%) after Bangladeshi households (47%).

Homelessness and ethnicity

It is difficult to obtain a national picture of homelessness by ethnicity, but we do know that in London, ethnic minority families, excluding the Irish, are three times more likely to be homeless than white families, and that ethnic minority families form 45% of the statutory homeless. Those of African Caribbean origin have the highest rate of homelessness.

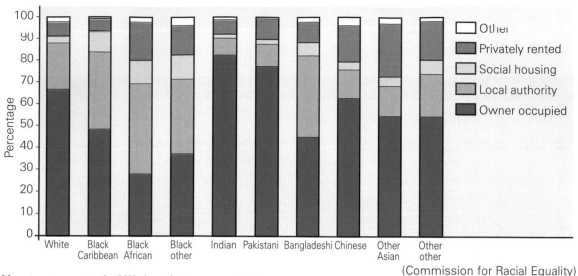

Housing tenure in the UK, by ethnic group, 1991

(Commission for Racial Equality)

Harassment

National statistics about harassment are difficult to find, but once again the figures that are available for London indicate that Asians living in local authority housing are the single group most likely to be at risk of harassment.

REVIEW POINTS

◎ Many groups of people suffer disadvantages in the housing market – two of these are women and the ethnic minorities.

◎ Women are less likely than men to be owner occupiers, mainly because of their lower incomes.

◎ Even after divorce or separation, when they obtain the family home because they have custody of the children, women may be unable to afford to pay the mortgage.

◎ Ethnic minorities are a diverse group with very different housing patterns. It seems that those of Indian origin are the most likely to own homes of an adequate standard – more so than any other ethnic group, including whites.

◎ Bangladeshis and those of African Caribbean origin are the least likely to own homes, and are more likely to have poorer-quality local authority housing.

REVIEW ACTIVITIES

1 What particular problems do women face in the housing market?

2 Why are women particularly hit by the decline in local authority housing, and by the 1996 Act?

3 What differences are there between the various ethnic groups in terms of their tenure patterns?

4 What differences are there in quality of accommodation and overcrowding between ethnic groups?

References

Anderson, I. (1993) Housing policy and street homelessness in Britain. *Housing Studies*, 8(1).

Blakemore, K. (1998) *Social Policy – an Introduction*. Open University Press, Buckingham.

Commission for Racial Equality (1999) *Housing and Homelessness*. CRE, London.

Kemp, P. and Rugg, J. (1998) *The Single Room Rent: its Impact on Young People*. Centre for Housing Studies, York.

McCarthy, P. and Simpson, R. (1991) *Issues in Post Divorce Housing*. Gower, Aldershot.

Murray, C. (1994) *Underclass: the Crisis Deepens*. Institute for Economic Affairs, London.

O'Callaghan, B. and Dominian, L. *et al.* (1996) *Study of Homeless Applicants*. HMSO, London.

Social Exclusion Unit (1999) *Rough Sleeping: Report by the Social Exclusion Unit*. Cm. 4008. The Stationery Office, London.

13 The Discipline of Social Policy

By the end of this chapter you should be able to:

◎ Understand and evaluate the different ways in which politicians and academics can define social policy, as well as showing an awareness of common ground between the two groups.

◎ Distinguish between different academic perspectives in sociology, and show how these can affect approaches to social policy.

◎ Critically consider the social scientific and ethical dimensions of social policy, and the relationship between social scientific research and policy decisions.

◎ Document and weigh the arguments of a range of political and social perspectives on social policy.

Lots of different groups in society have an interest in social policy – among them, politicians, academics and various lobby groups. This chapter looks at the sometimes different ways in which various groups define and seek to influence social policy.

Politicians, in particular, are the makers of social policy. They draw up (sometimes with the help of academics, sometimes not) and implement policies that affect us all – policies on education, health, social services and so on. Academics (notably, social scientists) are the thinkers of social policy. Some academics try to persuade policy-makers to implement particular ideas, whereas others want to contribute to an intellectual debate irrespective of whether this has practical consequences.

The relationship between social policy research (an academic process) and social policy practice (a political process) is a complex one. Academics have a reputation for probing issues to do with research methods and ethics, whereas politicians are renowned for concerning themselves with practical, 'down-to-earth' matters. These representations shouldn't be pushed too far, but they do contain more than a grain of truth.

In an important sense, politicians (and those academics who advise them) are the big movers of policy. But theirs' aren't the only voices. Other groups in society, particularly those that actively lobby policy-making politicians, are part of the discourse, even though people in power don't always act upon their arguments. Among the more prominent of these lobby groups are feminists, anti-racists, the unemployed and low paid, disabled people and environmentalists.

This chapter considers political, academic and other approaches to social policy issues. It examines 'theory into practice' matters, with particular reference to social scientific, ethical and party political debates. A large part of the chapter is taken up with a consideration of the theoretical perspectives that various ideological approaches bring to social policy. We identify a 'historical trail' of Tory, Whig and socialist perspectives leading to 'traditional' British social policy. We also describe and explain how representatives of groups in society that are often marginalised are challenging the 'received wisdom' of the traditional party political approach.

The definition of social policy problems

Some social policy academics are as interested in how politicians think about social problems as they are in the problems themselves

When does a social issue become a 'social policy problem', and who says so? There are no 'rules' for deciding what a social policy problem is. Nevertheless, it's possible to identify different ways in which social phenomena come to be 'problematised'. In particular, we need to consider the different roles and approaches that politicians and academics play in the process of defining social policy problems.

An example of policy priorities

In the run-up to the 1997 general election, Tony Blair (the Party leader) said that the Labour Party had three priorities: 'Education, education and education'. A year and a half later, in a speech to the Labour Party Conference in Blackpool on 29 September 1998, when he was Prime Minister, Tony Blair again referred to the challenge facing British schools, saying 'There is no task more important than yours, for in your hands lies the future of our children'.

We can be certain that, for Tony Blair, education is a crucial social policy issue. He has defined it as such, and a Prime Minister's definitions have major consequences. New Labour was elected on a manifesto to put education at the centre of public policy, and Blair is determined to do just that. But is he right? Is education more important, for example, than poverty? Who decides what social issues are of pressing importance and which ones are less substantial? In particular, whose decisions carry most weight when it comes to defining what constitute social problems in the first place?

In addressing these questions, it's important to consider what the French philosopher Michel Foucault refers to as discourse. By **discourse**, Foucault means a way of defining the social world, and he pays particular attention to the definitions of the powerful. 'Education, education, education', is Tony Blair's discourse, and a Prime Minister's vocabulary is privileged. It's an agenda-setter and it makes things happen.

Deciding what should appear on a social policy agenda is a value judgement. But once the die is cast, the implementation of a social policy must take account of objective factors. Thus, for example, concrete educational policies are (or should be!) based on empirical research findings – for example:

- Which measures are likely to promote 'lifelong learning'?
- How can we best enhance the learning opportunities of children who have special educational needs?

Addressing the Labour Party Conference in 1998, Tony Blair once again placed education at the centre of public policy

347

◎ What can be done to ensure that all pupils have access to information technology?

◎ How can we encourage more people to become teachers?

Discourses in social policy

There are lots of different 'voices' jockeying for position in the field of social policy. In the UK today, New Labour politics represents the official discourse, but other opinions also enter the fray. Women, minority ethnic groups, the jobless and the low paid, and the disabled all lobby politicians to implement social policies that will promote equality of opportunity for people who face social barriers. Although the government exercises the final decisions in areas of national social policy, politicians do listen to the electorate. There's no guarantee that MPs will act on what the people want but, if popular views are ignored, there's no guarantee either that the people will return their local members to power at election time.

New Labour takes this matter seriously. Shortly after its election in 1997, the government set up a 5000-strong focus group to gauge public opinion on key policies and public services. According to politicians, the so-called Peoples' Panel will narrow the gap between politicians and voters, thereby making government more accountable.

Social policy problems: political and academic definitions

Politicians sometimes suggest that they live in the real world and that academics occupy ivory towers. In this respect, politicians – according to them – deal with practical policy issues, whereas academics play with theories. Academics counter with the assertion that politicians rush headlong into policy implementation without paying sufficient attention to research findings, being activists rather than reflective practitioners.

These are, of course, caricatures. Not all politicians and academics fit the unflattering images that each *sometimes* has of the other. That said, caricature does sharpen conceptual clarity, and is sometimes used (though not in the unflattering sense) in social science for precisely this purpose. Social scientists refer to a caricature that captures the essence of a social phenomenon as an **ideal type**. In this context, the term 'ideal' has nothing to do with morals. Rather, it describes a good model. For example, when a social scientist uses the ideal type 'professional', this is shorthand for

someone who has a very high level of expert knowledge, such as a teacher, doctor or social worker.

The political definition of social problems

Keeping with the theme of Tony Blair's views on education, the Prime Minister is in no doubt that educational under-achievement is a social problem. According to him 'there are too few good state schools. Too much tolerance of mediocrity. Too little pursuit of excellence' (Labour Party Conference Speech, 29 September 1998). Blair isn't likely to ponder *how* educational under-achievement comes to be construed as a social problem. For him, it *is* a problem because there's evidence that it's actually happening.

Politicians often adopt this 'taken for granted' approach to public issues, as indeed do members of the general public. One of the key differences between politicians and 'the public' on the one hand and academics and lobby groups on the other, is that the first two groups take things for granted and the second two groups take nothing for granted. As a politician, Tony Blair is more interested in dealing with social '*problems*' than in *problematising* (adopting a searching intellectual or challenging stance towards) what come to be defined as social problems from the outset.

If we had to frame the Prime Minister's outlook in sociological terms – something that he would be unlikely to do explicitly – we would say that his approach is rather *functionalist*. Tony Blair evidently believes that the *function* of social policy is to do battle with social problems, thereby helping to build a healthy, stable society.

The academic definition of social problems

Academics are usually more interested in how social phenomena become 'problematised' than in the social 'problems' themselves. Why, they ask, is it that powerful figures, like a British Prime Minister, decide to place some social issues centre-stage and let others slip off the policy agenda? By problematising definitions of what constitute important social issues (especially, social 'problems'), these academics raise an important question: Which powerful people in society say that some social issues merit more public attention than other?

We can, of course – and academics do – raise other questions. For example, a relevant question would be 'Do the opinions of the powerful carry more momentum than the opinions of "ordinary" people when policy agendas are formulated and implemented'?

It's important to mention that not all academics are interested in debating how certain issues are defined as social problems. Some, rather like most politicians, contend that it's more important to tackle, rather than philosophise about, social problems. Consider crime, for example. The chance of being a victim of burglary is higher in the UK among people from ethnic minority groups. It's therefore more sensible, argue 'let's get real' politicians, to tackle this problem than to debate whether or not, and in what way, it is a problem. That's why criminologists who work for the Home Office are commissioned to do 'cause and cure' research, rather than to ponder what comes to be categorised as burglary, homicide or robbery.

Having suggested that it's not *always* easy – nor, indeed, appropriate – to distinguish between 'political' and 'academic' definitions of social policy problems, we'll continue to look at what the academics have to say by considering an important subject that professors of social policy often draw upon: sociology.

persuade policy-makers to implement their ideas, whereas others just want to contribute to an intellectual debate.

◎ Other groups in society, particularly lobby groups, join the discourse, but their views aren't always heeded by policy-makers.

◎ Politicians often treat social policy problems as givens. Once problems have been identified, they tend to believe that the most important thing is to tackle them.

◎ Academics are more inclined to 'problematise' by asking, 'Who says this is a problem?' Some academics adopt a 'politician's' view, and seek ways of solving social problems.

REVIEW POINTS

◎ Various social groups have an interest in social policy – among them, politicians, academics and various lobby groups. Politicians are the makers of social policy. Academics (notably, social scientists) are the theorists. Some academics try to

REVIEW ACTIVITIES

1 Why is it important, in social policy terms, to acknowledge that some voices are more powerful than others?

2 In what various ways do politicians and academics define social policy problems?

3 Do you think it's possible for an academic to study a social problem without expressing a value judgement?

4 Do you think it's possible for a politician to study a social problem without expressing a value judgement?

Sociology and social policy

First, we'll examine how sociologists explain human social behaviour. Then we'll be in a better position to understand how some human social behaviours are defined as social problems.

Human social behaviour is the result of biological inheritance and individual psychology, but it's also influenced by social factors. The sociologist W. G. Runciman (1998: 1), makes this point when he writes:

'You, like myself and every other human being in the world, are at the same time three things. First, you are an organism – that is, a living creature born ... of one male and one female parent from both of whom you have inherited your genes. Second, you are an organism with a brain, and therefore a mind ... Third, you are an organism with a complex mind living in regular contact with other organisms with complex minds, and therefore you have a social life in which you have relationships with other people to which you and they attach a meaning.'

Some soldiers risk life and limb for the honour of the regiment

'Sociology', continues Runciman (1998: 1), 'is the scientific study of human behaviour under the third of these headings.' It takes account of biology and psychology, but the focus is on the social dimension of human behaviour. Let's try to unpack these different but interrelated influences by considering, as an example, what motivates a soldier to advance against enemy fire. Biology plays a decisive role: adrenaline is pumped into the bloodstream, priming the body for action. Psychology is also important: the soldier feels but controls fear. Sociology is crucially involved too: some soldiers risk life and limb for the honour of the regiment.

Because human social behaviour typically occurs in groups, sociologists are particularly interested in studying social groups: armies, companies, families, gangs, households, hospitals, prisons, schools, trades unions and so on. Within these social groups, individuals have **roles** – that is, positions in clearly defined social settings (or **structures**, to use another term) – as well as corresponding parts to play. Thus, in a family, an elder daughter or a son occupies a position that carries certain social obligations with regard to other family members. For example, they may feel that they have to babysit a younger brother or sister at times.

Roles bind the individual to the 'social', forming a tight connection between the two. But things go in both directions. We're born into an existing society that influences our behaviour, but we, in turn, bounce back and make our mark on society. Consider, for example, a teenager who agrees to babysit a younger sister, but contests a parental decision about what time to return home at night. Here we find both **consensus** (complying with a social rule, or **norm**, as it's called) and **conflict** (disagreement with convention) coexisting within the same social group – in this case, a family.

It's therefore perhaps not surprising to learn that, within the discipline of sociology, **consensus theory** (also known as **functionalist theory** because of its emphasis on interdependent social functions) explains why individuals sometimes accept existing practices, and that **conflict theory** (often referred to as **Marxist theory**, after its 'founding father', Karl Marx) spells out why, from time to time, individuals oppose convention. There's also a third main perspective, **social constructionist theory**, that explains how individuals follow custom in certain circumstances and construct new forms of conduct in others.

All of these theories have a bearing on social policy because they all help us to understand the relationship between the individual and society. Consensus theory, for example, can demonstrate how social policies, such as state education, affect the way we think and behave. Conflict theory can show how other social policies, such as zero-tolerance policing, stir up opposition in certain communities. Social constructionist theory can offer insights into how important it is for 'non establishment' figures, such as disabled groups, to have a voice in social policy.

In general terms – and we recognise that there are exceptions – functionalist sociologists and many politicians share the view that 'social problems' such as suicide, crime, and unemployment are actual social behaviours or social conditions that upset the social order, and need to be tackled through solution-focused social policies. There's little discussion here about who decides what constitutes a social problem in the first place. For example, the functionalist sociologist Emile Durkheim regards suicide not only as a major social problem, but also as a scientifically measurable 'social fact'.

Functionalist academics maintain that suicides are 'caused' by an amalgam of biological, psychological and sociological factors (for example, depression, coupled with a sense of worthlessness and social isolation). They also argue that suicide rates can be accurately measured and documented by medical and legal experts – notably coroners. Functionalist academics and many politicians trust the experts – in this case, coroners – to provide reasonable approximations of the extent of suicide, as well as likely explanations of its various causes. They also believe that knowledge of the causes of suicide can help social policy-makers to find ways of reducing the problem.

An 'alternative' way of looking at suicide, one adopted by a number of social constructionist sociologists, is that suicides are 'socially constructed' by 'experts' who interpret unusual deaths. For example, a coroner might interpret the signs that 'add up to suicide' differently to you or me. Moreover, doctors may, on occasion, feel pressured to present an obvious suicide as something otherwise; perhaps, for example, as a death by misadventure.

Ultimately, say social constructionists, suicides are deaths so defined, whether or not the definitions are factually accurate. Here we have a sociological perspective that *problematises* the issue of suicide by raising important questions as to how certain deaths are defined as suicides. While official suicide statistics help sociologists to identify the causes of suicide, these statistics are the products of complex social processes. Social constructionists, such as Jack Douglas (1967) and J. Maxwell Atkinson (1973), contend that coroners play an important interpretive role in the compiling of suicide statistics.

A social constructionist perspective is more likely to be adopted by academics than by politicians. Politicians tend to treat social problems such as suicide as givens. By contrast, academics of a social constructionist leaning contend that we first need to understand how some deaths are socially constructed as suicides *before* saying that suicide is a social problem. It would be incorrect, however, to suggest that social constructionists aren't concerned about people killing themselves. They are. But, at the same time, they want to alert us to the problem of taking official suicide statistics at face value without considering how the statistics are compiled.

We haven't considered the conflict theorist perspective on suicide because the big debate on this issue is between functionalists and social constructionists. That said, academics who adopt a conflict theory view are more likely to side with functionalists in arguing that suicide is a real social phenomenon and has real social causes.

However, conflict theorists aren't as convinced as functionalist academics and politicians that the problem of suicide can be effectively tackled through social policy. They think that more radical social transformations, such as the total elimination of poverty in society, are needed to reduce suicide rates significantly. This isn't to say that Marxists are, in crude terms, anti-social policy and pro-revolution. For, as Fred Pincus (1997) argues, social policies that improve working-class lives, that promote ethnic and gender equality, that expose negative aspects of capitalism, and that foster working-class unity and political mobilisation deserve the support of Marxists.

REVIEW POINTS

- Different sociological perspectives play a role in how academics view social policy.
- Functionalists (like many politicians) advocate policies that solve social problems and promote stability.
- Marxists prefer radical restructuring to piecemeal tinkering, but support affirmative policies that help the oppressed and the poor.
- Social constructionists remind us that non-establishment voices can make a difference in policy terms.

REVIEW ACTIVITIES

1 How do different sociological theories relate to outlooks on social policy?
2 What do functionalist sociologists and some politicians share in common?
3 What does it mean to say that social constructionist sociologists *problematise* the issue of suicide?
4 How might the *problematisation* of social problems be relevant to the study of social policy?
5 Why might a Marxist support a particular social policy measure?

Social policy: social scientific and ethical issues

In a 'perfect world', *social policy* would be the *application of social scientific knowledge in the pursuit of human social needs*. In such circumstances, policy responses to social problems would be carefully judged and based on objectively researched 'evidence' of need. There would be an appropriate response to a real problem. At times, however, policy-makers draw up social policies without regard to the findings of social scientific research. Thus, for example, ideology, personal preferences and 'common sense' – all poor substitutes for science – can and do, at times, play a greater role than social scientific research in informing social policy decisions.

Social policy: part science, part ethics

In reality, social policy is based on an amalgam of objective evidence and subjective opinions. Social scientists provide evidence-based results, and policy-makers decide, on the basis of political and ethical considerations, what to do with the findings. When policy-makers heed social science and act on empirical evidence, social policy becomes an applied social science. However, the 'acting on' bit necessarily involves a value judgement – for it goes beyond saying *what is* (an objective statement), to claiming *what ought* to be (an ethical proposition).

For example, a large body of empirical evidence shows that being disabled in the UK increases the risk of being poor. Applied social science offers a number of 'ought to' ethical solutions to this, including:

- ◎ substantially increasing disability benefits for people whose disability is so severe that they can't work
- ◎ investing a lot more public money into making the built environment accessible for people who are otherwise disabled by it, thereby enhancing their life chances

In what ways do these proposals contain both applied social scientific logic and ethical value judgements?

That's a tough question! Our reply is that *the social science part* is the logic that underpins the following assertion:

If X (in this case, being disabled) 'causes' Y (here, heightened risk of poverty), then Z (for example, more benefits for the severely disabled) is likely to reduce Y.

The ethical part is to contend that, once we

have the scientific evidence to give severely disabled people a better economic future, it's morally right to act on the findings of social science.

Value judgements also feature at the beginning of a research project. A social scientist makes an initial value judgement, for example, when he or she decides to investigate poverty instead of, say, transport. One field of study is valued over another. It's only during the investigative stage of a project that values become a barrier to objective research and must be put on hold.

Some people think that social scientists should collect evidence and then step aside, letting politicians and other powerful people decide what to do next. In this situation, the social scientist *allegedly* adopts a position of so-called **ethical neutrality**:

> 'Here is what I have found out about poverty. It's now up to the government to decide what to do with the findings. I'm neutral.'

This is the argument that social science should pursue knowledge for its own sake, and leave policy to others. Advocates of the position see an important role for economics, sociology and other social sciences as *pure* (that is, 'ethics-free') disciplines: 'Theirs is not to reason why, theirs is but to find the facts!'

It could, however, be argued that the claim of ethical neutrality is really an excuse for ethical indifference. Isn't it both good science and good morals – once we know, for example, why disabled people have access difficulties in the built environment – to advise the Housing Minister on solutions to the problem? Has a social scientist done his or her job properly if he or she just leaves her 'raw' data on the minister's desk and walks away? It's important to add that the decision 'not to get involved' is itself a value judgement. The very act of choosing not to follow through one's research in an applied sense involves making a moral judgement.

Many of the theorists who have made major contributions to sociology – one of the key disciplines that social policy draws on – argue that pure social science and applied social science are both worthwhile, and that the latter often, but not always, arises from the former. Put another way, we need to get the basic principles right before considering whether they have a useful application.

But if scholarship helps us to make society a better place, we shouldn't shrink from saying so. Max Weber (1864–1920), a 'founding father' of sociology, said that he had no time for an indifferent social science. He argued that social scientific findings should be put to good use. Importantly, Weber also contested the view that an ethical stance necessarily compromises scientific objectivity, noting that 'an attitude of moral indifference has no connection with scientific objectivity'(Weber, cited by Lee and Newby, 1986: 172).

Weber wasn't alone among the founding fathers in thinking that an ethical social science would benefit society. For example, August Comte – the French social scientist who, in the 19th century, first coined the term 'sociology' – also believed that social science should give social policy-makers the knowledge to improve society. Comte even envisaged a 'sociocracy' – a society led by sociologists who would design practical and ethical policies.

Another famous 19th-century social scientist, Karl Marx, argued that 'scientific socialism' – a fusion of social science and left-wing politics – would make for a better and a more just society. Durkheim, who was both a sociologist and a socialist, also supported the argument that social science should be used for the good of humanity.

As the 19th century progressed, social policy-makers increasingly heeded social scientific findings. Such data provided them with hard evidence about the causes of social problems, as well as helpful leads on possible solutions. In Britain, for example, pioneering social scientific work by Charles Booth and Seebohm Rowntree, in their separate surveys, disclosed that older people were very vulnerable to poverty. These early social scientists found that half of all people dying over age 65 were dependent on Poor Law (state) assistance in their last years. However, only one in nine would have had recourse to such relief before the age of 60.

In the light of such figures, it was unconvincing to suggest that poverty was the fault of the individual or that the problem could be adequately addressed through a combination of existing statutory measures and prudential doses of charity. It was time for something different and something better. It was time for a welfare state.

The UK was one of the first nations in the world to develop a welfare state, and it did so on the basis of an overriding concern to tackle the social problems that social scientific research had exposed. As the 20th century gathered pace, more and more evidence provided a conclusive case for well informed state intervention. Today, the government employs full-time social scientists to advise them on social policy. Since the 1997 general election, the doors of Number 10 have been open to 'Third Way' (see pp. 54–55) gurus from the London School of Economics, among whom the director of that famous institution, the sociologist, Anthony Giddens, figures prominently.

In some countries, particularly, Nordic ones, social scientific research is used in the service of socialist and centre-left *ideologies* (belief systems). In ethical terms, this research helps politicians to provide protection for individuals whose social well-being is at risk – people who are disabled, single parents, the unemployed and other marginalised groups.

Right-wing views also have an ethical role to play in social policy development. For example, a right-wing think tank (see p. 11), the Centre for Policy Studies (CPS) – founded in 1974 by Margaret Thatcher and Keith Joseph – bases its policy proposals on the value of free markets. The ideas of the CPS have influenced social policies on council house sales, privatisation and restructuring taxes to favour traditional families during the 1980s.

The Adam Smith Institute (another UK right-wing think tank, established in 1977) has also influenced government action. The Institute's advocacy of the distribution of nursery vouchers and doubling the number of assisted places for 'bright' students from low-income families to attend private schools became official policy under the Conservatives. Today, its social scientists train government officials across five continents.

Irrespective of what the politics are, value judgements are an inescapable (and, arguably, a desirable) fact in social science. The point is to recognise them and, whenever possible, to avoid letting them affect the inquiry stage of social science. For this is the investigative period, the time when it's important to be as detached and objective as possible.

Policy-oriented research in the social sciences makes good sense because it provides *empirical* (factual) findings upon which policies can be more reliably based. While ethical judgements enter social policy decisions (for instance, prioritising a children's play centre over another scheme), once a decision is reached, its implementation can and

Bullying at school is a worldwide problem, but it can be tackled effectively by applying the insights of social scientific research

government uses the objective findings of atomic physicists to go to war? Is it morally right for a social services department to use sociological data on income distribution in order to means test welfare claimants?

Notwithstanding these important questions, social scientists should be involved in key policy-making roles. Social science relies on the sufferance of people in society, and good must flow from social science to society. Some people think it's right for social scientists (and here we cite a passage from the Edexcel Foundation AS/A Level Social Policy syllabus) to address:

> '... the development and implementation of policy measures in order to *influence the circumstances of individuals*, rather than [just] the more general study of those circumstances themselves.'
>
> (brackets added)

In this spirit, social science needs to adopt both a *descriptive* (saying what is) and a *prescriptive* (saying what ought to be done and what can be done) stance when it comes to understanding and tackling social problems. Nor should the issue just be about *reacting* to social problems. Social scientists have much to say about *proactive* best practice. This means getting things right before problems start. For example, the Norwegian government commissions social scientific research into ways of tackling bullying at school so that the knowledge gained can be put to good *preventive* use in social policy initiatives. One of the leading figures in this research is Dan Olweus, a Swedish psychologist who works at the University of Bergen in Norway.

Dan Olweus (1997) has trialled a number of anti-bullying measures, and has produced a list of good practice pointers. Importantly, these include setting up whole-school anti-bullying policies. Once in place, such policies can nip the problem in the bud or, better still, create a social climate in which bullying is kept at bay.

Although the social sciences help to develop effective evidence-based social policies, politicians don't always follow research recommendations. In 1980, for example, the Black Report on inequalities in health (which contained evidence from the sociologist Peter Townsend) disclosed that good health was linked to good nutrition, high-quality housing, access to the National Health Service, shops that sell healthy food and decent incomes.

should be guided by social scientific principles. This requires the social policy analyst *dispassionately* (without prejudice) to judge which strategy will probably work best. That, in turn, involves consulting a wide range of people, listening to what they have to say, weighing up their arguments, incorporating them where feasible, and producing a plan that has a good chance of success.

Consider, for example, deciding how best to make the built environment of the city, town, suburb or village where you live more accessible to people who are disabled. How can we ensure that, in addition to the views of 'able-bodied' social policy experts, the voices of the disabled are acted upon? They are experts too – some might say, the real experts! It needs to be added, of course, that some social scientists are disabled.

Next, taking into account a given budget, how can we produce affordable policy proposals? Economists need to be consulted here, and perhaps some hard decisions have to made. It might, for example, be considered desirable to equip all commercial and public buildings with wheelchair access, but what do we do if the funding doesn't stretch that far? In short, given financial constraints, how do we do the best we can – not *for* but *with* – the people whose lives are most likely to be affected by the envisaged policy?

It isn't easy to try to be objective while also having strong views on particular policy issues. But all scientists – natural (for example, physicists) and social (for example, sociologists) – face the same dilemma. Is it justifiable that a

In plain terms, the data showed that ill health among poor Britons was probably more linked to their standard of living than to what the health system could or couldn't do for them. Sir Douglas Black included this evidence in his report some 20 years ago to the then Prime Minister, Margaret Thatcher, and had the report buried for his pains. Sir Donald Acheson told Tony Blair the same thing in the late 1990s – poverty is a killer.

Politicians often claim that they have a finite budget, and that when it comes to combating poverty they can only spend what the pot contains. But there's also the important consideration of *how* to spend existing funds. Thus, for example, in the wake of the late-1980s implosion of the old Soviet empire, 'Western' governments such as that of the UK now spend proportionately much less money on defence than they did during the Cold War. This means that more money is available for health, education and social welfare.

The issue isn't just about spending priorities. When, for example, US politicians can win votes for 'getting tough on drugs', not all of them want to hear from social scientists that:

> 'A dollar's worth of drug treatment is worth seven dollars spent on the most successful law-enforcement efforts to curb the use of cocaine.'
>
> (Joseph Treaster, 1994; cited by Livingston, 1996: 495)

The fact that this finding was reported by Rand, a Californian research organisation that has close links with the US Federal government, and whose research into how to curb cocaine use was partly funded by the White House, didn't prevent the White House from rejecting Rand's main arguments. It seems that, for some politicians at least, it is just too risky to endorse social scientific research findings that might cost votes.

REVIEW POINTS

- Ideally, *social policy* would be the *application of social scientific knowledge in the pursuit of human social needs*. This is what 'founding fathers' such as Comte, Durkheim and Weber envisaged.

- While the social sciences (particularly, sociology) provide social policy-makers with ideas and evidence, thus helping them to make sound policy judgements, researchers make value judgements about what to study and how to use their findings. This is why ethical issues cannot and should not be side-stepped.

- It's up to politicians whether or not to heed the findings of social policy research. Some do, and some don't.

REVIEW ACTIVITIES

1 How do science and ethics become intertwined in social policy?
2 What did Max Weber mean when he said he had no time for an indifferent social science?
3 Why should social scientists be involved in key policy-making roles?
4 While it's important to consider the size of the public spending pot, why is it also important to consider how to spend the pot?
5 How might politicians respond when faced with a finite public spending pot that doesn't stretch to the funding of two different but equally important social policy measures?

Political perspectives on social policy

Different societies, and different groups within the same society, have different views on the role of social policy. This involves not just specific social policies, but also the economic and political contexts in which policies are framed. For example, New Right politicians, as will be seen, favour minimal political intervention in economic markets. So when we're discussing perspectives on social policies, we have economic and political backdrops in mind as well as particular initiatives.

Ultimately, politicians make the big social policy decisions in society. In the United Kingdom, Old and New versions of Left and

Right politics are crucial here. These perspectives carry weight because they form the *dominant discourses* (voices of the powerful). Middle way (or Third Way, as it's now commonly called), communitarian and social democratic positions are increasingly finding direct expression in these same discourses, particularly, in Blairite 'New Left cum Centre-Left' politics.

Less high-profile, but nevertheless influential, have been the voices of feminist, anti-racist, disabled, unemployed and low paid, and environmental groups, whose opinions are largely articulated through lobbying.

First, we examine the historical origins and development of Left and Right perspectives, plotting changes as well as continuities. Much of the discussion here focuses on mainstream politics, which is the arena in which social policy issues are debated and formulated at government level.

Next, we investigate Third Way, communitarian and social democratic approaches. With few exceptions, these perspectives are wedded to New Left thinking, and have thus become part of the everyday vocabulary of Blairism. The terms 'New Left' and 'New Labour' are used interchangeably, because New Labour is a particular kind of New Left government.

Finally, we look at feminist, anti-racist, disabled, unemployed and environmental group approaches to social policy. These platforms often (but not exclusively) operate outside of mainstream politics.

Traditional and emerging perspectives on the Left and Right

If we want to find the origins of left-wing and right-wing perspectives on social policy, we must go back quite a few centuries to the time of Queen Elizabeth 1, whose reign saw the setting up, in 1598 and 1601, of the Poor Laws (see pp. 355–358). These statutes, implemented in a period when left–right had more to do with military parade grounds than politics, established founding principles for a system of social security that has fuelled heated political debate ever since.

The debate on the Poor Laws came to a head in the early 19th century, when aristocratic politicians, some of Tory leanings and others of Whig disposition, got into a dispute over aristocratic duties and working-class self-help. The old-style Tories (whose politics had much in common with that of pre-Thatcher Conservatives) favoured a 'moral' rather than a 'free' market economy, and argued that aristocratic privilege conferred public

duties, particularly in relation to the welfare of the poor.

The Tories' political opponents, the Radical Whigs (the precursors of later Liberals and present-day New Right thinkers) supported free market economics and complained that the old Poor Laws led to 'subsidised idleness'. The Whigs favoured social reform and argued that state-funded education would root out dependent poverty by promoting a national work ethic.

For these important historical reasons, our starting point is the early 19th century, a period that heralded the emergence of a new view of the role of government in the affairs of the nation.

The Old Right

Political parties were not as clear-cut in the early 19th century as they are today. Nevertheless, conservative opinion found a mouthpiece in a political grouping known as the Tories. The term 'Tory' was first used in 1679 to refer to those who wanted James, Duke of York, to succeed to the throne. Tories in general were very pro-monarchy. In 1832, the Tories took on a new name, forming one of the two main political parties of Britain, the Conservative Party. However, the term 'Tory' stuck, and is still used today to denote the Conservatives.

In the early 19th century, most Tories were upper-class landowners. They accepted hierarchy, but believed that privilege carried public duties, both classic features of the Old Right perspective. Tory landowners were often benefactors in their local communities, providing for the welfare needs of the rural poor. They contributed towards cottage repairs, subscribed to Anglican schools for poor children, set up fuel and clothing charities, distributed free bread and allotment plots, and supported hospitals and dispensaries. The Old Right belief in *noblesse oblige* (that high position also carries responsibility) was enshrined in common law, giving villagers the right to buy corn at a fair price. The historian E. P. Thompson (1971) has termed this system a **moral economy**. This type of economy is significantly different to that of the capitalist **free market**, where supply and demand, not ethics and duty, take precedence.

The more important distinguishing characteristics of the Old Right are as follows:

- *noblesse oblige* (notably expressed as *paternalism* – 'fatherly duty')
- honour
- hierarchy

- ◎ king and country
- ◎ land
- ◎ Anglicanism
- ◎ the amateur ideal

While Old Right values endure up to this day in High Tory circles, the impetus of industry and its alternative ideology were to prove irreversible. As the British Industrial Revolution gained pace, new economic forces confronted conventional social relations. Traditional expressions of *noblesse oblige*, with their roots in a static, hierarchical order, were out of step with the new realities of a socially mobile, market-driven, capitalist economy. The Tories couldn't prevent the industrial nation coming of age, but they tried to muffle the impact of hard-edged capitalism on conventional rural values. This inevitably pushed them into an ideological confrontation with the new barons of industry, and also with the members of their own social class – notably Whigs – who had broken ranks by showing sympathy to the industrialist cause.

When, however, in 1846, one of their own, the Conservative Prime Minister, Robert Peel, also went over to the other side by opening corn prices to free market forces (a major concession to the capitalist class), opposition to economic and social reform became increasingly untenable. At the time, Peel's repeal of the Corn Laws split the parliamentary Conservative Party. The old guard found it hard to accept that a Conservative would support the *laissez-faire* (let the market decide) principles of the capitalist class.

However, under another Conservative premier, Benjamin Disraeli, unity was gradually reforged. Henceforth, the Conservative Party would embrace free market capitalism. Vestiges of an older-style patrician Toryism still lived on, but *laissez-faire* had won the decisive battle. The new ideology lies at the heart of Conservative Party thought today.

The first stirrings of *laissez-faire* thinking in upper-class circles came not from the Tories, but from another aristocratic political grouping, the Whigs. A prominent figure here was the early 19th century MP, Samuel Whitbread, who sought to reduce Poor Law expenditure through public investment in mass schooling.

In 1807, Whitbread tabled a Poor Laws Bill that proposed the levying of rates for the support of schools to teach working-class children reading, writing and arithmetic. This important bill, an early instalment in a series of debates leading to the first main government grant for elementary education in 1833, challenged many aspects of the prevailing orthodoxy. In particular, it foreshadowed the gradual replacement of the old Poor Law with one based on the principle of self-help. Thatcher's New Right Conservatism, with its emphasis on individual effort, captured this same spirit, making her more of a Whig than an 'Old Right Tory' in outlook.

Not that the Old Right was against educating the poor. In the early 19th century, the genie was out of the bottle and schooling was here to stay. The big debate centred on the funding and role of popular education. Whereas reformist Whigs fought for state-funded schooling of the kind that would encourage the poor to rise above their station, die-hard Tories favoured charitable support for a popular education that didn't promote inflated social ambitions.

The Tories were to lose this battle. Reformist Whigs, such as Whitbread and Henry Brougham, had laid the groundwork for a more openly bourgeois society, in which old hierarchical habits and deference-based authority were destined to crumble. Having started its programme of subsidies to education in 1833, Parliament had effectively endorsed a policy of state intervention.

In line with their revised view of the English working class, reform-minded politicians continued to legislate for a society in which dependent poverty would become replaced by self-help. Following the report of the Royal Commission on the Poor Laws in 1834, social policy took a much harder line towards cash help for the poor.

The Commission's main recommendation was that unemployment benefits should only be provided as a last resort, and that all able-bodied individuals would have to work, even if this meant entering a workhouse. Conditions in workhouses were deliberately made harsh, in the hope that the poor would seek work elsewhere. The philosophy of the 1834 Poor Law was in line with the capitalist doctrine of *laissez-faire* which, in this case, meant letting the poor fend for themselves in a free labour market.

Conservative Party ideology, while generally embracing *laissez-faire* economics after Peel repealed the Corn Laws in 1846, also advocated government efforts to redesign market forces when they threatened public aims. This perspective, sometimes described as the 'kinder face of capitalism', continued into the 20th century, and expressed what have come to be known as traditional Tory values.

SOCIAL POLICY AND WELFARE

These values endorsed (as did Old Labour values) the development of a welfare state that would provide a safety net within an essentially capitalist economy. The safety net could only be provided if politicians from the Left and the Right were prepared to make conscious efforts to redesign markets for public aims. The theories of a Cambridge University economist, John Maynard Keynes, were to play a profound role here.

According to Keynes, macro-economic policy (the manipulation by government of public spending, taxation, borrowing and interest rates) can help policy-makers to build a full employment society. On this reckoning, left to its own devices, *laissez-faire* isn't to be trusted, which is why the state must play a role in the economic and social affairs of the nation.

We'll return to Keynes shortly. Meanwhile, it's pertinent to point out that the Old Right's trust in Keynesian economics came under increasing challenge in the 1970s from a modern version of the classical free market model – **monetarist theory**, also known as **Chicago School Economics** (not to be mistaken with Chicago School Sociology). Prominent in this counter-attack was the American economist Milton Friedman, whose argument for an updated form of *laissez-faire* was to help Margaret Thatcher rediscover Whiggery in her particular brand of New Right Conservatism.

The New Right

Margaret Thatcher was a memorable Prime Minister. During her 11 years as Conservative Prime Minister from 1979 to 1990, it became possible to speak of a Thatcherite mind-set. Dubbed 'the Iron Lady', Thatcher's style of Conservatism was, of course, quite different from that of her predecessors. Old Conservatives, whom Thatcher derided as 'wets', argued (like 19th-century Tories) that the poor needed a helping hand from the rich when times were hard. Thatcher (like 19th-century Whigs) prescribed a different medicine: standing on one's own two feet.

At the heart of the Thatcherite ideology lay a New Right set of core values:

- free economic markets
- minimal state intervention in social welfare
- means testing
- privatisation
- individual choice and responsibility

- self-help and individualism
- family (the mum, dad and two children kind)
- duty
- respect for law
- country and patriotism

According to New Right thinking, the welfare state, far from ridding the nation of poverty and ignorance, prolongs these problems by undermining personal and family responsibilities. Excessive welfarism, it's alleged, has created an 'underclass' of people trapped in a 'dependency culture', both of which are economically and morally damaging to welfare recipients and taxpayers.

A powerful version of the New Right perspective is found in Friedman's argument that human beings are essentially self-interest maximisers. According to Friedman's **rational choice theory**, economics can explain all manner of human social behaviour on the basis of self-interest and supply and demand. Thus, for example, marriage is considered less in terms of love and more in relation to 'What do I gain by marrying this person?' Similarly, people commit suicide when remaining lifetime utility hits zero.

From the standpoint of New Right philosophy, there isn't any behaviour, however seemingly emotional or compassionate, that can't be explained by the tools of economic analysis. Strip the gloss away and the underlying structure reveals the common pursuit of personal interest. This doesn't mean that the New Right simply endorse survival of the fittest. Like Adam Smith, from whom they draw enormous inspiration, New Right thinkers believe in the providential (favourable) design of the market economy.

Thus, for example, in their book *Operation Underclass*, Madsen Pirie and Iain Smedley (1994) argue that the urban unemployed would be helped by social policies that promote free market ethics. They therefore propose 'green card' tax and National Insurance exemptions for companies that hire the long-term unemployed, and opportunities for people to start businesses in so-called 'green light' estates without regulatory burdens. A third recommendation is for a benefit buy-out scheme that would enable long-term unemployed people to draw future benefits in advance as a lump sum to help fund a new business.

The problem, of course, for the New Right today is that their arguments don't carry the same weight in Labour government circles as they did during the premierships of Thatcher and John Major. Nevertheless, as indicated earlier, New Right arguments have influenced New Labour policies. Before looking at the New Left, we'll first consider its predecessor, the Old Left.

The Old Left

Noblesse oblige and *laissez-faire* weren't the only ideologies in 19th-century Britain. Other voices – those of the poor – were stirring. Partly in response to the distress caused by the reformed Poor Law, working people developed their own self-help movement along socialist lines. This socialist outlook was 'new' then, but, over time, it has become known as Old Left. Trades unions, co-operative savings 'banks' and friendly societies were to play a conspicuous role here.

The Labour Party had its roots in 19th-century socialism, a political belief which grew out of opposition to industrial capitalism. Socialism's most notable proponent at that time was the German philosopher and social scientist Karl Marx, who had settled with his family in London. Marx argued that English society was divided into two main social classes: capitalists who made big profits, and workers who received meagre wages. Workers were typically employed in factories by capitalists and, according to Marx, were overworked and underpaid. He wanted things to change so that goods and services in society would be distributed on the basis of people's needs, rather than on their class position. This, in essence, is what 'traditional' (some would say *real*) socialism stands for. It's here that we find the origins of what is now termed Old Left thinking.

Marx looked to the Chartists whom, in 1852, he called '... the politically active portion of the British working class ...' (cited in Bottomore and Rubel, 1975: 206), as a socialist party-in-waiting. He thought that the Chartists' bid for **universal suffrage** (mass voting rights) would '... be a far more socialistic measure than anything which has been honoured with that name on the Continent. Its inevitable result, here, is the *political supremacy of the working class*' (Bottomore and Rubel, 1975: 207). Marx was to be disappointed. In the 1868 general election, a number of working-class voters supported the Tories.

Notwithstanding this setback, in 1890, a number of trades unions joined with three socialist sects to form the Labour Representation Committee. The Labour Party was in the making. By 1906, a separate and self-styled Labour Party had gained 29 seats in the House of Commons.

The first brick of the British welfare state was, however, to be laid by a Liberal government which, in 1909, introduced a non-contributory (you don't have to contribute payments to receive benefit) pension scheme. A five-shilling 'Lloyd George Pension' (named after the then Prime Minister) became payable from age 70 to men and women.

The government estimated that the pension would cost about £6–7 million. However, by 1914, the actual costs had almost doubled, to £12.5 million. As an indication of the inadequacy of the old system, the Poor Law had earmarked only £2.5 million for the relief of the elderly poor. Liberal politicians next focused on sickness and unemployment, introducing a National Insurance Act in 1911, which produced compulsory health insurance, employees and employers each paying flat-rate contributions.

Approved friendly societies provided minimum cash benefits that could be topped up by extra contributions to the societies themselves. A state contribution also provided entitlements for workers who weren't previously insured through a friendly society. This flexible partnership between state and non-state welfare providers lasted for 37 years, until finally replaced, in 1948, by the National Health Service and other state-funded arrangements.

By the 1940s, many of the basic elements of a welfare state were in place. There were contributory benefits for old age, sickness, unemployment and widowhood, as well as a special safety net for the elderly and the jobless. But provision was patchy and poorly coordinated.

It fell to Sir William Beveridge (1879–1963), who had a keen interest in the problem of unemployment, to bring together a disparate range of welfare benefits into a single coherent framework. Beveridge was the son of a British civil servant and attended the University of Oxford. He was to become Director of the London School of Economics, as well as Liberal MP for Berwick on Tweed.

Influenced by Seebohm Rowntree's research into poverty, Beveridge produced what was to become an important part of the 1945–1951 Labour government's plan for a welfare state. Beveridge's proposals, published as an official report in 1942, set itself the task of tackling the five 'giant evils' of want, ignorance, squalor, disease and idleness.

The Beveridge Report became an instant bestseller, and has exercised an important influence on social policy to the present day.

People queued up to buy copies, and the then Archbishop of Canterbury, the Left-leaning William Temple, said that the report embodied the Christian ethic. It was Temple who, in 1941, introduced the term 'welfare state' into the English language, But it didn't catch on, and Beveridge hated the term because of its totalitarian and 'free hand-out' connotations. Clement Attlee, the postwar Labour Prime Minister who largely implemented the Beveridge Report, first resisted the term, but then adopted it in his 1949 broadcast to the nation.

In this manner, a Liberal MP's blueprint became a concrete social policy under a Labour government. At the time, Labour politicians would have described themselves as forward-looking – but yesterday's radicalism is today's convention, which is why we now refer to them as Old Labour.

Although there were differences of emphasis between Labour and Conservative governments between 1948 and 1979, Ken Blakemore (1998) has characterised the period as one in which cross-party agreement existed about the benefits of a welfare state. In that respect, both the Old Left and the Old Right generally supported expanding the state welfare.

There were, however, some 'even older' Old Leftists (mainly from the Marxist stable) who expressed doubts about a welfare system whose purpose was to soften, not dismantle, the impact of capitalism. These critics also pointed out that the main beneficiaries from the welfare state were the middle class, not the poor. They added, correctly, that welfare reform didn't significantly redistribute wealth.

Notwithstanding these criticisms, it's worth noting that income differentials (not the same as wealth – **income** is money, while **wealth** is property) did significantly narrow during the period from 1940 to 1975. Moreover, there was a greater equalisation in access to basic services, as well as improvements in educational achievement, health and life expectancy, during the same time span.

The economic theory that underpinned the broad consensus between Old Labour and Old Conservatism was provided by John Maynard Keynes (1883–1946), whose book *The General Theory of Employment, Interest and Money* (1936) founded modern macro-economics. Keynes, who had the ear of Conservative and Labour politicians, distrusted the free play of market forces, believing that these could cause havoc, leading to slumps and unemployment. Only governments, said Keynes, could rectify the problem, by bringing the free market into line.

According to Keynes, economics, in applied form, was a moral social science to be used in the service of humankind. In that spirit, he dedicated one of his books, *Farewell to Treasury*:

> 'To the economists – who are the trustees, not of civilisation, but of the possibility of civilisation.'

Throughout his life, Keynes campaigned for full employment as the guiding principle of a civilised society. In this quest, he urged governments to tackle the spectre of unemployment through enlightened economic policies. Prominent here was his advocacy of the view that government, through official action and social design, should ensure that people had jobs.

For without work, not only do people become poor, but they don't have the money to buy goods and services. This, in turn, makes matters worse because, when companies can't sell their products, they go to the wall, and even more workers are laid off.

Nor did Keynes think that low wages were a good thing because, like unemployment, they reduce the demand for goods and services. Were he still alive, he would have undoubtedly supported the decision of the European Union member states to introduce a minimum legal wage.

Keynesian economics were translated into concrete policies in America when President Franklin D. Roosevelt's New Deal was launched in the 1930s. In that period of the Great Depression, millions of Americans were out of work, and bread lines sprang up throughout the country. 'Brother, can you spare a dime' went the words of a popular song.

The New Deal provided Federal funds to put the jobless into work – planting trees, creating fish, game and bird sanctuaries, tackling stream pollution and, very innovatively, painting murals inside and outside of public buildings. It also set up a system of insurance for the old, the disabled and the unemployed, drawing on employer and employee contributions. Put simply, the New Deal laid the groundwork for the US version of a welfare state.

The Keynesian confidence that government economic policy could lift economic growth and bolster near full employment exercised a powerful influence on 'Western' economics right up to the 1970s. Around that time, however, the New Right

American economist, Milton Friedman, launched a strong counter-attack.

Friedman argued that governments couldn't spend their way out of unemployment without creating accelerating inflation, the root cause of which is excessive growth of the money supply. Instead, said Friedman, they should revert back to 'good old' *laissez-faire*, letting the economy gravitate to a 'natural' rate of employment determined by market forces rather than by government intervention.

Friedman's economics, as already indicated, were adopted in Britain by Margaret Thatcher. They were also, indirectly, to have an effect on the Labour Party which, in the 1980s, was starting to show signs of a split between Old Left socialists and market-friendly New Left thinkers. Much of the ensuing debate between these two camps centred on a long-standing socialist goal in the Labour Party's constitution, the now defunct Clause IV – a pledge to the public ownership of the means of production, distribution and exchange. Clause IV committed the Labour Party, at least on paper, to the goal of placing factories and services into public ownership.

In reality, the nearest Labour had ever got to Clause IV was the nationalisation of key services (for example, the Post Office and the railways) and utilities (for example, coal and steel). The policy of **nationalisation** (the buying up by government of big industries and services) is designed to remove the commanding heights of the economy from corporation bosses. It seeks to re-orient production away from private profit-seeking and keep it in line with public need. Thus, for example, placing a railway company into public ownership might lead to more services in rural areas, even if this means running at a loss.

Nationalisation received its launch in 1945, when the then Labour government lit the fuse by inaugurating a massive programme of state enterprise. In the 1980s, however, it encountered a staunch opponent in Margaret Thatcher, who set about replacing it with privatisation. Slowly but surely, first under Thatcher and later under John Major, privatisation wrested control from the public sector. Gas, water, railways and a whole host of other state-run concerns went back into private ownership. Old Labour protested, but couldn't halt the process.

Then Labour leader, Neil Kinnock, contested Major in the 1992 general election on a ticket that toned down Old Labour chest-thumping and offered a less socialist (namely, New Left) alternative. But he lost the fight. The next Labour

(The Observer, 10 May 1998)

Has Blair put the final touches to the switch from Old to New Labour

leader, John Smith, tragically died of a heart attack in 1994. Tony Blair subsequently took up the mantle and promptly coined a new political slogan: New Labour. In 1995, Blair persuaded his party to ditch its long-standing, Old Labour attachment to nationalisation, when a special conference in April of that year removed Clause IV of Labour's constitution.

According to Mark Garnett (1996: 7), it was a decision that was, '... the most potent of Blair's determination to change his party's ethos'. Remarkably, Blair had succeeded in adopting a New Right approach and re-packaging it in a more 'palatable' form: New Left politics.

Before examining New Left politics, we'll end this section by outlining the central values of the Old Left:

- working class improvement
- anti-capitalist
- social and economic equality
- nationalisation
- Keynesian economics (that is, state intervention to control market forces)
- strong welfare policies
- universal social security

The New Left

Tony Blair became Prime Minister on 1 May 1997 as the result of an historic Labour landslide and a spectacular Conservative rout. Labour won 419 of the 659 House of Commons seats, a large 177-seat majority. The Conservatives held on to just 165 seats, and the third main party, the Liberal Democrats, increased their seats to 46 in total.

Two days after he entered 10 Downing Street, the *Financial Times* (3 May 1997) reported that the remarkable extent of Tony Blair's transformation of Old into New Labour (or today's New Left, as it's also known) was shown by the market response to the Labour landslide: UK gilts and equities rose, and sterling hardly wobbled. In times past, a Labour victory would have spelt a fall in stocks and shares, and in the pound.

While it's true that Blair doesn't have a monopoly on New Left thinking, he is the Prime Minister, so his particular blend of New Left politics has a profound impact on social policy, and is therefore worthy of study. For Blair, a New Left – or New Labour, as he prefers to call it – view of society is characterised by a readiness to move towards the centre, to bridge the breach between the Old Left and the New Right. Unlike Old Labour, he believes that the state has often got things wrong. Unlike New Conservatism, he believes that government has an important role to play in social welfare.

Blair believes that work is the surest route out of poverty. That's why New Labour welfare policy is based (in the Prime Minister's words) on, 'work for those who can; security for those who cannot'. Echoing this sentiment, Principle One of the Department for Social Security's document, *New Contract for Welfare: Principles into Practice* (1998) reads:

> 'The new welfare state should help and encourage people of working age to work where they are capable of doing so.'

New Contract for Welfare heralds the abandonment of social insurance as the cornerstone principal of the welfare state. *The Observer's* Comment column (1 November 1998, p. 28) describes this decision as one which 'brought the curtain down on Labour's twentieth-century commitment to social democracy as a means to social justice', and as an entry into 'the conservative domain of the welfare state as a means-tested, discretionary safety-net for the deserving poor'.

Critics contend that Blair, far from stepping beyond the old ways, isn't much far removed from New Right politics. Thus, for example, Martin Jacques (*The Observer*, 18 October 1998, p. 31) says that 'for all the hyperbole, it is the continuities rather than the ruptures that characterise

the Blair era: the refusal to raise income tax and the acceptance, for the first two years, of the Tories' spending plans'.

However, New Labour insists that it's breaking with the past: not just with Thatcherism, but also with older forms of Labour politics. Blair urges a return to first principles by raising the question of what we want the welfare state to achieve. He believes the answer lies in a Third Way that doesn't dismantle welfare but reforms it on the basis of a new contract between citizen and state, with each having responsibilities.

While it bills itself as a centre-left political party with a belief in community, compassion ('tough love' version), and public service, one might reasonably argue that just as pre-Thatcher Conservative governments learned to live with Old Labour nationalisation, New Labour is coming to terms with New Right privatisation. In that context, it's apt to point out that New Labour's vision of the third millennium welfare state involves a partnership between public spending and private saving. This is why the government is promoting the idea of the 'Stake-holder Pension', a portable, private, second-tier provision. The government is also committed to the principle of encouraging people on low incomes to save more through Individual Savings Accounts.

Although there's some truth in the assertion that Blair is re-packaging some of the ideas of the New Right, it's also true that, while the Conservatives wanted to live with capitalism, the New Left doesn't want to live with it unchanged. Blair wants to socialise capitalism in order to prevent it from being something that isn't benevolent. There are strong echoes here of Keynesianism, of market economics with a left-wing tilt.

Perhaps then, rumours of the death of Old Labour might be premature. *Observer* reporter Ian Aitken (*The Observer*, 25 October 1998, p. 28), has gone so far as to suggest that Labour Chancellor Gordon Brown, for all his expressions of New Labour prudence, is operating a public spending policy of which Keynes would have approved. Spending lots of billions of pounds on health and education, in spite of a slowdown in the British economy, is Keynesian economics of the plainest kind. But, notwithstanding the retention of a Keynesian foothold at the Treasury office, the readiness of New Labour to look for a new direction rather than return to the old rhetoric of Left and Right – of socialist and capitalist – is echoed in the Party's 1997 manifesto, *New Labour Because Britain Deserves Better* (1997). In seeking to implement its manifesto promises, New Labour is increasingly adopting a more centrist approach to politics, one which replaces the traditional ideologies of Left and Right, one which looks to the Third Way.

The Third Way, social democracy and communitarianism

The Third Way – sometimes also called 'post-modern social democracy' – is a new centrist approach to politics. Its goal is to combine the free market with a social conscience. Some Third Way politicians also advocate the replacement of the welfare state with a 'communitarian state' in which all citizens are stakeholders.

A relative newcomer to the political stage (at least, in its New Labour form), Third Way politics neither advocates *laissez-faire* nor wholesale state interference. Instead, it promotes the development of social policies – especially in the area of education and training – whose purpose is to foster personal responsibility, community and a shared sense of national destiny. The big idea here is 'mutuality': a civic spirit that links rights with obligations and balances individualism with community.

For some commentators, the Third Way comes over as a middle-of-the road fudge, a bit of this, a bit of that, and perhaps a few new ideas along the way – pick-'n'-mix politics. Not so, says Blair, who argues that the Third Way is taking institutional shape and even starting to put down some social roots. In support of this argument, Blair can turn to Anthony Giddens, a sociologist who is widely seen as the Prime Minister's intellectual mentor.

In his book, *The Third Way* (1998), Giddens accepts that there isn't an alternative to capitalism. Instead, he says, the debate is about how far and in what ways capitalism needs to be regulated. Giddens favours quite a lot of regulation, including a gigantic global regulator to police reckless money market speculators. The message, according to Giddens, seems to be that we must live with capitalism, but not in the raw. Defenders of the Third Way (who, in 2000, included British Prime Minister Tony Blair, US President Bill Clinton, and German Chancellor Gerhard Schröder) insist that it offers a viable alternative to the stale and tired debate between Left and Right. In this respect, say its proponents, the Third Way offers a framework of ideas that bind a range of political themes.

The glue that is responsible for the binding is **communitarianism**, a philosophy that is derived from the work of the American sociologist, Amitai Etzioni. In his book, *Spirit of Community* (1993), Etzioni laments the passing of community and embraces the goal of building a 'supracommunity': a society of communities. Communitarians argue that, that through a commitment to the welfare of the community, individuals acquire a sense of personal and civic duty. Through communitarianism, says Etzioni, the selfish 'I' is played down and the collective 'we' is developed. In this way, the celebration of self yields to the avowal of communal responsibility. Moreover, the role of social policy becomes one of promoting the common good, of building what some American social scientists call a 'moral ecology'.

The 1990s saw a concerted effort by the New Left to reclaim the moral ecology of community and to place it above selfish individualism, statism and traditional Left and Right politics. As early as 1990, Gordon Brown (Labour Chancellor of the Exchequer since 1997) invoked the ideal of community in an *Observer* article. In 1993, Hillary Clinton proposed in the *Washington Post* that people should serve their communities, and in *The Guardian* in 1995 Blair argued that 'community' best summed up the beliefs of the New Labour Party. It's important, in the midst of these proclamations, to acknowledge that 'community' is a contested concept. For example, according to some commentators, the Reagan–Thatcher years were characterised by pseudo-community policies: care in the community, community policing and defended communities. 'What community?', came the retort.

We must also pay attention to the different ways in which different groups define community. Some people see community in religious terms, others in feminist, political and social forms, others in ethnic settings, and yet others in geographical environments. And, of course, for some of us, community combines all of these factors. The communitarian ideal of community is one in which strong rights also presume strong responsibilities. Thus, for example, if I have the right to a well-paid job, I also have the responsibility to provide for my continuing prosperity in old age by paying into a private pension scheme, thereby easing the burden of welfare costs on society as a whole. If, on the other hand, illness and unemployment prevent me from taking out a private pension, then I have the right to receive a decent pension from the state.

In addition to their attachment to communitarianism, Third Way politicians often describe themselves as upholders of 'social democracy'. According to Blair, the Third Way is the road to renewal and success for social democracy. Free from outdated ideology, says Blair, his Third Way takes essential values of the Centre and Centre-left and applies them to a changing world.

The Prime Minister's interpretation of social democracy is that it represents a significant departure from the statist politics of the Old Left. For Blair, a social democracy is one in which the people's voice gets a proper hearing, which is why public opinion is widely solicited by the present government. Critics, of course, regard this as clever rather than committed politics.

Does social democracy have a distinctive economics? The answer is no. Social democracies around the world come in different shapes and sizes, and adopt different economic principles. In the UK, the preferred approach is to forge a positive relationship between bosses (private and public) and workers within a market-friendly climate. In New Zealand, which also regards itself as a social democracy, policy-makers have embraced quite unbridled *laissez-faire* principles.

In Norway, yet another social democracy, Keynesian economics are alive and kicking. Writing in *The Guardian Weekly* (12 April 1998, p. 19), Larry Elliott argues that, by passing 'the three traditional tests of social democracy – jobs for all, reducing inequality and increasing democratic control over the economy', Norway has managed to keep the faith. According to Elliott, Norway is a 'Milton Friedman'-free zone, where social democratic governments still believe that generous maternity leave, decent pensions and fair unemployment pay are signs of a civilised nation.

Judged against these standards, the UK's market-friendly version of social democracy appears very different. It also parts company, in certain respects, with the new swathe of centre-left policies in France, Germany and Italy, whose economic policies have a distinctively Nordic look

---

Over here, Tony Blair's Britain … over there, a left-leaning future

Britain   Prime Minister Tony Blair
- Tighter laws on asylum, including restrictions on benefits.
- The implementation of an EU directive that limits the length of the working week to 48 hours. A new right to take your employer to an industrial tribunal for compensation over unfair dismissal, if you have been employed by the company for a year or more. New laws to make recognition of trades unions easier. A £5 billion welfare-to-work programme.
- Removal of the subsidy to the nuclear power industry, but no plans to shut plants.
- A lower age of consent for gay men.

France – Prime Minister Lionel Jospin
- A civil solidarity pact to give legal recognition to non-married couples who have been together for more than three years, including gays and lesbians.
- A major youth employment scheme, aimed at creating 700 000 jobs – half in the public sector.
- The working week cut from 38 to 35 hours without loss of pay.
- The judicial system to be completely overhauled, to restore public confidence in its independence and efficiency.

Italy – Prime Minister Massimo d'Alema
- A commitment to a 35-hour working week.
- The promotion of employment in the poorer south.
- Reform of the outdated legal system.
- Active promotion of women's rights, including within the new Cabinet.
- Reform of the electoral system away from proportional representation, to undermine the influence of tiny factions.

Germany – Chancellor Gerhard Schröder
- Every economic policy to be judged on its impact on unemployment.
- The tax burden on low- and middle-income families to drop by about £1000 a year.
- Citizenship law will be changed to allow millions of foreigners to become full German citizens.
- All nuclear power stations will be shut down, gradually but irreversibly.
- Equal opportunities legislation will be binding on public and private employers.

about them. The snapshot profiles on page 364 – of economic and social policies in Blair's UK and in other European countries where social democracy also prevails – make the point.

Differences apart, Third Way, communitarian and social democratic (centre-left version) commentators also have certain common goals. What they want, in social policy terms, are:

- citizen stakeholding (that is, investing, as a partner with government, in welfare)
- more participatory democracy
- a balance between civil rights and personal responsibility
- community spirit
- regulated capitalism
- harmony between bosses and workers

Up to now, we've examined dominant political perspectives on social policy. They're dominant because, more than other outlooks, they exert a daily influence on the lives of ordinary Britons. In the next section, we consider some of the alternatives that offer critical perspectives on current welfare provision and different solutions.

REVIEW POINTS

- Lots of different voices have important things to say about social policy. The dominant discourses enjoy ascendancy in government circles, where debates ensue between Left and Right, and other political hues.

- The historical trail of Left, Right and Liberal politics, and the implications that these positions have for social policy, goes back at least 200 years. Of particular importance was the early 19th century debate between the Whigs (the forerunners of the New Right) and the Tories (the forerunners of the Old Right) on the role of the state in Poor Law reform.

- New Labour approaches to social policy hold sway in government today. These are characterised by a move towards the centre, bridging the breach between the Old Left and the New Right. Unlike Old Labour, Blair believes the state has often got things wrong. Unlike New Conservatism, he

believes government has an important role in social welfare.

- The Third Way, sometimes also called 'post-modern social democracy', is a new centrist approach to politics. It combines free market economics with a social conscience.

- Some Third Way politicians advocate the replacement of the 'welfare state' with a 'communitarian state' in which all citizens are stakeholders.

- Social democracies around the world come in different shapes and sizes, and adopt different economic principles. In the UK, the preferred approach is to forge a positive relationship between bosses (private and public) and workers within a market-friendly climate. In New Zealand, which also regards itself as a social democracy, *laissez-faire* principles are to the fore in social policy. In Norway, another self-proclaimed social democracy, social policy-makers have kept faith with Keynesian economics and therefore support high levels of public spending.

REVIEW ACTIVITIES

1 Briefly outline each of these perspectives on social policy: Old Right, New Right, Old Left and New Left.

2 What happened in 19th-century Britain that led to a new approach to dealing with 'social problems'?

3 Define the terms *laissez-faire*, **nationalisation** and **privatisation**.

4 What's the main difference between the economics of John Maynard Keynes and that of Milton Friedman? How might this difference affect alternative approaches to social policy?

5 Where does Tony Blair stand on the role of the state in social policy?

6 Why is it difficult to define the Third Way?

7 What are the central principles of **communitarianism**?

8 How do notions of 'social democracy' differ between the UK, New Zealand and Norway?

Other voices in social policy

White middle- and upper-class men occupy the commanding political heights in the UK today. Few are disabled, more (but still relatively few) are women, and none are low paid or unemployed. This state of affairs generally means that the voices of feminists, minority ethnic groups, disabled people, the unemployed and the working poor, and environmentalists are marginalised. Now it's time, in this book at least, to bring the concerns and aspirations of these *important* groups to the fore.

Although, in the following sections, we sometimes refer to a 'lobby' or a 'movement' in the singular (for example, the Women's Movement), we recognise that this is a shorthand description of a social phenomenon that, without exception, contains various strands of thought. It would be more accurate therefore to talk of 'lobbies within lobbies' or 'movements within movements'.

The feminist lobby

Feminists are united in their identification of and opposition to the oppression of girls and women. But feminism comes in different forms. Pamela Abbott and Claire Wallace (1997) have identified four broad types of feminism:

- *Liberal/reformist feminism*. Feminists of this outlook argue that women and men are innately equal, but that socialisation works against this by discouraging women from regarding themselves as equal to men, and by encouraging men to be either accepting or complacent about this. Liberal/reformist feminists advocate the passing of anti-sexist legislation to protect women's inherent rights to be treated as equal.

- *Marxist feminism*. Feminists of this outlook believe that capitalism oppresses both sexes, but that women suffer more. Women are socialised into a 'domestic' role that is, by and large, a form of unpaid labour. Marxists believe that the main beneficiary of motherhood is capitalism, which obtains new and disciplined workers without incurring any costs to itself. Women in paid work generally receive lower pay than men, which also benefits the capitalist system. Marxist feminists have little faith in piecemeal social reform. They seek to fight gender inequality through political struggle.

- *Radical/revolutionary feminism*. Feminists of this outlook argue that gender inequalities are largely caused by **patriarchy** – male domination that oppresses women. Like Marxist feminists, they adopt a revolutionary stance in their pursuit of gender equality. Unlike Marxist feminists, they generally prefer to keep men outside of women's affairs.

- *Socialist feminism*. Feminists of this outlook claim that both patriarchy and capitalism create problems for women. They thus combine aspects of radical feminism and Marxist feminism, but are noticeably less fervent about revolutionary struggle. Socialist feminists aim to influence social policy in a manner that brings about more justice for women. Some of them become Labour MPs.

In relation to the last point, it's relevant to point out that many more women are MPs than previously. Of the 419 Labour MPs who were elected in the 1997 general election, 101 were women, and other parties added a further 59 female MPs.

Women's voices, of course, are more often expressed outside the formal corridors of power: less like shots heard around the world, but more like ripples of change, to borrow from Geraldine Ferraro, a US advocate of women's rights. This doesn't mean that the feminist lobby has no impact on social policy. The history of the suffragettes' movement in Britain (which took root in the 1860s) belies that assumption. In 1884, women actually came close to winning the vote, but lost when Prime Minister William Gladstone sent out a 'whip' (that is, a politician who seeks to ensure that members abide by the party line) against the proposed legislation. It wasn't until 1918 that women over the age of 30 got the vote: the age was subsequently lowered in 1928, to 21, the same as for men at that time.

The Women's Movement (in its various feminist hues) has continued to play a prominent role in public policy debates. It has played a crucial role, for example, in working to end sex discrimination and promoting equal opportunities for women and men. Key victories in these areas were the **Sex Discrimination Act 1975** (amended and broadened in 1986) and the **Equal Pay Act 1975** (amended in 1984).

The Sex Discrimination Act makes its unlawful to discriminate on sex grounds. Specifically, sex discrimination is prohibited in employment, education and advertising, and when providing housing, goods, services or facilities. It's also unlawful to discriminate because a person is married. The Equal Pay Act says that women must receive the same pay as men when they do equal work.

It's important to realise that women's struggles for equality, justice and peace now have a strong global dimension. Not just in the UK, but in other parts of the world too, patriarchal structures and the social policies that they generate are under attack from women. Noteworthy in that context is the work of the Women's Environmental and Development Organization (WEDO), which describes its mission as one of:

> 'actively working to transform society to achieve a healthy and peaceful planet, with social, political, economic and environmental justice for all through the empowerment of women, in all their diversity, and their equal participation with men in decision-making from grassroots to global arenas.'

A staunch advocate of gender issues at the 1992 Earth Summit in Rio de Janeiro, WEDO organised the World Women's Congress for a Healthy Planet in 1991. It produced the Women's Agenda 21, which women have used worldwide as a blueprint for advocacy at United Nations conferences since then. While the mainstreaming of a women's perspective into national and global policy-making is still a long way off, WEDO has become an important agenda-setting body at these conferences. Its co-founder, Bella Abzug – former congresswoman and feminist at the barricades, who died in 1998 – urged women not to ask permission to claim their rightful place on the planet.

Another organisation working for women's rights is the Working Women's Forum in India. A mass movement of poor women workers, the Forum is seeking to reverse patriarchy by developing its own grassroots social policies. It has set up consciousness-raising workshops on food sharing within the home, on training and employment for girls for financial independence, and on the need for girls and boys to share household chores.

Women's voices don't always get acted upon by male policy-makers, but words uttered publicly can and do take on a moral force and, given time, can and do change policies. Illustrative of the power of public rhetoric to change public policy are the campaign speeches of Dr Martin Luther King, whose influence on equal rights for black Americans is examined in the next section.

First, though, we'll summarise key feminist perspectives on social policy:

- better representation in Parliament
- anti-sexist legislation
- equal opportunities
- education and training with girls and women in mind
- global consciousness-raising

The anti-racist lobby

At the 1991 Census, just over 3 million (5.5%) of the then 55 million people in the UK didn't describe themselves as white. Half of this group are of South Asian origin (that is, of Indian, Pakistani and Bangladeshi descent), and 30% are black. Most racial discrimination in the UK is based on colour, which means that this visible minority of 5.5% of the population are in the firing line.

As with women, but even more so, ethnic minority groups are poorly represented in Parliament. However, representatives from ethnic minority communities advise and lobby government on racial issues. Notable in this context is the **Commission for Racial Equality (CRE)**, which was set up under the provisions of the **Race Relations Act 1976**. The CRE receives an annual Home Office grant, but works independently of government. One of its current aims is to increase public awareness of the barriers to equal access for ethnic minority women, particularly in employment, and of the action needed to remove these obstacles.

Before looking at the UK experience, we'll first consider one of the most successful campaigns mounted by black people in pursuit of equal rights: the American **Civil Rights Movement**. The origin and development of this movement serve as an exemplary case study of ethnic minority lobbying, and its victories have inspired anti-racists throughout the world.

We'll begin with an act of civic courage. On 1 December 1955, a black American woman, Rosa Parks, refused to give up her seat on a bus to a white man who wanted it. Her action, alongside protests by other black people against institutional racism,

Montgomery, Alabama, 1958. Unaware of who he is, two police officers arrest the American civil rights leader, Martin Luther King, for 'loitering'

- twice as many black people than white people were unemployed
- of employed black people, 75% had menial jobs
- the rate of infant mortality among black people was double that among white people
- at the beginning of 1967, twice as many black people were combat soldiers in Vietnam compared to white people

King combined social scientific rigour with a civil rights leader's determination to put things right. His solution, echoing the findings of some social scientists today, was to re-slice the national pie. King said that 'true compassion is more than flinging a coin to a beggar; it understands that an edifice which produces beggars needs restructuring' (King, 1969: 178).

He added that:

> '... a nation that continues year after year to spend more money on military defense than on programs of social uplift is approaching spiritual death. America, the richest and most powerful nation in the world, can well lead the way in this revolution of values. There is nothing to prevent us from paying adequate wages to school-teachers, social workers and other servants of the public to insure that we have the best available personnel in these positions which are charged with the responsibility of guiding our future generations. There is nothing but a lack of social vision to prevent us from paying an adequate wage to every American citizen whether he be a hospital worker, laundry worker, maid or day laborer. There is nothing except shortsightedness to prevent us from guaranteeing an annual minimum – and *livable* – income for every American family.'
>
> (King, 1969: 179)

set in motion the Civil Rights Movement, which led to the **Civil Rights Act** of 1964. This and subsequent legislation heralded a radical change in American social policy, ultimately ensuring that all black Americans must be given equal treatment with white people under the law.

A leading figure in the struggle for equal rights for all Americans, irrespective of the colour of their skin, was the black sociologist Dr Martin Luther King.

A graduate of sociology from Morehouse College, Atlanta, King argued that while black Americans had at last been 'spared the lash of brutality and coarse degradation', to keep murder at bay 'is not the same thing as to ordain brotherhood' (King, 1969: 13).

As a good social scientist, King exposed the extent of the social problem that he sought to overcome before putting forward policy proposals. In 1969 he revealed, for example, that in the 1960s, black Americans endured massive inequalities:

- half of all black people lived in substandard housing
- black people had half the income of white people

King's example has encouraged minority ethnic groups around the world to put pressure on white majority governments to ensure that their civil rights are guaranteed and protected in law. It was, of course, precisely this kind of pressure that eventually brought down a racist white minority government in South Africa.

Closer to home, anti-racist groups in the UK continue to challenge the spectre of racism in our multi-ethnic society. Consider the death of Stephen Lawrence, a young black man stabbed to death on a London street in 1993. Stephen's parents, Neville and Doreen Lawrence, were named Media Personalities of the Year in 1999 at the Race in the Media Awards organised by the Commission for Racial Equality. They won this award because the sheer force of their determination to find out why and by whom their son was killed has stirred the nation into confronting racist violence. Piers Morgan, editor of *The Daily Mirror*, which sponsored the award, said that 'without their tenacity, their determination not to be fobbed off and their unflinching quest to get justice for their son Stephen, the McPherson Report and its far-reaching ramifications for tackling institutionalised racism would never have happened' (Commission for Racial Equality, 1999).

Violence towards black and Asian people has long been commonplace in the UK. Brick Lane, for example, a destination for newly arrived Asians, is an area that has attracted racist activists from all over East London to engage in 'Paki bashing'. The council still fits flats with fireproof letterboxes, to protect Bangladeshi homes against arson attacks.

Not only do black and Asian people fare worse than white Britons as victims of crime, but they also suffer disproportionately in relation to unemployment, low pay, poor housing and bad health – and this despite the **Race Relations Act 1976**, which outlawed direct and indirect discrimination on grounds of race! Moreover, black people are twice as likely to be unemployed as white people, and when they have a job, it's more likely to be low paid and in the semi-skilled or unskilled sector. Pakistanis and Bangladeshis are the poorest groups in British society, high male unemployment and low pay being important contributory factors: 60% of people from these two minority ethnic groups are poor – this is much higher than the poverty rate among white people.

Economic hardship isn't always linked to racism, but it doesn't help to be from a minority ethnic group in a society in which black and Asian workers form the bottom stratum of the working class, as well as encountering discrimination at work and in school on a sometimes daily basis.

In their efforts to combat racism and build a more just society, anti-racist lobby groups, among whom the Commission for Racial Equality is especially prominent, support:

- anti-racist legislation
- equal opportunities
- public awareness about racism

The unemployed and the working poor

Current social policies on tackling poverty are based on an employment economy that defines the norm for adult men, and, increasingly, adult women, as being in paid work. David Blunkett, currently New Labour's Minister for Education and Employment, is clear on this, noting that:

> 'welfare-to-work draws directly on Labour's deep traditions. 'Work not dole' was the cry 60 years ago, and that's exactly what the New Deal is all about.'
>
> (*The Observer*, 1 November 1998, p. 31)

The 'got to do something about the jobless poor' theme has a long history. In Elizabethan times, the 'idle poor' risked cruel physical punishment, in Victorian times the workhouse, and today the latest raft of job-creation schemes. The 'right' to work thereby becomes, if we're not careful, an *obligation* to work, however meaningless the job and however low the pay. Yet, as a by-product of the kind of 'welfare' that enforces an employment orthodoxy on the poor, Kevin Dixon (1998) identifies the rise of communities, co-operatives and alternative work projects in many parts of the UK. These include militant

The anti-poll-tax movement is one example of successful direct action by poor people

369

urban anarchists, rural co-operators, New Age travellers and Green activists.

What most of these groups have in common, says Dixon, is an antipathy towards alienating employment. Their methods of resistance to official policy range from direct protest (for example, not paying the poll tax), lobbying (for example, through claimants' unions), and creating alternative lifestyles (for example, setting up local bartering schemes). While the anti-poll-tax movement is an example of successful protest by poor (and other) people, opposition by claimant groups to government policies on welfare have usually been blocked. In part, this is due to what Paul Bagguley (1998: 50) terms:

> '... the marginalization of the "poverty lobby" from decision-making over social security policy.'

This isn't just a UK experience. In France, for example, despite a long history of mass demonstrations by unemployed people for adequate benefits and the right to work, it has become increasingly difficult for the poor to organise collectively and make their demands heard. But they haven't given up. There are still many attempts by the jobless to achieve an organised voice (Chopart et al., 1998).

In Scotland, the Scottish Poverty Information Unit (SPIU), which promotes widespread debate and discussion on welfare reform, makes the important point that there will always be people in society who cannot work in paid employment: the severely disabled, the old, carers, and parents looking after children. These people, says SPIU, must be protected and must therefore receive decent benefits.

SPIU also wants more recognition for the many people, mainly women, who work in an unpaid capacity. Yet the government appears to be reinforcing the invisibility of unpaid work by consistently referring to 'workless families'. The UK welfare state has often discriminated against unpaid workers. For example, women have been unable to contribute to pension schemes because their careers have been interrupted by child-bearing and -caring roles. If , as the government insists, society has an obligation to assist in the upbringing of children, then, says SPIU, lone parents must be guaranteed a decent standard of living should they decide to stay at home and look after their children.

While unemployment undoubtedly causes considerable hardship, one of the main historical causes of poverty in the UK has been – and still is, in many instances – low wages. Indeed, many welfare recipients are part of the working poor. However, in lobbying terms, the low paid have had more success than the unemployed. For example, the Low Pay Commission (set up in 1997 to advise the Prime Minister on a national minimum wage) had meetings with low-paid workers. The Chair of the Commission, George Bain, has said that some of the homeworkers who attended these meetings made him understand the need to address the worse cases of poverty wage exploitation.

Advocacy for the low paid is also mounted through regional low pay units, which seek to influence local and national policy-makers on employment rights and pay. These organisations raise public awareness of the problems of poverty pay and bad employment practice, and provide advice and support for the low paid. Trades unions campaign and lobby for better wages too – and have tried, unsuccessfully, to obtain a national minimum wage of two-thirds median earnings. Interestingly, this formula might be adopted in Ireland.

Significantly, the working poor are more likely to get a sympathetic hearing than the unemployed because the assignment of moral fault in New Labour's UK is on the jobless, not the low paid. Moral condemnation is reserved for those who are not only poor, but who also shun the principle of self-help. Thus the poverty of a low-paid dishwasher is seen as being different from the dependency of an able-bodied welfare recipient.

New Labour says that it wants to help people in the former category. As Gordon Brown (Labour Party Conference speech, 1998) puts it 'the New Deal is about real employment with a future, not dead end jobs'. One wonders, though, whether the current minimum wage of £3.60 an hour is enough to turn a job into a prospect with a future!

In terms of social policy initiatives, the unemployed want:

- adequate benefits
- choice, not compulsion
- real jobs
- recognition of and adequate benefits for people who cannot work
- recognition and provision for unpaid workers

The working poor seek:

- ◎ a minimum wage
- ◎ good working conditions
- ◎ public awareness of the problems associated with low pay

The disabled lobby

Disabled people are less likely to enjoy the same rights as 'able-bodied' people in the UK. Being disabled also increases the risk of being poor, often because of increased living costs and reduced earning power. Disabled people are making strong representations for full inclusion in society. They're insisting that enabling technologies, particularly in education, work and transport, are crucial if the disabled are to be 'designed' into mainstream. Importantly, they're shifting the policy debate away from 'welfare eligibility' to 'social rights' (see Chapter 8, pp. 239–240).

The disabled people's movement is made up of a variety of lobby groups, some run by able-bodied people, and others by self-organised disabled people. However, self-advocacy is gaining momentum. More and more disabled people are telling social policy-makers that the people who know best about the needs of the disabled are the disabled themselves.

An important area in which self-advocacy groups are making progress is in right of access to the built environment. Illustrative of this is an early 1970s success story in California. At that time, Berkeley City Council (close to San Francisco) was successfully lobbied by the disabled community to provide kerb ramps. At first, the public works division balked at the idea, but disabled people refused to give in, and council funds were eventually allocated for ramping the kerbs.

Like so many other local protest movements, the kerb ramps became the litmus test for a wide range of other access reforms in public places, public transportation and at work. Of course, there is much to be done, not just in the USA but also around the world. In Spain, for example, the unemployment of disabled women is three times higher than the national figure, which is why the Women's Institute there is developing a pilot project on new ways of work for this particular group. Discrimination against disabled people is widespread in the UK, not just in job terms but also in relation to emergency evacuation, risk of poverty, access to buildings and a whole range of other areas.

In an effort to remove the social barriers that disabled people encounter, the National Disability Council is currently advising the government on measures to reduce or eliminate discrimination. Another lobby group, the British Council of Disabled People (BCODP), *run and controlled* by disabled people, is petitioning the government to implement a full package of civil rights legislation. The aim is to provide equal employment opportunities for the disabled by guaranteeing them accessible public transport, properly funded mainstream education and training, and non-discriminatory work practices.

BCODP has provided expert input on a number of government issues, including the Disability Living and Disability Working Allowance and consultation on the Citizens' Charter. It is also represented on the Disability Rights Task Force, set up by the Labour government in 1997 to consider the establishment of a Disability Rights Commission.

Despite lobbying activities, disabled people in the UK still encounter major access problems in most walks of life – at work, on transport, in the built environment and so on. Disabled women especially believe that their particular needs are not being sufficiently taken into account by service providers.

According to a 1995 Joseph Rowntree Foundation report, disabled women say that they:

- ◎ Feel not only marginalised in society as a whole, but also within the disability movement and the women's movement.
- ◎ Encounter difficulties obtaining access to information, housing, safety, transport, employment and education. Lack of access to transport is a major problem, and leads to isolation at home.
- ◎ Face patronising attitudes and are offered little choice of the kinds of service that they might receive.
- ◎ Are rarely able, if they have suffered sexual abuse, to receive proper support from women's refuges and rape counselling services.
- ◎ Seem to experience isolation and an extremely low quality of life in residential care and in long-term hospital units.

It appears as though problems that non-disabled women and disabled men face in society are exacerbated for disabled women. This is why it's crucially important that the disability movement

– in its campaign for access to the built environment, social inclusion, empowerment, civil and human rights, as opposed to 'welfare eligibility' and charity, more self-advocacy and enabling technologies – wages an even harder struggle against the particular problems facing disabled women.

The environmental lobby

Global industrialisation is placing life on Earth seriously under threat – the primary product of industry is pollution. About 350 million metric tons of hazardous waste are produced worldwide each year, of which about 90% comes from rich nations. Although the situation looks bleak, environmental lobby groups (often collectively referred to as the Green Movement) are rising to the challenges facing the planet's environmental degradation. Some environmental groups work within the political mainstream. Others operate as non-governmental organisations (NGOs).

As an electoral force, the environmental movement is relatively young. The first environmental party in Europe started in Britain in 1973. Green parties soon developed in other European countries, and some of them gained seats in national assemblies. A big break came in 1983, when the German Greens (*Die Grünen*) won close to a million votes and gained 28 seats out of 497 in the German Federal parliament. Recently, *Die Grünen* became the third political force in Germany, and a Green politician, Joschka Fischer, became the country's Foreign Minister. Given that several European environment ministers are now Greens, Juan Behrendt, secretary general of the 27-strong group of Green deputies in the European Parliament, thinks that it's time to paint Europe green! The map below shows the state of play in 1998.

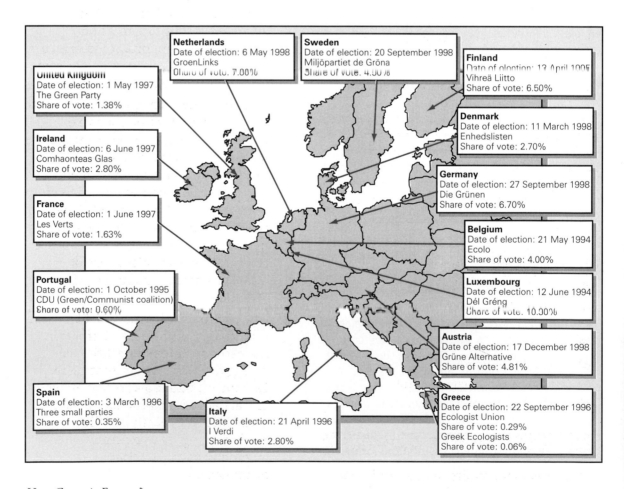

How Green is Europe?

In 1993, the European Federation of Green Parties was formed, with a mandate to speak on behalf of Greens in Europe. This body promotes the development of a sustainable and socially just Europe, seeking eco-development, peaceful conflict resolution, and the right to a healthy and clean environment. Over the past ten years or so, many issues championed by the European Green Movement have gained popular support, and the movement is now able to influence policy-making in many national parliaments, as well as on local councils.

Outside of mainstream politics, the environmental lobby exists as a powerful pressure group, in the form of NGOs, that exerts considerable force. Prominent among these NGOs is Greenpeace which, with nearly 3 million members around the globe, continues to 'bear witness' to environmental abuse by establishing a well publicised presence at the scene. Greenpeace's campaign for more eco-friendly forestry practices has been so successful that new forests in Austria, Canada and Germany are being logged in accordance with its guidelines. In these operations, 'clearcutting' (stripping every bit of standing vegetation in a forest) is prohibited. Enough old and dead trees are left to provide habitats for birds and insects, and to nourish new growth.

Greenpeace and other environmental NGOs have a long list of objectives – clean beaches, protected oceans, renewable energy, communal land rights, and nuclear disarmament, to name just some. As for politics, a British multinational company that asked for an expert briefing on Green power received this advice: count on the Greens being a force to reckon with (Castle and Butler, 1998).

By way of a summary, the environmental lobby is calling for:

- better representation in Parliament
- public awareness about global dangers
- eco-friendly politics
- social justice
- peaceful conflict resolution
- rights to a decent environment
- nuclear disarmament

REVIEW POINTS

- In the main, white middle- and upper-class men occupy the commanding political heights in the UK. Few top politicians are disabled, not many are women, and none are low paid or unemployed.

- This means that the voices of feminists, minority ethnic groups, disabled people, the unemployed and the working poor, and environmentalists are often marginalised.

- Feminists are seeking to achieve – with some notable success stories – better representation for women in Parliament, anti-sexist legislation, equal opportunities, education and training with girls and women in mind, and global consciousness-raising.

- The anti-racist lobby is fighting for anti-racist legislation, equal opportunities and more public awareness about racism. It has achieved some important victories but – in the UK at least – not on the same scale as those won by women.

- Disability advocacy groups continue to wage concerted action for social policies that will improve access to the built environment, foster social inclusion, increase empowerment, guarantee civil and human rights as opposed to 'welfare eligibility' and charity, promote self-advocacy and provide enabling technologies. In this struggle, the particular needs of disabled women require special attention.

- The environmental movement, which is increasingly finding a platform in mainstream European politics, is calling for better representation in Parliament, public awareness about global dangers, eco-friendly policies, social justice, peaceful conflict resolution, rights to a decent environment and nuclear disarmament.

REVIEW ACTIVITIES

1   Briefly, what are the four main types of feminism identified by Pamela Abbott and Claire Wallace?

2   Why is the late Dr Martin Luther King still an important figure in anti-racist lobbying?

3   With reference to any two of feminist, ethnic minority, disabled, unemployed and low paid, and environmental lobby groups, describe how these groups have sought to influence social policy.

4   What are the particular problems faced by disabled women in UK society?

5   Why is it both ethically and social scientifically necessary to bring the aspirations of marginalised groups into debates about social policy?

References

Abbott, P. and Wallace, C. (1997) *An Introduction to Sociology: Feminist Perspectives*, 2nd edn. Routledge, London.

Atkinson, J. M. (1973) Societal reactions to suicide: the role of coroners' definitions. In: *Images of Deviance* (ed. Cohen, S.). Penguin, Harmondsworth, pp. 165–191.

Bagguley, P. (1998) Collective action and welfare recipients in Britain. In: *Beyond Marginality?* (ed. van Berkel, R., Coenen, H. and Vlek, R.). Ashgate, Aldershot, pp. 39–57.

Blakemore, K. (1998) *Social Policy: an Introduction*. Open University Press, Buckingham.

Bottomore, T. and Rubel, M. (eds) (1975) *Karl Marx: Selected Writings in Sociology and Social Philosophy*. Penguin, Harmondsworth.

Castle, S. and Butler, K. (1998) *The Independent*, 31 October, p. 18.

Chopart, J.-N., Eme, B., Laville, J. L. and Mouriaux, R. (1998). The collective action of welfare recipients in Europe. In: *Beyond Marginality?* (ed. van Berkel, R., Coenen, H. and Vlek, R.). Ashgate, Aldershot, pp. 59–94.

Department for Social Security (1998) *New Contract for Welfare: Principles into Practice*. The Stationery Office, London.

Dixon, K. (1998) Strategies for survival: poor people's movements in Britain. In: *Beyond Marginality?* (ed. van Berkel, R., Coenen, H. and Vlek, R.). Ashgate, Aldershot, pp. 21–37.

Douglas, J. D. (1967) *The Social Meanings of Suicide*. Princeton University Press, Princeton, New Jersey.

Etzioni, A. (1993) *Spirit of Community*. Fontana, London.

Garnett, M. (1996) *Principles and Politics in Contemporary Britain*. Longman, London.

Giddens, A. (1998) *The Third Way*. Polity Press, Cambridge.

Keynes, J. M. (1936) *The General Theory of Employment, Interest and Money*. Macmillan, London.

King, M. L. (1969) *Chaos or Community?* Penguin, Harmondsworth.

Labour Party (1997) *New Labour Because Britain Deserves Better*. The Labour Party, London.

Lee, D. and Newby, H. (1986) *The Problem of Sociology*. Hutchinson, London.

Livingston, J. (1996) *Crime & Criminology*. Prentice Hall, Upper Saddle River, New Jersey.

Olweus, D. (1997) *Mobbing i Skolen (Bullying at School)*. Universitetets forlaget, Oslo, Norway.

Pincus, F. L. (1997) Toward a Marxist view of affirmative action. *Critical Sociology*, **23**(2), 89–103.

Pirie, M. and Smedley, I. (1994) *Operation Underclass*. Adam Smith Institute, London.

Runciman, W. G. (1998) *The Social Animal*. Harper-Collins, London.

Thompson, E. P. (1971) The moral economy of the English crowd in the eighteenth century. *Past and Present*, no. 50, 76–136.

Internet sources

Commission for Racial Equality (CRE) (1999) *CRE Media Awards Honour Lawrences*. Press release, 23 April: http://www.cre.gov.uk/

Joseph Rowntree Foundation (1995) *The Experiences of Disabled Women*. Social Policy Research 81, Ref. SP81, August: http://www.jrf.org.uk/

Women's Environmental and Development Organization (WEDO): http://www.wedo.org/frmain.htm

Index